RUDOLF SERKIN

Rudolf Serkin PHOTOGRAPH BY DON HUNSTEIN. REPRODUCED WITH PERMISSION

RUDOLF SERKIN

A Life

Stephen Lehmann and Marion Faber

OXFORD
UNIVERSITY PRESS

2003

OXFORD

UNIVERSITY PRESS

Oxford   New York

Auckland   Bangkok   Buenos Aires   Cape Town   Chennai
Dar es Salaam   Delhi   Hong Kong   Istanbul   Karachi   Kolkata
Kuala Lumpur   Madrid   Melbourne   Mexico City   Mumbai   Nairobi
São Paulo   Shanghai   Taipei   Tokyo   Toronto

Published by Oxford University Press, Inc.
198 Madison Avenue, New York, New York 10016

www.oup.com

Oxford is a registered trademark of Oxford University Press

Library of Congress Cataloging-in-Publication Data
Lehmann, Stephen.
Rudolf Serkin : a life / Stephen Lehmann and Marion Faber.
p. cm.
Discography: p.
Includes bibliographical references and index.
ISBN 0-19-513046-4
1. Serkin, Rudolf, 1903–1991   2. Pianists—Biography.   I. Faber, Marion.   II. Title.
ML417.S46 L44 2003
786.2'092—dc21   2002002384

1 3 5 7 9 8 6 4 2

Printed in the United States of America
on acid-free paper

For Steve, Rachel, and Dinah—MF

For Carol, Joanna and Rogers, and Paul—SL

ACKNOWLEDGMENTS

We owe a large debt of gratitude to the many people who have aided, advised, and encouraged us during the years we have spent preparing this book. Our first thanks are to Rudolf Serkin's family, most especially his children, Ursula Serkin, Elisabeth Serkin, John Serkin, Peter Serkin, Judith Serkin, and Marguerite Serkin; his nieces, Anna Buchthal, Traute Merz, and Lene Mezger; and his grandson, Christopher Serkin. We came to them as strangers, and they have been unfailingly open, generous, and supportive. We have also relied heavily on the kindness of Rudolf Serkin's friends, students, and colleagues in sharing with us their memories and perceptions. Some of the participants in those conversations appear in the "Voices" sections in the text proper. Their contributions form a significant part of this book, for which we are most appreciative. We would also like to thank Shmuel Ashkenasi, Marguerite and Björn Andreasson, Lotte Bamberger, Luis Batlle, Stephanie Brown, Hedwig Busch, Anthony Checchia, Orlando Cole, Edgar Curtis, Evelyne Crochet, Judith Dorian, Eugene Drucker, Mary Lynn Fixler, James Freeman, Lady Ilse Gombrich, Gary Graffman, Byron Hardin, Bice Horszowski, Leon Kirchner, Anton Kuerti, Robert Levin, Cecile Licad, Yo-Yo Ma, Bernard Meillat, Freya von Moltke, Veronika Jochum von Moltke, Paul Moor, Ken Noda, Harvey Olnick, Peter Orth, Murray Perahia, Leslie Parnas, Pia Passigli, Edith Peinemann, Cynthia Raim, Paula Robison, Ned Rorem, Mstislav Rostropovich, Friede Rothe, Frank Salomon, Shoji Sato, András Schiff, Peter Schoenbach, Judith Sherman, Ignat Solzhenitsyn, David Soyer, Lee Stone, Silvia Tennenbaum, Michael Tree, Benita Valente, Piero Weiss, May Wenner-Fahrländer, and Felix Witzinger. And we remember with gratitude those of Serkin's friends and relatives whom we interviewed who have since died: Amalie and Hugo Buchthal, Lotte Busch, Felix Galimir, Albrecht Goes, Sir Ernst Gombrich, Katharine Graham, Barbara

Kempner, Lord Yehudi Menuhin, Sol and Bertha Schoenbach, Henriette Speiser, and Victor Weisskopf.

We are grateful to the many scholars, librarians, archivists, and others who have made available to us documents and information from institutional holdings and personal collections: Claude Abravanel, Richard Bartnik (Carnegie Hall Archives), Dr. Thomas Blubacher, Vera Brustle (Curtis Institute), Wolfgang Burbach (Brüder-Busch-Gesellschaft), Brian Cornell (Library of Congress), Carol Faris (Marlboro Music School and Festival), Yonah Gershator (Columbia Artists Management), Jane Gottlieb (Juilliard School), George Huber (Swarthmore College), Kevin LaVine (Music Division, Library of Congress), Christian Limbeck-Lilienau, Hilde Limondjian (Metropolitan Museum, New York), Philip Maneval (Marlboro Music School and Festival), Bob Matuozzi (Washington State University Library), Viola Morse, John Roberts (University of California), Robert Schmitt Scheubel (Technische Universität, Berlin), Joanne Seitter (Curtis Institute), Peter Spiro, as well as the staffs of the Deutsches Exil Archiv (Die Deutsche Bibliothek, Frankfurt), Hoover Institution Archives, Musikakademie Basel, the Max-Reger-Archiv (Karlsruhe), the Paul Sacher Stiftung (Basel), the Arnold-Schönberg-Institut (Vienna), the Staatsbibliothek zu Berlin–Preußischer Kulturbesitz, the Schweizerische Landesbibliothek, the late Isaac Stern, the University of Pennsylvania Library's Interlibrary Loan Department (David Cohen and Lee Pugh), Music Library (Marjorie Hassen), and Rare Book & Manuscript Library (Michael T. Ryan and Nancy Shawcross), and the Music Library of Yale University.

Luis Batlle, Anna Buchthal, Wolfgang Burbach, the Curtis Institute of Music, Lene Mezger, the Marlboro Music School and Festival, and Peter Serkin provided the photographs and other illustrations that so enrich our text. To them and to the artists (or their estates or representatives) and studios we offer our thanks: Camera One, Pete Checchia, George Dimock, Margo Feiden Galleries, Dorothea von Haeften, Don Hunstein, Clemens Kalischer, George Krause, Christoph Lehmann, Virginia Leirens, Woodrow Leung, and J. M. Snyder.

We gratefully acknowledge the support of Swarthmore College in providing research funds, the archival assistance of Joanna Curtis, Hyorim Lee, and Jennifer Traub, and the technical help of Karen Jones and Michael Jones.

For information, advice, and help of every imaginable kind we thank colleagues, friends, and family in the United States and Europe, especially Sara Bershtel, Jane Bryan, Michael Burri, Barbara Casalini, Steven Cerf, Paul Dry, Beverley Eddy, Erik Entwistle, Mel Faber, Sharon Friedler, Jeffrey Garrett, Stephen Grosz, Steve Hannaford, Philip Hart, Lynne Heller, J. Dennis Hyde,

ACKNOWLEDGMENTS

Elise Jackendoff, Steven Jaffe, Jeffrey Kallberg, Avi Kempinski, Mark Kuperberg, Erich Lehmann, Nicola Luckhurst, Michael Marissen, Barbara McDonald, Benjamin Nathans, Jim North, Joel and Rivka Perlmann, Tully Potter, Anne Raunio, Willis Regier, Constance Reid, Cristina Remenyi, Bettina and Rolf Sabersky, Bernard Saffran, Dena Schoen, Klaus Schreiber, David Toccafondi, and Patricia Zander.

The accompanying CD would have never come about without the persistence of Paul Farber, the generosity and technical wizardry of Ward Marston, and the financial help of Swarthmore College, Marlboro Music School and Festival, and an anonymous donor. Peter Serkin kindly listened to the tapes provided by the Library of Congress and recommended the selection of pieces for the CD.

A few people took upon themselves the burden of a close and careful reading of the entire manuscript, offering detailed suggestions for improvements and corrections. The book is a much better one for their help, and to them we owe a special debt of thanks: Anthony Checchia, Elizabeth Lewis, Matthew Lore, Martin and Lore Ostwald, Carol Sabersky, Elisabeth Serkin, John Serkin, and Judith Serkin. Any remaining errors are, of course, our own. Paul Farber has been endlessly insightful and informative in his musical guidance over the years; we could not have written this book without him. Our thanks, too, to our editors at Oxford University Press—Judith Hoover, Maribeth Payne, Niko Pfund, Kim Robinson, Jessica Ryan, and Ellen Welch—for their patience and friendly guidance.

Our greatest thanks go to Irene Serkin for entrusting us with this project and giving us so much help and support along the way. She facilitated many of our interviews, and her blue eyes would often beam with delight when we told her of these encounters. We remember her with affection and wish she might have lived to see this book.

Robert Silverman, "Serkin: An Interview—Part One," *Piano Quarterly,* vol. 26, no. 100, Winter 1977–78. Copyright String Letter Publishing, P.O. Box 767, San Anselmo, CA 94979-0767; stringletter.com. Reprinted with permission.

Steinway Project Interview, Rudolf Serkin with Elizabeth Harkins, October 6, 1980, Brattleboro, VT. Oral History American Music, Yale University, Vivian Perlis, Director.

CONTENTS

CD CONTENTS

The compact disk that accompanies this book contains recordings of live performances by Rudolf Serkin at the Library of Congress.

1. J. S. Bach (1685–1750): French Suite No. 5 in G major

    Allemande
    Courante
    Sarabande
    Gavotte
    Bourrée
    Loure
    Gigue

2. Felix Mendelssohn (1809–1847): Three Fantasies, Op. 16

    Andante-Allegro-Andante in A minor
    Scherzo in E minor
    Andante in E major

3. Felix Mendelssohn: Rondo capriccioso in E major, Op. 14

4. Felix Mendelssohn: Songs without Words, Op. 62, no. 1 in G major ("May Breezes")

5. Felix Mendelssohn: Songs without Words, Op. 67, no. 4 in C major ("Spinning Song")

6. Frédéric Chopin (1810–1849): 12 Etudes, Op. 25

No. 1 in A-flat major (Allegro sostenuto)
No. 2 in F minor (Presto)
No. 3 in F major (Allegro)
No. 4 in A minor (Agitato)
No. 5 E minor (Vivace)
No. 6 in G-sharp minor (Allegro)
No. 7 in C-sharp minor (Lento)
No. 8 in D-flat major (Vivace)
No. 9 in G-flat major (Allegro assai)
No. 10 in B-minor (Allegro con fuoco)
No. 11 in A-minor (Allegro con brio)
No. 12 in C-minor (Molto allegro, con fuoco)

Produced by Ward Marston and taken from the original lacquer disks, except for the "Three Fantasies" and the "Spinning Song," which were taken from a pre-existing transfer of the original disk (now lost). Although a pitch waver can be heard in the second half of the recording of the French Suite, it was felt that the value of the performance merits its inclusion. 1. April 14, 1950. 2. December 10, 1946. 3., 4., 6. May 5, 1948. 5. December 10, 1946.

The memory is a living thing—it too is in transit. But during its moment, all that is remembered joins, and lives—the old and the young, the past and the present, the living and the dead.

EUDORA WELTY
One Writer's Beginnings

RUDOLF SERKIN

"Why should anyone write about *me*?" Rudolf Serkin was known to ask. "All I did was practice, practice, practice." Although possessed of great charm, playful and quick, he was also a private person and mistrustful of speech, and for much of his life he fended off interviewers, journalists, and would-be biographers. Responding to a request for a radio interview in 1942, he cabled that in front of a microphone he felt like Harpo Marx.[1] In his eighties he wrote to a friend, "To talk about Bach or Mozart or Schubert or any great music, my tongue would freeze in my mouth."[2] And when the German magazine *Stern* asked him for an answer of twenty lines or less to the question *Aimez-vous Brahms?*, he replied, "Unfortunately I do not have the talent to express in words what I feel about Brahms's music. 'This music is among the greatest and deepest and . . .' You see: I can't even express that clearly. I am happy when I am allowed to play and listen to Brahms."[3] Performers, he felt, had no business making pronouncements. His stance was elusive and protective. He hated public speaking and would noisily push chairs around to distract attention from his appearance in a German film about the Marlboro Music School and Festival that was shown there every summer. He was also a famously delinquent correspondent. Busy as he was, he had little time for writing letters, but perhaps here, too, his reluctance came from a deeper source.

"You really want me to tell you my life?" he asked a French interviewer. "But there are biographical notices on the record jackets, aren't there?" She pressed on: "Why don't you talk to me about what isn't on your record jackets?" "Eh bien," he was quoted as replying (the interview is rendered in French) as he eased into a well-mined repertoire of anecdotes that he embellished and varied over the years and that themselves deflected attention, like the chairs in the Marlboro dining room.[4]

How, then, to understand and describe the life of such a reticent man? The challenge is not made easier by Serkin's particular perception of what is appropriately private and public: he did not mind referring in a speech to having suffered as a boy from "a very embarrassing diarrhea" before an audition, but to a question about his relationship to contemporary music he answered, "I prefer not to tell you . . . It would be too difficult to explain. Too intimate."[5] When the same interviewer asked him whether he suffered from stage fright: "That's a question you should never ask! I don't want to know the artist who has no stage fright. Everyone has it. But let's forget about it, it's too intimate, too intimate . . ."[6] "It's too personal," he told Isaac Stern, who in a televised interview in honor of his seventy-fifth birthday asked him about Adolf Busch, the person to whom he was probably closest in his life. Stern was nothing if not persistent, but Serkin would not be drawn out.[7]

And yet, Serkin had a strong, if ambivalent, sense of his own history. He made several trips to Europe with his children and grandchildren to show them the sites of his early life; he held on to piles upon piles of letters from parents, siblings, friends, children, and grandchildren. He went to considerable lengths to document the history of the Marlboro Music School and Festival that he helped found in 1951, carefully preserving the programs and publishing them at regular intervals in a bound volume known as the Red Book. He knew that he was part of an enterprise with a history to be recorded, and surely he was just as aware of the centrality of his role in it. Furthermore, by virtue of his powerful intelligence and the strength of his convictions, Rudolf Serkin was a naturally dominating figure. But he was happiest operating more or less invisibly, behind the scenes: the more closely attention was focused on his person, the more uncomfortable he would become and the more likely he would be to recede.

Why, then, to return to Serkin's question, should anyone write about him? Although there are some notable exceptions — Joseph Horowitz's interviews with Claudio Arrau (1982), Peter Heyworth's two-volume biography of Otto Klemperer (1983, 1996), Peter Ostwald's study of Glenn Gould (1997), and Bruno Monsaingeon's film *Richter the Enigma* (1998) — accounts of the lives of performing musicians are not necessarily engrossing. And yet, when one considers the scope of Serkin's achievements, the complexity of his character, and the sheer drama of his life, one can only turn his question on its head and ask: How could one *not* write a biography about him?

At the apex of his career in the 1950s and 1960s, Serkin was a towering presence in American culture: a musician of unquestioned authority and success who conveyed and represented his art as an ethical activity; an embodiment and disseminator of European culture, the energizer of a vision, and a power-ful figure in the world of classical music and its politics. His life—he was born in 1903 and died in 1991—spanned nearly the entire twentieth century. He spent his youth among the cultural elite of Schoenberg's Vienna and his early adulthood in Germany and Switzerland in the fertile, tense period between two World Wars. Arriving in America in the mid-1930s, part of the great migra-tion from central Europe, he was among the best known of the scholars and artists who infused American educational, scientific, and cultural institutions at all levels with European cultural impulses, both forward-looking and con-servative. His benign, bemused, bespectacled face—as unlikely an icon as one could imagine—adorned the cover of dozens of recordings and was recog-nized everywhere. Though some listeners and critics may have preferred Horo-witz's brilliance, or Schnabel's interpretative imagination, or Rubinstein's exu-berant warmth, it was Rudolf Serkin, artist, teacher, and shaper of musical institutions, whose unshakable commitment and vitality had the more pro-found impact on the culture of classical music in the United States.

Given the richness of such a life, we have taken the evasiveness and modesty of his character, and his insistence that he was nothing more than a musical workhorse, as a challenge and an invitation to a deeper understanding.

In contrast to Serkin, his wife, Irene, who published a collection of the corre-spondence of her father, the violinist Adolf Busch, believed that it would be both appropriate and important to document his life. Shortly before his death, Serkin consented to her wish and submitted to an interview with the biogra-pher Irene had chosen (who later withdrew from the project), but by then he was ill and too weak to participate actively. For that matter, his consent to a biography probably signaled a collapse of his resistance rather than a change of heart.

In preparing this biography without Serkin's participation, then, we have relied wherever possible on primary sources: Serkin's correspondence (from his own papers and numerous other archival collections), unpublished accounts by relatives, programs, reviews, and memoirs of associates.

Serkin saved whatever the mail happened to bring: greeting cards, requests for autographs, letters from fans ("You are my bosom friend through many records from my childhood"), proselytizers ("Mr. Serkin, are you a Christian? Do you trust Christ as your own personal Saviour?"), businessmen seeking endorsements (for Beethoven's Inn in Virginia), and schoolchildren on assign-ment ("I would like to know if you have ever studied Latin and if so how much you have learned and how much you have needed it in your profession"). He saved hateful, anonymous notes ("Pounding on the piano is *not* music. There are millions of people over the world who play beautifully—like *Horowitz!*"), as well as requests from cookbook compilers soliciting recipes from celebrities ("You and your mom would be in good company . . ."), uncashed checks, and on and on, endless detritus washed up by the U.S. Postal Service onto a mountaintop in southern Vermont. The haphazardness of this archival flood suggests that though Serkin threw little away, he saved more from indifference than with a purpose. For a biographer, such a randomly assembled resource is both a gift and a curse. On the one hand, it preserves much suggestive and surprisingly useful material that a more selective culling might have discarded; on the other, it leaves huge gaps, swaths of missing correspondence, programs, reviews, and itineraries. And the files of many of the institutions with which he was associated (Marlboro and Carnegie Hall being notable exceptions) were, if anything, even less systematic in documenting their own history.

Nonetheless, our source material has enabled us to reconstruct the course of Serkin's life and the development of his art with some accuracy. We have also interviewed a wide selection of people who spoke to us about him from various perspectives. Because we did not know him personally and to ensure that he be evoked as fully as possible, we have included ten of these interviews in our book. Although we have edited the interviews, the original conversations that resulted in these texts were as wide-ranging as they were illuminating, and we have attempted to retain something of that conversational tone and flow.

We have organized the book into two sections. Part I provides a linear narrative of Serkin's life with emphasis on his European roots and the impact of his move to the United States. Part II focuses, with the help of the interviews, on three key aspects of his work, particularly as it unfolded in America: his art and career as a pianist; his activities as a pedagogue, including his long association with the Curtis Institute in Philadelphia; and his key role in institutionalizing a redefinition of musical values in America through his work as artistic director of the Marlboro Music School and Festival in Vermont. The book concludes with a discography by Paul Farber that documents an essential part of Serkin's achievement.

In writing of our subject, we usually call him simply "Serkin." Many of the people we interviewed would speak of "Mr. Serkin," even some who had known him well for decades. To many others he was "Rudi," which we use for the boy and when it is necessary to distinguish him from other Serkins. With his widow we enjoyed a relationship that grew to be quite close; not to refer to her as "Irene" would have seemed stilted and forced.

A project such as this is inevitably shaped and constrained by its timing. By the time we began our project, many of Serkin's contemporaries had died, especially, of course, those who had known him when he was young. The philosopher Karl Popper, a friend since their youth in Vienna and the last survivor of Serkin's adolescent communist associations, died a few weeks before our scheduled interview. Yet, as Serkin himself died only fairly recently, the world is still full of people who have a personal stake in his story. Although our portrait of Serkin is as true as we could make it, we had no desire to invade the privacy of those who were close to him. In the centenary year of his birth, we attempt to provide a narrative of Serkin's long life, a sense of its significance, and the historical context in which it unfolded. In the end, however, the essential core of Serkin's life was music, and it is in his music making that his life's deepest truths are expressed.

Part One

CHAPTER ONE

Beginnings: Eger and Vienna

> *Art comes not from ability but from necessity.*
> —ARNOLD SCHOENBERG

SERKINS AND SCHARGELS

Like Rudolf Serkin himself, his family surname resists pinning down. Sarkin, Sorin, Soric, Surin, Suris, Suric, Surman, Sorkin, Surkin, Syrkin, Scherkin, and Sirkin are some of its variants, the last two employed by Rudolf's father, Mordko, who also went by Mordechai, Marcus, and Max.[1] Derived from *Sarah*, it was a fairly common metronymic surname among Jews from the area now called Belarus. When an Irving Syrkin wrote to inquire whether he might be a relative, Serkin answered, "My father always told me that there was only one family Serkin; so I feel we must be related somehow."[2]

Mordko Chazkelewitsch Serkin came from the town of Disna in Belarus, the heartland of eastern European Jewry, once part of Poland but in Russia's "Pale of Settlement" when he was born there in 1860. He was a musician whose life was dragged down by bad luck, poor choices, and a talent that was probably inadequate to his calling. When Rudi was 9, he wrote a song for his father's birthday that began with the words *Wie kommt's, dass Du so traurig bist*—Why are you so sad?

Mordko was the atheist son of an orthodox Jew, a shoemaker (or possibly a tanner, or both). Working with leather was something of a family tradition:

one of Mordko's brothers was also a shoemaker, and Mordko himself ran a shoe repair shop for a time and later eked out a living making shoe polish in Vienna during the First World War.[3] Mordko left home at 16 to escape his family, religious orthodoxy, and conscription into the Russian army. Having been educated only in the Talmud, he taught himself Russian (free, it was noted, of a Yiddish accent).[4] His German, however, was Russian-accented, and he maintained a sentimental allegiance to Russia all his life. Mordko Serkin's gift was his voice. After working for several years as a cantor in Poland, he went to Berlin to study at the Stern Music Conservatory, only to be expelled from Prussia along with the other Russian students in the spring of 1881 in the aftermath of the assassination of Czar Alexander II.

Austria-Hungary was the obvious next place to go. There, during the previous decades, the government had enacted a series of reforms that removed burdensome restrictions from the lives of its Jewish subjects, leaving them free to move around, settle down where they wished, and participate in the Empire's developing economy. Mordko Serkin headed to the Austrian capital, where, for a time, he sang minor roles in minor operettas. For the next ten years he plied the Habsburg provinces as cantor and stage singer.

In 1892, while performing in the northern Bohemian spa of Teplitz, he met his future wife, Auguste Schargel. The Schargels were Jews from the Galician town of Jaroslav (now in southeastern Poland, near the Romanian border). A part of the postemancipatory Jewish migration that moved westward geographically and upward socially, the Schargels consented to the marriage of their 18-year-old daughter to the 32-year-old singer, but on condition that he abandon his stage career. In exchange, they set him up in business. Amalie (known as Maltschi), Serkin's sister and the family memoirist, speculated that going into business might not have been a big sacrifice for their father: "Maybe he saw that he was not going to be successful on the stage and was even happy to slip into a bourgeois life."[5]

Mordko and Auguste Serkin's first child, Wilhelm (Willi) was born in 1893, followed by Robert in 1895 and Charlotte (Lotte) in 1897. Mordko opened a series of stores in northwestern Bohemia and persisted in his restless ways, moving with his family from Teplitz to Karlsbad and back again to Teplitz. In August 1897, now nearing 40, Mordko registered himself, his wife, and their three young children with the authorities of Eger, a town of close to 24,000 in the westernmost corner of Bohemia, hard by the German border.

The Serkin-Schargel marriage cannot have been an easy one. Auguste Serkin later admitted to her youngest daughter, Marthl, that an early love for another man had always cast a shadow on her feelings for her husband.[6]

*Auguste Schargel
and Mordko Serkin,
April 27, 1892*
COURTESY OF ANNA
BUCHTHAL

Auguste's many letters to Rudi are written in a sad and muted, perhaps depressed voice. Mother and son seem to have been emotionally distant. Mordko, a musician with proletarian roots and strong opinions, was by all accounts a more expressive personality, with a sometimes wicked humor that Rudi would inherit. "And now, my dear son," he wrote to Rudi, announcing the unexpected marriage of his daughter Lotte in 1922, "I have some family news that will surely interest you: Fritz and Lotte have taken it upon themselves to obtain the legal rights that will permit them to sleep together."[7]

EGER

Bohemia, where Rudolf Serkin was born, has long been something of a question mark on the map of Europe. A part of the Habsburg Empire since the seventeenth century and with a population part Czech and part German, it had a fractured identity all its own. Even today, "It's Greek to me" translates into German as *Das sind mir böhmische Dörfer*—It's all Bohemian villages to me.

Eger (belonging to Austria-Hungary), now known as Cheb (in the Czech Republic), was a town thoroughly German in character and outlook—not merely German-speaking, but more closely linked to Germany than to the Austrian Empire of which it was a part. Eger's citizens were "more German than the Germans."[8] Readers of Schiller know Eger as the site of the assassination of General Wallenstein in 1634, and it was long a stopping-off place for Germans on their way to the nearby spas of Karlsbad, Marienbad, and Franzensbad.

Although Jews had lived in Eger since the Middle Ages, the town had never welcomed their presence, expelling them repeatedly. During the century's final decade, the period in which Mordko Serkin moved there with his family, its Jewish population doubled to about 550, less than 3 percent of the overwhelmingly Catholic population.[9] Eger, meanwhile, "had become a byword for anti-Semitism,"[10] a hotbed of German nationalism, and a home base for Georg von Schönerer, the notorious anti-Semitic demagogue, who for several years represented the Egerland in the Austrian parliament and was an early inspiration to Adolf Hitler. "The self-respecting citizens of Eger," writes historian Elizabeth Wiskemann, "were not expected to buy from Jews nor to have anything to do with them socially."[11] Maltschi remembered Christian children throwing stones at her.[12] A café in Eger posted a sign forbidding entrance to "Jews, Czechs and dogs."[13]A Christmastime boycott in 1909 would have targeted Mordko Serkin's notions store on the Bahnhofstrasse, the street that links the train station to the market square.[14] The animosity was returned: "a cross between Austrians and apes" is how one Serkin characterized Eger's Germans.

In 1938, when Eger, along with the rest of what was by then known as the Sudetenland, was handed over to Hitler's Germany, the local citizens welcomed the takeover as a long-overdue homecoming: *Heim ins Reich*. After the war, Eger's Germans were put into trains and dumped onto the German side of the border. Today Cheb is a Czech-speaking town of 31,000, lovely and picturesque, with a historic, oblong, cobblestone market square (where the house in which Rudolf Serkin was born still stands), though the street vendors are as likely to be Vietnamese as Czech.

The first Serkin child to be born in Eger was their fourth, Susanna, called Suse. A second cluster of four children came in relentless succession a few years later: the oldest, Rudolf, on March 28, 1903, Amalie in 1904, Martha (Marthl) in 1906, and finally Paul in 1907. Rudolf was a popular name among the Jews of the Empire in the years following the suicide of the liberal Crown Prince Rudolf in 1889, but given the strong antimonarchist views of Serkin's father, this would be an inconceivable namesake. According to one family story, Rudi and his seven brothers and sisters were all named after opera characters. *La Bohème* received its Vienna premiere in 1897: might Rudolf Serkin's antecedent be Puccini's Bohemian poet Rodolfo?

Serkin later told several of his children that as a young boy he had overheard his mother confiding to a neighbor that he was an unwanted pregnancy that she had hoped to abort: it had been more than four years since her previous child, and she had no desire for more. What does a child do with such a memory? Perhaps this early experience of himself as a contingent, accidental, almost defiant presence, where nothing, least of all love, was a given, helps to account for Serkin's tendency to deflect aggression inward, or express it covertly, or to transform it in his art.

During their seventeen years in Eger, the Serkins lived at no fewer than six different addresses, the moves, presumably, occasioned by the needs of the growing family and perhaps also by financial exigencies. Serkin's fondest memories were of a house on the edge of town with a large, untamed garden, chicks, ducks, and a sheep named Dolci. He was to love animals all his life. However difficult their years in Eger, the Serkins would look back affectionately on the German-Bohemian market town, especially after the extreme poverty and near starvation that awaited them in Vienna.

JEWS IN POVERTY

In 1926 the *Egerer Zeitung* published an article by Armin Wilkowitsch, Eger's cantor and resident Jewish historian, about Serkin, then 23 and already famous. Its self-promoting tone offended Rudi's oldest brother, Willi, who fired off a strongly worded letter to the author. Wilkowitsch, in turn, sent Willi's letter on to Auguste Serkin, accompanying it with his own furious response:

> Permit me to send you this "thank you letter" from your son for all I have
> done for you and your dear family. You will remember how the *Egerer Neue
> Nachrichten* attacked your late husband when I wrote the first report on Rudi's
> concert! How they described you as being persecuted by the Russian government,
> how they described Rudi as a bow-legged Jew-boy who could bang out a few
> notes, etc. . . . Have you totally forgotten what we have done for your family? Of
> course we were too polite to mention that we had gone deep into our pockets on

your behalf, that I had lent my money to you for your business *without interest* for years. That I traveled to Frankfurt to get money for you . . . that I paid for the journey for you and your family [from Eger to Vienna] without asking for recompense . . . Everything thrown into the sea of forgetfulness?[15]

This angry letter touches on two issues that figured significantly in Serkin's life: his early experience of poverty and his Jewishness. In interviews he spoke of his family as "bitterly poor." During the worst years of the war in Vienna his father's sour joke was that being full is the fantasy of someone with a stomach ailment. But if early poverty and hunger left psychological scars, they were not apparent; although Serkin enjoyed the material comforts his success brought him, his tastes were modest, and he had no arriviste interest in luxury or display. Still, at the core of his sense of himself, the experience of his family's poverty stayed with him. Sitting as an old man with his wife on a hotel balcony overlooking Switzerland's Engadine Valley, he allowed that he hadn't done badly "for a poor boy from Vienna." And of an old Swiss friend, Serkin said repeatedly that the strength of their bond had come from their shared experience as "the children of poor people."[16]

Serkin's Jewish origins were a subject about which he spoke little. Mordko was a freethinker and outspokenly antireligious. Wrote Maltschi, "He had no truck with priests or Judaism: 'It's all a fraud!'"[17] He closed his business on the Sabbath, but only as a concession to Eger's Jews.[18] Something of Rudi's early attitude toward religion can be inferred from the handwritten story outline of a four-act play that he wrote in adolescence, in which God "sits on a throne of velvet, smoking a pipe and drinking a schnapps, surrounded by angels and similar vermin . . . He is somewhat *shicker* [drunk]." (Serkin's penchant for parody continued into later adolescence, and as an adult he would be both ironic and playful, with a well-known tendency toward practical jokes and scatological humor.)

Serkin's relationship to Judaism never changed, and like most of his siblings, he married a non-Jew. Irene Serkin maintained that in the early 1930s her husband was strongly attracted to Christianity and considered converting, but to avoid any impression of disloyalty at a time when Jews were so vulnerable, he decided against this step. In letters to his wife, he alludes now and then, usually ironically, to being Jewish; clearly he recognized it to be a part of who he was. "Merry Christmas," he wrote Irene in 1983, "from the old Jew Rudi." But the prevailing attitude in the world in which he moved was that to insist on an ethnicity whose religious content had been abandoned was a retrograde tribalism, even a caving in to the worldview of the Nazis. (Violinist Alexander

Schneider, by contrast, was preoccupied with Jewishness to the point of obsession and took delight in writing Serkin about what he called his *Idisiche nischome*, his "Jewish soul.")[19] Though Serkin's attitudes toward matters Jewish were inevitably complex, he neither rejected nor embraced his Jewish origins, but rather confronted with integrity the psychological and social conundrums of being a non-Jewish Jew.

CHILD PIANIST

Serkin maintained that his father had tried to make musicians of all his children and forced them to study either violin or piano with an insistence that Serkin thought unwise (this became the explanation he later offered for having handled the talent of his own son, Peter, with such diffidence.)[20] He claimed that his musical talent first expressed itself at age 2, when he tried to play on the piano "what I heard from my brother,"[21] but according to Maltschi, his musical gift was first recognized when he burst into tears while listening to one of his older sisters practice: "It's all wrong, it's all wrong," he is said to have wailed to his father.[22] Serkin first played the violin, but detested it, finding the sound too close to his ear.

At 4 (or possibly 5) Rudi started studying piano with Camilla Taussig, with whom he took daily lessons until he was 9.[23] Of her, he wrote:

> My first teacher Camilla Taussig was a very sweet woman but scary to look at. She was very short (when I was five I already had outgrown her), and she had an enormous hunchback and very long fingers like spiders. Besides she cooked for me after specially good lessons (as a reward) a hot beer soup, a Czech national favorite, and made me eat it. But I loved her, and I never did throw it up.

Serkin told Dean Elder, his interlocutor in the most extensive interview he ever granted, that he first performed in public when he was "5 or 6" in Franzensbad, the spa neighboring Eger, though he gave different versions of this event at different times.[24] His first documented performance was a recital of Fräulein Taussig's students in Eger's Hotel Kronprinz Rudolf on June 6, 1909. The program lists Lotte Serkin, Robert Serkin, Willi Serkin . . . and *der kleine Serkin*—little Serkin. Rudi, of forty participants the only one whose given name was not printed, was 6.

The program testifies to a remarkable level of musical culture in what were, after all, provincial backwaters. It began and concluded with piano transcriptions from Beethoven's Fifth Symphony. Of the remaining thirty-six (!) works,

Rudi Serkin COURTESY OF ANNA BUCHTHAL

most were by long-forgotten nineteenth-century composers of pedagogical and salon pieces, such as Gustav Lange and Fritz Spinder, but also represented were Mendelssohn, Chopin, and Schubert. Rudi played Hirschberg's E-minor Fantasie and Stephen Heller's *Trotzköpfchen*. (Charles Rosen: "I can die happy without ever hearing another piece by Heller.")[25] The overwhelming presence of Jewish names among Miss Taussig's students attests to Eger's rigid social divisions as well as to the lively participation of Jews in a culture from which, only some fifty years before, they had been largely cut off. A local paper gave young Serkin his first review: "Little six-year-old Rudi Serkin delighted his audience with his extremely precise playing, earning him his first well-earned laurels."[26]

The following year Serkin began music theory lessons with a local chorus director. A year later—he was 8—he penned a bit of doggerel (whether his own or copied, we don't know) on the subject of theory that expressed some of the musical values he was to articulate and exemplify for the rest of his life:

Musik verschönert das Leben,
Ihre Theorie ist wichtig,
Drum greife nie daneben,
Und spiele immer richtig.[27]

Loosely translated:

Since music gives life grace,
And its theory is crucial,
The notes must be in place,
And errors unusual.

It must soon have become obvious that Serkin's talents exceeded Eger's normal standard. He applied to the conservatory in Prague but was rejected as too
young. (As an 18-year-old he would be turned away by Ferruccio Busoni in
Berlin for being too old.) When the Polish-born violinist Bronislav Huberman
and his accompanist, the Viennese virtuoso Poldi Spielmann, performed in
Eger, Rudi (then 8 or 9) appeared before them to play etudes by Czerny, Kuh-
lau, and Köhler. It was said that "they looked with astonishment at the tiny
magician."[28] A few weeks later Mordko and Rudi traveled to nearby Pilsen to
play for the Viennese pianist Alfred Grünfeld (1852–1924), who was giving a
concert there. Grünfeld was sufficiently impressed to encourage 9-year-old
Rudi to move to Vienna to study with Richard Robert.

VIENNA

According to Serkin, Grünfeld not only suggested that he study in Vienna, but
actually took him there.[29] Although Grünfeld came from Prague, after moving
to the imperial capital, he became *the* Viennese pianist—"the embodiment of
Vienna."[30] The Viennese pianistic style of the time, of which Grünfeld was the
apotheosis, stressed virtuosity, but also sensuality of tone, passion, "optimistic,
carefree pleasure in life, a warm, beautiful, kind humanity, with a distaste for
'depth,' ponderousness, exaggeration, and hardness"—these associated in Vienna
with a German style.[31] Serkin later described Grünfeld's playing as "incredibly
beautiful."[32] He was a special favorite of the city's Jews, a passion spoofed by a
contemporary joke in which a Viennese Jew remarks, "Of the Jewish holidays I
observe only Grünfeld's concerts."[33] Grünfeld was unquestionably a serious
musician, whose programs favored relatively pedal-free Bach, Mozart, Beethoven, Schubert, Chopin, and Brahms, in addition to nineteenth-century
miniatures, especially, it need hardly be added, the waltz.[34]

Richard Robert (1861–1924), the teacher to whom Grünfeld sent Serkin,
was a prominent figure in Viennese musical life, though he lacked the international reputation of the city's most famous piano pedagogue, Theodor

Richard Robert COURTESY OF PETER SERKIN

Leschetizky. Born Robert Spitzer, he studied with Julius Epstein (a teacher of Mahler's), Franz Krenn, and Anton Bruckner. (Although Serkin was one of the few major Austro-German pianists of his generation whose pedigree did not descend back through Liszt and Czerny to Beethoven, he could, through Krenn's teacher Ignaz Xavier Seyfried, trace his musical lineage to Mozart.) Robert taught piano, composition, and conducting, composed, wrote music criticism for Viennese newspapers, edited the journal *Musikalische Rundschau*, and briefly headed the New Conservatory of Music, where Grünfeld served on his board of directors.

After Robert's death in 1924, his student Wilhelm Grosz published an obituary that provides fervent testimony to the impact he had on his students as a man, teacher, and musician:

> Words are not adequate to convey what he meant to us, his many students, who loved him like a father . . . He didn't have a "method," nor did he form "piano players" (how he hated all these words) but he was to all of his students the most loving guide into the deepest essence of music, whose secrets he knew like no one else . . . Living as he did in the works of the great Masters gave him a reputation among some as a reactionary, but most unjustly.

Anyone familiar with Serkin's reputation as a teacher will recognize much of him here: the importance of technique, but only as it serves musical goals, rejection of "method," and the affinity with the canonical composers of the German-Austrian tradition. George Szell, also a Robert student, wrote a similar testimonial for Robert's sixtieth birthday in 1921 that stressed, in addition to his musical qualities, his "kindness, his integrity, modesty, and readiness to help."[35]

In moving from the provinces to Vienna (then with a population of two million, the world's sixth largest city), Rudolf Serkin was following a well-beaten path: Sigmund Freud, Alfred Grünfeld, Karl Kraus, Gustav Mahler, Joseph Roth, and Artur Schnabel had all done the same. But unlike these other Jewish boys, Serkin, 9 years old, was sent to live with complete strangers. Even young Clara Haskil, who had left her native Romania to study with Robert some years before Serkin, had come to Vienna with a bachelor uncle.

Serkin boarded with "a petit-bourgeois Jewish family" chosen by Robert, where he was lonely and homesick and wet his bed.[36] They were, Serkin said later, "terrible people."[37] He lamented to his parents:

> I am not able to practice at the Weissbergers, even though I have to! First, Else's piano teacher arrives. Then she practices herself. When Frau Weissberger has a headache I'm not allowed to practice. Then Else's singing teacher arrives. Then the others arrive to practice. Then the customers arrive, and visitors, and I'm not allowed to practice then either. And then the whole day is gone. I am allowed to go for a walk only when Frau Weissberger is at home. I can go for a walk whenever and for however long I want to. I'm going to tell her that, too. I am homesick, but it will pass when Lotte comes, at least someone from the family!!! Frau Weissberger is *very* unfriendly now. I can't stand her!!!! It's already cold here.

Mordko and Auguste Serkin in Eger, ca. 1913. Sitting between them, their three youngest children: Amalie, Paul, Marthl. Standing: Lotte COURTESY OF ANNA BUCHTHAL

Please write *often*. Mama should send me trousers and gloves. Also send winter socks. I am healthy. Many kisses, Your Rudi.

In spite of his complaints, there is a tone of resolve—to practice, to move about in freedom, to resist the restrictions his landlords impose, to prepare for the winter—that is remarkable in a 10-year-old child and no less characteristic of the man he was to become. With his sign-off declaration, *I am healthy,* he reassures his parents and declares both his physical well-being and an impressive resilience. Subsequently, he lodged with "an old lady with one leg" who, he said, made him chase her around the dining table.[38]

In the summer he returned to Eger. A letter from Richard Robert to Rudi testifies to the boy's great good luck in having come to this teacher:

> *My dear Rudi,*
> *Your letter, which reported your safe arrival in Eger, made me very happy. Too bad that your lamb and Mazi were no longer there, but fortunately you now have*

many more chickens, who will keep you busy. I hope you are romping around and getting a lot of fresh air.

I want you to regain your strength, so that you can work hard again in the fall. In order that you don't do anything but laze about in the summer, you can start again to practice two to two and a half hours. The most important thing, dear Rudi, are the technical exercises, which have enabled you to progress so far in such a short time. Practice these exercises twice a day (mornings and afternoons half an hour each time), but attentively, with a large, beautiful, singing tone, as if you were playing a melody.

Additionally, please practice the following:
Bach, 2-Part Invention No. 14 (B-flat major)
Bach, 3-Part Invention No. 6 (E major)
Weber, E minor Sonata, 1st movement
Let me know when you are finished with these exercises—when you have practiced them with one hand and two hands, emphasizing each in turn and with clarity—and I will send you new ones. At the difficult passages, emphasize alternately the first, then the second, third, fourth notes, etc., as you did it for me. I am very curious to see how you study on your own, since you will also work alone in Vienna.

Dear Rudi, I want to say once again that the main thing is for you to come back home strong and healthy, so that if in the summer you sometimes practice a bit more or less, or not at all, it doesn't matter to me at all. *You are a good, hard-working boy and you deserve to romp around to your heart's content. So have a good time, play more with your brothers and sisters and with the animals than on the piano, climb on the trees and—write me now and then how you're doing. Soon the vacation will be over and you'll begin work.*

I am very much looking forward to seeing you here again in a few weeks. I have become very fond of you in this short time, and we are good friends already, aren't we?

One notes the admonition not to practice too much—a wish that many would harbor for the mature pianist with at least as much fervor as Robert did for the boy.

Robert and his wife, Laura, were enormously kind to the gifted children who studied with him—they had none of their own—even dedicating a corner of their living room to toys purchased especially for shy Clara Haskil.[39] Irene Serkin recounted that when Rudi played for Robert, he would look at the bust of Beethoven at the end of the piano to see whether he was smiling in approval, and that Laura Robert gave him lessons in "manners." In later years Serkin remembered the many times he played transcriptions for six hands and three pianos with George Szell (then Georg Széll) and Hans Gál.[40] He also remembered with distaste the Weber sonatas and rondos Robert forced him to play.[41]

After studying with Robert for some years, Serkin wrote him that he needed to broaden his musical education and would seek another teacher. Robert responded supportively and congratulated him on his maturity and growing independence. The following week Rudi showed up at Robert's at his usual time and resumed his lesson without either teacher or student referring ever again to the exchange of letters.[42] Indeed, Serkin turned up at Richard Robert's for at least one lesson long after he had left Vienna and established himself as a concert pianist.[43]

During Serkin's second year in Vienna, events back in Eger took a dramatic turn for the worse. Maltschi writes:

> My father's business partner turned out to be a crook. He stole all the liquid capital and disappeared "to America," as one said at the time, meaning simply: gone forever. We were declared bankrupt and most of our personal possessions were sold off to satisfy the creditors . . . And in Eger someone who had been through a bankruptcy sale was all but an outcast. So off to Vienna. To begin a new life, and above all to be reunited with Rudi.[44]

Ominously, the Serkins left for Vienna on the same day as the call for general mobilization that signaled the start of the First World War in August 1914. Met in Vienna by Mordko, who had traveled ahead to find lodging, they found his face "yellowish" and his eyes sad. "He seemed suddenly shrunken."[45] Mordko Serkin, however demoralized and defeated, did his best to maintain a semblance of a "normal" family. Nonetheless, it is not difficult to imagine the degree to which Rudi, whose father had failed not once but repeatedly, must have felt the weight of the responsibility that his gift had conferred on him.

Their first apartment was in a "dark, narrow street,"[46] Pfluggasse, about a mile northwest of St. Stephan's Cathedral on the periphery of the Ninth District, known for its concentration of middle-class Jews, and not far from the Roberts' apartment on the Liechtensteinstrasse. Serkin remembered it as a "kind of ghetto" frequented by prostitutes who gave him candy.[47] Subsequently the family moved further north, to a top-floor apartment in a five-story walkup on the Döblinger-Hauptstrasse, a busy thoroughfare on the unfashionable edge of the comfortable Nineteenth District, across from an old Jewish cemetery and immediately outside the Gürtel, or Belt, that demarcates the limits of central Vienna. Though presumably chosen for its proximity to Richard Robert's flat, it was also a part of the city that Mordko Serkin knew well, having lived there in the 1880s. That the Serkins chose not to move into the heavily immigrant, Jewish, eastern European Second District suggests how decisively the family had broken from its origins.

Mordko Serkin never recovered from the disaster that befell him in Eger. In Vienna he lived a hardscrabble existence, doing his best to help keep the family afloat by manufacturing soap ("very bad soap," according to Maltschi) and shoe wax.[48] His two older sons vanished into the war and were reported killed, until they eventually turned up as Russian prisoners. Maltschi remembers "a difficult adjustment—in school we were Russian, Jewish, and Czech [i.e., Bohemian]: enemies, despicable and ridiculous."[49] Given that by their own reckoning they were not Russian (except for Mordko), Jewish only in name, and Bohemian by happenstance, the Serkins must have found their outsider status particularly irksome and in some ways worse than it had been in Eger.

Cruelly, Susanna, their fourth child and the sibling to whom Rudi felt closest, died in 1919 at the age of 20 of a brain embolism (or tuberculosis, depending on the account). Her death affected Rudi profoundly. Over a year later he wrote to a family friend in Eger: "It is very difficult for me to write you. My sister Suse died on May 4, 1919. I must ask you not to write either my parents or Lotte for the time being, since this could only result in their getting terribly upset. My parents, brothers, and sisters are doing relatively well. I have nothing to say, except that it is your duty not to go under."[50] *I have nothing to say*—even as a 17-year-old he struck this note, and withdrew.

Conditions in Vienna during the war were wretched, probably the worst of any city in western Europe. Serkin never forgot the hunger. In a letter to her future husband, Serkin's youngest sister, Marthl, wrote that the war had exposed the absence of love between their parents and destroyed their family.[51] In 1922, eight years after coming to Vienna and four years after war's end, Mordko died there, 62 years old, "a worn-out and disappointed man."[52]

What is striking about Serkin's childhood is the extraordinarily high degree of instability that he had to contend with as a young boy. His parents were uprooted in the extreme, completely separated from their own backgrounds, for many years virtually nomadic, and enjoying, even when settled, few of the ties that normally link family and community. Mordko's bankruptcy and the family's departure in disgrace from Eger and final slide into permanent poverty marginalized them even further. As personalities, Mordko and Auguste could hardly be called rock solid. That this enormously gifted and intelligent son of theirs would himself become a restless and inwardly rootless man is hardly surprising, nor is it difficult to see why a person growing up as Rudolf Serkin did

Mordko and Auguste Serkin COURTESY OF ANNA BUCHTHAL

would invest the one stable point in his life—music—with almost divine attributes.

FRAU DOKTOR

If Richard Robert was Serkin's first big lucky break, his second was Eugenie Schwarzwald (1872–1940), known as Genia, or Frau Doktor, a remarkable and controversial figure, "much loved and much hated, over-praised and maligned."[53] Serkin would later say that he owed her his entire education. Over thirty years older than Rudi, she formed the beginnings of his adolescent intellectual and social development, became a second (in some sense, perhaps a first) mother, and remained the object of Serkin's devotion even beyond her death. When, as an old man dying of cancer in Vermont, he was asked by his daughter Elisabeth whether there was anyone he would like to see, he said that the one person he would still want to talk to was Frau Doktor Schwarzwald.[54]

Schwarzwald was born Eugenie Nussbaum near the town of Czernowitz, as far east in the Empire as Eger was west and later home to a vital literary culture.

*Frau Doktor
Schwarzwald, 1932*
COURTESY OF
PETER SERKIN

As a child she moved with her family to Vienna. Later, she earned a doctorate in German literature and married Hermann ("Henne") Schwarzwald, a brilliant and ambitious economist and administrator, who was to work in the upper reaches of the Finance Ministry and is credited with keeping Austria's economy afloat after the First World War. Frau Doktor sported short hair, spoke German "with a Slavic accent," and looked "like one of the Roman emperors."[55] Vienna could not contain her energy, and her network extended to Scandinavia—the Danish writer Karin Michaelis was a close friend—and even to America: the journalist Dorothy Thompson, who knew Schwarzwald in Vienna and had turned to her in a depression, credited her with saving her life.[56] The Schwarzwalds lived more or less openly in a menage à trois with the charming and attractive Marie ("Mariedl") Stiasny, who would later follow them into Nazi-imposed exile and nurse them in their last days in Zürich, where Hermann Schwarzwald died in August 1939, Genia a year later.

Eugenie Schwarzwald is the subject of an extensive literature, most of it in memoirs of Viennese artists and intellectuals who studied or taught in her schools, participated in her salon or in the many events and institutions that she organized.[57] Many of them are not particularly kind. Robert Musil, who described her in his diaries as "this juxtaposition of doing good and doing herself good" (*dieses Nebeneinander von Wohltun und Sichwohltun*) immortalized Schwarzwald as the slightly absurd *saloniste* Diotima in his novel *The Man without Qualities*.[58] Elias Canetti found her "a well-intentioned bore" whose conversation was "a hopeless jumble."[59] Among the harshest of her many detractors was the writer Karl Kraus, whom the Schwarzwalds had supported and hosted, and whose newspaper *Die Fackel* Serkin read avidly. Kraus renders a cruel portrait of the Schwarzwalds in his drama *Die letzten Tage der Menschheit*—a self-serving, self-deluding, altogether ludicrous couple falling over themselves as they rush from one miscalculated good deed to the next.

More generous, Alice Herdan-Zuckmayer (a Schwarzwald school alumna who married the playwright Carl Zuckmayer) sensed something beyond the off-putting manner: "I felt for the first time that there was a secret, and began to suspect that behind her overflowing tenderness, the ardent embraces, the declarations of love, lay an area so protected that no one was allowed in."[60] It seems fair to speculate that this well-camouflaged reserve was something Eugenie Schwarzwald and Serkin recognized and loved in one another.

When Richard Robert first brought Serkin to Schwarzwald on July 11, 1915, Rudi was a 12-year-old musical prodigy, she an educator and social activist in her early forties.[61] Schwarzwald's views on pedagogy were outspokenly progressive: learning, she believed, should take place "without pain and boredom, and should bring only joy."[62] According to one account, Serkin was one of the "few selected boys" to attend Schwarzwald's girls school—a story that has, however, no basis in fact.[63] Serkin asserted throughout his life that because of the demands of the piano he enjoyed no formal schooling of any kind, and there is no evidence to the contrary, though he did occasionally perform in Schwarzwald's school.

Schwarzwald's girls' school in the center of Vienna was the most prominent and stable of her many projects. She also founded Austria's first coeducational elementary school, wartime community kitchens, and countless other projects and charities. In 1916 she started a fresh-air fund for Viennese children, Wiener

Kinder aufs Land, by which they could escape the heat and squalor of the city's wartime summers for farms, rural estates, and retreats in Austria and Slovenia. Maltschi remembered the camp in Topolschitz (now Topolšica, in Slovenia) that she and Rudi attended as "pure paradise."[64] Herdan-Zuckmayer, another Topolschitz alumna, conveys something of the 15-year-old Serkin's insouciant charm and self-confidence: "Once some important officials were expected at Topolschitz, from whom Fraudoktor was hoping for some favors . . . Rudi came [to perform], as always, in his swimming suit, having also put a tie around his neck, otherwise nothing."[65] Another veteran of the Schwarzwald camps wrote to Serkin years later recalling memories of lectures by Willi Schlamm (who in the United States was to become an editor of the right-wing *National Review*), Karl Popper whistling a symphony, and especially Rudi himself, biking down the mountain, his legs in the air, bare chested, with a red cloth around his neck.[66]

Through Schwarzwald, Rudolf Serkin made a number of extraordinarily talented friends; in addition to Popper, who described Serkin as his oldest friend,[67] they included the physicist Victor Weisskopf, the painter Oskar Kokoschka,[68] and the architect Adolf Loos. For Loos's sixtieth birthday in 1930 Serkin wrote a characteristically charming tribute:

> When I was twelve years old, I met Adolf Loos . . . In the children's camp at Topolschitz there was a small pool, which was fed by a thermal spring. There Loos taught me a somersault: you had to jump, do a complete turn, and land with your feet on the water. Endlessly patient, Loos demonstrated the somersault at least thirty times. Never have I learned something more thoroughly. I can still do the somersault today, and when I do it, I always think with love and gratitude of my teacher, Adolf Loos.[69]

Reading descriptions of Schwarzwald's school and camps, it is impossible not to think of what was later to become the Marlboro ideal: its purposefulness, the relative informality of its style, but above all the pleasure in the ongoing creation of a community based on meaningful activity, collaboratively undertaken. "The feeling of community came alive in everyone," wrote Paul Stefan, a prolific and ubiquitous chronicler of the Viennese music scene.[70] Stefan evokes a sense of somewhat self-conscious other-worldliness that also characterizes Marlboro: "There's no consumerist one-upmanship, no gambling or cards, no noisy bar, no idle plunking on the piano, no dilettantism to torment frayed nerves. From somewhere far away the newspapers report on the usual ugliness."[71]

EARLY CONCERTS

Serkin embarked on his career as a concert performer during these Viennese years, although Mordko Serkin refused to market his son as a touring Wunderkind. "I'm not going to spoil his childhood!" he is supposed to have said.[72] If Serkin did not tour as a child, he did, from the age of 12, help to support a family of ten.[73]

His earliest concerts, then, all took place in Vienna. He gave his first "professional" concert on February 1, 1916 — he was not yet 13 — at Vienna's first musical address, the Grosser Musikvereinssaal, the ornate, second-floor hall just off the Ring. The program featured the Berlin Royal Opera soprano Claire Dux, then at the height of her fame. Oskar Nedbal conducted. For the 12-year-old Rudi Serkin it was a distinguished debut indeed. He performed Mendelssohn's virtuosic, spirited G minor Concerto, Op. 25, a work he would continue to play throughout his career and was credited with having revived. Although most of the program was Dux's, it was the 12-year-old Rudi who was the evening's star:

> This Wunderkind performed the difficult and beautiful concerto, which has been unjustly neglected by the great pianists, with a clear and calm objectivity, with an agility of finger and a clean, fluid technique [*Passagentechnik*] that suggest an unusually musical and well-instructed talent. Particularly notable: the secure sense of rhythm, the transparent phrasing. His touch itself is extraordinarily powerful, although he has not yet developed the multi-colored sound palette whose mastery is obligatory for a modern piano virtuoso.[74]

It is astonishing how accurately the critic of the child pianist in 1916 pinpoints the very qualities that reviewers would discern in Serkin's playing throughout his seventy-year career: the technique, the musicality, above all the rhythm and the power, as well as the relative inattention to tonal color. Notice of Serkin's performance extended as far as Leipzig, where the *Neue Zeitschrift für Musik* also gave him a glowing review.

He gave his first public solo recital later in the same month, playing a program of "sonatas and short pieces" by Mendelssohn, Schubert, Bach, Scarlatti, Chopin, Schumann, and Liszt, "all receiving," according to one critic, "a surprisingly mature interpretation, balanced in its whole as well as in its details." Serkin continued to charm and move audiences and critics in the recitals and concerts that followed. In December 1917 he performed Beethoven's Third Piano Concerto with Franz Schalk and the Tonkünstler Orchestra in a celebra-

Rudi in Vienna
COURTESY OF
PETER SERKIN

tion of the anniversary of the composer's birth. In these early years in Vienna he also played the Mozart C minor and Grieg concertos with young George Szell conducting the orchestra of the Konzertverein.

TRANSITIONS: JOSEPH MARX, POLITICS

Serkin had not undergone a formal, conservatory-based musical education. Richard Robert, who himself had been the director of the New Conservatory, no doubt saw a training in composition as a necessary part of a musician's preparation, and at about the time of his Vienna debut, Serkin began studying composition, counterpoint, and harmony with Joseph Marx (1882–1964).

Rudi

Marx, though relatively young himself, was regarded as an epigone. Vienna's modernists disapproved of him. The composer Ernst Krenek described him as a "hugely fat and noisy man," who "in later years was to become a spear-carrier of the mindless Teutonic reactionaries and a forerunner of the Nazis."[75] Marx's songs, Serkin wrote later, were "very warm and lyrical but rather on the sweet side."[76] A letter from Serkin to Marx, written in the 1960s, was grateful beyond politeness and acknowledged their affinity as musical traditionalists. Marx, for his part, remembered Rudi as cheerful and highly gifted.[77] The scores of some songs that Serkin wrote during the time of his work with Marx, dedicated to his sweetheart of the time, Lisl Sinek, have survived among his papers. According to the musicologist Jeffrey Kallberg, they are written in a "popular" and somewhat indistinctive style.[78]

At home and through Schwarzwald, Serkin was immersed in a thoroughly politicized atmosphere: it was said of Mordko that he expressed his anti-Habsburg convictions so forcefully that Auguste would close the windows to keep the neighbors from hearing, and that he thought of moving back to Russia after the Revolution there.[79] As Rudi's own political awareness sharpened, he began to doubt his calling as a musician, thinking he needed to devote himself to something more useful, and for a time he toyed with the idea of becoming a carpenter.[80]

After war's end, Serkin was able to bring politics and music together by playing regularly for workers as well as for large groups of children (whom he also taught) from working-class, politically active families housed by Vienna's socialist government in a wing of Schönbrunn Castle, the eighteenth-century Habsburg palace on the southwestern side of the city. "We had our own revolution in Vienna, a small one," he told Otto Friedrich.[81] On one occasion at Schönbrunn, Serkin, a good sport if ever there was one, offered up his head to a group of eager boys who had acquired a set of hair clippers. After they sheared a strip straight down the middle of his scalp, he prevailed on them to finish the job by shaving off what remained.[82]

SCHOENBERG

It was but a short step from political to musical rebellion. In 1918, as the war was ending, Adolf Loos introduced the 15-year-old Serkin to Arnold Schoenberg (1874–1951), then in his mid-forties, at a concert at the Schwarzwald school, where Schoenberg had taught after-hours classes.[83] The meeting resulted in one of the most significant and problematic associations of Serkin's life. Given the political and social ferment in a city whose conservative taste in music was, in the words of pianist and scholar Charles Rosen, "the most uncompromising in Europe,"[84] the bracing, passionately austere climate of intellectual, moral, and aesthetic rigor practiced by Schoenberg and his followers ("artistic and intellectual Puritanism")[85] had a powerful and lasting impact on Serkin.

Serkin later expressed his alienation from Vienna by describing it as a city that was "very—how shall I put it—conscious of its own importance."[86] Paul Stefan entitled his 1913 account of the atmosphere of bitterness and defeat among Mahler's Vienna supporters *Das Grab in Wien*: The Grave in Vienna.

He provides a grim list of what he calls "the Austrian foibles": "lack of persis-tence, fear of anything new, a platonic love of action (as Frau Doktor calls it), a cold heart and lack of hospitality, a frame of mind that can only be called *petit-bourgeois* and bureaucratic, a need to dominate."[87] This was the Vienna that Mahler and then Schoenberg worked so hard to overcome—a struggle into which young Serkin threw himself whole-heartedly. When Serkin informed Richard Robert of his decision to study with Schoenberg, Robert "nearly cried," Serkin wrote, "but our relationship remained the same."[88]

For about two years, Serkin played "nothing but contemporary music."[89] The years of his association with Schoenberg, 1918 to 1920, span the middle of a fallow period in Schoenberg's compositional activity, coming between his "first" and "second" revolutions, between the total chromaticism that marked the so-called emancipation of the dissonance and the invention of the twelve-tone system, which he developed in the early 1920s.[90] It has become common-place to recognize in Schoenberg the continuities with and affirmation of prin-ciples represented in the music of Wagner and Brahms.[91] Nonetheless, as Charles Rosen writes, "What should be emphasized here is the sense of scan-dal, the consciousness of moral outrage aroused by Schoenberg's work after 1908."[92] The protective way that Schoenberg's followers grouped around him was both a response to their pariah status—Ernst Krenek writes of having to approach Schoenberg through his "bodyguards"[93]—and also an accommoda-tion to Schoenberg's rather authoritarian personal style. He took as students not only aspiring composers but many performing musicians, like Serkin.[94] According to one of Serkin's fellow students, Schoenberg would include one student in the class who was wealthy enough to pay for the others. In Serkin's class, it was a Dutchman who knew what was happening and "didn't mind at all."[95] "It was very informal," Serkin told Otto Friedrich. "Once, I wrote a rondo for piano and I brought it to him. He looked at it, and then he said, 'Serkin, I'm going to cut out all the parts that you like best.' . . . And he did. All the extra things . . . He wanted only the essentials."[96]

However pathbreaking Schoenberg's compositions, his pedagogy was tra-ditional: a complete mastery of theory, he believed, was the necessary founda-tion for a creative musician.[97] As texts Schoenberg used his own *Harmonielehre* (published in 1911 and dedicated to Mahler) and Heinrich Bellermann's classic *Contrapunkt*, first published in 1862. Schoenberg emphasized objectivity, the striving for truth, whether in composition or in performance, and "clarity and precision."[98] According to the prospectus of Schoenberg's Society for the Pri-vate Performance of Music (Verein für Musikalische Privataufführungen), "The only success that the artist should have here is that which should be most important to him: to have made the work and thus its author understand-able."[99] The atmosphere that characterized his classes was that of the work-shop, and his relationship to his students was one of master-apprentice rather than master-disciple.[100]

"No," Serkin corrected Isaac Stern, who suggested that Adolf Busch was the decisive influence on him, "it was Schoenberg. Busch just added to it. It was Schoenberg." Schoenberg gave Serkin an aesthetic that was ethically based and an institutional model for implementing it. Like Schwarzwald, Schoenberg taught Serkin at an early age what total dedication could achieve, how it was possible for, indeed incumbent upon visionaries and idealists and outsiders to transform their commitments into meaningful action with endless work and sacrifice. It was a lesson Serkin would always carry with him.

Serkin's years with Schoenberg coincided closely with the life span of Schoenberg's Society for the Private Performance of Music (1918–1921), which had its initial performances in the Loos-designed auditorium of the Schwarzwald school.[101] Charles Rosen again:

> The Society was an extension of Schoenberg's teaching; it was, at least in theory, an instrument of education and not of propaganda. Contemporary works were at last rehearsed for as long hours as needed to be played well: music that required more than one performance to be understood was repeated several times at sub-sequent concerts. The center of interest was to be the music itself, and the per-former was relegated firmly to second place . . . Above all, the music was to be withdrawn both from the dictates of fashion, which inflated and deflated reputa-tions arbitrarily, and from the pressures of commercialism.[102]

Applause was forbidden, and Serkin later remembered with pride that after he once performed a piece of Schoenberg's, the audience was moved to stand—silently. Each piece would typically receive ten to twenty rehearsals, an intensity of striving that Schoenberg is said to have learned from Mahler. (Not that Schoenberg was always such a perfectionist. Serkin remembered playing second viola to Schoenberg's cello in the Mozart quintets: "I didn't play well—but bet-ter than Schoenberg.")[103] Adding to the strong emphasis on community and learning that Serkin had absorbed through Schwarzwald, the Verein gave him an institutional model that fused musical, cultural, and educational ideals. He was to implement important aspects of this model, though under very different circumstances, thirty years later at Marlboro. And like Schoenberg, Serkin was to become a powerful force at the center of something that his friend the pianist Claude Frank described as "like a cult," adding quickly, "a good cult."[104]

One of 60 panels from a
quilt Irene Serkin made
for her husband's sixtieth
birthday. This one depicts
Serkin on the viola
(right) playing with
Schoenberg (second from
right).

Serkin's own performances in the Verein—he was its youngest performer
—spanned a wide range of material, including Josef Suk's *Erlebtes und Erträumtes*,
an eight-hand version of Berg's Op. 6 orchestral pieces, five pieces collected
under the title *Exotikon* by the Czech composer Vitézslav Novák, Schoenberg's
Three Pieces, Op. 11, and a four-hand arrangement of Stravinsky's *Petroushka*
with fellow Schoenberg student Edward Steuermann. "People started throwing
things at me," Serkin said. "Sometimes the police were called in."[105] After a concert in Prague in March 1920 in which Serkin and Steuermann played Debussy's
En blanc et noir, Anton Webern wrote Alban Berg, "The public finally broke
through the prohibition on applause. It was a big success, especially for *Steuermann and Serkin*."[106] (Serkin knew both Webern and Berg well and studied
Berg's Piano Sonata, Op. 1, with the composer.)

How fully Serkin had become a part of the Schoenberg camp is evident
from contemporary accounts and later memoirs.[107] In 1920 Erwin Stein described
Serkin's refusal to accept a fee for performing at the Verein in a letter to
Schoenberg: "To my suggestion that he doesn't have to play for people for free,
he said he doesn't play for people at all. A great guy!"[108] Nonetheless, Serkin
began to feel, as he expressed it in later years, that he could no longer perform
the music of Schoenberg and his circle "with honesty." He told others, simply,
that he "was tired of it." After Serkin's death Karl Popper wrote Irene that he
and Rudi had tried, together, to learn to love modern music, and that, together,
they gave up.[109] Otto Friedrich quotes Serkin: "Schoenberg was a fantastic

man. I loved him. But I could not love his music. I told him so, ̣
forgave me. He said, 'It's up to you to decide whether you want t̤
side of the barricades or that one.'"[110] About Schoenberg's piano piɛ
said—the persistent use of metaphors of war and revolution spẹ   ̣ᴇ
time—"I had to tell him I didn't like them . . . He looked at me as if I were a
soldier who had deserted."[111]

Serkin's need to break away must have been festering for some time before
it broke into the open. As early as February 1920, nine months before the rup-
ture with Schoenberg, he wrote Maltschi from Harthof, a Schwarzwald-run
country boarding school outside Vienna: "I am so glad to be at Harthof, and
not to have to associate with all these small people in Vienna. I want to learn a
lot, and then go away, far away."[112] Yet practically to the end of their association, Schoenberg seems to have been unaware of Serkin's unhappiness. Responding to a suggestion by the Dutch conductor Willem Mengelberg that some of
his students should join him in Amsterdam, Schoenberg wrote in October—
this was a month before Serkin's defection—recommending Serkin and
Steuermann, "both of *the very first!!!* order . . . I can guarantee you that soon
both of them will be famous—each in his own way."[113] That Serkin would
have revealed so little of his disaffection before acting on it was consistent with
his need to keep surfaces smooth. There can be little doubt that his sudden
departure surprised Schoenberg and contributed to his implacable displeasure.

By the time of his break with Schoenberg, Serkin was a guest in some of the
most distinguished houses of the Viennese intelligentsia, even outside the
Schwarzwald circle. The writer Arthur Schnitzler, whose son Heinrich was also
a Richard Robert student, writes in his 1920 diary that he attended a Serkin
concert and had him to tea, along with Richard and Laura Robert, George
Szell, and others.[114] Even in Serkin's earliest years in Vienna, according to
Wilkowitsch, he played "in the first boudoirs of Vienna's aristocracy" and was
presented with his own Bösendorfer. But factionalized as Vienna was, Serkin
cannot have found it a comfortable place after he left Schoenberg, who refused
from then on to have anything to do with him.*

---

* Schoenberg was not to put him entirely out of mind, however. In 1922, in a letter to Alexander Zemlinsky, he described a young pianist as "a kind of female Serkin—a sensation"
(October 26, 1922, Arnold-Schönberg-Institut, Vienna), and he listed Serkin among his
former students in a roster he prepared for an autobiography in 1944 (Nuria Nono-
Schoenberg, ed., *Arnold Schönberg 1874–1951; Lebensgeschichte in Begegnungen* (Klagenfurt:
Ritter Klagenfurt, 1992, p. 390). But Serkin was not among the former Schoenberg students
who contributed a photograph and vita in an album compiled for their teacher on the occasion of his fiftieth birthday in 1924.

"Schoenberg never forgave me," Serkin laments in the Stern interview, adding that he "couldn't stand it in Vienna any more. I felt I was *suffocating*!" (In old age his memories of Vienna seem to have been entirely positive, focusing on his involvement with Schwarzwald, Schoenberg, Loos, and Kokoschka.)[115] But he always spoke warmly of Schoenberg: "I loved him," he told Isaac Stern. "I adored him. He was warmhearted, gay, and funny." Serkin's and Schoenberg's paths did not cross again, though Schoenberg and Adolf Busch were to enjoy a friendly backstage encounter in Los Angeles in 1937, and, according to Peter Serkin, his father had considered playing Schoenberg's Piano Concerto in the late 1940s as a way of repairing the breach.[116]

What course Serkin's life would have taken had he not met Adolf Busch and left Vienna for Berlin at this juncture is anyone's guess. He had been bound for Paris, where he intended to study with Hungarian-born Isidor Philipp (1863–1958), the great "modern" educator of a long series of excellent French pianists,[117] at the time a professor at the Paris Conservatoire. Serkin included Philipp in some accounts and omitted him from others. He told Isaac Stern that he was part of a Schwarzwald-organized cultural program that was "to bring Viennese culture to Paris," and Otto Friedrich quotes him as saying that he was to go to Paris to study with Philipp, be treated for tuberculosis, and work at the Hôtel de l'Opéra.[118] According to a Columbia Artists Management's press release from the 1960s, Serkin was going to Paris to join Loos and Kokoschka, accompany Elsie Altmann (Loos's wife) in her dance recitals, and "introduce the works of Schoenberg in Paris."[119]

It was, however, not the ticket to Paris (which he lost, the often-told story goes, thus missing his train) that took Serkin out of Vienna in 1920, but a ticket to Berlin, and it was paid for by Adolf Busch. The encounter with the great German violinist signals the major turn in Serkin's biography. The rest of his life followed from his relationship to this man.

The most reliable of many versions of this first meeting is probably told by Leonie Gombrich (the mother of Ernst Gombrich and a former student of and assistant to Leschetizky).[120] Busch and his wife Frieda were in Vienna, where he had been concertmaster of the Konzertverein Orchestra from 1912 to 1918, and where his daughter Irene had been born in 1917. Seeking a replacement for his Vienna accompanist, who had become ill, Busch turned to Leonie Gombrich. She contacted her friend, the Swedish musician Kalle Söderberg, who recommended Serkin. Unable to find Rudi's address, they went to the police for the information, whereupon Busch wrote to Rudi and invited him to the Gombriches' house on the Gumpendorferstrasse. Leonie Gombrich describes the encounter:

We had just sat down to afternoon tea, when the maid came in and said, "There's a young lad outside who says he's been told to come." As a precaution, she would not let him into the room. I went out and recognized Rudi immediately. I took him in right away. He was terribly shy, but we all took a liking to him at once, even before we had heard him perform. There are many anecdotes about this tea, many of them invented by Adolf.

After the tea, Rudi played. Adolf was enchanted and nudged Frieda and me the entire time. Then Adolf said, "Wouldn't you like to play a little Chopin?" Rudi answered very shyly but very decidedly, "I'd rather play Bach." He made a tremendous impression on all of us. Adolf said: "The way the boy plays, you see the whole score in front of you."

Adolf and Frieda withdrew, then asked Karl [Gombrich, Leonie's husband] and me to join them for a war council, and very quickly it was decided that Adolf and Frieda would have Rudi live with them in Berlin. Rudi was thrilled when Adolf and Frieda invited him and, movingly, said, "I hope that someday I can do something so kind for you—for you and others."[121]

Busch suggested that Serkin should go to Berlin to study with Ferruccio Busoni (who, as it happens, was a close friend of Isidor Philipp's). "The next day," concludes Leonie Gombrich, "father Serkin came, and everything was settled."

"The Venerable Firm of Busch & Serkin"

> *I don't give a damn about anything relating
> to success and advancement in the world . . .
> Our way of making music, Toscanini's way,
> yours, Rudi's and mine (including my
> quartet), is nevertheless the right way
> and the "enduring" way!*
>
> —ADOLF BUSCH TO FRITZ BUSCH (1927)

BERLIN

The violinist Barbara Kempner, who was studying with Busch in Berlin, remembered the telegram from Adolf and Frieda that had preceded young Serkin's arrival, alerting the maid to the visit of a gifted young pianist whom she should point straight to the bathtub.[1] The story sounds unlikely— Serkin was, after all, 17—but it shows how he was perceived, as a kind of "wild child" whom Frieda and Adolf had taken under their wing to educate and acculturate.

The Busches themselves had moved from Vienna to Berlin just a few years earlier, when Adolf Busch was appointed to succeed Henri Marteau at the Hochschule für Musik in the position first held by the great violinist Joseph Joachim. In comparison to the young man they were taking in, the Busches, though not yet 30, were well established and relatively settled, with a young daughter and a large house in the suburb of Lichterfelde. They were also a very powerful pair of personalities. Both came from musical backgrounds. Busch's father was a cabinet maker and fiddler who made and repaired string instruments; his brother Fritz was to become one of the outstanding German conductors of his time, and his brother Herman became the Busch Quartet's cellist. Frieda's father, Hugo Grüters, was a conductor and *Musikdirektor* of the city of Bonn, described by a contemporary musicologist unenthusiastically but not without admiration as "a capable musician, free of the ambitions of the modern type of conductor."[2] Frieda's mother was of Dutch Jewish background. Frieda herself had a modest musical gift; she sang and played the clarinet and the piano, sometimes serving as her husband's accompanist.

Adolf was on his way to becoming the most revered German violinist of his time, described by none less than Thomas Mann as *the* German violinist[3]—the incarnation of an ideal that encompassed his physical qualities (tall, handsome, and usually described as blond, although in fact his hair darkened as he matured), as well as his character and artistic attributes (both straightforward and deep). Although best known today as the primus of the Busch Quartet, he regarded himself primarily as a composer. He was possessed of an enormous talent, a musicianship of selfless and compelling conviction and commitment, and a direct, warm, and highly charismatic personality. Artur Schnabel—not one to be taken in—first came across the 16-year-old Adolf playing in Fritz Busch's orchestra in Riga, "a blond boy, touchingly different from the rest," his face revealing "devotion" and "independence."[4] There are not many people who knew Busch who did not find him extraordinarily attractive in every way, his appeal the more powerful for being artless. His flaw—it was consistent with his spontaneous and open nature—was his capacity for rage: he was what the Germans call *jähzornig*—prone to outbursts of great fury.

His wife's was a more complicated and controversial personality. Her detractors, and they were numerous, described her as socially ambitious, opinionated, and bossy. She was quick to find fault and to convey her disapproval. Admirers were drawn to her generosity and intensity. Serkin's brothers and sisters, in whose lives she figured significantly during what one called the Hitler years, disliked her greatly; they regarded her as controlling and renamed her *Unfriede* (strife, discord). Her energy, which enabled her to manage her husband's (and, for a period, Serkin's) career and then earn a doctorate in political economy when she was in her forties (with a dissertation that was at least partly ghost-written, according to family stories, by her brother Otto), probably served to hold together a less than stable personality. Maltschi, who was later to live with the Busches and her brother and help look after young Irene, met Adolf and Frieda for the first time when they came to Vienna with Rudi in 1921. She wrote that she "fell under Frieda's spell immediately": "She was very pale and had too little chin. But her face was illuminated by penetrating, very light blue eyes. Her face was extraordinarily lively and expressive."[5] Yehudi Menuhin, who spent two summers studying with Busch in Basel, remembered Frieda with studied neutrality, describing her in his autobiography as "a small, wiry, vigorous woman of high and earnest principle . . . [who] had energy to spare for me when I was in trouble or at fault."[6]

Frieda's family, the Grüters, were *Bildungsbürger*—passionately devoted to high culture as educated Germans understood it, especially to Germany's musical tradition and its literary classics. Although not necessarily hostile to contemporary culture, the aesthetic of the *Bildungsbürger* was inherently conservative, and, as filtered through the Busches, it had an immediate and lasting impact on the young Serkin. Although he played Schoenberg's music for the family at the 1920 Busch Christmas tree-trimming in Berlin, soon afterward he was writing Maltschi of his new enthusiasms with the insistent single-mindedness of a recent convert: "You have to read Goethe's *Wilhelm Meister: Lehrjahre* and *Wanderjahre*! And if possible the Greek tragedies by Sophocles (*Antigone, Oedipus*, etc.). *And then Shakespeare!* . . . If you go to concerts, go only to classical, real music. Nothing modern! *Bach*, Mozart, Beethoven, Schubert." *Nothing modern!*— this less than a year after he had been performing in Schoenberg's Society!

Writing Maltschi in September 1921 on the occasion of her seventeenth birthday, Serkin offered a credo on courage, conviction, change, and autonomy that reveals a remarkably introspective disposition for an 18-year-old:

> I believe that with everything that one does, and with everyone with whom one interacts, one has a *genuine* feeling (for me it's only a feeling), which, however, is usually suppressed by something else (prejudice, habit). What is essential is to recognize that feeling and to liberate it from the others . . . I believe, then, that one shouldn't be afraid of leaving something to which one is usually bound by habit or other minor things.

The meticulous attention required to tease out deep truths and the fidelity to what has been discovered and recovered with such effort—Serkin is, of course, reflecting on his own immediate past here—these would remain unspoken watchwords for the rest of his life.

In the same letter Serkin expresses shame and regret at having acted badly toward his father and with indifference to his mother while he was still living with them in Vienna. He then goes on to link this private failure with his activist politics: "I used to believe that to 'help' workers was more important than my nearest surroundings. Now I believe differently. Think about it: all that *I* with my body can do directly for humanity is on a small scale . . . What's ethically the highest is to help those closest to us and push everything else to the side." In another letter to Maltschi written in the same period Serkin again implicitly disavows his earlier, more radical stance, distancing himself even from Schwarzwald: "Better to be a bit of a philistine than in this youth movement. So be careful with what you let influence you, be it scouting, Schwarzwald . . ."

The ground for Serkin's renunciation of all involvements excepting only music and the private sphere had no doubt been prepared in Vienna; he had, after all, left Schoenberg and was planning to go to Paris to study with a musician of a much more mainstream cast. But Adolf and Frieda provided Serkin with a persuasive alternative to his Vienna life and its commitments, drawing him into a very close family governed by a single-minded, quasi-religious devotion to music. Later, in America, Serkin would explore wider arenas for his energies and talents, but together with Adolf and Frieda Busch he dedicated the next fifteen years to his art and his career. He may have regretted having treated his parents badly, but it was regret from a distance. Though he remained a loyal and dutiful son and brother, the stronger tie was now to another family.

Relatives have blamed Frieda Busch for the distance that came between Serkin and his own family: she was manifestly a snob, and the Viennese Serkins would not have been up to her standards. And once Serkin was in her family, she seems to have wanted all of him for Adolf, Irene, and herself. Nonetheless, not all the responsibility can be laid at Frieda's feet, nor is it difficult to see why Serkin, himself still a boy, would cast his lot with a family so rich in vitality and talent and so tightly fused by a life in music.

Since the nineteenth century Vienna and Berlin have been considered antipodes: heart-wit; feminine-masculine; southern charm–northern vigor. "Vienna and Berlin, the two complementary halves of the German essence."[7] Schnabel, who had made the move more than twenty years before Serkin, characterized the contrast as one between Viennese servility and German obedience.[8]

In the 1920s both cities were still reeling from the economic consequences of the war. But Berlin, with a population close to 4 million (twice Vienna's), was Europe's third largest city and more important than ever as a gathering

Auguste Serkin and her sons. Sitting: Paul, Auguste, Rudi. Standing: Willi, Robert COURTESY OF LENE MEZGER

point for new energies. Vienna, having lost its significance as a political and economic center along with its empire, had become irrefutably and irredeemably provincial. A "musical market second to none in the world,"[9] Berlin offered opportunities that were correspondingly greater than could be found in Vienna. In the mid-1920s there were twenty-one concert halls in Berlin (eight of them large) that offered some six hundred concerts in the winter season.[10] Serkin played most frequently in the Singakademie (which seated 1,010, or 1,321 with stage seats) and the 1,036-seat Beethoven-Saal (in terms of prestige, Berlin's Carnegie Hall), larger than ideal for chamber music and recitals, and both very close in size to New York's Alice Tully Hall (1,096).[11] (London's preferred venue for chamber music, Wigmore Hall, by contrast, has a capacity of about 540 seats.)

For Adolf Busch, Berlin versus Vienna was not an issue. He had moved back to Germany for a job at the Hochschule für Musik (resigning after a year and a half, when the neo-Romantic Viennese Franz Schreker was appointed director), and the manic postwar modernist milieu for which Berlin was to become so famous—"the golden Twenties"—was hardly his style. Musically there was a steady back and forth between the two cities—in the months after moving to Berlin Serkin himself returned to Vienna for numerous concerts,

*Frieda, Adolf, and
Irene Busch, 1924*
COURTESY OF PETER
SERKIN

among them the Schumann Piano Concerto for Richard Robert's sixtieth birthday ("outwardly in constant motion and inwardly with almost feminine delicacy, according to one review),[12] and Beethoven's Triple Concerto with Busch and Paul Grümmer.

Once in Berlin, Serkin plunged almost immediately into Germany's hyper-active musical life. On January 25, 1921—he had been in the city hardly two months—he and Busch played an evening of three Beethoven sonatas at the Singakademie under the aegis of Germany's best-known concert agents, Wolff & Sachs, as part of an ongoing Beethoven cycle. In early March Serkin audi-tioned, successfully, for the Düsseldorf conductor Karl Panzner; toward the end of March he and Busch gave recitals—their soon famous Sonata Evenings —in Bremen and Munich. On April 1, Busch, Serkin, and Paul Grümmer were back in Berlin performing the Beethoven Triple Concerto.

The next evening, April 2, saw the genesis of what was to become the most famous of all Serkin anecdotes. Busch and Serkin gave a Bach-Mozart Evening in the Beethoven-Saal, where Serkin played the piano part in Bach's Fifth *Brandenburg* Concerto. "The surprisingly generous but stylistically perfect" performance of the first movement's brilliant cadenza reaped the pianist a "spontaneous and special success," wrote the critic Paul Schwers.[13]*

The audience's enthusiasm was such that Busch urged Serkin to play an encore. Serkin asked for a suggestion, and when Busch jokingly proposed the *Goldberg Variations*, Serkin took him at his word and played through the entire forty-five-minute work. (There is no mention of the encore in Schwers's review.) Serkin had probably studied the *Goldberg Variations* with Richard Robert, who had published an edition of them. Serkin told Dean Elder that he had played them after one of Schoenberg's seminars in 1918 and that Schoenberg was unfamiliar with them.[14] The story of the *Goldberg* encore has itself been given numerous variations: depending on the particular version, at the conclusion of the performance remaining in the audience were only Adolf and Frieda Busch, Albert Einstein (or sometimes the critic Alfred Einstein, though he was not living in Berlin at the time), Artur Schnabel, and/or one of Leonie Gombrich's daughters. This was presumably the last time Serkin ever played the *Goldberg Variations* as an encore, but it was a work with which he became closely identified during his years in Germany and Switzerland.**

Berlin's most eminent musical personality in the early interwar years was the great pianist and composer Ferruccio Busoni, who had returned there from Zurich in 1920, summoned, like Schreker, to help build the cultural life of the

---

* A later iteration of Serkin's Fifth *Brandenburg* with Busch has been preserved on a hair-raising recording from 1935. Isaac Stern's excited prose conveys the impact of Serkin's performance of the cadenza in Prades in 1950: "I will never forget hearing him in that rehearsal: all of us in the orchestra just sitting and listening to his cadenza start slowly and begin to build, and then build and build, and suddenly march across the musical landscape with giant boots, and end with a musical volcanic eruption of sheer ecstasy, a climax that leaped out of the piano and roared its way into the coda, at which point we made our orchestral entrance, playing the final few measures, and then finishing the last chord and suddenly jumping to our feet and screaming like crazy, 'Bravo! Bravo!' It was one of those astonishing musical moments when everything that could be done with a phrase was done—and a little more." *My First Seventy Years* (New York: Knopf, 1999), 91.

** The 1920s saw a flowering of *Goldberg* performances. They were, of course, played before that—Brahms is said to have performed them—but rarely.

The industrialist Otto Krebs, Adolf, Irene, and Frieda Busch, Serkin COURTESY OF
PETER SERKIN

new Republic. Once in Berlin, Serkin wrote to Busoni—who is supposed to
have told his students, "In order to get beyond being a virtuoso, you first have
to be one"[15]—and asked for a lesson. He got no answer, but in May and
December of 1921 he heard Busoni perform the last twelve Mozart concertos in
Berlin.[16]

During this period Serkin and Busch prepared Busoni's second violin
sonata for performance. Busoni gave them an audience and was pleased with
their performance. (He told Serkin he was too old for lessons, but that he
should attend as many concerts as possible and play with more pedal.) Shortly
afterward, Serkin and Busch heard Busoni and Egon Petri play the same piece
(on November 16, 1921 in the Beethoven-Saal, in an arrangement for two
pianos) at twice their tempo. Serkin: "We had tried to play slowly and with dig-
nity, since the sonata develops from a Bach chorale. Now we had to relearn it,
in order to play it in his spirit."[17] (Busoni died in July 1924. His successor at the
Musikhochschule was Arnold Schoenberg.)

In the course of this first year with the Busches, Serkin became a full-
fledged family member in all but name. In the summer he spent a vacation
hiking with Adolf and Frieda in Arosa in eastern Switzerland, in October he

joined them in celebration of the seventieth birthday of Frieda's father in Bonn, and in November they all traveled to Weimar to play at the dedication of Holzdorf, the estate of the industrialist Otto Krebs, where they were to spend summer vacations in the years ahead.

During the same time, Busch's and Serkin's performing lives were becoming increasingly fused. In 1921 they gave "sonata" concerts in Breslau, Wiesbaden, Duisburg, Vienna, Hannover, Copenhagen, and Göttingen, frequently playing Beethoven, Busoni, Reger, and Schubert, sometimes Brahms and Mozart, with occasional solos (a Bach partita for Busch, Schubert's *Wanderer Fantasy* for Serkin) added into the mix.

Serkin's first year as a full-time concertizing pianist was busy, though at the time it seemed but a warm-up for the year to come. "I am practicing quite a bit," he wrote Maltschi in September. "I have, after all, a lot planned for next year." In January 1922 he played the Reger concerto with Wilhelm Furtwängler and Vienna's Tonkünstler-Orchester, with which he had made his debut only six years earlier. As an enthusiastic critic for the *Neues Wiener Tagblatt* wrote, "With Serkin and Furtwängler this work, which has been performed before, received its premiere."[18] (Serkin was to perform under Furtwängler only one more time in his life. Some years later, playing the continuo part in a Bach concerto in which Busch was the soloist, he incurred the conductor's wrath by honoring a request covertly conveyed by Busch to follow his—slower—tempo rather than Furtwängler's, thus pulling the orchestra with the piano and giving the victory to Busch. Furtwängler, supposedly, never spoke to Serkin again.)[19]

From a letter Serkin wrote on March 7 to his parents in Vienna, one gets a sense of the intensity of his activity in 1922, taking him as it did through Germany and to Switzerland, Austria, Czechoslovakia, and Italy:

On the 22nd I went from Berlin to Bonn, where I played Beethoven's G major concerto with orchestra. Then I had eight days to learn a Mozart concerto, which I played in Magdeburg. Then a concert in Kassel, back to Düsseldorf . . . Then two concerts in Cologne, where we got a good rest. Then Berlin again, where I played one Bach concerto and one Mozart concerto yesterday. Busch also played two violin concertos. Tonight we are playing together in Potsdam for a benefit.

That July, Mordko Serkin died. With Rudi now a steady and reliable source of financial help, his mother stayed on in the family apartment in Vienna. On September 13, 1922 Serkin held his first Berlin solo recital in the Singakademie, giving the premiere of Busch's new C minor Piano Sonata, with its Reger-like double-fugue finale.[20] He also appeared with Busch at occasions like the Strauss

Week in Vienna (March) and the Reger-Bach Festival in Heidelberg (October), in addition to the sonata recitals and performances with members of the Busch Quartet in various combinations (trio, piano quartet).

COLLABORATION

From the very beginning, reviewers and the public recognized the special quality of the Busch-Serkin duo, the Basel critic Erich Wolff, for example, describing "the still unknown pianist" Rudolf Serkin in 1922 as "a partner equal to [Busch] in every regard," possessing "a quality of intellect and expressive forcefulness that is actually unheard of for his age."[21] (When he played in Basel again in December of the following year, however, the review in the *Nationalzeitung* trounced the performance, faulting his lack of technical care and wild use of the pedal and suggesting that he needed to concertize less and practice more.)[22] In October 1922 Alfred Einstein observed, "Serkin is not merely the 'accompanist' of Adolf Busch, but already a performer with a sense of style similar to Busch's, similar in his great talent (an infinitely far cry from virtuosity), and strangely similar in a sensibility that is soft without being weak or feminine."[23] Before the end of the year they were playing before sold-out houses, and by 1925 they were such an entrenched fixture in Germany's musical life that a critic described them as *Busch und Serkin, die bewährte Firma*: "the venerable firm of Busch & Serkin."[24]

The Busch-Serkin collaboration quickly established itself as a unique partnership in the history of modern "classical" performance. Though they are sometimes singled out as pioneers in their genre—two musicians of the highest caliber regularly playing programs of the highest quality as equal partners—they were not without precedent: Schnabel and Carl Flesch first began playing together in Berlin in 1908, to be joined soon afterward by the Belgian cellist Jean Gérardy, much as cellist Paul Grümmer, and then, in 1926, Herman Busch, were to come together with Busch and Serkin to form the Busch Trio. Schnabel later paid tribute to Busch and Serkin: "Compositions for piano and one other instrument are often performed. But—with the exception of the Adolf Busch–Rudolf Serkin ensemble—they are hardly ever played by two persons equally equipped. Mostly it is, as I would say, a *prima donna* and a footman."[25]

Equally equipped they may have been, but Busch was unquestionably the senior partner. Reviewing in 1978 the reissue of a 1943 recording of Beethoven's Sonata No. 8 in G, Op. 30, no. 3, the critic Joseph Horowitz wrote of Busch and his impact on Serkin:

*Adolf Busch and
Rudolf Serkin*
PHOTOGRAPH BY
WILLOTT. COURTESY OF
PETER SERKIN

It is a performance absolutely free of affectation or superfluous detail, motivated
by an integrity that is not merely dutiful, but fierce. Mr. Serkin's marvelous con-
tribution is indispensable, but it is Busch who makes the stronger impression.
In fact, one cannot listen to such playing without inferring that key elements of
the pianist's style—the ability, for instance, to keep the line taut at the softest
dynamic levels—are very likely drawn from the example that Busch set.[26]

Horowitz's insight is corroborated by a recollection of Serkin's student Seymour Lipkin, who once asked Serkin in Busch's presence the tempo of a particular piece. Serkin turned to Busch: "Adolf, what is our tempo?"[27]

"Transposed Heads." From the April 1, 1933 issue of the Swiss magazine Sie und Er
COPYRIGHT RINGIER AG, ZOFINGEN, SWITZERLAND

By the end of the decade, Busch and Serkin were—this is very rare in chamber music—playing together from memory. When Busch played programs of shorter, more virtuosic pieces rather than the great German classics, he chose other pianists (Schnabel's "footmen") such as Hubert Giesen. On such occasions the printed program carried the banner "Adolf Busch: Violin Evening. At the piano: Hubert Giesen" rather than the by then customary "Busch-Serkin Sonata Evening." (The extent to which Busch and Serkin became identified with one another is vividly illustrated by a doctored photograph that appeared in the April 1, 1933 issue of the Swiss illustrated weekly *Sie und Er*, showing them with "transposed" heads: Busch's head on Serkin's body, at the piano, and Serkin, similarly, on the violin.)

It would not be too much to say of Busch and Serkin that for them the personal was musical and vice versa: both were musicians in every fiber of their being. Their affinity drew on similarities in temperament, outlook, and musical background, though there were significant differences between them. Isaiah Berlin applies Schiller's distinction between the "naïve" artist (who has an unbroken relationship to himself, nature, the world, etc.) and the "sentimental" artist (who strives to recreate a lost wholeness) to describe the contrast between Verdi (naïve) and, for example, Wagner (sentimental). Berlin quotes Schiller, "The poet . . . *is* either himself nature, or he *seeks* her," and continues:

> The first of these, Schiller calls *naiv*, the second, *sentimentalisch* . . . The naïve
> artist is happily married to his muse. He takes rules and conventions for granted,

The Busch Trio: Rudolf Serkin, Adolf Busch, Herman Busch COURTESY OF PETER SERKIN

uses them freely and harmoniously, and the effect of his art is, in Schiller's words, "tranquil, pure, joyous." The sentimental artist is in a turbulent relationship to his muse: married to her unhappily . . . He cannot be at rest . . . Hence the effect of the sentimental artist is not joy and peace, but tension [and] conflict.[28]

It is a contrast that also works for Busch, who was straightforward, direct, and unselfconscious, and Serkin, who was none of these. The paradigm drawn by Schiller and revived by Berlin does not apply in every detail to Busch and Serkin, but it helps to sharpen the contrast between the two musicians and to account for the particular power they exerted in combination.

One of their strongest bonds was a shared line of descent from and devotion to the music of Max Reger. Both Adolf and Fritz Busch had been close to Reger personally and made his music their cause. (Fritz Busch took his fiancée to a rehearsal of Reger's *Hiller Variations* conducted by the composer and asked her to tell him "truthfully" whether she liked it or not: if not, "there could be no thought of marriage! . . . After the general rehearsal . . . we agreed that we could carry on with the marriage.")[29]

Serkin probably first came into contact with Reger's compositions through Richard Robert, whose inscribed copy of the Reger Piano Concerto Serkin later owned. (Serkin's student Anton Kuerti happened upon it in Vienna, purchased it for $5, and presented it to Serkin.) In the years with Schoenberg, himself strongly influenced by Reger,[30] Serkin became more deeply immersed in Reger's music. Indeed, in Schoenberg's Society for Private Musical Performances Reger was performed more frequently than any other composer.

Although neither Reger (who died in 1916) nor Busch, nor, ultimately, Serkin followed Schoenberg in his radical reworking of the classical tradition, the specific musical sensibility that Serkin developed while studying with Schoenberg went into the mix of qualities that enabled him to be such a natural partner to Busch. "What Reger shares with Schoenberg—," writes the musicologist Walter Frisch, "and what is . . . rare among composers working in an advanced chromatic language and with larger instrumental forms at this time—is the ability to control broad spans with a fusion of harmonic tension, subtle phrase structure, and thematic construction"[31]—precisely the musical features to which Busch and Serkin attended as performers in their own playing.

Serkin, finding himself musically at home with Busch, added to their partnership the energy of his own high-strung temperament. Busch described their way of working together—today one would use the word *synergy*—in a 1938 article:

I do believe that ensemble playing offers better opportunities for deepening the purely musical approach [than solo playing] . . . In my work with my ensemble partner and son-in-law, Rudolf Serkin, frequent examples of this have arisen. In the Sonata in G major, Opus 30, Number 3 of Beethoven, to offer but one example, the composer's indications are *"molto moderato e grazioso."* In my own readings of this movement, I inclined to emphasize the *molto moderato*. Serkin, in his turn, wishes the *grazioso* to be emphasized. Both of us had the composer's indications to support our views. Where should the distinction be made? We talked it over, argued about it; each tried it in the other's way, and then we talked some more. Finally, we put the sonata aside for some days and then came back to it afresh. The second time, each had considered the other's wishes to the point of evolving a new, unified conception. I obeyed the *grazioso* indication by taking the *tempo* a shade more slowly, though not entirely slowly. And thus we worked out a reading which suited us both and which, we believe, comes closer to the composer's indications than either of us would have been able to accomplish alone. That particular kind of experience never could be attained by solo playing alone, where one is of necessity in accord with one's self.[32]

How characteristic of Busch, a lifelong stranger to ambivalence, is the last sentence!

To the audiences of the 1920s and 1930s, Serkin's playing exemplified a style that was thoroughly modern, even when it was applied to a traditional repertoire. "Objectivity," *Sachlichkeit*, was the byword of the day. It was used to characterize the rejection of an earlier era's *Schwulst* (floridness and pomposity) and self-indulgence, a struggle in which Mahler (himself a father-in-spirit to Schoenberg) had been a pioneer a generation earlier. Mahler's biographer Henry-Louis de la Grange writes of "Mahler's famous *Sachlichkeit*," going on to quote a colleague of Mahler's at the Opera: "He was only interested in the thing itself."[33] It is in the context of this legacy that a Stuttgart reviewer described Serkin as an "objective musician, who indeed practices his art for the sake of the matter at hand."* Not everyone regarded Serkin's objectivity favorably. A Berlin critic, after conceding that "it is hardly possible to play the piano better than he does," described Serkin as an "*up to day* [*sic*] youth, infected by that movement which shirks from any expression of feeling and the concomitant wealth of nuance."[34]

The most prominently articulated musical feature of this objectivity was the insistence on a fixed beat: said Serkin, "For any music, the pulse should remain unified, with a certain flexibility. In the *Appassionata* or the *Waldstein* Sonatas, I think a tempo that is not unified is"—the verdict is unambiguous—"a crime."[35] In a 1983 interview he said, "In the early years of my concertizing, secondary themes [*Seitenthemen*] were played twice as slowly as the exposition. We younger players protested strongly to this by playing at constant tempi—strictly 'classical' in today's sense." (In the intervening years, however, his position had softened, for he added, "But, I have to say, when I hear it again on old recordings, I'm ashamed of myself.")[36]

The second feature of objectivity in performance that Serkin strove for was clarity: clarity of structure, clarity of tone, clarity of musical thought and intention. Busch's observation when he first heard Serkin play at the Gombriches—"The way the youngster plays, you see the whole score in front of you"—goes to the heart of their shared approach to music, and Busch recognized it the moment he heard it in the younger musician.

---

* The "objectivity" of musicians like Busch and Serkin should not be confused with the "New Objectivity" (*Neue Sachlichkeit*) movement in art and literature that developed in Germany after 1923, though they shared certain features and arose from related impulses. The only association by Busch and Serkin with any aspect of *Neue Sachlichkeit* was with the Bauhaus in Dessau, where they played several times.

Busch and Serkin PHOTOGRAPH BY LOTTE MEITNER-GRAF. COURTESY OF ANNA BUCHTHAL

Busch, too, exemplified the modern, objective approach and did so with an intensity of concentrated passion that gave his playing a highly individual, transcendently intimate quality. Something of his attitude is captured in a letter he wrote to his brother-in-law Otto Grüters after a performance by his Quartet in 1927: "Playing interestingly is nothing—anyone can do that; but playing rightly [*richtig*], as we can do, no one else can do that—not even us."[37]

After establishing the collaboration with Serkin, Busch began to feature the piano with new frequency and centrality in his own compositions. In 1922, in addition to the Piano Sonata, Op. 25 (dedicated to Otto Grüters), he wrote a sonata for piano and violin (Op. 21) and began a piano concerto (Op. 31) that he completed in 1924. The concerto was dedicated to Serkin, who gave its first performance with Fritz Busch in Dresden on December 19, 1924. He performed it several times in the course of the next two years and arranged a version for two pianos that was published by Breitkopf in 1928.[38]

Not all the composing was serious. In August 1924 Busch and Serkin agreed

Serkin and Karl Doktor (Busch Quartet violist) COURTESY OF PETER SERKIN

to join forces to write a serenade for Frieda's birthday. Each was to write the other's part, which, naturally, they made as difficult to play as they possibly could. For Irene (then seven) a double bass was procured, on which she played her part, written for the open strings, except for the very last note. In the slow movement, Serkin, who, according to his son Peter had a passion for jazz at the time, played the saxophone.[39]

Gifted as they were, and in those days still high-spirited, the Busch-Serkin family had a penchant for practical jokes of a musical kind and the ability to carry them out. Happening once to see the score of a little-known Scarlatti sonata on Serkin's piano while Serkin was momentarily out of the house, Fritz Busch, who possessed a powerful musical memory, looked at the part for a few minutes, and then, when Serkin returned, sat at the piano to play it casually from memory, as if he had known it all his life. Serkin, who thought he would be rescuing a lost piece from oblivion, was crushed.

DARMSTADT

Early in 1922 the Busches began to think about moving from Berlin. Otto Krebs (1873–1941), an industrialist and art collector who had made his fortune manufacturing steam boiler parts and whose son studied with Busch, built them a house in Darmstadt, on the site of the famous Jugendstil-oriented artists' colony established on the Mathildenhöhe, a slope that rises on the eastern side of the city, where the house still stands.[40] There were many advantages to this arrangement. The terms were easy (Krebs let them stay rent-free). Darmstadt was a cultured town with an active musical life—a bit sleepy, but without Berlin's edginess, its heyday as an arts and design center definitely behind it. Its location just south of Frankfurt positioned Busch and Serkin well for their frequent tours. And Annele ("Addi") Andreasson, the wife of the Busch Quartet's second violinist and a close friend of Frieda's, also lived in Darmstadt and was able to help look after Irene when the Busches were away.

There was, in any case, little in Berlin to hold them. They had associated, to be sure, with the cream of the capital's social and cultural life (including Albert Einstein, keen amateur fiddler), but their only close and enduring friendship had been with Francesco von Mendelssohn (1901–1972). Known as Cesco, von Mendelssohn was an actor and a gifted cellist, with whom Serkin occasionally performed. Heir to enormous wealth—paintings of El Greco, Rembrandt, and van Gogh adorned the walls of his house—he enjoyed the best musical and social connections, and he was a lifelong and generous friend to the Busches and to Serkin.* Aside from von Mendelssohn, Busch and Serkin had forged few enduring ties in Berlin; there hadn't been, it seems, the time or the need.

---

* Mendelssohn's sister, Eleonora, was married for a time to the pianist Edwin Fischer. His cousin, Lilli, was the wife of Emil Bohnke, who was the violist of the Busch Quartet in 1919–1920.

They moved into the new house in Darmstadt on December 15, 1922. The town was to be their principal residence for the next four years. They were frequently on the road, their tours taking them throughout Europe, as far as Sweden (where they met the Nobel family), Finland (staying in the German embassy), Spain, and England.

They loved Italy, where they and the Busch Quartet enjoyed a responsive and loyal following. In Modena, two men in the audience stood up in the middle of a quartet performance and sank into one another's arms, crying, "Che bellezza!"[41] In 1923 the diminutive Polish-born pianist Mieczyslaw Horszowski (1892–1992) first heard Serkin and the Busch Quartet in Milan, marking the beginning of a close association that was to last almost seventy years. (Horszowski is said to have remembered a Busch Quartet-Serkin performance of the Brahms G minor Quartet, Op. 25, from the 1920s as one of the most beautiful he heard in his very long life.)[42]

Busch and Serkin's first London appearance took place in Wigmore Hall (where their pictures still adorn the Green Room) in May 1925. The opening-night hall was virtually empty, but the audience was enthusiastic and became even more so (and larger) in the course of the three-concert series.[43] (Serkin was to give his first London solo recitals in Wigmore Hall with two concerts in February 1932.)

Spain, on the other hand, was a catastrophe. In Barcelona the audience was so noisy and inattentive that Busch and Serkin stalked off the stage. The management tried to mollify them by explaining that concerts gave young people their only opportunity for getting together, but the musicians insisted that they would not resume the performance until the audience was shushed. The announcement was made, Busch and Serkin returned to the stage, and the audience did as asked but was "icy." After it was all over, Busch raged (Grüters uses the term *Tobsuchtanfall*—a temper tantrum of the highest order), threatened to break off the tour, and swore never to play there again.[44]

Serkin prospered. In Berlin he stayed in the Hotel Adlon, at the time the epitome of sophistication and luxury. In 1926 he wrote Maltschi, "I'm getting richer and richer, and soon I'll be drowning in money." When Serkin's sister Marthl married a Protestant pastor in 1929, he presented the newlyweds with a Bechstein piano. He worked hard, practicing six to eight hours a day when he wasn't touring. His infrequent letters to Maltschi tell of a life full of pleasure and delight, vacationing with the Busches on the shores of Lake Como, on the Riviera, and in Switzerland, where they skied in the winter and hiked in the summer, usually around Arosa. Until 1930, when he and the Busches had a falling out with Krebs, they spent the last weeks of each summer on his estate at Holzdorf rehearsing and preparing for the concert season ahead.

BASEL

Living in Darmstadt was convenient, but for the Busches and Serkin it was, like Berlin, more a base of operations than a real home. According to Maltschi, "They didn't know one single person from Darmstadt" during their years there.[45] When not traveling, they cultivated hobbies and shared enthusiasms: for a time it was biking, and the three would take long trips through the Hessian countryside. Busch and Serkin also became devotees of electric trains and Meccano, the French-made metal construction sets, and Serkin cultivated a passion for fish and kept an aquarium. Busch expressed the wish to move back to Vienna, where, so went the fantasy, he would head up a music school with six students.[46]

In the end, they settled on the Swiss city of Basel, located on the Rhine at the point where Switzerland, France, and Germany meet, with a population of about 150,000.[47] In April 1927 the Busches and Serkin moved into a princely house (what the Germans call a *Villa*) named Die Zosse (an obsolete word for "brewery," after an earlier structure on the site): St. Albanvorstadt 96, a few steps from the Rhine and not far from the center of town. (It was in this house that Menuhin studied with Busch. He remembered Serkin as a pale young Jewish man, practicing, and rather under Frieda's thumb.)[48] They wouldn't move again for another five years, and then it would be a short trip across the river.

Why Basel? Irene claimed that the real reason was that her mother wanted to study at the university there. (In 1936 Frieda would be awarded a doctorate for her dissertation, *Tributes and Their Effects, Studied with the Example of the French Payments after the War 1870–71*.) Later, Germany's deteriorating political climate was sufficient to justify the choice of Switzerland, but 1927 was early still, and it is hard to know now to what extent that explanation for their move is reasoning after the fact. Basel had long been a haven for refugees and emigrés, and it was in many ways more of a European than a Swiss city.[49] Ernst Krenek, who had settled in Zurich three years earlier, wrote about the impression of wealth and stability Switzerland made on him, coming from "impoverished Austria and hectic Germany."[50] Basel was a transportation junction, old, lovely, rich, and deeply cultured, a famous center of learning. Perhaps most compelling of all, the Busches had a number of devoted friends there—the patrician Vischers, the painters Jean-Jacques Lüscher and A. H. Pellegrini,

as well as a host of musicians—with other friends in nearby Zurich (the conductor Volkmar Andreae and his wife) and in Geneva (the Honeggers). Basel
was to be the Busch-Serkin home for the next twelve years, and a happy choice
it was.

In Basel, finally, they put down roots. In January 1928 the Busches and
Serkin hosted a house-warming party with 134 guests in attendance. The Busch
Trio played Reger and Schubert, and Frieda and Irene sang the letter duet from
the third act of *The Marriage of Figaro*. Busch and Serkin continued to tour,
concertizing regularly in Germany, Switzerland, England, Austria (where Serkin gave two concerts at the 1928 Salzburg Festival) and Italy, where they played
privately for Eleonore Duse and Maxim Gorki. In April 1928 they ventured as
far as Leningrad. Returning to Basel, Serkin wrote Maltschi, "I don't know
much more about Russia than I did before," but he found it, nonetheless, "a
wonderful country."

He maintained his ties to old friends like Frau Doktor Schwarzwald, though
his busy schedule could get him into trouble. Arriving at the station in Basel
for a visit with Serkin in May 1928, Schwarzwald found herself standing alone
on the platform: Serkin, it turned out, had left town. She made her way to the
Busch home, where Frieda and Irene took her in: "First I admired your enchanting garden," she wrote Serkin, "then I stood, moved, at your desk and
piano, and then, in your music room, I shed tears."[51] During these years Serkin
continued to attend Schwarzwald's summer gatherings at the Sommerheim
Seeblick in the Austrian alps.

It was not only his old friends but also new ones who enriched Serkin's
years in Basel. It was there that he came to know Albert Schweitzer, who was
from nearby Alsace and attended the Busch-Serkin concerts in Basel and in
Strasbourg and Mulhouse.[52] In Basel Serkin grew friendly with Vladimir
Horowitz, whom he had first heard playing Chopin's Ballade in G minor at
Francesco von Mendelssohn's house in Berlin[53] and with whom he delighted in
playing four-hand piano.[54] Through Horowitz he met Rachmaninoff, who
lived near Lucerne in central Switzerland.* With the Basel-born conductor and

---

* Peter Serkin wrote, "Horowitz suggested a visit to introduce my grandfather and my father
to Rachmaninoff . . . Adolf and Rudi really hit it off with Rachmaninoff. They loved his sense
of humor and sarcastic wit. The three pianists, Rachmaninoff, Horowitz, and my father took
turns playing four-hand music together, mostly sonatas by Mozart, of which Rachmaninoff's
favorite was the one in B-flat major, K. 358. I think that maybe the only pianist who impressed
my father pianistically more than Horowitz was Rachmaninoff, whom they both adored."
David Dubal, *Remembering Horowitz* (New York: Schirmer Books, 1993), 151–152.

patron Paul Sacher he performed the C minor Mozart Concerto, K. 491, in November 1935. Above all, it was during this time that he became close to Arturo Toscanini (1867–1957).

TOSCANINI

The Busches had first met Toscanini late in 1921, when they attended the famous *Falstaff* performance with which he reopened La Scala after its postwar refurbishing; Serkin first heard Toscanini in Zurich in 1926, saying later of his performance of Brahms's Second Symphony, "It was an incredible revelation. It was architecture with passion."[55]

Toscanini, the Busches, and Serkin attended one another's performances, and their friendship grew. In May 1930, when Serkin and the Busches made the trip to London to hear another Toscanini concert, Toscanini invited Busch to perform with him in the United States in the fall of 1931. The contract signed in September, a very happy Frieda wrote her brother Otto, "Adolf's musical dreams are thus fulfilled."[56] In October they met up again, this time in Zurich, where Toscanini attended a rehearsal of the Busch Quartet, after which he said that though he knew Beethoven's quartets by heart, this was the first time he had really heard them. After the cavatina of the Op. 130 Quartet he cried, embraced Busch, and said that these were the two most beautiful days of his life. Later, in the car with the Busches and Serkin, he kept repeating, "O questo adagio."[57] Half a year later, in May 1931, Busch and Serkin, in Milan for a concert, played "for hours" for Toscanini. According to Irene, they had scheduled the concert as a pretext to give them a chance to see Toscanini, who was under virtual house arrest after being attacked by fascists in Bologna. In her informal memoirs Irene describes a series of events involving her parents' and Serkin's efforts to liberate Toscanini that could be straight out of a spy thriller, with secret meetings, false trails, and a smuggled letter.

The infatuation of Toscanini and the Busches and Serkin for one another arose from an intensely experienced musical affinity. George Szell, who first heard Toscanini in 1930, later enumerated the qualities that he had found so epiphanic: "The clarity of texture; the precision of ensemble; the rightness of balances; the virtuosity of every section, every solo-player in the orchestra . . . in the service of an interpretive concept of evident, self-effacing integrity, enforced with irresistible will power and unflagging ardor, [setting] new, undreamed-of standards literally overnight."[58]

For the rest of his life, Serkin was to include Toscanini along with Schoenberg and Busch in the trio of musicians who most strongly influenced his own musical development. "He was the confirmation of what I had learned in Vienna with Schoenberg: clarity," he told Robert Jacobson.[59] The musicologist Richard Taruskin, who provocatively describes Toscanini as "the great cross-over artist of the twentieth century," ascribes his particular appeal and success to the way he applied the values of the French-Italian opera tradition to the Austrian-German instrumental tradition: "He defamiliarized the repertoire and made it new again, in performances of staggering technical mastery and irresistible visceral appeal." Although Toscanini was an avatar of pre-Romantic musical values, "the force of his example was such that it has become an absolute standard in our time. It defines 'modern performance' of the German classics."[60]

At the time of their closest contact, Toscanini and Busch were both mature and fully formed musicians (in 1931 Toscanini was 64, Busch 40), and it is fair to say that theirs was as much a mutual confirmation as it was a discovery; Serkin, on the other hand, was still in his twenties, and the impact on his play-ing of Toscanini and all he represented was correspondingly greater. If Tos-canini stoked the fire of Serkin's natural intensity, he may also have contributed to a sometimes relentless pace and an increasingly obsessive striving for per-fection, described harshly by Edward Steuermann (referring to Toscanini) as "the barbarism of perfection."[61] But Serkin told an interviewer, "Others got stuck with this aspect of perfection and precision only, but this was just a part of him."[62]

DEVELOPING CAREER

For much of the 1920s Serkin performed primarily with Busch. Their Sonata Evenings typically featured performances of Bach, Beethoven, Schubert, Brahms, and Reger for violin and piano together, and, for either, often a major solo piece: the Schubert B-flat Sonata, D. 960, Schumann's *Kreisleriana*, Brahms's *Variations on a Theme by Paganini*, or Reger's *Bach Variations*, to take examples from 1924 to 1925. (By 1929, the solo works had largely dropped out of their programs, which then took on a more austere character.) The pro-grams of the Busch Trio changed little over the years, consisting uniformly of three trios, often one each by Mozart, Beethoven, and Schubert, with a Reger trio, sometimes Tchaikovsky, Dvořák, or a trio by Busch himself substituting for one of the three great Viennese. Occasionally, too, Serkin performed in piano quartets and quintets with members of the Busch Quartet.

When Serkin did play solo programs in his early career, they could be sur-prisingly varied and long. Pianist and Serkin student Richard Goode came across a very early Serkin program: "I remember it contained not only the Reger *Bach Variations* . . . but the Sixth *English Suite* of Bach and pieces like Granados's *Goyescas* and Liszt's *Campanella*. And it went on and on." He was told that because Serkin didn't play many solo programs in those days, "he wanted to get everything in. I was amazed at the repertoire. The Reger and the Bach you would associate with him, but the *Goyescas*—that surprised me."[63] In addition to these "mixed" programs, in his early years Serkin performed programs consisting solely of major works, typically including a Beethoven sonata, a Schubert sonata, and Reger's *Telemann Variations*. Except for the absence of the big Chopin and Liszt sonatas in his programs, Serkin's repertoire in this period was characteristic of German taste at the time, similar to the programs of pianists such as Edwin Fischer and Elly Ney. (Eastern European pianists, by contrast, usually featured French and Russian works, as well as Liszt and Chopin, in addition to the German composers.)

In the course of the decade Serkin became one of the most popular musicians in German-speaking Europe. As early as 1925 a Viennese journalist described him as "by far the most significant among young German pianists" —an impressive assertion, even if one has to make allowance for local pride and friendship: this being Vienna, the writer had known Serkin as a boy.[64] A review of his performance with Busch at the 1929 Leipzig Bach Festival stands for many:

> Serkin's playing could not have been more beautiful, with astonishing independence of the hands, clear, transparent, masculine in his conception of the so-called *Goldberg Variations* . . . The artists came together for a performance of the F minor Sonata and the Sonata in G major for Violin and Figured Bass (a previously unknown work of which this was the first performance), thus offering a true feast for the ears and for the heart.[65]

Germany's most talented and respected critic of the interwar years was Alfred Einstein, who between 1922 and 1932 wrote ten reviews of Serkin's performances, initially for the *Münchener Post* and beginning in September 1927 for the *Berliner Tageblatt*. During Serkin's early years, Einstein was often less than enthusiastic. He criticized a 1924 performance of Beethoven's *Emperor* Concerto for being that of a "lovable teenager,"[66] and in the same year he accused Serkin of substituting energy for musically shaped phrasing.[67] By the 1930s, however, he had become consistently positive, even enthusiastic: "Schubert's Impromptus Op. 90 are so beautiful one could weep . . . [Serkin] is almost thirty and at his peak: may he never leave it!"[68]

Inevitably, there were opposing voices. A Dresden critic, reviewing Serkin's 1927 performance of Beethoven's Fourth Concerto there, dissented sharply from the majority opinion, writing that, although "amazingly gifted," Serkin "never serves the work: with the theatrical extravagance of an expert, he plays only Serkin."[69]

Halls were often sold out, and reviewers regularly describe the audiences as worshipful, though Otto Grüters's chronology bears with some regularity the note "poorly attended," and now and then even "very poorly attended." In 1928 a Viennese critic reviewed a concert "that did *not* take place": "The very important pianist Rudolf Serkin . . . canceled this year's recital. He didn't put forth the usual excuses . . . but instead declared openly and manfully: I'm canceling my concert because of 'lack of public interest.' For the many pianists who play on in spite of a lack of interest: an example that should be emulated."

Although there is some truth in the frequently made assertion that Serkin's European reputation was based primarily on his partnership with Busch and that his fame as a soloist blossomed only in America, it derives more from the slowness with which perceptions change than from the realities of Serkin's career. In 1924–1925 roughly a quarter of his sixty-five bookings were solo recitals or with orchestra, but eight years later they constituted fully half of what was projected for the 1932–1933 season, before political events changed everything. From reviews it seems that the decisive shift to a more active solo career occurred in 1928.[70] It is likely that it was a conscious choice, made with the active encouragement of Adolf and Frieda: Busch and Serkin had been playing together for seven years, their move to Basel the year before marked a fresh start, and in March 1928 Serkin turned 25 and may well have been deemed old enough to make his own way.

By 1929–1930 Serkin's recitals began to take on a more defined character, typically focusing on a Beethoven sonata (most frequently Op. 53, the *Wald-stein*), with groupings of Chopin appearing on most programs, together, often, with Bach and Reger. Serkin's concerto repertoire in these years is less comprehensively documented. We know that he played the Reger concerto, at least three of the Beethoven concertos, several of the Mozart concertos, both Brahms concertos, Schumann, and Richard Strauss's *Burleske*. (As late as 1939 he performed concertos and solo works in the same program, the Brahms Second Piano Concerto, for example, as well as Schumann's *Abegg Variations*, two of Mendelssohn's *Songs without Words*, and a Chopin Etude.)[71]

In spite of the fact that by the end of the 1920s Serkin was the sole performer in something like half of his concerts, he continued to be ineluctably linked to his older partner in people's minds. As late as December 1932 a

reviewer wrote, "The man with whom Adolf Busch, the most German of violinists, cultivates the classical art of German sonatas with unattained perfection
will always find a most warm welcome among us, whether with Busch or
alone."[72] (Given the date—barely a month before Hitler's accession to the
chancellorship—one has to wonder whether the reviewer stresses both Serkin's
link to Busch as well as Busch's German qualities in an attempt to legitimize
the Jewish pianist.)

COMPOSER AND RECORDING ARTIST

In the summer of 1927, as plans for Serkin's more active solo career were taking
form, Busch persuaded him to try his hand at composing. He wrote a one-
movement, fourteen-minute string quartet in a modern (but not serialist) style
that was given its first performance by the Busch Quartet in Berlin on October
14. Alfred Einstein, who had recently made the move from Munich to Berlin,
reviewed it condescendingly, though not without admiration as "a little quartet, an embryo of a quartet, more or less what the English call a Fantasy Quartet, a cyclic sequence of fast and slow, of *perpetuum mobile*, and lyric monody,
of dreaminess and emotion; pretty and well-constructed, with a few nice harmonic details and sentiments, and a human statement without excess, without
a false note." (Serkin's composition soon dropped out of the Busch Quartet's
repertoire, only to be revived in 1963 by Felix Galimir, Samuel Rhodes, Michael
Tree, and David Soyer, as a surprise for Serkin's sixtieth birthday. The gesture
was well-intended, but, according to Galimir, who genuinely liked the piece,
Serkin was embarrassed and annoyed.[73] A write-up of a later performance in
the *New York Times* characterized it as "dark and moody . . . gray, tense.")[74]

Serkin began to record in the late 1920s. His first effort was on piano rolls with
the Freiburg firm of Welte. Its Welte-Mignon recording and playing mecha-
nisms had yielded over five thousand rolls since 1904, rendering ghostly, auto-
mated performances by many of the period's best-known composers and
pianists, including Saint-Saens, Grieg, Fauré, Mahler, Paderewski, Debussy,
D'Albert, Strauss, Busoni, Scriabin, Ravel, Respighi, and Bartók.[75] The company did very well for a while—the United States was an especially lucrative
market—but its fortunes began to slide after the First World War. In 1927–
1928 Serkin made the short trip from Basel to Freiburg to record Schubert's C
minor Sonata, D. 958, the *Goldberg Variations*, Beethoven's F major Sonata,
Op. 10, no. 2, and four Chopin Etudes for the Welte rolls. Over fifty years later
a Basel musicologist doing research on the Welte rolls sent Serkin a long ques-

tionnaire (which he probably never answered), in which he quotes back to him his unhappy reaction in 1959 when he heard his Welte-Mignon performance of the Chopin Etudes: "I'm actually very distressed. I hope this wasn't me! I never played them so slowly and so unclearly . . . The Welte system surely has good features, but in this matter [tempo] it doesn't seem to reproduce the artist's performance . . . It's out of the question that our taste has changed so much, at least not mine in such a relatively short time."[76]

For all its supposed literalness in rendering a pianist's performance, with regard to tempo the technology is highly unreliable: the Welte-Mignon *Goldberg Variations*, as released commercially in 1992, sound inhumanly fast. According to Peter Serkin,

> When it was played back for my father, he was aghast. He said, "No, that's absolutely wrong. I don't play it in that tempo. It's much, much too fast." And Mr. Welte said, "Oh, just a minute, then, Rudi." He went to the back of the piano, flicked a switch, and it was fine . . . As far as I can tell, the recording—the recent CD reissue of the old piano rolls of my father's performances of Bach's *Goldberg Variations* and the Schubert C minor Sonata with a couple of Chopin Etudes— was quite a distortion. Those preparing this CD probably didn't make the needed adjustment which Mr. Welte had made at the time, resulting in ridiculously fast tempi. And I doubt that the keys were pushed down from that roll with the same sensitivity and voicing with which they were originally played. Not only that, but I think the use of the damper pedal is very changed and made cruder in the process. So I find that those recordings should be listened to very skeptically.[77]

In October of the same year that Serkin was recording for Welte, he and Busch began to explore the new and vastly improved electric recording technology using microphones that was quickly superseding the earlier "acoustic" means of recording (based on horns that funneled the sound into grooves on wax disks). Electric recordings opened a new world of tonal quality and with it vast new markets: by 1929 150 million recordings were being sold annually in the United States, and another 30 million each in England and Germany.[78]

Serkin and Busch made their first recording, Beethoven's Sonata Op. 30, no. 3, in Berlin in 1928 for the Electrola label (a subsidiary of the Gramophone Company, which, in turn, was half-owned by the U.S. company Victor). The recording needed polishing and in the end was never released, because Kreisler and Rachmaninoff had beaten them to it by a month. On October 24, 1929 they recorded the Bach G major Sonata again in Berlin—this was to be their first released recording—followed two years later in London by the Brahms

G major Violin Sonata and the Allegretto from Reger's F-sharp minor Sonata, Op. 84 (their only Reger on disk), among others, all with His Master's Voice (the label of the Gramophone Company).

The pace of their recording in London picked up considerably in the early 1930s, and by the time they moved to the United States, HMV had added key works from the Busch-Serkin sonata repertoire as well as Serkin's *Appassionata* and his performance of the pellucid Mozart E-flat Concerto, K. 449 (his only pre-U.S. solo and concerto recordings) to their growing catalogue. Except for Serkin's 1928 *Goldberg Variations* for Welte, which was technically not a sound recording at all, the landmark recording of large sets of keyboard works was the prerogative of an older generation of pianists: Schnabel recorded the thirty-two Beethoven sonatas (1932–1939); Edwin Fischer, the *Well-Tempered Clavier* (1933–1936); and Wanda Landowska, the *Goldberg Variations* on the harpsichord (1933).

RIEHEN

By 1931 it must have become evident to the Busches and Serkin that they had become *Wahlverwandte*—relatives by choice—in the ten years that had elapsed since the Busches' impulsive invitation of November 1920. They decided to build their own house, one that would give Serkin more independence (he was 27), while enabling them to continue to live together as one family. After considering a property near Geneva with Adolf Abel, the architect brother of Frieda's friend Addi Andreasson, they settled on a site in Riehen, a suburb of Basel with some 6,400 inhabitants,[79] twenty minutes by tram east of the center of town and a short walk from the German border crossing at Lörrach. Although the style was inspired by Abel's own house in Munich and by Goethe's garden house in Weimar (surely Frieda's idea),[80] the distinctive feature of the Riehen property was its architectural mirroring of the Busch-Serkin family constellation: the two houses (a smaller house for Serkin and a larger one for the Busches, sharing one address, Schnitterweg 50) were joined at the center, connected by a library. Building the houses was a costly undertaking, for which Busch incurred a large debt that was soon to become a significant source of worry.

Circulating as they did among Basel's cultural and social elite, the Busches and Serkin shared friends: the Vischers; the Barrels (director of the Basel pharmaceutical company Hoffmann-La Roche); the art collector, German-born Robert von Hirsch and his niece and her husband, Gertrud and Hans Ritz; Paul Häberlin, a philosophy professor; the writers Albert Steffen and Felix

Schnitterweg 50, Riehen COURTESY OF PETER SERKIN

Moeschlin; the painters Jean-Jacques Lüscher and Adolf Pellegrini. Thomas Mann, who left Germany for Zurich in 1933, was a devoted fan, attended their concerts regularly, and paid his respects in the Green Room afterward.[81]

In 1931 Pellegrini painted a portrait of Serkin (the same year in which he did his third portrait of Busch and a painting of the Busch Trio), an activity he later described in an obituary that appeared in a Basel newspaper after Busch's death:

> How did I paint [Serkin's] portrait? He practiced hours on end—that's well known—and when practicing, one doesn't sit still, but I set to work, and finally we both had enough. He stood up, looked at me carefully and critically, and said (typically of him): "You . . . you're not even sweating!" Only then did he look at the picture. Ever since then it's easy for me to explain the difference between music and painting.[82]

(In Vermont, the portrait was to hang behind the piano in the Serkins' living room. The Serkins liked to tell visitors that Horszowski, first seeing it, took one

*Rudolf Serkin by A. H.
Pellegrini, 1931*
COURTESY OF LUIS BATLLE

look at the position of Serkin's hands and exclaimed, "You were playing the
Busoni Toccata!" which Serkin supposedly confirmed. The Uruguayan-born
pianist Luis Batlle, however, to whom Irene later gave the painting, insists that
the picture does not show enough of the hands or fingers for the story to be
credible.)

Serkin also enjoyed a group of his own friends, independent of the Busches,
none of them musicians. A number of them gathered weekly at the so-called
Stammtisch (regular table) in the Café Spillmann, overlooking the Rhine in the
heart of Basel. These included a director of the Sandoz pharmaceutical company, an art curator and gallery owner, a geologist, a pediatrician, an architect,
and Serkin's closest Swiss friend, Hans Oertli, a doctor and passionate moun-
taineer, whom Serkin joined for hikes in the Alps when his schedule allowed it.
And there were girlfriends: Irene remembered seeing girls on his arm (and not
liking it).

"For us the years in Riehen were the happiest of our lives," Serkin wrote in
1985, in some ways a surprising acknowledgment, given what was going on a
few hundred meters down the road.[83] The Baslers, too, would look back fondly

on the years when the Busch-Serkin family was among them: a 1954 tribute to Busch, for example, remembers April 17, 1936 as "a day that has become a part of Basel's musical history," an all-family concert with Fritz, Adolf, and Herman Busch and Rudolf Serkin performing the Beethoven Triple Concerto and the Brahms Double Concerto.[84] However historic and cultured, Basel was small and rather provincial, and these great and famous musicians unquestionably enriched the city and its musical life.[85]

DARKNESS

On January 30, 1933, Hitler became the Chancellor of Germany. Nothing was ever the same for the Busches and Serkin, in Germany or anywhere. For the next two months the situation was uncertain and seemed fluid. On February 14 Serkin concluded an agreement to play the B-flat Piano Concerto at the Brahms Festival, scheduled for May in Hamburg, celebrating the centenary of the composer's birth in that city. Adolf Busch and the Quartet were also invited to participate. In March Busch and Serkin continued to play in Germany, and enthusiastic reviews described full and enthusiastic houses.[86] The critic of the *Süddeutsche Zeitung* wrote pointedly (and bravely, for the terror was already well underway), "In this ensemble neither player is *der Führer* and neither is the one being led [*der Geführte*]."[87] The reference could hardly have been unintended. Serkin later told Otto Friedrich, "People told us not to go . . . but . . . Busch said, 'We will go, and if anyone makes any trouble, I will break my violin over his head.' So we went, and he took a new violin, not his Stradivarius. In Stuttgart, a man stood up in the audience and gave the Hitler salute, and Busch stopped playing and shouted at him: 'Put your arm down!' So he put his arm down, and we went back to playing."[88] On March 28 (Serkin's thirtieth birthday) storm troopers showed up to disrupt the Serkin-Busch concert in Düsseldorf, but apparently thought better of it in the face of an audience demonstratively supportive of the musicians.[89] (The May issue of *Die Musik* noted simply, "The audience was enthusiastic about Busch-Serkin's ideal performance of several Beethoven sonatas.")[90]

The point of no return came on April 1, a Saturday. The Busches and Serkin were in Berlin, where the Busch Quartet was to play Haydn's *Seven Last Words*. It was the day of the so-called *Judenboykott*, the state-sponsored, nationwide demonstration against Jewish-owned stores and businesses. Busch was so upset by what he saw that he returned immediately to Riehen and sent a telegram to his German agent canceling the remaining concerts:

I regret that with my sudden cancellation by telegram I necessarily placed you in an unpleasant position. Thanks to the impression made on me by the actions of Christian countrymen against German Jews, with the intention of forcing Jews from their professions and robbing them of their honor, I have come to the end of my emotional and physical strength, so that I felt obliged to break off my concert tour in Germany.[91]

One is hard-pressed to think of another prominent German who expressed his solidarity with his Jewish fellow countrymen so openly and directly. Although Busch no longer lived in Germany, the cost of cutting himself off from its ador-ing and knowledgeable audiences was enormous—emotionally, artistically, financially. It has been said that because Frieda was "half-Jewish," Busch could not have done other than he did, but there were, of course, many men and women in comparable situations who were much more circumspect. Maltschi was at the house in Riehen when her brother arrived with Adolf and Frieda: "[Adolf's] sense of shame was difficult for an onlooker to witness. We were all in this chaotic mess, without future and facing every imaginable difficulty. We were the persecuted, but he felt responsible. He was ashamed to be a Ger-man."[92]

Between trains in Frankfurt on their way back to Basel, the Busches and Serkin ran into the Nazi violinist Gustav Havemann, who defended the new regime, telling them: "The Movement isn't directed against artists like Ser-kin."[93] What they didn't know was that Havemann, in an effort to enlist Hitler's patronage for the Brahms Festival to which Busch and Serkin had been invited, had written to its organizers on March 30, suggesting that they "of course" would engage only "German artists."[94] The Hamburg Philhar-monic Society acceded quickly and informed Serkin, by then back in Basel, that his participation was no longer welcome. Busch and the Quartet with-drew from the Festival.

There was no difficulty finding replacements: Havemann stepped in for Busch, the Havemann Quartet for the Busch Quartet, and for Serkin, Elly Ney. (In the same month a competing Brahms festival was held in Vienna under the patronage of Reichspräsident Paul von Hindenburg, with Schnabel—whose scheduled series of Brahms chamber music in Berlin with Huberman, Piati-gorsky, and Hindemith had also been canceled—playing both Brahms con-certos under Furtwängler.)[95]

Toward the end of April 1933, arriving in New York with Busch for his first U.S. concert, Serkin was described in the New York press as having "displayed no animosity toward the Hitler régime, saying that he had not been upset by the trouble in any way."[96] Perhaps he was unwilling to display his wounds publicly, or it may be that he did not wish to add fuel to Nazi charges of Jewish "propaganda" abroad, with which they justified persecution against the Jews at home. In any case, describing the episode to Otto Friedrich years later, he seemed to have completely forgotten what had actually occurred: "In Hamburg, the Busch Quartet was going to give a concert, and the news came that Hitler was going to attend. The official in charge of this wrote a letter to Busch, telling him to get a different violist and a different cellist (he was not a Jew but married to a Jew)."[97] The story as Serkin tells it is plausible. Karl Doktor, the violist of the Busch Quartet, was indeed Jewish, as was the wife of Herman Busch, the unnamed cellist. But it is not what happened.

With the break between Busch and Germany now public and, in a sense, official, the German press let loose. On May 3 the *Schwäbischer Kurier*, a Stuttgart paper, wrote under the headline "Swan Song," "It has always been incomprehensible to us why the violinist Adolf Busch chose the Jew Rudolf Serkin, who performed virtuosically but lacked all warmth and soul, as his standing accompanist . . . We'll gladly do without artists whose heart belongs ever more to Jewry than to their fellow Germans. Herr Adolf Busch has turned his back on his fatherland for good cause. He says *For the time being*. Our wish is: *forever*." In 1934, after Busch and Serkin had complained to the music publisher Kistner & Siegel about the "Heil Hitler!" with which they closed their letter—"We strongly object to this greeting. We live here in Switzerland, which means that we find this formulation insulting"—the Darmstadt *Hessische Landeszeitung* threatened: "If Misters Busch and Serkin feel they can no longer play in the new Germany, we will be sure that they find out what it means to vilify the faith of the German *Volk* in this way."[98]

Busch, "*the* German violinist," was a particularly painful thorn in the Nazis' side: that he, who could so easily have played along, chose to break ranks, and do it so publicly, enraged them. A stock Nazi accusation against him was that he had moved to Switzerland to evade taxes. The 1935 dictionary of Jewish musicians described Busch as a "violinist in Switzerland. His pianist is the Jew Serkin," who, in turn, is listed as "accompanist of the Aryan violinist Adolf Busch."[99] The Nazis tried to cajole Busch into returning—his reply to them, "First hang Hitler, hang Goering," has been quoted often—and they supposedly offered to declare Serkin an "honorary Aryan" if that is what it would have taken to bring Busch back. Hearing reports of mounting opposition to the Nazis and of "more and more courageous people," Serkin wrote Fritz Busch of his hopes for "a heroic time in Germany."[100] By 1936, however, he was advising the husband of his sister Marthl to quit his position as a pastor in Germany and emigrate to Switzerland: "Only one SA man has to make a fuss and no one will dare stand by you."[101]

Having moved into their new house and with Germany now off limits, the Busches and Serkin worked their way into local life. In April 1934 they performed in the village church with the Riehen Men's Choir at a benefit concert for the local deaf-mute asylum. The gesture was deeply appreciated, and in August the two musicians became honorary members of the choir, which came to the house on the Schnitterweg to make the presentation and serenade them in the summer evening. Soon afterward, in 1935, the Busches became Swiss citizens. Serkin had to wait another two years to do so, presumably (according to one Basel friend) because of anti-Semitic prejudice.

It was a cruel time. Old friends accused them of "dirtying their own nest," and in 1934 Pellegrini and Busch had a political argument in the Café Spillmann so fierce that for a while they broke off their friendship.[102] When a compromised Munich friend, the Norwegian-born caricaturist Olaf Gulbransson, sent Serkin a presentation copy of his autobiography in 1934, Serkin returned it, writing, "I have to make a great effort to expel our friendship from my heart, but I am angry and want to be."[103] (Years after the war, when Serkin was performing in Munich, he and Gulbransson's widow reconciled by letter.) When old friends came to Riehen and informed Busch that they had joined the Party "to be left in peace," he broke off the relationship, as he did with an unnamed pianist (according to Irene, this was Edwin Fischer), who had called Busch, saying, "Where the Jews may no longer play, a good time will begin for us."[104]*

Busch and Serkin continued to concertize where they could, together and separately, but with the loss of Germany and the financial burden of the new house, they needed to look for new sources of income. Busch was forced to sell his second Stradivarius. The idea of forming a small chamber orchestra (with Serkin on the continuo) came to fruition early in 1935, first with a concert in Basel and then in Florence's second Maggio Musicale (Musical May).

The Florence performances became legendary. The concerts were preceded, according to Frieda Busch, by sixty-eight rehearsals.[105] Alfred Einstein, now

---

* The Jewish pianist Konrad Latte gives a very different account of Fischer's behavior during the Nazi time. See Peter Schneider, *Und wenn wir nur eine Stunde gewinnen* (Berlin: Rowohlt, 2001), 88–90.

writing for the London *Daily Telegraph*, wrote with enthusiasm of "two unforgettable evenings at the Pitti Palace of genuine Bach."[106] The chamber orchestra played the six *Brandenburg* Concertos in a lean, clean, energized style that marked a turning point in the way Bach was heard. It was the first time that the *Brandenburgs* were played as a cycle in Italy. Typically of Busch, the orchestra, which he led from the first violin stand, included not only virtuosos like the great French flutist Marcel Moyse and his son Louis, but family and friends— Swiss, German, English, French, and Italian. It was Irene's first occasion to perform, and years later she described how another violinist came up to her after one of the early rehearsals to "congratulate" her: "You finished ahead of everyone!"

In September the series was repeated in Basel (with Toscanini in attendance), in October in London (where they were recorded onto fourteen shellac disks), and the following year (in which they added the four Bach orchestral suites) in Brussels and again in England. Busch, wrote a German musicologist, "carried the spontaneous interaction of chamber music over into baroque orchestral works and united brilliance and intimacy. Adolf Busch brought a new tonal realization to Bach's music."[107] Paul Sacher later wrote with mild disapproval of Serkin's playing the continuo part on the piano in the Basel performances but conceded that "in other aspects he was already approaching the performance practices of the eighteenth century."[108]

In spite of their own precarious finances, Busch and Serkin were frequently asked to donate their services to the various causes of the day, and they responded generously. Hans Deichmann remembered such an occasion in Paris in the fall of 1934: "[Serkin] had come to give a piano recital for German emigrés at the Quaker Meeting House . . . The recital took place in a small hall, and the lights were dimmed as Rudi played. The audience was made up almost exclusively of exiles—all one heard was German. Many were crying, overcome with emotion and gratitude."[109] One source of additional income for Serkin was his private students. It was during his Basel years that Serkin began to teach in earnest (see Chapter 5).

MARRIAGE

On January 20, 1935, Serkin and Irene Busch announced their engagement. (Irene told the story that Serkin proposed by saying that he had bought her a "herring" in Basel, making a pun on *Ehering*, the German word for "wedding ring.") They had lived essentially as brother and sister for fifteen years; just a few years earlier Serkin had written Irene that he hoped her arm was better so that they could soon box again. Irene, who was 3 when Serkin came into her

Rudolf and Irene Serkin, May 31, 1935 COURTESY OF PETER SERKIN

family, had no memory of a life without him. She remembered Rudi as a big brother who rescued her on his bike when, 3 years old, she was wandering about, lost, in their Berlin neighborhood. As a little girl, she would announce, using Serkin's nickname, *"Ich heirat' den Bubser"*: I'm going to marry Bubser. She had been a lonely child, and Rudi, a joker and a teaser, surely helped balance the high degree of control Frieda exerted over her daughter. For his part, Serkin's choice of bride would also allow him to continue in his longtime role of adopted son. By marrying Irene, Rudi would remain tied to the Busches to the end.

In the months before the wedding, Otto Grüters had written to the Busches urging against the marriage; he and his wife thought Irene was too young and immature. Frieda, his sister, was furious, and Serkin wrote a firm letter in defense of the step he and Irene were about to take: "When you Grüters," wrote Serkin, "get disoriented by your excited thoughts, I'm glad to be a sign-post in the desert."[110]

A family friend, writing Serkin from Germany after Frieda's death, remembered, "When I saw Frieda for the last time, after she poured out her heart about the badness of mankind, she said she would never have given Irene to any man other than Rudi, 'the best man in the world.' "[111] Perhaps the trauma of 1933 had drawn them all that much closer. In his wedding toast Busch downplayed the significance of the change within their family: "Our child is moving to the house next door, a little furniture gets moved around, and all four of us stay together just as always."[112]

They married in Basel on May 31, 1935, Irene still three weeks shy of her eighteenth birthday, legally underage and requiring dispensation. A few days before the wedding, Serkin received a letter from his brother Willi, informing him that their ailing mother was lying "with four working-class women" in the third-class ward of a Viennese hospital. The Vienna family seems not to have been invited to the wedding. As the entire event, according to Irene, was very much Frieda's show, the numerous and impecunious Serkins would presumably not have added to the tone she was seeking. The night before the wedding Irene's Girl Scout troupe came to the Riehen house to sing in honor of the occasion. Many years afterward Henriette Speiser, one of the Scouts, asked Serkin if he remembered their serenade. "And how! You trampled our lawn."[113] (She claimed it was the fault of the Riehen Men's Choir.)

After the civil wedding in Basel (there was no religious service), the couple went next door to the study of Eduard Thurneysen, the distinguished Basel pastor and theologian, who then baptized Irene. (Adolf and Frieda had left the Protestant Church in protest during the First World War, and Irene, born in 1917, had not been baptized.) Because Austrian law, to which Serkin was still subject, would not have allowed a wedding between people officially of two different faiths, she could take this step only after she had become Serkin's wife. Returning to Riehen, Irene changed clothes for the wedding reception, while Serkin, preparing for his forthcoming concerts in England, practiced the Chopin Etudes.

CHAPTER THREE

American Pianist

As long as we could listen to Rudolf Serkin, we were released from the horrors of our time. Can one say anything more about an artist?
—ELIAS CANETTI (1991)

FIRST TOURS

If there was one thing Irene Serkin hated, it was to be called a refugee. "We were *not* refugees. We came here for Rudi's career!" she insisted again and again. She was asserting what was in her view a statement of fact. Perhaps she was also recoiling from the image of the refugee that the conductor Robert Shaw (urging his chorus to sing more boldly) articulated in 1943: "Meek, squeaky little things. No self-respect. Standing in corners, hiding behind doors, ducking into subway stations, peering out from under rugs. Refugees."[1] Serkin himself, asked to supply biographical information for a refugees' Who's Who, replied, "I do not feel that I have the right to be included in the Dictionary of outstanding emigrés. I have been fortunate to live in Basel, Switzerland, since the late twenties, and therefore I was spared the threat of physical persecution."[2] (He was included anyway, as was Busch.)

Unlike the many thousands of Germans and Austrians waiting with increasing desperation and quickly diminishing financial resources for visas and tickets giving them safe passage out of the hell that their home had become, the Serkins and Busches, by the time of their move to America, drew on Swiss bank accounts and carried Swiss passports. Nonetheless, they felt increasingly insecure in their Riehen house, lying, Irene remembered, so close to the German border that they sometimes unwittingly strayed into German territory during their weekend walks. One Basel acquaintance remembered the atmosphere in the city as "black." Given Busch's status as a German icon and his uncompromising hostility to the Nazis, the family felt particularly vulnerable. Like other Swiss at risk, they secured a haven, a rented house in central Switzerland, deep into the Emmental Valley.

Serkin first performed in the United States in 1933, when he came over with Busch and the Quartet for a single concert. His arrival had been preceded in 1931 by a *New York Times* article that described him as "one of the most commanding pianists of the age" who played to a Berlin audience that was in a state of "almost hysterical delight."[3] On the morning of April 24, the Busch Quartet gave its first American concert at the Coolidge Foundation's Festival of Chamber Music at the Library of Congress. On the 25th—it was the last concert of the Festival—Busch and Serkin gave one of their vintage Sonata Evenings. The review in *Musical Courier* described the increasingly enthusiastic reactions of the invitation-only audience from the opening Bach Sonata in G ("stentorious applause"), to the Reger Sonata in E minor, Op. 122 ("receiving even a greater ovation"), to the concluding Beethoven Sonata in E-flat, Op. 12, no. 3 ("thunderous appreciation").[4]

Serkin next came to America in 1936, this time for a three-city tour. Three years and four journeys later he stayed—for the rest of his life. The rapidly deteriorating political climate in Germany and the resulting migration of artists and intellectuals to the United States in the 1930s make it difficult to see Serkin's move there in any other context, but European musicians had, in fact, been crossing the Atlantic for many years, leaving Europe not for their lives but for their livelihood: for new opportunities, for celebrity, and for income. By the beginning of the twentieth century "musicians were being groomed for the world celebrity market, with America as the ultimate goal."[5] A list of soloists who appeared with the Cincinnati Symphony in the 1920s gives a sense of the quality of European-born musicians who were touring the American hinterlands in the decade before Serkin came over: Wilhelm Backhaus, Béla Bartók, Pablo Casals, Alfred Cortot, Carl Flesch, Walter Gieseking, Myra Hess, Josef Hofmann, Vladimir Horowitz, Bronislaw Huberman, Wanda Landowska, Nicolai Medtner, Ottorino Respighi, Heinrich Schlusnus, Joseph Szigeti, and Jacques Thibaud. An exchange between Richard Strauss and Mahler from thirty years before conveys the enduring European attitude:

Mahler, naturally anxious to know what kind of reception he might expect in America, asked Strauss, who had already been several times across the Atlantic: "Isn't it nonsense for me to be going to work in New York, where none of the pre-conditions for understanding what I am trying to do are found?" To which Strauss simply replied: "But Mahler, you are and remain a child. Over there you get up on the podium and do this—(he waved an imaginary baton)—and then you go to the cashier and—(a gesture of counting money)."[6]

This is not to say that Serkin's move to America took place in a political vacuum: the Nazi ascendancy to power in Germany had, after all, led directly to diminishing opportunities for European engagements. To be sure, Busch and Serkin could still play in much of Europe, but nothing could compensate for the enormous gap left by Germany. Had there been no Hitler, would the Serkins and Busches have settled in America? Surely not. For Busch the years in the United States were to prove exceedingly difficult, and even had America enticed Serkin with its wealth and new opportunities, it is unlikely that he and Irene would have left her parents alone in the conjoined houses in Riehen or that he would have ended his partnership with Busch.

Organized by Sol Hurok and dominated by Toscanini, at the time 68 and in his last season with the New York Philharmonic–Symphony, Serkin's first American tour had taken two years to plan and was completed in two weeks in February 1936. It was a short but effective introduction to concertizing in America, described by Serkin in a series of lively, almost giddy letters home to Irene, then about three months into her first pregnancy. Arriving in New York harbor, Serkin had not yet stepped off the boat when a telegram from Tos-canini greeted him on board. Whisked through customs as Hurok's agent greased palms, he settled down at his room in the Astor Hotel in Times Square and practiced at Steinway Hall on West 57th Street "to strengthen my weak muscles." (At other times he would also complain of pain caused by "the sud-den stopping of muscle activity" if he took a break from the piano.)[7] Having given himself a workout, he proceeded to Toscanini's apartment, also in the Astor: "He was *very* sweet," he wrote Irene, "but so was *I.*" In his letters back to Riehen, Serkin tracked the mood swings of the volatile and pampered Toscanini: "I don't think [his cold] is bad, but he takes it as a major illness."

The tour that would culminate in Serkin's three New York/Toscanini con-certs was brief: he had wanted more engagements, but in the end it was the best he could get out of Hurok, who must have regarded the truncated tour as a test of the young pianist's marketability. It began with a quick trip to Baltimore for a recital (Bach, Beethoven, Brahms, and Chopin) on a snowy night at the Peabody Institute. The audience was small and the piano poor, but the *Sun* gave him a good review.

From there he continued to Chicago, where he gave an afternoon performance of Beethoven's Fifth Piano Concerto. The conductor was Frederick Stock, then 63, German-born but long a fixture in Chicago. Serkin liked him but was contemptuous of his musicianship: "I tricked him a few times to get him to pay better attention. After which the concert went fairly well." The reviews in the *Daily Tribune* and the *Daily News* were positive, though not uncritical. (In Chicago Serkin was particularly taken with the aquarium, which he described as "the most beautiful in the world. From the guppy to the manatee.")[8]

Serkin hurried back to New York to hear the fifth concert in Schnabel's Beethoven cycle—he played the *Hammerklavier* Sonata—"but it wasn't beautiful. Insanely rushed and incomprehensible."[9] Ironically, given their fundamentally different attitudes and styles, there would be no pianist to whom reviewers would compare Serkin as frequently in the course of his long career as Artur Schnabel (1882–1951). Their repertoire and backgrounds were similar, and Schnabel's U.S. career was peaking precisely at the time that Serkin's was beginning to take off.[10] Serkin enjoyed describing how Schnabel would tactlessly grill him after concerts, asking, "Why did you play such and such a passage this way? Why not this way?"[11] According to Alexander Schneider, after one concert Schnabel appeared and said to Serkin, "Dear Rudi, you have practiced enough in your life, I think it is about time you start making music and enjoying it."[12] Serkin and Schnabel are said to have liked and enjoyed one another, but Serkin disapproved of the older musician's laxness, feeling that it set a bad example; Schnabel, for his part, thought Serkin deficient in imagination.*

Nor was Serkin uncritical of Toscanini's concert the next evening, February 13: except for Dvořák, "not a single good piece," though it was "beautifully played." Afterward he joined the party at Jascha Heifetz's: "It was quite nice. Tosca gets very peppy around beautiful women and somewhat indecent." Strangely, Serkin made no mention of Toscanini's surprise announcement—it appeared in the next morning's papers—that he was resigning from his position as director of the New York Philharmonic-Symphony.

---

* In 1935 Serkin approached Schnabel about playing a Bach two-piano concerto together with Busch's chamber orchestra, but Schnabel turned him down, saying he would only play it with his son, Karl Ulrich.

THE TOSCANINI CONCERTS

The day before his first concert with Toscanini Serkin wrote: "My only wish is that I play decently for the Maestro tomorrow. I've worked enough."[13]

On Thursday, February 20, Serkin played Beethoven's Concerto No. 4 (known among Viennese musicians a few generations earlier as the "ladies' concerto") and Mozart's then rarely performed last concerto (K. 595) with the New York Philharmonic-Symphony in Carnegie Hall. "I discovered to my surprise," Serkin remembered, "that [Toscanini] scheduled the Beethoven concerto for the first part of the program and the Mozart for the second. When, after the performance I asked him why, he said with a smile, 'I thought you might be nervous and it is easier to overcome nervousness with Beethoven than with Mozart.' I adored Toscanini."[14]* Beethoven's Fourth Concerto became a staple in Serkin's repertoire, but Toscanini never conducted it again after a second broadcast with Serkin in 1944. Nor did he and Serkin ever perform together again, though they continued to see one another socially.

On February 22 Serkin wired his report to Riehen: "Went well Maestro satisfied great success happy home soon." He had every reason to be pleased. The concert, performed initially on a Thursday evening and then repeated Friday and Sunday afternoons (the last for live radio broadcast) was reviewed by at least six New York papers. It received the highest possible praise from critic Olin Downes in the *New York Times* and from the *Herald Tribune*'s Lawrence Gilman. (Downes: "We have seldom heard a pianist's performance which so admirably combined the most penetrating analysis with artistic enthusiasm and warm feeling.")[15] *Musical Courier* deemed it "a tremendous popular and critical success."[16]

In Serkin's own view of his life, this was his "big break." Next to the claim in the draft of an article that "Serkin can point to no prize competition or discovery that suddenly 'made' his career" he penciled an oversize question mark and one word: "Toscanini."[17]

After finishing his last concert with Toscanini on Sunday afternoon, Serkin cabled Irene the good news: an offer by Sol Hurok to undertake a major U.S. tour. The "ultimate plum" was his. Serkin's agent in Paris, Paul Schiff, wrote him, "with this success your material needs are now secure for a long time to

---

* In the course of his career, Serkin was to play 110 more concerts with the Philharmonic, the last on February 20, 1986, fifty years later to the day after the first; by contrast, he played only nine times with the Vienna Philharmonic, the major orchestra of the city of his musical roots.

Adolf Busch, Rudolf Serkin, Arturo Toscanini, Frieda Busch, 1936 COURTESY OF
BRÜDER-BUSCH-ARCHIV, HILCHENBACH

come."[18] Serkin maintained contact throughout the summer with Hurok, who
proposed a tour of the Soviet Union with Busch and suggested a recording
with Toscanini.[19]

This second, 1936–1937 tour was a brutal affair that the Serkins—Irene
accompanied her husband for much of it—would long remember. Beginning
in Oberlin, Ohio, on December 8, it took them up, down, and across the East,
Midwest, and South, a marathon stretching from Winnipeg in the dead of winter to Oklahoma and New Orleans, back and forth from Birmingham to Dallas
to Memphis, with four separate sets of concerts in Canada, and a final series on
the East Coast that concluded in Albany on March 9. Doing their best to
endure with good grace the vast distances, the extremes of climate, floods,
inattentive audiences, and the monotony of American cities and hotels, Serkin
wrote the Busches that he and Irene "are also [like the cities and hotels] always
the same, always happy, and more or less tired."[20] They missed their infant
daughter, Ursula, born the previous June. Irene Serkin harbored difficult
memories of the long stretches of time she had spent as a child farmed out to
family friends while her parents were on tour, and after this first trip Irene preferred to let her husband travel alone until the children were older.

CARNEGIE HALL AND REGER

In terms of Serkin's subsequent American career, the most important event of the 1936–1937 tour was his Carnegie Hall recital debut on January 11. It was advertised on the same page of the *New York Times* as forthcoming concerts by Jascha Heifetz, Myra Hess, Josef Hofmann, Lauritz Melchior, Erica Morini, and Joseph Szigeti, among others. New York had replaced Berlin as the center of the classical music world. Once again Olin Downes outdid himself in praise of Serkin's playing. Jerome D. Bohn of the *Herald Tribune*, too, was ecstatic: "One of the most magnificent accomplishments in the field of pianism." Serkin's program was characteristic of those he would perform for the next fifteen to twenty years: Beethoven, Sonata Op. 53 (*Waldstein*); Reger, *Variations on a Theme by Bach*; Mendelssohn's *Rondo capriccioso*, Op. 14; two Schubert impromptus; four Chopin etudes. Downes was impressed by the seriousness of the selections (no "show pieces" were his words), but what thrilled him (and Bohn) was the Reger, which he compared to the great sets of Beethoven, Brahms, and Schumann variations.

The New York critics were right to zero in on this part of Serkin's first Carnegie Hall recital program as its most distinctive and noteworthy element: his ardor for Reger remained unabated, as did his determination to continue to champion the composer, who was largely neglected in American concert halls. Busch and Serkin had performed the Reger E minor Sonata in their first American concert together at the Library of Congress, and Serkin was to be the first pianist to perform Reger's concerto in the United States—on November 16, 1945, with Dimitri Mitropoulos in Minneapolis.*

Almost three years after Serkin's first Carnegie Hall recital, in December 1939, Busch and Serkin played Reger's Suite in F ("In the Old Style"), again with a vigorous thumbs-up from the *Times*. When Serkin programmed Reger's *Variations on a Theme of Telemann* for his fifth Carnegie Hall recital in November 1940, however, Downes, who had begun to complain about the pianist's hard tone and "conventional" playing, lost his patience: the piece, he wrote, is "a series of tricks, and not inspired metamorphoses of an idea" by a "garrulous" composer.[21] Serkin, as far as we know, never played the *Telemann Variations* in public again.

---

* He was to regard the performance with Mitropoulos, which was preceded by a full week of rehearsals, as one of the highlights of his musical career; so successful was it that they had to repeat the last movement. Years later Szell rejected Serkin's suggestion to perform the Reger, letting Serkin know that he could not "stomach it." Serkin responded with uncharacteristic alacrity that he was "surprised, disappointed . . . and hurt."

Dimitri Mitropoulos and Rudolf Serkin PHOTOGRAPH BY FRED FEHL.
COURTESY OF PETER SERKIN

LETTERS HOME

The two seasons that followed Serkin's 1936–1937 tour continued the earlier pattern: extensive U.S. schedules in the winter, comprising a mixture of solo concerts and orchestral appearances, with the significant addition of Adolf Busch for the duo concerts for which they were so famous in Europe. In the winter of 1937–1938 they played the Beethoven violin sonata cycle (as was their practice, from memory) in a landmark series of concerts in Boston, New York, and Washington. Toscanini, who had just arrived from Europe to conduct the new NBC Symphony, attended at least the first of the Town Hall concerts.[22] "A rare and sustained pleasure" is how Irving Kolodin described the experience, noting also "that a few additional listeners could have been accommodated in the hall."[23] Only by the third concert did it fill up.[24]

In January 1938 Serkin played for the first time under the auspices of the New Friends of Music, an organization founded the year before by the enterprising department store executive Ira Hirschmann to promote chamber music in New York. Serkin and Busch, along with Schnabel, Feuermann, and countless other European musicians, would play regularly during the war years for Hirschmann's series, which was held in the 1,500-seat Town Hall on West 43ʳᵈ Street. Supposedly modeled on Vienna's Gesellschaft der Musikfreunde, the New Friends of Music was sometimes called "Old Friends of Artur Schnabel."[25] Although Hirschmann was devoted to chamber music, and to a very wide range of it, his tight control over programming resulted in regular clashes with the Busches and Serkin, who were not used to being told what they had to play. When the U.S. season concluded in the spring, the families returned to Basel through the fall for more concertizing and some rest.

When Serkin was on the road, he sent a steady stream of letters to Irene. From Peoria, the first venue of his 1937–1938 tour (October 26), he sent a postcard:

> The first concert is over . . . I had all manner of handicaps to overcome for the concert. A small piano (but brand new), a hall seating about 2,000 (small, as I was told in New York), buttons on my shirt that kept popping open, a white vest with a tear, able to play the piano for only 10 minutes (because of the glissando, but this time in the Liszt), a piano chair that was too high, cloth-only curtains that muffled the sound . . .

From Lawrence, Kansas, on November 8:

> I played in a huge hall, with two echoes. Old piano and the keys could be pressed down only with the greatest effort . . . The chauffeur was very nice and invited me to eat a Barber Cut [i.e., barbecue] with ale. Saying no was out of the question, and it was absolutely delicious. It is a negro specialty, very spicy.

Further west, he wrote Adolf and Frieda in a less cheerful mood:

> There's not a cloud to be seen here. I don't think I could endure this eternal sun—it makes one quite nervous. I'm not in the rosiest mood in any case. Traveling alone like this is depressing . . . Luckily I've got my own piano. The local pianos are a catastrophe—I try them everywhere I go. Right now I'm in a remote area, past El Paso (dirty and ugly) and Phoenix (clean and ugly), but the surrounding countryside must be very beautiful.

Even though conditions for touring performers had improved greatly since the 1920s —audiences and critics were considered to have become more discerning and more receptive[26]—Serkin had not yet made his peace with the American continent even after the war:

One could easily go into a steep decline here, because the whole environment has so little of art in it. The halls sometimes (like in Albuquerque) a hideous *playground* [Serkin uses the English word, meaning gym], the audience fairly clueless [*ahnungslos*], although open to beauty. But a beautiful piano is then a great joy, because if on top of everything else, I'd have to play on a poor instrument, I'd just be playing for the check. So I play for my own pleasure, and for Steinway & Sons.[27]

But he was often upbeat and positive, commenting frequently on the friendliness and warmth of the people he met, and his letters were always charming and playful. He teased Irene, "Don't think about money, you Swiss housewife. Be—or at least try it out—an *American girl!*"

EMIGRATION

The back and forth between Europe and America that began in 1936, although strenuous given Serkin's continued concertizing in Europe before and after the American tours, might have continued indefinitely but for the deteriorating situation in Europe and the opening of an attractive and ultimately irresistible position in the United States. On March 12, 1938, German troops entered Austria. Serkin's mother and most of his brothers and sisters were trapped in Vienna, where they were vulnerable to a level of anti-Semitic violence that astonished even the Germans. Meanwhile, Italy began to adopt increasingly aggressive anti-Semitic measures. In May 1938 (the same month as Hitler's state visit to Rome) Serkin and the Orchestra da camera Adolfo Busch performed several *Brandenburg* cycles in Italy, but by October Adolf struck that country, too, from his schedule. Of the major European countries in which Busch and Serkin concertized regularly, by the end of 1938 only England and Switzerland were still open to them. (France had never been especially receptive to Busch or Serkin. When they played there in 1936, the audience consisted mainly of the small number of German refugees who could afford the tickets.)[28]

Soon a musical government-in-exile began to take shape. In the summer of 1938, the Swiss city of Lucerne hosted a new festival, an anti-Salzburg, with Toscanini its most prominent participant. Adolf Busch was the orchestra's concertmaster, and the members of his Quartet served as leaders of the other string sections. In the Lucerne Festival's first summer Busch and Serkin gave a sonata recital. Serkin attended the second Festival in 1939, though he didn't play. Horowitz performed the Brahms Second Piano Concerto with Toscanini (Horowitz's father-in-law since 1933) at the last concert on August 29. Three days later the Germans invaded Poland.

Life in Switzerland began to sour. Irene felt that their Basel "friends" (the quotation marks are hers) disapproved of the family's developing ties to America. "I'm really afraid," Irene wrote in a dark moment, "that it's all over between us and our friends, certainly for a while."[29] Though her fears were exaggerated, those left behind in Basel could indeed be prickly, especially when criticism came from what they saw as the easy safety of distant America ("darkest America," in the words of one of Serkin's Swiss friends).

On his October 1937 crossing from Le Havre to New York on the Cunard White Star *Georgic*, Serkin made the acquaintance of "two young Italian composers, who seem to be a bit fey [*huch*] but very nice."[30] (For the most part Serkin seems to have been rather unconcerned about homosexuality, regarding it as a distinction without a difference. Indeed, though he responded swiftly and without mercy to musical offenses, he was generally tolerant about people's personal lives. When an interviewer told him that Arthur Rubinstein had gotten involved with a younger woman, he replied simply, "He did it all his life. Why should he change now?")[31] The two "Italians" were Samuel Barber, then 27, and the 26-year-old Gian Carlo Menotti. Both had studied at Philadelphia's Curtis Institute and Barber, especially, developed a close relationship to its founder, Mary Curtis Bok.[32] After the encounter on the *Georgic*, he and Menotti brought Serkin to Mrs. Bok's attention, and on December 27, 1938 she offered him a position at the Institute. With secure employment and a steady income thus assured, the Serkins embarked on the move to the United States in the fall of 1939.

BEGINNING AGAIN

Throughout their lives, Busch and Serkin, like many successful musicians, enjoyed the support of well-connected and philanthropic patrons, both in Europe and in America, whether in the form of privately organized concerts, a home (Otto Krebs), a summer sanctuary (again, Krebs), or a car (Francesco von Mendelssohn). The affection between the Serkins and well-placed and wealthy friends was, for the most part, genuinely felt on both sides. Serkin was too naturally confident in his relationship to music and too selflessly devoted to its cause ever to feel that anyone owed him anything, and his appreciation of those who supported him never abated.

Both Serkins were drawn to powerful and intelligent older women, who responded in turn to Serkin's charm and intelligence and to Irene's youth and openness. For Serkin Eugenie Schwarzwald had been the prototype of the woman activist, though she lacked the wealth and the exalted social position of her American successors. In the Berlin-Darmstadt-Basel years Frieda Busch consumed all the emotional space, but by the time the families had come to America, her grip on her daughter and son-in-law inevitably began to loosen.

In addition to Mrs. Bok, two other women, Agnes Meyer and Rosalie Leventritt, became important figures for the Serkins and the Busches, giving them decisive support and guidance in their early American years. Agnes Meyer (1887–1970), the wife of *Washington Post* publisher Eugene Meyer, was a tireless promoter of educational and cultural causes. The daughter of Germans, she had a penchant for high culture, especially German culture at its highest. (Her published correspondence with Thomas Mann comes to a book of over 1,100 pages.) She was exceedingly well connected, interceding for the Serkins when they had visa problems in their immigration in 1939 and arranging for Serkin's sister Maltschi and brother-in-law Hugo Buchthal in London to be given a visa application appointment in 1941. The Serkins were regular guests at the Meyer estate in Mt. Kisco, New York, where Mrs. Meyer liked to have Serkin perform after dinner. Thus in June 1940 he and the Busch Quartet gave a "house concert" in Mt. Kisco in which they played the Brahms and Schumann quintets for an audience that included Thomas Mann, who recorded the experience in his diary as "magnificent."[33] Serkin also played at family occasions like Eugene Meyer's funeral in 1959 and Agnes Meyer's eightieth birthday in 1967. Irene Serkin, especially, was devoted to Mrs. Meyer, who addressed her in correspondence as "darling child" and in 1950 became godmother to the Serkins' fourth daughter Judith Agnes.

If Agnes Meyer was formidable and severe, Rosalie Leventritt (1891–1976), known to her friends as Winnie, was a charming, Jewish, Alabama-born New Yorker. She funneled her energies and financial generosity into good causes of a musical nature, most famously the Edgar M. Leventritt Foundation, which she established in 1939 in memory of her husband, a New York lawyer. Indeed, according to an interview given shortly before her death, it was Serkin who inspired the eponymous competition: "After my husband passed away, I thought about what I could do in his memory. *Not* a marble statue. Rudi Serkin, a good friend of ours, said young musicians, if they were good enough, could always get a teacher to teach them for nothing. But where did they go from there? So we set up the Leventritt Competition."[34]

From its inception, she involved Serkin as advisor and judge, and "the Leventritt"—which in its early years awarded the winner an appearance with the New York Philharmonic-Symphony Orchestra (the prize later grew to include other engagements and cash)—quickly established itself as the most elite and prestigious of American classical music contests. The first competition was

Rosalie Leventritt in the 1970s
COURTESY OF PETER SERKIN

open only to pianists.[35] The first jury (in which both Adolf Busch and Serkin participated) awarded the prize to Sidney Foster, a Curtis-trained pianist who had studied with David Saperton and Isabelle Vengerova. At the conclusion of the 1940 competition Mrs. Leventritt wrote to thank Serkin, suggesting that its success rested to a large extent on his efforts.[36]

Once more or less permanently in New York in the winter of 1939–1940, the Serkins made a series of moves from Manhattan to Dobbs Ferry to Great Neck, and then, to shorten the commute to Philadelphia, back to Manhattan in April 1941, into a penthouse apartment at 49 East 96th Street. The Busches took a small apartment directly below. In 1943, after neighbors began to complain about Serkin's constant practicing, the family moved again, this time to 850 Park Avenue. This apartment was one floor above Rosalie Leventritt, who would have no objection to hearing Serkin whenever he was at the piano.

Serkin established himself as a major presence in the American musical world with astonishing speed: within a very few years he had become one of the best-known pianists in the United States, a friend and advisor to three of the country's most generous musical patrons, and a teacher in one of its most prestigious conservatories. He participated in high-profile occasions such as the Gabrilowitsch Memorial Series in which he played five concertos in Carnegie Hall with Leon Barzin and the National Orchestral Association between January and March 1939, and the opening of the New York Philharmonic-Symphony 1940 summer season in the 6,000-seat Lewisohn Stadium. In the first Carnegie Hall recitals reviewers observed the large number of empty seats, but by war's end Serkin was playing to a full house. In 1946 Irving Kolodin acknowledged that he was "something of the season's pianistic lion,"[37] and in his March 1947 Carnegie Hall recital not only was the house sold out but "there was also a stage full of listeners." Harold Taubman noted that he had become "a box office attraction to equal the most successful."[38]

BUSCH IN AMERICA

Moving to the United States required Serkin to adjust, and adjust he did; for Busch, the consequences of exile and dislocation were terrible. He could no longer be German, but what was he if not German? And America did not embrace him. The sonorities of his "German" style sounded thin and dry to American taste, which had been shaped by the brilliant virtuosity of the Russian-born Jascha Heifetz. "It is difficult for me," Busch wrote in 1941, "with my way of making music. Rudi (as a piano player) has it easier. People haven't yet fully recognized that one can play the violin so as to make music, and not simply so as to show that one can play the violin."[39]

Serkin did what he could to help Busch get concert engagements, assuring managers that he would join the violinist if it would increase ticket sales. In their joint recitals they were given equal billing, as they had been in Europe. Serkin encouraged other musicians to perform Busch's compositions (suggesting, for example, to the Budapest String Quartet that they perform Busch's Piano Quintet together),[40] but the discrepancy between their fortunes in America was hard on both of them. In 1942, as a partial remedy for the scant bookings, Busch assembled a small chamber orchestra on the model of the European group he had first pulled together in 1935 for the Florentine *Brandenburgs*.

Busch Chamber Players. Serkin at the piano, Irene Serkin on the left (in the white blouse) COURTESY OF PETER SERKIN

At their second concert (March 27) Serkin again played the solo in the *Brandenburg* Fifth. Though he continued to perform with Busch's group, given Serkin's crowded calendar Busch regularly turned to other pianists to join the Chamber Players, among them Serkin student Eugene Istomin and Mieczyslaw Horszowski.

Busch described the American music scene as he experienced it in a letter to their Swiss friend May Fahrländer in August 1942:

> Here in this country everything has first of all to be big—they have the biggest houses, the biggest halls, the biggest orchestras (also the best ones), the biggest virtuosos, the biggest audiences for these virtuosos, etc. However since chamber music is always and everywhere intended for a smaller, though cultivated audience, but the programs have been set for decades by managers and virtuosos (with bad taste and lust for the American dollar), the audience has to suffer, and *does* suffer, quite literally, still today.[41]

Serkin wrote to Busch's Basel friend Benedict Vischer, "The whole 'art life' [*Kunstleben*] here is a mixture of the best with the most repulsive."[42]

On December 1, 1940, not yet 50, Busch suffered a major heart attack. Though he would recover, its shadow hung over him until his death in 1952. Serkin described the harrowing circumstances of the attack in a letter to the Vischers in Basel:

> We were to play the last concert of a complete cycle of Beethoven's violin sonatas in Town Hall in New York. Adolf was very nervous, and he complained about the lack of blood in his left hand. After the first sonata (C minor, Op. 30) he said he had terrible pains in his chest. Since he had played so well, I thought it was nerves and convinced him to try the next sonata. He played it wonderfully too, but the pain had become so strong that we asked for a doctor in the audience. He immediately forbade Adolf to continue, which he probably couldn't have done anyway. He said right away that it might be a thrombosis, and that it was serious. After ten minutes [Ira Hirschmann] came and asked me to play a solo in the place of the *Kreutzer* sonata in order not to upset the audience too much. I played the *Appassionata*; but with what feelings you can easily imagine.[43]

According to Ira Hirschmann, Karl Ulrich Schnabel ("a relentless critic") "to this day vows it was the most remarkable rendition of the Beethoven opus he has ever heard."[44]

Less than two weeks after the Town Hall concert—Busch was still in the hospital—Frieda Busch wrote to Elizabeth Sprague Coolidge about Busch's "broken heart," broken by his hatred for Germany. "I hated too much," she quoted him as saying. "That is nothing for me, I will never hate again."[45] Busch's career as a violinist was essentially destroyed. Little illustrates the American reversal of his fortunes more poignantly than a letter written to Robert Lowell by Elizabeth Bishop in January 1950, during the time when Bishop was Poetry Consultant to the Library of Congress: "Serkin and a violinist are giving two concerts at the Library."[46] Serkin had become a name; Busch, an anonymous fiddler.

"A DROWNING MAN"

As if the worries about Busch were not anguishing enough, Serkin was receiving a steady stream of letters from relatives, friends, and acquaintances pleading for him to rescue them from the Nazis, whether with money or affidavits for visas or, if they were safely in England or America, with help getting them jobs. They saw in Serkin their last best hope.

His own immediate family was his first concern. That not one of them perished at the hands of the Germans was in no small part due to his efforts. He regularly sent money to his mother, who had managed to find refuge with her youngest daughter in neutral Switzerland after the *Anschluss* in 1938. (She died there in May 1944.) His oldest brother, Willi, emigrated to Australia; his youngest, Paul, after being imprisoned by the Nazis, to New Zealand. Lotte and Robert escaped from Vienna to Lithuania, and from there to Kenya, where Lotte, bitterly unhappy at first, wrote Serkin frantic, furious letters imploring him to get her anywhere, but out, blaming him for acceding to what she perceived as Frieda's evil manipulation of their destinies. Maltschi was in England. After Robert fled Kenya (where he had attempted suicide) and returned to Basel, Rudi managed to get him the necessary papers and the money to reach the United States, where he ended up in St. Louis. In their wartime letters, his brothers and sisters expressed gratitude but some resented what they perceived as his indifference. Only Robert was beyond saving. Long unstable, he sank into illness and depression and killed himself in 1943. Paul wrote Rudi from New Zealand and tried to ease his feelings of guilt. Once the war was over, relations between Serkin and his siblings became much less tense. After what everyone had been through, they were grateful to have one another.

Those who turned to Serkin were under no illusion about how drastic their situation was. "It is," wrote a supplicant on behalf of Adolf Pines, a relative of Serkin's about to be deported from Vienna to Poland, "a question of life and death."[47] Serkin's papers contain scores of these letters. An appeal from Pines himself is typical: "You are so well known in the USA and surely also have connections, that you will be able to help me find the needed funds. You might consider this an imposition, but I can't describe my situation to you in a letter. So I ask you again, *urgently*, to help me."[48] He helped many: Richard Robert's former assistant Anka Landau; the singer Lotte Leonard; his first teacher, Camilla Taussig, who had been expelled along with the other Jews from Eger when the Germans marched into the Sudetenland in 1938; the widow of Richard Robert, unable to get out of Vienna; and Genia Schwarzwald, safe in Switzerland, but ailing. Camilla Taussig and Laura Robert both died before they could be rescued (had that, indeed, been possible). Serkin wrote Anka Landau, "I'm afraid to ask what's happened to our other friends. Anka, it is terrible to be so helpless!"[49] He continued to have close contact with Genia

Schwarzwald until her death in 1940. They corresponded regularly; he performed at a benefit concert on her behalf in New York, visited her when he returned to Switzerland, and comforted her when her husband died in August 1939. Almost exactly a year later, her life in ruins, she died of cancer.

"I am leaving soon for a concert tour and I feel like a drowning man," he wrote an acquaintance in 1942.[50] Given the expectations his friendliness and air of welcoming accessibility aroused, friends would sometimes find themselves disappointed. One friend rebuked Serkin in 1941, "Don't forget: many times I asked if I could speak with you, and you didn't even take the trouble to find out what I wanted to say or ask." "You are a great artist, whereas my boast is to be the better friend," wrote another, characterizing the asymmetry that many of Serkin's relationships entailed.

Although Serkin did not have the stable social circle in America that he had enjoyed in Basel, he made friends, among them Samuel Barber and the Vienna-born psychoanalyst and amateur violinist, Richard Sterba. (In 1954 Sterba and his wife Editha published a psychoanalytic study of Beethoven. Serkin responded flatteringly after reading it, though privately he was derisive.)[51] And together the Serkins enjoyed a wide group of friends and acquaintances, most of them from the elite of the New York–area emigré community: Justin Thannhauser and his wife Käte, art dealers through whom the Serkins acquired much of their own collection that included works by Marc, Utrillo, Kokoschka, Pissarro, Delacroix, and Munch; and publishers Kurt Wolff and Helen Wolff, who were themselves good friends of the Sterbas and the Thannhausers.

Serkin was lively and gregarious, even enchanting in good company. The range of his appeal stretched from *Washington Post* owner Katharine Graham, the daughter of Eugene and Agnes Meyer, who was devoted to him, to the German-born historian Erich Kahler, who, after a brief acquaintance, wrote Serkin that he was drawn to him from their first meeting by "that natural, undeviating feeling of attraction, connection, and belonging . . . that one calls friendship."[52] It is difficult to overstate the intensity of the deep and close affection that Serkin evoked in many, many people. And yet, his shyness, commonly said to be misleading, was truer and went deeper than most people realized, and that was probably part of his appeal. The warmth of feeling on his side could be genuine, but the gregariousness went only so far and in the end he kept people at arm's length. If there were people who thought they knew him well, those who knew him best were not among them. Music was probably his only real company. To one friend he seemed "like a wanderer in the desert."

To New York's community of German and Austrian refugees, Serkin and

Busch were a remnant of the culture they had loved. There was probably little in Manhattan that evoked the Berlin or Frankfurt or Vienna of the 1920s and early 1930s as powerfully as the Busch-Serkin recitals in Town Hall. In their book *Escape to Life* Thomas Mann's children Klaus and Erika Mann devote a chapter to a private concert given by Busch and Serkin at the Muschenheims in New York. Although the chapter bears the title "A Musical Evening," music is not really its subject. The Manns were fascinated—who wouldn't be?—by an audience that included Jascha Heifetz, Albert Einstein, and Toscanini. But the real focus of their interest was the duo Busch-Serkin, whom they saw as the embodiment of German and Jew. (In this context it is probably relevant that Klaus and Erika Mann were, themselves, children of a "mixed" marriage.) Busch is described as "big, fair, and broad-shouldered, like a Westphalian peasant youth," whereas Serkin is "small, slim, dark." Serkin's "dark" head is contrasted with Busch's "rubicund face," his fair hair, his resemblance to "woodcarvings in old German churches." The Manns quote Einstein: "That is Germany, that is the true, the best Germany . . . and what a testimony it is, if such were needed, against all the imbecilities of 'Race.' Can anyone imagine a more perfect unity, a purer fusion than that created by those two—the fair and the dark, the Aryan and the young Jew?"[53] It is a passage that surely would have made Busch and Serkin squirm, casting them as it does in the language of race even as it argues against racism, but in the 1930s and 1940s there was no getting away from thinking of this kind.

VERMONT

During the war years, the two families, unable to return for their Swiss summers, began to spend the warm months between the concert seasons in southeastern Vermont, in the hill country west of Brattleboro. The surrounding landscape immediately endeared itself to the homesick emigrés, as it reminded them of the countryside they had left behind. Serkin would claim that it was like the Vienna Woods; for Irene, it evoked the Jura foothills, near Basel; the violinist Gösta Andreasson was reminded of Sweden, and his wife, who came from Stuttgart, thought it just like the Black Forest. The small and relatively intimate scale was more familiar than the big cities and endless spaces of their travels, and yet they were only hours from major urban centers.

With gasoline rations lifted at war's end, the Serkin and Busch families were free to live in Vermont year-round. They bought 125 acres on a hilltop in Guilford, near the Massachusetts state line. (Later, Adolf took a smaller acreage on an adjacent property.) "It is very beautiful here," Serkin wrote his sister Marthl.

"Many hills, wild forests, and nice, straightforward people."[54] Strapped for cash, and himself lending to Busch,[55] Serkin followed the advice of his friend Horowitz and made the down payment for the Vermont property with the money he owed the Steinways for the hire of their pianos. "Just don't pay them. They will wait," Horowitz said. (Some years later, over dessert "at a very elegant dinner club," Theodore Steinway said to Serkin, "Rudolf, everybody has to pay his bills, eventually. Now it's your turn.")[56]

Meanwhile, the family continued to grow: like Ursula, Elisabeth Hedwig was born in Switzerland; John Arthur (named after Hans Oertli and Toscanini, who declined to be the child's godfather, claiming that all the fathers of his godchildren died after the honor was conferred) was born on Beethoven's birthday, 1942; Susan followed in 1945; Peter Adolf was born in 1947, Judith Agnes in 1950, and finally, in 1959, the same year as the birth of their first grandchild, their seventh and last child, Marguerite Dorothy, named after Eugene Ormandy's wife, Margaret, and the Vermont writer Dorothy Canfield Fisher. "They have all the good qualitys [sic] of the mother and grandparents, without the defects of the father," Serkin wrote to his friend Frances Dakyns.[57]

Some of the children attended a one-room schoolhouse at the bottom of the hill, and Irene sold pies at the county fair; nonetheless, it is easy to overplay Serkin's activities as a Vermont farmer. (When mistaken for Serkin and asked about his farm, Rubinstein supposedly quipped, "Serkin is the farmer; I'm the pianist.") A black couple was brought in as domestic help, and local farmers were hired to do the hands-on farmwork. But Serkin participated in the management of his small farm as actively as his schedule allowed: a 1950 letter from Columbia Artist's Management bears a penciled note in his hand: "How much space per sheep in barn?"[58] According to his son John: "My father knew the farm would provide important learning opportunities for his children. He also wanted to be a participant in that Vermont tradition, working and improving the land. However, within a few years it became obvious that the farm would never make money. My father was very proud when, on occasional years, it broke even. Even though it was a financial burden, he kept it going for the children."[59]

Stories about a famous Jewish pianist from Vienna running a Vermont farm were irresistible, and journalists and program writers made the most of it. In February 1951, following a benefit Serkin gave for the Philadelphia Orchestra, a Farmall Cub tractor was wheeled onto the stage and presented to the pianist as a gesture of gratitude and affection. *Harvester World* later reported that "Serkin gingerly climbed up on the seat, flipped his full dress coat

Philadelphia, February 1951, with Peter Serkin COURTESY OF PETER SERKIN

tails behind him, and guided his shining red tractor as it was pushed slowly across the stage."[60] Photographs appeared in the papers the next day showing Serkin onstage, atop the new tractor with his son Peter. Irene claimed that the tractor was too small to be usable. Not surprisingly, the story took on a life of its own. "Farmer Serkin," announced the headline of a story in a Buffalo program the following December. In 1965 a Rotterdam newspaper—Serkin was to perform there for the first time in thirty-six years—reported that friends had given the pianist a tractor that he then drove himself from New York to Vermont.[61]

Having a home in rural New England, the Serkin-Busch family acquired a base outside the tight New York–Philadelphia axis. In this way it was not unlike their move from Berlin, first to Darmstadt and then to Basel, by which they set themselves apart and asserted their autonomy as a family, and also as artists, making a clear separation between themselves and the cities in which music was so obviously a business. Because Serkin could not be far from Curtis during the school year, they lived from 1956 until the mid-1970s primarily in Philadelphia, in the Rittenhouse Square neighborhood near Curtis. For a time

The Serkins' house in Guilford, Vermont, ca. 1949 PHOTOGRAPH BY CHARLES LEIRENS.
REPRODUCED WITH PERMISSION

they also lived in New York again, but as Irene wrote Eugene Ormandy, "Rudi is against Vermont, and I'm against New York, so we agreed on Philadelphia."[62] (The most beautiful of their houses, Irene said later, was the first of their three Philadelphia residences, at 2004 Delancey Street, where they lived from 1956 to 1963.) The younger children went to the Bank Street School in New York and Philadelphia's Friends Select and boarded at the Putney School in Vermont. The summers, always, were spent in Marlboro (about 20 minutes from Guilford by back roads), and when Serkin left Curtis in 1976, they moved back to Guilford, this time permanently.

FAMILY MATTERS

For the Serkins the war and the years immediately afterward were a period of great trial. "We are all fine," Serkin wrote a friend early in 1940, "but very sad. It is a terrible time we live in."[63] The many strains began to take their toll on the Serkins' marriage. Irene became "difficult"—depressed and angry. In Serkin's life, she felt, she and the children had taken a back seat to Frau Musica. Nonetheless, when on tour, he wrote home frequently, and his letters, intimate

Irene Serkin,
New York
PHOTOGRAPH BY
SHELBURNE STUDIOS,
NEW YORK.
COURTESY OF PETER
SERKIN

and loving, represent an impressive record of constancy. "I love you more than ever," he wrote Irene in 1958, "and it's not because I'm so far away, but more and more, I just don't tell you about it nearly enough. And sometimes we're both so overtired that our overirritated nerves confuse it with irritation. Maybe our lives will become quieter one day, or sometimes you could come with me on these trips—that would be nice."[64] From his 1960 tour of Asia, which he enjoyed immensely, leading him to speculate jokingly that he was himself of Asian descent, he wrote, "Prepare yourself for your Asian husband, who will love you even more that your previous Austrian, Swiss, and American husbands."[65]

Adoring her father, Irene had more of her mother in her than she cared to admit, and, like Frieda, she could be blunt and undiplomatic. (They also shared a name: *Irene,* the Greek equivalent of *Frieda,* means *peace*—something neither was given much of to enjoy in life.) She was deeply vulnerable, but this was not the side of herself she generally showed. She played the violin, and if she had no particular talent for it, what mattered in the household in which she was raised was that you played with love: skill was a bonus. This was not her husband's attitude, and that, too, was a source of tension.*

In August 1946, Frieda Busch died of lymphatic cancer in the Serkins' Vermont house. After her death Adolf and Rosalie Leventritt talked of marriage, though Busch subsequently changed his mind, fearing that she would not be able to tolerate the stressful life of a concertizing musician. On October 7, catastrophically, the Serkins' infant daughter Susan (named after Serkin's favorite sister, who had died in 1919) was killed in a crib accident while the Serkins and Busch were in Iceland. "It is so infinitely difficult to grasp or comprehend," Serkin wrote Maltschi. "And it hurts so badly . . . Irene and I are making an effort—a big effort—to keep the children from noticing how we really feel."

And finally, after a short, happy second marriage to Hedwig Vischer, Irene's closest childhood friend from Basel, and with the prospect of future work on the Curtis faculty, Adolf Busch died at the age of 60 of a heart attack in Guilford on June 9, 1952, leaving two small sons. With Busch's death both Irene and Serkin lost the person who was probably most important to both of them. Thanking Hermann Hesse for his condolence letter, Serkin wrote, "That Adolf Busch is no longer alive is incomprehensible. Our lives were so richly intertwined that to me the boundaries between death and life now often seem blurred."[66] He wrote Irene's uncle, Otto Grüters: "How can one ever express the sadness, except in music! I have no strength, and as much as I'd like to, I have no consoling word to say to you. Adolf was a part of myself, or rather: I was a piece of him, and after the initial numbing pain, it often seems to me that I can no longer feel anything."[67]

Serkin, by then almost 50, escaped into a routine of performing, recording, teaching, and practicing, practicing, practicing.

Serkin was a loving and often playful father. His daughter Elisabeth recalls their "Elephant Game": "In the early morning, still in bed, he'd make an elephant out of his hand, and I'd make an elephant out of my hand, too, and the elephants would have a conversation. This was a game he had played with my

---

* Once, when Serkin had asked an acquaintance, a surgeon and an amateur violinist, how he could show his gratitude for a generous donation to Marlboro, the surgeon replied that he would like Serkin to accompany him through some violin pieces. "All right," said Serkin, "but I won't ask you to let me operate on *you*."

Rudolf and John Serkin, Guilford, Vermont
COURTESY OF PETER SERKIN

mother when she was a child."[68] But he was often absent, on the road much of the time and otherwise in the studio. (Ursula Serkin: "When he was younger, my father did a lot of things with us, like hiking. But as he got older, he had to practice more and more.")[69] And the household was a busy one. Marguerite Serkin remembers the years in Philadelphia:

> There were always so many people involved in our lives. My mother always had two or three people she was looking out for, starving students invited for meals, one would be our dog walker, another my baby sitter, and other people, too, musicians visiting from Europe . . . and with six of us kids, our friends and various pets, it was pretty wild. It was an open household. My mother controlled every aspect of it: if I left a book upside down or even closed in the living room, it

would be on the stairs within five minutes to go upstairs. She was tough . . . but I guess she had to be, because it was *so* busy and there was so much going on.[70]

To ensure that the children had at least some time with their father, Irene saw to it that each one accompany him on at least one European tour. Elisabeth remembered attending his recitals: "Sometimes he would give special encores . . . He knew that I loved a particular piece, and he would play it for me. And when my mother was in the audience and he played an encore for her, it was like an 'I love you.'"[71]

His relationships with his daughters by and large seem to have been less complicated than with his sons. In the 1960s the difficulties between Serkin and teenage Peter became widely known, and, in an era when adolescent rebellion was daily front-page fare, the struggle between the Old World father and long-haired son took on an emblematic quality in the press.[72] Peter had first been seen on stage at his father's side turning pages; he made his debut when he was 11 (the Haydn D major Concerto under Alexander Schneider at Marlboro). In 1961 father and son performed at Marlboro for the first time in public (Adolf Busch's *Theme and Variations for Piano*, 4 Hands, Op. 63), and that fall, at a Philadelphia Orchestra Pension Fund concert, they gave the first of many performances of the Mozart Concerto in E-flat for 2 Pianos (K. 365), with Peter on *Piano secondo* because his father thought Peter should play the part that Mozart himself played. "He wanted to do much more collaboration than I wanted," said Peter. "I had the feeling I could have spent the rest of my life playing the Mozart Double Concerto with my dad. I'm sure I could have been much more easy-going about the whole thing, much nicer. But it was difficult."[73] Peter, gifted son of a gifted father, struggling to find his own way, had no contact with his father at all from the late 1960s through much of the 1970s. Though father and son eventually reconciled, it was a painful time for the family. A *New York Times* journalist portrayed a regretful father: "Rudolf Serkin clenches his fingers like the talons of a bird. '. . . I didn't give him much encouragement—I didn't know.'" "I will defend myself," he continues, recounting the manner in which *his* father had forced music on *him*: "From the time I was 4 years old, he made me practice—and *paid* my older sister to watch me. I wasn't getting anything out of it, I felt, while she got paid for doing nothing. You can see that I would be reluctant to push Peter. When I discovered his gift, I was confused. A child feels that he must be like his father. You have an obligation to tell him not to make the same mistakes."[74] *A child feels that he must be like his father*—well, yes and no.

In addition to Peter, two other Serkin children became professional musicians: John played the French horn in a Florida orchestra (later he became a piano technician), and Judith is a cellist based in Vermont. Ursula is a social worker, Elisabeth a sociologist, and Marguerite is a writer and translator. Grandchildren abound, among them several musicians.

EUROPE AGAIN

"For pianists and lovers of piano music," wrote the pianist David Burge, "the years immediately following the end of World War II were good ones. Piano recitals, whole seasons of piano recitals were major events in the musical life of city after city in the United States and in Europe."[75] Notwithstanding the change in American cultural life, some of the European musicians who had settled in the United States, like Schnabel, chose to return permanently when the war was over. Friends from Switzerland wrote to ask Serkin whether he would move back, but with his large and Americanized family and his property in Vermont, there was no question of returning to Europe to live. Furthermore, as he wrote after the war, "This country has been very good and kind to us, and I am deeply grateful. I was permitted to do all the music I wanted, and it was *music* which helped keep me up."[76] Furthermore, the Busches and Serkin were nervous about what they saw as "business as usual" attitudes toward Nazi musicians in postwar Switzerland. Frieda wrote Ira Hirschmann, "It seems you have to be a Nazi to get permission to work in Switzerland."[77] The Baslers were peeved by Frieda's letters as they made their rounds of the city: "We just shake our heads," one friend wrote Serkin.[78]*

When Serkin first returned to Europe in 1947—he performed in Switzerland, Italy, and England, with Busch as well as in solo recitals and with orchestras—he reacted to the countries in which he had spent his youth and early maturity with great ambivalence. Being back in Switzerland was "nerve-wracking," he wrote Irene.[79] (Not that he wasn't warmly welcomed: a Swiss critic wrote about being so caught up in the emotion of Serkin's concert in Zurich that he was no longer able to lay claim to his position as impartial listener.)[80] "When the first excitement of recognition is over," Serkin wrote, "what is left is a terrible homesickness. I feel like an American tourist here . . . I didn't realize

---

* After the war and half a year before her death, Frieda was quoted in *Time* on the subject of her husband's brother and sister still in Germany: "We don't even know if they are living, and we don't want to" (January 7, 1946, p. 43). She subsequently wrote to Benedict Vischer that the *Time* article was "all lies" (Grüters, *Adolf Buschs Lebenslauf*, May 14, 1946).

how deeply I have already taken root in America." Although he was still "very tied" to Basel,[81] seeing their houses in Riehen again, he "didn't feel the slightest trace of emotion. I don't even think they're that pretty."[82] After a conversation with his old friend Hans Oertli, he wrote Irene, "I'll be glad to be back in happy America, where people have *fun*. I also prefer American audiences."[83] In Italy, he found the disparity between rich and poor "terrible": "You've got to admire England, where everyone has the same—little." From Milan, Serkin wrote, "The hotel is good, but it used to be the Gestapo headquarters, and I don't like the walls that must have seen such terrible things. Everything is knotted up with the past, wherever you look."[84] Summing up the 1947 trip he wrote that it was "*necessary*, if only to regain the perspective that one loses so easily in America. But it's no pleasure trip."[85]

In 1948 Serkin and Busch spent a month in September and October concertizing in Colombia, Puerto Rico, Cuba, and Mexico. In Bogotá the orchestra and conductor were so poor, Serkin wrote, that Busch offered to play with the orchestra's violins during Serkin's performance of the *Emperor* Concerto. Serkin wrote Irene from Cuba, complaining about the heat, but looking forward to "the dear U.S.A.! You see what a Yankee I've become."[86]

Not long afterward, the Serkins became U.S. citizens. Serkin's daughter Elisabeth said it plainly: "My father loved America. It was liberating, coming to a country where anything was possible."[87] Serkin and Irene spoke German with one another, but English was the common language at home. Marguerite Serkin remembers: "Although his accent was abominable, his English was impeccable, his grammar and vocabulary flawless. But I did coach him on one or two words that he just couldn't pronounce. One of them was 'wool.' He would say 'vool.' The other was 'sword.'"[88]

In 1949 they returned again to Europe (this time with the children), playing in the third Edinburgh Festival.* Though it was a different Europe and a different Serkin from before the war, the European tour was henceforth a fixture in Serkin's life.

---

* After he and Busch canceled a planned 1951 appearance in Edinburgh, Serkin did not play there again until 1964, when he performed seven Mozart concertos in two concerts (among them the Concerto in E-Flat for 2 Pianos, K. 365, with Peter). It was there that he met Mstislav Rostropovich (with whom he later recorded the Brahms sonatas) for the first time.

Rudolf and Irene Serkin leaving for Europe, with John, Peter, Elisabeth, Ursula (left to right), 1949

PHOTOGRAPH BY ENELL INC., JACKSON HEIGHTS, NY. COURTESY OF PETER SERKIN

PRADES

In 1947, the same year as Serkin's postwar return to Europe, the violinist Alexander Schneider (1908–1993) went to the small town of Prades, on the French side of the Pyrenees, to pay homage to Pablo Casals (1876–1973), then 70. The encounter between the solemn Spanish cellist and the ebullient, Russian-born violinist was to be of significant consequence for the musical world of the second half of the century. Refusing to perform in any country that recognized Spain's fascist government, Casals was leading a hermitlike existence, completely withdrawn from public life. Schneider and Casals quickly became close. With the financial help of his friend and patron Elizabeth Sprague Coolidge, Schneider returned to Prades for longer stays and began to encourage Casals to perform in the United States: "If you wish you can have Rudi Serkin play with you, even God Himself," he wrote Casals.[89] When Casals wouldn't budge, Schneider proposed a festival in Prades, an idea that seems to have originated with Mieczyslaw Horszowski, though Schneider claimed it as his own.[90]

Serkin was one of the elite group of musicians (including Joseph Szigeti, Isaac Stern, Horszowski, and Eugene Istomin) invited to participate in the first Prades Festival in 1950, the bicentennial anniversary of Bach's death. The reunion between Serkin and Casals (their first meeting is usually dated to Berlin in 1920) occasioned the often-told story of their picking up the thread of a disagreement from decades before about a *ritardando* that Casals had wanted in the opening *tutti* of Beethoven's Fourth Piano Concerto: "How do you play Beethoven No. 4 now?" he asked Serkin in Prades.[91]

The first Prades Festival opened at 9 P.M. on Friday, June 2, with a performance by Casals of the first Bach Cello Suite. At the third concert a week later Serkin played the Fifth *Brandenburg* Concerto with Szigeti and John Wummer and, the next evening, the *Chromatic Fantasy and Fugue*, the *Italian* Concerto, and the *Goldberg Variations* (described by Horszowski in his diary as a performance of "incomparable beauty, understanding and mastery").[92] He would not agree to record either the *Brandenburg* Fifth (because he had done it with Busch)[93] or, not liking Casals's phrasing, the Bach D minor Concerto.[94] Nonetheless, he wrote Irene, "Casals is a wonderful, lovable man, who makes music with love and spirit, somewhat Spanish, but in Bach, too, a lot of fire can be beautiful."[95] The Festival (coinciding with the summer of Marlboro's beginnings in Vermont) was by all accounts an unforgettable event in the lives of many of the participants, and the bringing together of Casals and Serkin after so many years was to have a major impact on the lives of both. That Serkin was pulled into Casals's orbit just when Busch was starting his own new family may not have been entirely a coincidence of timing: Serkin was never afraid of associating closely with strong musical personalities; indeed, he was drawn to them, and their strength seems to have helped fuel his own.

The second Casals Festival took place in 1951, this time in Perpignan, considerably larger than Prades and about twenty-five miles to its east on the Mediterranean coast. Serkin was accompanied, as he had been in 1950, by his teenage daughter Ursula. Living conditions were simple: Serkin, Ursula, Horszowski, and three others stayed in a villa rented by Rosalie Levintritt, where they shared one shower, one toilet, and one sink and had no running water after 8 in the evening. Probably inevitably, the second Festival was remembered as a bit of a let-down after the first. Once again, Serkin played the *Goldberg*

Variations. Performing the Bach and Beethoven sonatas with Casals was not without its difficulties: "In many ways, Casals plays differently from what I am used to hearing, but with such concentration and great feeling that we found our way after all." It was in Perpignan that Serkin and Casals also recorded the E-flat major Mozart Concerto, K. 482, with Serkin's own cadenzas. The following year Serkin sent Hermann Hesse a copy of the recording, writing of the great pleasure that the performance had given him and Casals and expressing the hope that the recording succeeded in conveying some of that joy.[96] (Later taking a dislike to his cadenzas, Serkin refused to play the concerto for many years.)

Serkin was not among the pianists at the third Festival. He must have complained, because Schneider apologized, writing that Serkin had said he would not be coming to Europe that summer and bending over backward to try to accommodate him in the schedule at the eleventh hour.[97] Serkin was back the following year, this time with his 10-year-old son John, and repeatedly after that. (He would also participate in the first Casals Festival in Puerto Rico in 1957.) Serkin stayed on after the 1953 Festival to complete the recording of the Beethoven sonatas that he and Casals had begun in 1951. He wrote Irene: "Much was and is different from the way I conceive it, but the intensity and the depth of feeling, and the absolute devotion to the work of art are exemplary. I am very happy and the [Beethoven] sonatas are unbelievably beautiful pieces." He found these recording sessions so strenuous that he canceled his scheduled concerts in Perugia and Palermo to recover.

ISRAEL, GERMANY

Israelis expected Jewish musicians to show their solidarity with their new country and lobbied intensely for them to concertize there. Serkin, who seems to have had little in the way of sentimental attachment to the Jewish state, took his first trip to Israel in 1952, four years after independence. (Adolf Busch had gone to Palestine in 1937, the first soloist to perform with the Palestine Orchestra.) It was not a happy experience. He complained in a letter to Irene that he was treated with so much deference that he felt isolated, in a "hybrid state between rest and imprisonment." After an initially positive impression,[98] he did not like working with the conductor Jascha Horenstein, resented the frequency (13 times) with which he had to play the Brahms First Concerto, and felt pushed beyond his limits and exploited.[99]

On a subsequent trip to Israel in 1961, Serkin opened the door of his hotel room in Tel Aviv one day to be greeted by a man who identified himself as

Ja'akov Serkin, the son of Serkin's brother, Robert, born in Russia after his sol-dier-father had returned to Austria after the First World War. His mother, who perished in the Holocaust, had told him of an uncle who was a famous pianist, and seeing an announcement of Serkin's forthcoming concert in a newspaper, he decided this must be the one. Rudi "kept touching his head and his ears and cried repeatedly, 'It's him! You're him!' "[100]

Germany, not surprisingly, posed a dilemma. Whether or not to perform there after the war was the subject of considerable debate, much as American music lovers argued about whether to boycott the postwar tours of German musicians with compromised reputations, such as Walter Gieseking (in 1949) and Elisabeth Schwarzkopf (in 1953). Busch resumed performances in his native country relatively early, in 1949, but, as he refused to play the sonatas he played with Serkin—the core of his repertory—with any other pianist, the German agents, he wrote, made "glum faces."[101] Jewish musicians responded variously. Yehudi Menuhin played in Germany almost immediately after the war, but Arthur Rubinstein never went back, though he met his German fans more than halfway by performing on the Dutch side of the German border. Schnabel wrote, "I don't want to go to a country to which I am admitted only because it has lost a war,"[102] and in his autobiography Alexander Schneider expressed his dismay that George Szell, Bruno Walter, and William Steinberg chose to return to Germany and Austria.[103]

In 1951 Serkin's Swiss manager began to encourage him to return to Ger-many. For twelve years Serkin resisted German importuning, though he per-formed for Germany's Chancellor Konrad Adenauer at the home of Busch's old patrons Dannie and Hettie Heinemann in New York in 1956. For some Ger-mans Serkin had become an icon of a lost culture. As early as 1952 the German writer Albrecht Goes published a story, "Was wird morgen sein," in which a character, a wounded soldier who had been a pianist, goes by the nickname "Serkin." Goes and Serkin were later to became friends, but at the time Goes wrote the story they had never met. Goes said later that it was "a small decla-ration of love."[104]

Illness forced Serkin to cancel what would have been his return to the Ger-man concert stage in January 1957 for a memorial concert for Adolf Busch organized by the industrialist and music publisher Günter Henle. Not for nothing had Henle been a diplomat, and if he thought he could lure Serkin back to Germany by asking him to participate in an event honoring Busch, he knew his man. The promise having been made, Serkin rescheduled with an all-Beethoven program held in Düsseldorf on May 31, twenty-four years after he had been disinvited from participating in the Brahms celebration in Hamburg.

The reception was enthusiastic, though not without traces of both sentimentality and anguish on the part of the Germans. One headline read: "Return of the Much-Beloved Brother." (Bach's *Capriccio on the Departure of His Beloved Brother* was on one of his first programs.) "We had to wait a long time for his return, painfully long," the review began.[105] He returned to Germany again that fall, and after that regularly. (He didn't play in Austria again until June 1962, finding Vienna "very melancholy—it's like visiting a cemetery.")[106] When Serkin went to Germany, Irene usually stayed behind: she was, he would joke, too German to forgive.

In October 1974 the German Consul General in New York informed Serkin that the President of the Federal Republic had awarded him Germany's highest civilian honor, the Grosses Verdienstkreuz (Great Cross of Merit). Freya von Moltke (an old friend from the Schwarzwald circle), responding to Serkin's request for help, sent him a draft text of a response, which gave him a place to start.[107] Serkin's refusal was gently worded but firm: "Please let me state that I am very aware that there is a New Germany, and that there is no continuity with the years of terror. That is why I concertize in Germany again—and gladly, and with love. But I can't escape the fact that a person's life has its own continuity, a fact that prevents me from accepting the German award."[108] Seven years later, in 1981, he accepted Germany's prestigious Order Pour le Mérite for Arts and Sciences. (Among its charter members were Mendelssohn, Meyerbeer, Liszt, and Rossini.) Presumably, the recent naming of Serkin's old friends (and fellow emigrés) Ernst Gombrich (1977), Victor Weisskopf (1978), and Karl Popper (1980) to the Order played a part in his nomination as well as his acceptance of it.

SUCCESS

When Serkin played in Europe in 1939, he was a European pianist; when he returned eight years later, he had become an American star. But his success was exacted at a cost: the treadmill of concertizing wore him down, physically and emotionally, and he often longed to get off. As Serkin and Busch were trying to find their way as musicians in America, the calamitous developments in Europe and the loss of the firm footing they had known there and all the difficulties of beginning anew in middle age had taken their toll. It was a radically different life from what they had known in Europe before the war, where their partnership flourished in a musical culture with very deep roots and their work was balanced by hiking holidays and, in Basel, a busy social life. In America Serkin became, increasingly, not only a servant to music but also its slave.

In a 1939 letter to Elizabeth Sprague Coolidge, Serkin described the exhaustion he was experiencing as a "poison."[109] In 1940 he suffered a severe case of boils, beginning with a lesion on his arm that required surgery and followed by what Frieda Busch described to Mrs. Coolidge as "7 furunkels and 3 carbunkels." [110] (According to Maltschi, he gave each boil a name: "What a joy when Beethoven would heal up and what misery when Brahms would turn up unexpectedly.")[111] He canceled his engagements for much of that year, leaving the family close to the edge financially and seriously worried about his future as a pianist. In 1944, in desperate need of rest, he came close to canceling another season. It was a motif that was to run throughout his life as a performer: when the strain became too much, it often took a somatic outlet, and he became ill and canceled concerts. (Schnabel, by contrast, seems not to have missed a single engagement until his mid-sixties.)[112]

At war's end he wrote his sister Marthl in a mood of deep depression: "Now, when we're allowed to feel again and to be happy, we are no longer able to. It's as if one's heart had burned out . . . I came close to having a nervous breakdown, and only music, work, and my family prevented it."[113] In the 1950s Serkin and Irene consulted a neuropsychologist, Dr. Israel Strauss, who in two stern letters portrayed Serkin's fragile emotional state.[114] In April 1952 Serkin burned his fingers badly enough that it was reported in the newspapers. And for much of his life he suffered from insomnia. "How did you sleep?" his manager Mary Lynn Fixler once asked him when she picked him up for a concert. "Not well," he answered. Wincing, he pointed his outstretched hand to the side of his head and moved it in a slow circle: "The music . . ."[115]

At the height of his career in the 1950s and 1960s, Serkin gave up to sixty recitals and orchestra concerts a year (about forty of them in the United States) in a season that stretched from October to May and took him across the country and, after the war, at least once annually to Europe. Given his teaching and administrative responsibilities, his active recording schedule, and the remarkable fact that with Marlboro taking up the summer, he had essentially no time off, his was an arduous life indeed. (Rubinstein, whose career was devoted solely to performing, appeared in an average of 120 concerts per year; Arrau claimed to have played up to 140 at his peak.)[116] His regular major-city recitals, like those in Carnegie Hall, where he played virtually every winter, year after year for fifty years, testify to a sheer doggedness unmatched by any other musician.* In venues like Chicago's Allied Arts series the number of Serkin's recitals

---

* Rubinstein played for the first time in Carnegie Hall in 1919 but not again until 1938, after which he played there more than any other pianist until his last recital in 1976, when he was almost 90.

—twenty-four between 1949 and 1977—was exceeded, again, only by Rubin-stein, who appeared twenty-nine times in the same period.[117] Tours demanded a monastic rigor, "the routine," he wrote, "of a vagrant pianist—'practice and practice and rest.'"[118] Having lost three seasons over the course of his per-forming career to poor health—fall/spring 1940, fall 1951, and spring 1976—from November 1978 to the fall of 1979 Serkin scheduled a full "sabbatical." To get away from Marlboro (the only year he missed in forty), he spent that sum-mer with Irene (on whom age was also taking its toll) in Switzerland.

In the course of his years in America, Serkin had been twice to Asia on tours sponsored by the State Department, first to India in 1956, where the American Consulate General in Bombay sent a dispatch back to Washington describing him with evident astonishment as "warm, friendly, and utterly charming."[119] Four years later he went on a much more extensive tour that took him to Korea, Japan, Taiwan, Hong Kong, Vietnam, Thailand, Malaysia, Singapore, and the Philippines. He loved Japan especially and won a devoted following there that brought him back again in 1965, 1978, 1979, and 1982.

The United States Information Agency helped sponsor a film on Marlboro for German television in 1957, and he performed three times in the White House (he and Irene also attended numerous dinners there), the first time in 1970 for Richard Nixon. Serkin's last White House appearance was to inaugu-rate a "young artists" series with the young violinist Ida Levin in November 1981. Serkin's technician, Franz Mohr, whom Serkin brought with him, writes that on their way to the concert after dinner Serkin confessed to being com-pletely uncomfortable there and wishing he were home in Vermont.[120] Serkin had received the Presidential Medal of Freedom in 1963 and was to receive the National Medal of Arts in 1988, along with honorary degrees from a host of universities all the way up to Harvard. Thus, the Americanization that had been accomplished through a transformation in his musical and family life and its ties and allegiances—he had, after all, six American children—was also manifested by the highest forms of official recognition.

Serkin's success in the United States may have been exemplary, but it was hardly representative: for every Serkin, scores of first-rate European musi-cians were scraping by in obscurity. Busch was the rule, Serkin the very rare exception.

In the small world of classical music, Serkin's position of perceived power inevitably invited resentment. Writing of the Leventritt award, Joseph Horo-witz observed, "Serkin was especially controversial. Even Serkin's detractors conceded his musical stature and admired his ideals of sacrifice and self-abnegation. But Serkin appeared to some to relish the power he wielded on the

Al Hirschfeld calendar COPYRIGHT AL HIRSCHFELD. ART REPRODUCED BY
SPECIAL ARRANGEMENT WITH HIRSCHFELD'S EXCLUSIVE REPRESENTATIVE THE
MARGO FEIDEN GALLERIES LTD., NEW YORK

Leventritt jury, or at Marlboro."[121] (In fact, according to Seymour Lipkin, who
served with both Serkin and Szell on a Leventritt jury, it was Szell who was the
dominating figure.)[122]

The last Leventritt competition, held in 1976 (Mrs. Leventritt had died earlier
that year), concluded without a winner. Horowitz quotes an anonymous,
angry finalist:

> After the final round, we were all herded into this room to await the result. And
> suddenly Serkin walked in. There he was with this big smile on his face—the one
> he wears when you know he's hiding something. And he said, "To me, you're all
> winners!" And he patted us all and swept out of the room. It was about ten minutes
> later that we found out that none of us were winners. It was an ugly little scene.[123]

Others, too, reacted to Serkin's public persona: Ned Rorem describes in his
diary how Serkin welcomed him at Marlboro "with a bear hug and tears of

gratitude," adding, "I'd have been more moved had I not seen this routine repeated with others."[124] Some of this can be ascribed to an ingratiating "Viennese" manner, some to his more personally rooted aversion to open unpleasantness and conflict. Serkin was not uncomfortable with power, but he did not like wielding it openly.

Comparing the Leventritt competition with that founded by Van Cliburn in 1962, Horowitz wrote:

> These two events, the one elitist, the other populist, are as different as Rudolf Serkin and Van Cliburn, as different as Serkin's wire-rim spectacles and Cliburn's occasional cowboy hat. They resonate with two distinct moments in America's high-cultural history, the first—of the forties and fifties—shadowed by Europe (its wars and refugees, its cultural colonization of the United States, its patina of worldly reflectiveness), the second—of today—bright with American optimism, gusto, and heedless naivete.[125]

Still, the Texas-born pianist had won the Leventritt in 1954 and, in 1956, two years before his victory at the Tchaikovsky Competition in Moscow, he spent a summer at Marlboro. There he must have undergone something of an immersion in its traditions of European musicianship, having performed, for example, Dvořák's A major Piano Quintet with Alexander Schneider, Felix Galimir, Lotte Bamberger, and Herman Busch. The bridging of cultures is captured in a photograph showing Cliburn at Marlboro playing four-hand with the 13-year-old James Levine from Cincinnati, an almost-empty Coke bottle set on the piano.

Until the end of his life, Rudolf Serkin devoted himself to establishing in the United States European musical traditions as he understood them. The range and impact of his efforts are the subject of Part II of this volume.

Part Two

CHAPTER FOUR

Performing

> *Imagine our lives: we live for no other reason than to play as well as we are able in the evening, and to that end everything else is cast aside or deferred.*
>
> —RUDOLF SERKIN (1936)

> *Striving for the unreachable is really quite splendid.*
>
> —RUDOLF SERKIN (1982)

At his sister's in London, while waiting impatiently for the cab to his concert, Serkin went to the piano to take advantage of the extra time. When the taxi arrived a few minutes later, his brother-in-law asked, teasingly, whether the concert would now be a better one. Serkin's answer, and he meant it: "It will be."[1] His convictions about music were unsparing, his psychology obsessive. He had his eye on one thing only: the truest possible performance. Everything else was a distraction. But as Serkin knew better than anyone, the striving toward this ideal required not only untold hours of solitary practicing but an intricate network of institutions, technologies, and people, each with its own needs and demands that had to be harnessed and harmonized into a smoothly functioning operation. In prewar Europe the scale was relatively small, and the institutions of musical life had evolved over a long time and, as it were, on native soil. The successful cultivation of his art with American audiences left Serkin with no choice but to entrust himself to the machinery of American cultural life. He got off to a bumpy start, but he was nothing if not a quick study, and he readily mastered the system so that, come evening, he could play as well as he was able.

THE BUSINESS OF MUSIC

Serkin's first experience of American managers in 1936 was not promising. Sol Hurok, assuming that he would manage Serkin's second tour, held on to a portion of his earnings in anticipation of future promotional expenses. Serkin retaliated by refusing to pay what he owed his Paris agent, Paul Schiff. In April 1937 Schiff complained to Serkin, "Again and again you assume that the manager is an evil to which one turns only when absolutely necessary. I don't think that this attitude best serves your interest."[2] Writing Maltschi, Serkin alludes to Hurok's "sliminess." His final word on the subject: "*Zum Kotzen* [It makes me puke]." (Never one to bear long-standing grudges, when Serkin ran into Hurok in London many years later, he wrote Irene, "He was especially nice, and his undisguised vulgarity has an almost refreshing effect.")[3]

Dropping Hurok, Serkin turned instead to NBC Artists Service (of which S. Hurok Attractions was an independent affiliate), which managed his 1937–1938 and 1938–1939 tours. In 1941 he and Busch switched managers again. The "industry" was being shaken up in any case: the Federal Communications Commission was about to force the networks (such as NBC) to divest themselves of their concert management businesses. Busch and Serkin went from NBC to what was then called Colombia Concerts Corporation, which had been founded by the famously powerful Arthur Judson in 1932. Between them, Columbia and the successor to NBC, the National Concert and Artists Corporation (which included Hurok Attractions, Inc.), were to have a lock on the American classical music business until well after the war. When Eugene Ormandy found out about the move to Columbia, he gloated in a letter to Serkin: "You may recall that I have been the one to instigate such an association years ago and if you had accepted my suggestion and the offer Mr. Judson made you, you would have avoided for yourself a lot of unhappy moments. Well, let us hope now that everything is going to be all right."[4]

Judson, who for a time managed both the Philadelphia Orchestra and New York Philharmonic, ran a supremely effective business, and Serkin stayed with Columbia Concerts (later Columbia Artists Management, Inc., or CAMI) for three decades. His day-to-day managers at CAMI were William Judd and Mary Lynn Fixler, and when they left CAMI to start anew in 1969 under the name Judd Concert Bureau (Judson had been forced out of CAMI six years before),

A lithograph of Rudolf Serkin, signed by the pianist, by the German-born painter Eugen Spiro REPRODUCED WITH PERMISSION, PETER SPIRO, LONDON

Serkin, along with the young André Watts, went with them. Judd and Fixler sweetened the deal by giving Serkin, now a senior superstar, a 5 to 10 percent reduction on the standard 20 percent commission and continued to represent him until Judd's death in 1987. Serkin stayed with Fixler, who had gone over to Herbert Barrett Management, but by then he was ill and had essentially stopped performing.

Although Columbia Artists had established a European division after the war to manage the work of its American musicians overseas, Serkin preferred to work with his own network of European managers: Walter Schulthess (hus-

Rudolf Serkin, 1940s
PHOTOGRAPH BY
ERICH KASTAN.
COURTESY OF PETER
SERKIN

band of the Hungarian-born violinist Stefi Geyer and himself an important figure in Swiss music) and Georges Payot in Zurich (Konzertgesellschaft Zürich) for Switzerland, Germany, and Austria; Emmie Tillett in London (Ibbs & Tillett, who also served as managers for Schnabel and Hess); Clara Camus and Irène Casillo (Propaganda Musicale) in Rome; and Michael Rainer in Paris (Organisation Artistique Internationale, later DARSA). In the last decade of his performing career, Serkin tried coordinating the various European managers centrally, first, in 1979 through his Basel friend, Henriette Speiser, and after 1983 through Michael Rainer. In Japan Serkin was represented by Kajimoto Concert Management.

His managers negotiated fees, arranged travel, coordinated his schedule, booked recital halls, and troubleshot as necessary. An example of the intricate details (and rigors) of his schedule during one autumn concert tour in Europe in 1962, when he was close to 60, as sent to him by Schulthess:

October 12: arrival in Berlin

October 14–16: 3 performances with the Berlin Radio-Symphonie-Orchestra: Brahms D minor concerto (fee: DM 9,000)

October 17: flight to Munich

October 18, 19: 2 performances (including radio broadcast) of Brahms B-flat major Piano Concerto (fee: DM 6,000)

October 20: recital of Beethoven, Op. 109, 110, 111 (fee: DM 4,000)

October 21: flight to Düsseldorf, recital of Schubert A major Op. post., 2 Impromptus, Fantasy C major, Op. 15 (no fee)

October 23: recital, Beethoven, Op. 109, 110, 111 (fee: DM 4,000)

October 24: flight to London

October 25: recital of Schubert Sonata, A major, Beethoven *Moonlight* and Op. 109, *Wanderer Fantasy* (fee: $1,000)

October 27: flight to Hamburg

October 28: recital of Schubert A major, *Moonlight*, Beethoven, Op. 109, Schubert Fantasy in C major (fee: DM 4,000)

October 29: flight to Amsterdam

October 30: recital of Beethoven, Op. 106, 109, *Waldstein* (fee: $1,000)

October 31: flight to Basel

Until the 1970s, his American tours were no less strenuous; April 1962, for example, found him in Philadelphia, Boston, Atlanta, Columbia, Miami, Cleveland, and New York for four recitals, nine orchestral concerts, and a recording session. America's larger cities (such as Washington, D.C., where he gave a total of something like eighty performances between 1933 and 1987)[5] and university towns (such as Ann Arbor, Michigan, where he played eighteen times between 1939 and 1980) came to know him well, as did favored European venues such as Florence (home of his friends Franco and Pia Passigli) and Perugia, where he had close ties to the Buitoni family and played sixteen times.[6]

Whatever the Serkin and Busch families had known about the American music business before they lived in the United States, nothing in their experience could have prepared them for its intense focus on the bottom line. Schnabel wrote of American music managers that "their desire was, along the line of least resistance, to sell as much as possible, as quickly as possible, to as many customers as possible."[7] It is unlikely that a European manager would have written Serkin about a possible engagement with the Busch Quartet in the manner of the Boston impresario Aaron Richmond, who complained about the low earning power of the Busch Quartet.[8] Judson and his staff (called "salesmen") used the undisguised language of the market—indeed, the slave market: Judson writes Serkin, "When we sold you for this Philadelphia Orchestra date . . .".[9] The script of the Steinway-sponsored radio program *Symphony Hall* dressed its product in the form of a Renaissance-era fantasy: "Just sit in your armchair, lean back and imagine that you are the Duke and that Rudolf Serkin and the Adolf Busch Chamber Players are in your stately drawing room—as in fact they are tonight!"[10] Columbia Records "officially" declared a Serkin Month in 1957 and again in 1966. Ten years later they held a "consumer contest" in San Francisco; some 150 Bay Area fans responded. For the prize of a "complete Serkin library," contestants were asked to name their favorite Serkin recording and to explain their preference in twenty-five words or less.

Another aspect of American concert life to which managers asked Serkin to submit in his earlier years was the occasional watering down of his programs: "I do not favor the *Goldberg Variations*," wrote one promoter, ". . . because of their length and because of the necessity of a more diversified program for our mixed audiences."[11] As late as 1948, Aaron Richmond suggested that he try "in so far as possible to include one or two familiar works."[12] Serkin may have chafed, but within fairly well-defined limits he accommodated himself to his audiences when it was necessary. Later, he could play whatever he pleased, and the issue went away.

Serkin's managers at Columbia Concerts ran a tight ship, and in the early years they expected Serkin to fall into line. When he didn't, the reprimand was swift and sharp. In October 1942, Serkin wrote Judson, "Not having the courage to phone you, I want to tell you in this way that I have accepted three engagements . . . Please don't tell me what you think about it, but I simply couldn't say no."[13] A week later, Judson, who liked to say that his ruddy complexion was not a sign of health but of "permanent rage" from working with artists,[14] wrote him exactly what he thought about it: "I want you to promise me that in the future, you will refer all of these requests to me before you answer."[15]

Though occasional tugs-of-war between Serkin and Columbia continued to take place, for the most part his managers succeeded in getting him to play by the rules of the American music business. Like other Columbia musicians he toured frequently in the 1940s and early 1950s (and, much less frequently, into the early 1970s) under the auspices of its Community Concerts organization, which packaged concert series across the country for small towns that lacked the administrative infrastructure for the arts enjoyed by larger cities, relying instead on local, nonprofit committees to organize and sell the series. According to pianist Gary Graffman, who describes the enterprise in his memoirs, musicians loathed "the sanctimonious attitude that pervaded the pandering"[16] to its audiences, but Serkin seems to have taken even this in his stride. His last manager, Mary Lynn Fixler, remembers him as uncomplaining and utterly without airs.

His fees varied from venue to venue, but in 1938 averaged about $1,000 ($12,000 in current dollars) per concert, and $1,200 ($14,500) for Busch and Serkin together, minus 20 percent to NBC for commissions and another 5 percent for expenses.[17] The discrepancy between what Serkin earned for solo recitals and what he got when he played with Busch caused Charles Rosen to observe, "He gave up a lot of money because he loved to play chamber music. That is the way a performer should look at his art."[18] More to the point, perhaps, was that he loved to play chamber music with Adolf Busch and felt keenly his responsibility to help secure his father-in-law engagements. By the end of his career in the 1980s, Serkin was earning between $20,000 and $25,000 per concert, and his manager was able to promise $50,000 in Hong Kong and Taiwan.

Serkin was remarkably generous in donating his time and art for good causes: benefits for refugees and the war effort in the late 1930s and 1940s, for Rosalie Leventritt's Young Artists, for a mental hospital in New York, for the Putney School in Vermont, Adlai Stevenson's presidential candidacy in 1956, the Casa Verdi home for retired musicians in Milan, and countless pension benefit concerts for orchestras. "We musicians are today the only messengers of understanding and peace," he wrote Irene from Vietnam in 1960.[19] As late as 1985, he played a benefit with the student orchestra at the Oberlin Conservatory.

Because he was invariably welcoming, it was left to Irene to run interference. To a complaining Kansas City concert manager she replied, "My husband gave me once and for all strict orders not to give out his address while on tour . . . Nobody knows better than I that my husband likes to oblige whenever possible. But while he is on tour, he has to keep his mind on his work and nothing else counts for him then."[20] Irene would later recall how her husband fled to his studio or to his bedroom with a book when visitors who had taken him up on his easily extended invitations arrived at their house. Guarding over Serkin's time and privacy was not a job that earned one popularity.

"Besides that brilliantly lit two hours onstage," wrote Guarneri Quartet violinist Arnold Steinhardt, "life on the road for us is probably not much different from that of a salesman for electrical wire."[21] Said Serkin, "The glamour—well, that's in the mind of the public. To us, it's a life of terrible hardships and disappointments, long hours, low pay, and a constant battle with a fickle audience."[22] The complaining tone is, in fact, not characteristic. More typical is the humor with which he wrote his Philadelphia tailor, a Mr. Lipshutz, to cancel a fitting because he was about to leave for a two-month tour: "Please don't be as angry as my dentist was, who threatens I shall lose all my teeth. I hope I won't come home naked."[23] It is clear from Serkin's letters home that besides the all-important musical focus of his work, the touring life had its compensations, including as it did convivial reunions with old friends: a friend from San Francisco recalled "that night at the 'Mark' following your concert, when we drank champagne cocktails and you consumed a variety of liquids, from quarts of milk to fruit juice, and pitchers of water, topped off with a hamburger."[24]

The long absences from his family, however, were difficult. "I long for you, *lieber Schatz*," he wrote Irene from Columbia in 1948, "and I miss the children, too. And it's no help when I tell myself that I should be pleased to have work and that the traveling and the separation from you happens to be my profession." That it was harder still on Irene and on the children there can be little doubt.

Before concerts Serkin became extremely nervous, and it often seemed that whenever he wasn't performing, he was preparing to perform. (His daughter Ursula put it well: "If he wasn't nervous, he got nervous wondering why he wasn't nervous.")[25] "After studying," he wrote a student, "the fear is reduced to difficulties, which can be overcome easier than the fear."[26] His grandson Christopher remembers that when they were once driving together from Milan to Florence, he observed his grandfather in the back seat pulling out his pocket watch and registering the time. Then he closed his eyes as if to sleep. Opening them some half hour later he said, "I'm still playing it a minute faster than I want."[27] His student Stephanie Brown: "While we were having dinner he would be practicing continuously on his leg in a very concentrated, specific manner. He was working out fingerings in pieces, or doing double thirds or something like that."[28] When a performance was finally behind him, he was manifestly relieved. His lively and engaging postconcert persona is nicely described by a fan remembering a winter concert in Bangor, Maine: "As you were signing autographs for a group of young girls, your pencil broke off. You hesitated for a moment, put a look of mock fierce rage on your face, and then placed the pencil in your mouth and pretended to be sharpening the end of the wooden pencil with your furiously chewing teeth. You did it all with such vigor and style that everyone in the room . . . broke out into laughter."[29] "It is probably your experience, too," he wrote a friend in Switzerland, "that one is forced to question the meaning of this short life and all that happens in it ever more frequently and intensely. One has to be thankful when one has a profession and a task that one loves, and I am."[30]

RECORDING

On the recording side, too, having made the move to the United States, Serkin soon settled into a very long and stable relationship. In his first years in America he was heavily recruited by RCA, the U.S. distributor for his European recordings on the Gramophone Company's HMV label, but the negotiations went badly. A year later the company informed him of its promotional efforts on behalf of his European recordings, which prompted a sarcastic letter from Serkin expressing his "thanks" for "announcing the formation of an 'artist exploitation department.'"[31] In May 1941 he signed with Columbia Recording Corporation—like Columbia Concerts Corporation, a subsidiary of CBS, which had bought it from American Record Company in 1938—and began to record in Columbia's venerable 30th Street studio (just east of Third Avenue) in New York. His first Columbia record was Beethoven's *Moonlight* Sonata (Op. 27, no. 2), begun in September 1941 and completed in April the following year. In December 1941 he recorded the *Kreutzer* Sonata (Op. 47) with Busch and the *Emperor* Concerto with Bruno Walter.

From 1941 through the war, his royalties brought in close to $1,500 a year. An industrywide ban by the American Federation of Musicians that stretched from August 1942 until it was suspended by the War Labor Board in June 1944 froze all recording activity for almost two years, reinforced by a war-imposed shortage of shellac, essential to the manufacture of records. Even so, by 1945 Goddard Lieberson, then director of Columbia Masterworks and a friend, was sending Serkin a royalty check with the comment, "Here is another Utrillo!"[32] Four years later Serkin sent Lieberson a telegram expressing the hope that his next check would be big enough for a new car, a new barn, "and Picassos and Klees."[33] There were ups and downs, but by 1957 his royalties had climbed to over $30,000 a year, a level he maintained through the mid-1960s.[34]

During the recording strike of the war years, RCA's contract with the Philadelphia Orchestra and its conductor Eugene Ormandy had lapsed. When the ban was lifted in 1944, the orchestra went over to Columbia, a move that signaled the end of Red Seal Records' domination of the classical music market.[35] The union of Serkin and Ormandy under Columbia became an enormously successful enterprise for all concerned, and together they recorded

Serkin's core concerto repertoire (Beethoven, Schumann, Brahms) as many as three times. For Columbia he also recorded many of the Mozart concertos with Alexander Schneider (most of them for the Mozart bicentennial in 1956) as well as a representative slice of his concerto repertoire with George Szell. With a few exceptions, most of Serkin's recorded chamber music was taped at Prades/Perpignan and Marlboro. Except for his 1944 Beethoven Fourth Concerto with Toscanini and RCA, Serkin recorded with no company other than Columbia Records until the 1980s, when he signed with Telarc for the Beethoven concerto cycle with Seiji Ozawa and with Deutsche Grammophon for his Mozart series with Claudio Abbado.

Rudolf Serkin made no secret of his distaste for recordings: "One's interpretation of a work can only have validity for that one performance . . . An artistic achievement cannot and should not be repeated. I look back at some of my performances recorded many years ago and I shudder and probably at some future date I will look back at performances recorded at this time and shudder again."[36] The number of his solo recordings released commercially is thus relatively small, focusing on a handful of Beethoven sonatas (and these repeatedly). He did no *Hammerklavier* until 1970, and Op. 111 was released only after his death. He recorded but three Schubert sonatas, not much Brahms, little Bach, Haydn, Mozart, or Schumann. He recorded the Chopin Preludes, Op. 28, in 1976, but they have remained in the Columbia/Sony vaults. His last solo studio recordings to be released were the Brahms Intermezzi and *Handel Variations*, and the C major Haydn Sonata, issued with his triumphal Reger *Bach Variations* in 1986. (Only with the advent of digital technology did he feel that a recording could do justice to the dynamic range of the Reger piece.) He also made digital recordings of the *Waldstein* and *Appassionata* Sonatas, but these were never released.[37] Probably no major instrumentalist of his time made as little of his solo repertoire available on recordings as did Serkin.

PIANOS

Serkin showed Steinway pianos the same loyalty he gave Columbia Artists and Columbia Records. His piano of choice in Europe had been Bechstein, and the Berlin-based company had provided him with two of their pianos for his Basel studio. By 1934 he switched to Steinway. Serkin explained, "When Hitler came to power there were two brothers Bechstein. One of them was my friend, Karl, and his father was a Nazi. Karl was not, so Karl was pushed out and the firm became Nazi and, of course, I stopped playing and wanted to play Steinways."[38]* When no Steinways were available—but only then—he played the Swiss Schmidt-Flohr.[39]

His relationship with the German Steinway company was rocky. Fearing (incorrectly, they countered) that they were singling him out with new charges and fees, he complained that they treated him as if he were a conservatory student.[40] Years later he explained that, though he "didn't quite realize it then," the Hamburg Steinways "felt embarrassed to take over an artist from another German firm."[41] "Bechstein I loved," he said, "but Steinways I learned to love."[42] (When he toured India in 1956, he was astonished to find that Bösendorfers, the piano of his Viennese youth, were everywhere. "At first he thought it would feel strange to go back to them after Steinways but, at the first touch, 'it was like coming home,' he said.")[43]

Once in the United States, he had a Steinway on loan (soon there were to be two), in return for which he lent his name, picture, and testimony to Steinway's advertising campaigns in concert programs throughout the country. Asked about the supposed differences between German and American Steinways, he dismissed them as "more or less snobbery."[44] After rejecting the possibility of sending a tuner along on the entire tour, Steinway provided "special" pianos for "really important dates such as Chicago, Boston, Washington, Baltimore, Philadelphia, etc.," because Serkin frequently found the local pianos of poor quality.[45] Serkin, Steinway, and the local sponsors shared the considerable expense associated with using, transporting, and maintaining highest-quality pianos for his performances. By 1948 Serkin's debt to Steinway had amounted to almost $10,000 (close to $70,000 in current dollars).[46] Sometimes Steinway would forgive a portion of the debt, and, very generously, the company provided its pianos to Marlboro at no charge.[47]

Before Serkin began touring with his own instrument, he liked to practice on pianos that offered extraordinary resistance, a preference for which his son Peter offers both practical and psychological explanations:

> He would elect to have pianos for his personal use at home that were particularly difficult to play, almost impossibly unwieldy, the idea being that if you then came across a difficult piano at a concert, it would still be an improvement over what

---

* Concerning this period, a recently published Bechstein promotional book, which also carries a photo of Busch and Serkin, states unabashedly, "The firm enjoyed the new state's favour, a state that was mindful of cultural prestige and supported the House of Bechstein in many a way." *The House of Bechstein: Chronicle* (Berlin: Bechstein, n.d.), 57.

you've been used to playing at home . . . There was the sense that his task was to serve music, but at the same time some kind of penance was involved, some grueling aspect. He was so hard on himself, and that would project into his relationship to practicing and to instruments, too. He wanted things to be even harder than they had to be.[48]

Serkin's student Claudette Sorel remembered her surprise at the effort it took to push down the keys of Serkin's piano when she first played for him in 1948: "Serkin was curious to see who would be the victor or victim."[49] In his later years Serkin's own piano accompanied him on his U.S. tours.

Serkin developed close relationships to his piano tuners, some of whom, like Franz Scheerer and Oscar Ekberg (in Vermont), were retained to accompany him on tours and called to solve problems with pianos in emergencies or to assist during the Marlboro season. The Steinway technician Franz Mohr tuned Serkin's pianos in Vermont approximately four times a year and accompanied him when he played at the White House. Serkin's oldest son, John, who had apprenticed with Ekberg, tuned for his father for the last decade of Serkin's life and worked as Marlboro's tuner during most of the same period. His father, he says, was "obsessed" with the evenness of his pianos: "I have seen him spend ten minutes carefully and slowly pushing down the keys one by one to check the aftertouch; after finally finding a note he felt had a slightly different feel, he would make a long face and announce, 'This piano is uneven.' "[50]

Like all pianists, Serkin performed emergency repairs himself when he had to, as when he ripped a broken string out of his piano in a 1965 New York concert with the Philadelphia Orchestra. Or he simply played on as if nothing was amiss: a Cincinnati critic described a piano that by the slow movement of Beethoven's Fifth Concerto "was flat enough to sour cream. Serkin, a real trouper and a real artist, didn't flinch."[51] In the Dean Elder interview he remembered "playing a concerto [when] the back leg of the piano cave[d] in. I tried to keep on playing, even with the keyboard tilted dangerously. But the audience thought it terribly funny and roared!" In the same interview he recalled other incidents: a chicken flying out from the piano during an open-air concert in Salzburg, and in another concert a ballet dancer's corset that he pulled from the sounding board after a choked-sounding first movement.[52]

Though Serkin himself once referred to the piano as a kind of "coffin with wires," an intrinsically recalcitrant instrument that had to be brought to life by the skills of a true musician,[53] he would also write of a particular piano as of a special friend: "Fortunately I had my old piano 203, whom I know and who knows me."[54] And sometimes he endowed his pianos with a female identity.

"With these three pianos," he wrote Irene, "I feel like the owner of a harem. My favorite wife is number 67. The others are also magnificent, but 54 has a few weaknesses in the middle and down below, and the other one is too thin."[55]

REPERTOIRE

The *New York Times* critic Harold Schonberg, who heard Serkin in recital after recital and should have known better, was stuck on the notion that Serkin played nothing but Beethoven. Only in his very last review of Serkin's Carnegie Hall recitals, in 1977, did he concede, "Mr. Serkin really does have an extensive repertory, from Bach through Bartók," adding, inevitably, "but, more and more, he concentrates on Beethoven, his greatest love."[56] Though it is true that Serkin played the music of no other composer as regularly, as frequently, and with the same degree of involvement and identification as he played Beethoven—Beethoven was the only composer whom Serkin included in every one of his annual Carnegie Hall recitals over fifty years—his active repertoire was much larger than he is normally given credit for. After Beethoven and Schubert, the composer he played most frequently in his Carnegie Hall recitals was Chopin, who was represented in over a third of the programs. Serkin told Dean Elder, "Chopin in many ways is closer to Bach and Mozart than to the Romantics. For me, he is one of the greatest composers, something that the public doesn't always realize because the brilliance and sonority in his music perhaps sidetrack from its depth."[57] He played the Etudes, Op. 25, frequently in the 1930s and 1940s and, more sporadically, through the 1950s; in the later years, he preferred to play the Preludes, Op. 28.

Serkin bundled his 1937–1938 recital programs into five different groupings for NBC to offer the local managers. They are representative of Serkin's programming through the 1940s.

I.

1. Beethoven, Sonata in C major, Op. 53 (*Waldstein*)
2. Brahms, *Variations and Fugue on a Theme by Handel*, Op. 24
3. a) Mendelssohn, *Rondo capriccioso*, Op. 14
   b) Debussy, 3 Etudes
   c) Chopin, 3 Etudes, Op. 25
   d) Liszt, 3 Paganini Etudes

II.

1. a) Scarlatti, 2 sonatas (A minor, C major)

b) Bach, *Capriccio on the Departure of His Beloved Brother*
2. Beethoven, Sonata in C major, Op. 53 (*Waldstein*)
3. Schumann, *Abegg Variations*, Op. 1
4. Chopin, 12 Etudes, Op. 25

III.
1. Beethoven, Sonata in C major, Op. 53 (*Waldstein*)
2. Brahms, *Variations and Fugue on a Theme by Handel*, Op. 24
3. Mendelssohn, *Rondo capriccioso*, Op. 14
4. Chopin
    a) Polonaise in F-sharp minor, Op. 44
    b) 4 Etudes from Op. 25

IV.
1. a) Scarlatti, 2 Sonatas (A minor, C major)
    b) Bach, *Capriccio*
2. Beethoven, Sonata B-flat major, Op. 106 (*Hammerklavier*)
3. Schumann, *Abegg Variations*, Op. 1
4. Chopin
    a) Polonaise, F-sharp minor, Op. 44
    b) 4 Etudes from Op. 25

V.
1. Bach, Partita in C minor
2. Beethoven, Sonata in A major, Op. 101
3. Reger, *Aus meinem Tagebuch,* 3 Pieces, Op. 80
4. Schumann, *Abegg Variations*, Op. 1
5. Chopin
    a) Polonaise, F-sharp minor
    b) Scherzo, B minor, Op. 20

For its time, this was fairly standard recital programming, though the addition of Reger was wholly Serkin. Only the first program made a concession to the then-common practice of concluding with compositions played primarily for their display of virtuosic fireworks. By American standards of the time these were highbrow programs, though not as uncompromising as those of Schnabel, who played only Mozart, Beethoven, and Schubert. From the point of view of Serkin's later reputation their most striking aspect is the consistent inclusion of Chopin.

The core of his repertoire, to be sure, was German: for solo piano, Bach (in later years the *Italian* Concerto replaced the *Capriccio on the Departure of His Beloved Brother*); Beethoven (most frequently six of the "name" sonatas, *Pathétique, Moonlight, Waldstein, Appassionata, Les Adieux, Hammerklavier*, and later, the three last sonatas and the *Diabelli Variations*); Brahms (*Handel Variations*, Op. 24, and the Intermezzi, Op. 119); some Mendelssohn (whose particular beauty Serkin rendered with great power); Reger (the *Bach Variations*); Schubert (the three Op. post. sonatas and the *Wanderer Fantasy*); and Schumann (*Abegg Variations*, Op. 1, and *Symphonic Etudes*, Op. 13, both much more frequently before the 1950s than later). (Serkin was one of the first pianists to perform Schumann's F minor Sonata, the *Concerto without Orchestra*, in the modern concert hall. Horowitz, who later made a specialty of it as well, claimed that it had taken Serkin eight months to memorize it.)[58]

Serkin tended not to play the Mozart sonatas until relatively late in his career, when he performed the A major Sonata (K. 331), two of the D major Sonatas (K. 311, K. 576), and the C minor (K. 457). With the exception of two sonatas that he played regularly (C major, Hob XVI:50 and E-flat major, Hob. XVI:52), he played little Haydn. On the other hand, he frequently included both Debussy (selected Preludes and Etudes) and Ravel (*Alborada del gracioso* and *Une Barque Sur l'Océan* from *Miroirs*) in his recitals all through the 1940s. Charles Rosen, writing that when he was young "Serkin was my strongest influence," remembered hearing him play Rachmaninoff and Debussy, "not well, I might add, but had he played it more often, he might have gotten the hang of the music. And I don't mean that in a malicious way."[59]

Under the headline "Serkin Presents Annual Recital—Pianist Adds Mendelssohn, Chopin, Mozart to Usual Program of Beethoven," Harold Schonberg begins his 1958 Carnegie Hall review with a truly careless observation that he made in one form or another again and again: "Ordinarily Rudolf Serkin, for his annual piano recital, will program three or four Beethoven sonatas and let it go at that."[60] In fact, only once until then had Serkin presented an all-Beethoven program in Carnegie Hall, and that was in 1954; in the intervening three Carnegie Hall concerts he played programs of Bach, Schubert, Brahms, Mozart, Mendelssohn, Schumann, and Martinů, in addition to Beethoven.

In the year after Schonberg's 1958 review, Serkin began indeed to perform Beethoven-only programs regularly, as if finally yielding to the stubbornly erroneous perception. Perhaps Schonberg had divined and anticipated Serkin's deepest wish. In any case, throughout the 1960s and 1970s he put together recitals that typically combined three of six Beethoven sonatas: the *Moonlight*, the *Waldstein*, the *Appassionata, Les Adieux*, the *Hammerklavier*, and Op. 109.

Serkin would mix and match freely, though he never put the *Appassionata* and the *Waldstein* on the same program. For variety he availed himself of ten other Beethoven works, including the *Diabelli Variations*. He chose the *Hammerklavier* more frequently than any other sonata, and when selected, it was always the concluding sonata. (It sometimes happened, however, that he followed the *Hammerklavier* with another sonata as an encore, as in Ann Arbor in 1961, with the *Appassionata*.)[61] In 1982 and again in 1986, Serkin played a large number of recitals in the United States and Europe in which he performed only the last Beethoven sonatas (Op. 109, 110, and 111).

In addition to his core repertoire and to pieces that he played rarely or occasionally (Rachmaninoff Preludes, Op. 32; Schumann's *Carnaval*; Weber's *Invitation to the Dance*), now and then Serkin incorporated music into his repertoire for short periods because of a particular meaning or purpose they served at the time. In the season following Busch's death in 1952 he frequently played his late father-in-law's C minor Sonata, Op. 25, published in 1925 and dedicated to Otto Grüters. (When Serkin told Rachmaninoff that he was going to play the Busch sonata, the Russian said, "If you want to crucify yourself, go right ahead.")[62] On his USIS-sponsored tour of Asia in 1960 he performed Barber's Sonata for Piano, Op. 26 (1949), though never before or after, and for two years (1957–1958) he included in his programs the sonata that the Czech composer Bohuslav Martinů had written for him in 1954, which then disappeared from his repertoire.[63] (According to Richard Goode, when Serkin played the sonata for the composer at the home of Benedict Vischer in Basel, Martinů was not happy with Serkin's "extraordinarily conscientious" performance, in which he did everything "right." At Martinů's urging, Serkin rethought his interpretation, "and Martinů was happy.") Serkin also gave certain anniversary years special attention, such as Busoni's 1966 centenary, in which he programmed the *Toccata* and *Berceuse*, and most notably, the Beethoven bicentenary in 1970, in which he announced a complete Beethoven sonata cycle—his first—to be played in Carnegie Hall.

The suggestion for a Beethoven cycle was first made by William Judd.[64] (When, a few years before, Irving Kolodin had asked him about the rumor that he was planning to take a year off to prepare a Beethoven sonata cycle, his answer was pure Serkin: "Who wouldn't like to play the thirty-two sonatas of Beethoven?")[65] In 1967 Serkin wrote Eugene Ormandy that he would finally "dare" to play and record the thirty-two sonatas: "I have dreamed of it for many years, but I always put it off until later, when I might play them better. But I think it's suddenly gotten late, and so I want to try it."[66]

The project was obviously a daunting undertaking. Asked by Alan Blyth in 1969 whether he had ever played the entire cycle, he replied, "No, I've never had the courage," saying nothing about the series planned for the year ahead.[67] In October and December 1970 he played fourteen of the thirty-two sonatas and the Op. 77 Fantasy, for the most part those already in his central repertoire.

SERIES OF EIGHT CONCERTS FOR SEASON 1970-71

RUDOLF
SERKIN

BEETHOVEN

ALL 32 PIANO SONATAS

Thursday, October 8, 1970
Friday, October 16, 1970
Wednesday, December 9, 1970
Wednesday, December 16, 1970

Tuesday, March 9, 1971
Tuesday, March 16, 1971
Saturday, April 24, 1971
Saturday, May 1, 1971

EVENINGS AT 8:30

MAIL ORDERS ACCEPTED NOW FOR SERIES SUBSCRIPTION (EIGHT CONCERTS)

First Tier Boxes & Parquet $48.00; Second Tier Boxes
$42.00; Dress Circle $36.00; Balcony (Front) $30.00; Bal-
cony (Sides) $24.00; Balcony (Rear) $18.00. All prices are
per seat. Boxes seat eight. Make checks payable and mail to
Carnegie Hall Box Office, P.O. Box 717, Radio City Station,
N. Y. 10019. Enclose stamped, self-addressed envelope.

carnegie hall

Auspices:
The Carnegie Hall Corporation in association with Judd Concert Artists Bureau.

*Announcement
of the Beethoven
series* COURTESY OF
PETER SERKIN

The immensity of the task of preparing the remaining eighteen sonatas, however, overwhelmed Serkin, coming as it did on top of the burdens of the Curtis Institute directorship, which he had assumed two years before. Early in 1971
he canceled the remainder of the series. The four concerts were announced
again for the 1971–1972 season, but these, too, never materialized. Rather than
culminating his life's work—he was now nearly 70—by expanding his repertoire to include all of Beethoven, he contracted, focused, and deepened, and
turned to the three last sonatas.*

---

* Schnabel, by contrast, played complete cycles of Beethoven four times, first in 1927; Arrau
in Town Hall in 1953–1954, in addition to earlier cycles in Latin America and over the BBC;
Horszowski played Beethoven's entire piano *oeuvre* in a series of twelve concerts in New
York's 92d Street Y between November 1954 and February 1955.

Serkin, of course, also played music in the privacy of his studio that he never performed in public. Chopin's Mazurkas, he felt, were too intimate for concert halls. "They don't help me to relax at all," he wrote Mischa Schneider. "They are much too sad."[68] And Peter Serkin remembers reading through Brahms's *Hungarian Dances* at the piano with his father at Christmas, with violinist Pina Carmirelli turning the pages, singing along and urging Peter to play slower.[69]

After Busch's death Serkin limited his performance of chamber music primarily to Marlboro. Given the demands of a soloist's schedule on the one hand and the intense rehearsals required by chamber music on the other, it is extraordinarily difficult for musicians to manage both. He only rarely teamed up with another violinist, the major exception being Carmirelli, whose playing, according to Peter Serkin, reminded Irene of Busch's in some aspects.[70] With Carmirelli he performed the Beethoven violin sonatas in New York and Washington in 1966. Serkin gave five performances with the Budapest String Quartet at the Library of Congress between 1955 and 1959, and in a remarkable series of nine concerts in 1963, 1964, 1966, and 1967 Serkin joined Alexander Schneider and Leslie Parnas in playing the complete Haydn trios—works he compared in importance to the Mozart piano concertos—[71]in New York's Metropolitan Museum, performing some of them in London and Prades in 1966 as well. With friends and Marlboro associates like Paula Robison, the Guarneri Quartet, and the Aulos Wind Quintet (in which his son-in-law, Rudolph Vrbsky, was the oboist) he occasionally performed works such as the Mozart and Beethoven wind quintets, and the Schumann, Brahms, and Dvořák piano quintets. And at 79 he performed and recorded the two Brahms cello sonatas —the F major Sonata for the first time—with Mstislav Rostropovich. The cellist recalled, "I was amazed at how well and how quickly Rudi had learned this very difficult sonata. He had such a purity, such a beautiful musical conscience . . . This record has stayed in my memory as one of the happiest experiences of our work together."[72]

Serkin's reputation as a specialist in the period from Beethoven to Brahms, indeed in Beethoven and in Brahms, was no doubt shaped to a large degree by his concerto performances and recordings. He played all five Beethoven concertos (and, less frequently, the Triple Concerto and the *Choral Fantasy*) and both Brahms concertos much of his life, and recorded them all repeatedly. (Of all concertos, he felt, Beethoven's Fifth Concerto was the "safest" if one is insecure about the conductor or orchestra.)[73] He occasionally played complete cycles of the Beethoven concertos, the last time with Seiji Ozawa and the Boston Symphony Orchestra when he was almost 80. Unlike the solitary, monastic aura of his recitals and the intimate give-and-take of chamber music, the concertos of Beethoven and his successors not only promised the large audiences assured by orchestral subscription series, but they offered the soloist participation in a particularly intense and rich form of musical drama.

In addition to the Reger concerto, from the nineteenth century he played Richard Strauss's *Burleske*, the two Mendelssohn concertos, and the Schumann concerto, and he revived Schumann's rarely played Konzertstücke. He even performed the Tchaikovsky Concerto at least once (in Oslo in 1938, and he was prepared to do so again with Ormandy in 1940, canceling only because of his boils).

From the twentieth century he played the second MacDowell Concerto, Op. 23, and the second Rachmaninoff concerto (at least twice in the fall of 1942),[74] the Bartók First Concerto, which he performed with Reiner, Szell, and Ormandy in the late 1950s and early 1960s, and the Prokofiev Concerto for Left Hand (in 1958, its first U.S. performance).

Eugene Ormandy (1899–1985), the conductor with whom Serkin was most closely associated during his American years (Ormandy's association with the Philadelphia Orchestra began in 1936), encouraged him early on to venture into a less rarefied musical atmosphere than that of the German classics. In 1942 he asked Serkin whether he would be willing to play the Khatchaturian Piano Concerto, "which is supposed to be a sensation."[75] Serkin responded a week later, "As much as I would like to study a new piano concerto, I definitely don't like this one, a mixture of the Grieg and the Tchaikovsky Concerto, modernized and dressed up . . . How would you feel about one of the 2 Konzertstücke by Schumann, together with a Mozart or early Beethoven Concerto?"[76] Ormandy's reply was testy: "You are so closely associated with Beethoven and Brahms that it might be advisable for your own sake to play something else . . . I have no other suggestions to make; the next ones must come from you."[77] They settled on two Beethovens and a Brahms.

Although Serkin played a wider range of concertos than his reputation might lead one to believe, the core of his concerto repertoire was undeniably circumscribed, as Serkin himself was keenly aware. He wrote Ormandy that he was sometimes tired of "repeating the same concertos" and needed "to stop playing with orchestras" for a while.[78] According to Claude Frank, he gave in under pressure from his managers but "declared that he would double the fee for a pair, three times for a series of three, and so on, hoping that no orchestra's budget would permit it. But it backfired on him: The orchestras paid what he 'wanted.'"[79]

In the late 1970s he began another huge and, given his age, wildly ambitious project: to perform and record all of Mozart's twenty-four piano concertos. It was an idea he had been considering for thirty years, at least as far back as 1946.[80] When the project began to take shape in 1979, this time with Claudio Abbado and the London Symphony Orchestra, Serkin described it as *waghalsig*, meaning both risky and foolish.[81]

Serkin's original plan was to perform the concertos in a three-year cycle, eight a year, in London and possibly in New York. Rosalie Leventritt's son-in-law, Ted Berner, negotiating for him in London, demanded $10,000 a concert (twice what the LSO had budgeted) and threatened to take the project to the New York Philharmonic. For a while it looked as if it would never get off the ground. But it was very close to Serkin's heart, and between 1981 and 1988 he and Abbado managed to record for release (if not perform in live concert) all but three of the major concertos. This would have been a complex project under the best of circumstances; undertaken by a man in his eighties, it was a remarkable achievement. Among the recorded concertos was that in E-flat major, K. 482, which Serkin had refused to perform since the 1950s because he could no longer abide the cadenzas he had originally written for it.[82] (The cadenza he played for the 1984 recording of the K. 482 concerto is much more conservative.) In the previous year he had refused to play Mozart's C minor Concerto for the same reason.[83]*

Another problem for Serkin was the *Coronation* Concerto in D, K. 537, for which Mozart had not written out the left-hand part. In 1988, ill and unable to perform, he devoted a part of his enforced rest to writing a version he liked, and by 1989 he thought he had one. "Of course no one could guess [what Mozart had in mind]," he wrote, "but I think that this new attempt is less bad than the printed version."[84] He also sought out every cadenza he could find, but "none of them seem to fit the *Coronation* Concerto, so I might have to 'commit my own sin' as Sir Donald Tovey once told me."[85] (Serkin had come to know the eminent English musicologist and composer through Adolf Busch.) By the spring of 1989, after finding satisfactory solutions to all the problems the concerto posed, he expressed a fervent, almost desperate desire to record it "as soon as possible," writing Deutsche Grammophon that he could organize vir-

---

* Richard Goode: "We all abhor cadenzas we've written! But, you know, mostly cadenzas are misfortunes unless Mozart wrote them. Myron Bloom once played two Mozart horn concertos at a Wednesday night informal concert at Marlboro. Mr. Serkin wrote the cadenzas. He said he was inspired to write them by sitting on the toilet. Very Mozartean!" Interview with the authors, New York, October 7, 2000.

tually the entire following season around this effort.[86] But by the fall, he was no longer up to the strain of traveling and recording.

Although Serkin's musical taste was firmly anchored in the past, he recognized and struggled with a responsibility to the music of his own time. He maintained friendly relationships with numerous contemporary composers, among them Aaron Copland, Roy Harris, Alan Hovhannes, Roger Sessions, and Karl Weigl, in addition to Martinů, his friend Samuel Barber, and Leon Kirchner. In 1940 he wrote the London music publishers Novello & Co. and asked them "to indicate to me some modern works for piano alone" that might be of interest to him.[87] When he refused to perform David Diamond's piano concerto in 1949 and, in 1954, the compositions of Jenö Takács, the composer and pianist who was James Levine's teacher in Cincinnati, he reaped bitter letters from the composers.[88] Marlboro, as we shall see, provided him with the opportunity to find a solution to this difficulty.

TEXTS AND SCORES

Serkin had a scholar's interest in the music he played, but he never confused his role as an active musician with that of a musicologist. And yet, he was among the most scrupulous of musicians in his approach to the historical bases of the music he was performing. Predicated on what is known as *Werktreue*, a conviction that the composer's intentions as indicated in the original score are paramount in interpretive decisions (Richard Taruskin: "the most fundamental tenet of our musical culture"),[89] Serkin consulted the manuscripts of the music he played whenever possible and sometimes traveled with manuscript facsimiles and first editions on his concert tours. He had a detective's determination to track down the original version to get at the composer's intent, before and beyond the interpretations and distortions made by any editor, even the most revered. Even so, Serkin's reputation as a rigid literalist is often exaggerated. To one interviewer he articulated a more flexible, conciliatory point of view: "I would encourage young people to follow their instincts really, as long as it doesn't contradict the markings."[90]

Serkin delighted in sharing his collection of manuscripts and early editions with his students and colleagues. He was particularly proud of a manuscript of the *Goldberg Variations* in the hand of Bach's student Johann Christian Kittel and the *Stichvorlage* (the copyist's score prepared for the engraver) of the Brahms A major Piano Quartet, Op. 26. He acquired the Brahms in January 1947 when Elisabeth Bondy, wife of the Viennese art collector Oscar Bondy, invited him and Busch to tea at her New York apartment and offered each a manuscript of his choice from her collection. Serkin selected the quartet because he felt he could learn from its many penciled-in corrections and changes. (Busch chose the Brahms Sextet, Op. 36, which Irene inherited and later presented to the Sacher Foundation in Basel.) After Serkin's death, Irene gave the quartet to the Brahms-Institut at the Musikhochschule Lübeck.

It is thanks to Serkin that a neglected passage in Mozart's Piano Concerto K. 595 was brought to light. During the rehearsals with Toscanini in 1936, Serkin had complained that the conductor took the second movement too quickly, a disagreement that he would settle when he returned to Switzerland. Because no institution in Germany would have obliged him, he asked Marthe Honegger in Geneva to send for a copy of the manuscript score from the Prussian State Library in Berlin. The manuscript proved Toscanini right—Mozart indicated the tempo of the second movement in cut time—but it also revealed a previously unknown seven-bar segment in the first movement after bar 46. When the Berlin manuscript was lost after the war, the Prussian State Library replaced it with Serkin's copy, which had been absorbed into Toscanini's archives.[91] Although most modern editions omit the missing bars, as do conductors in performance, the authoritative edition of Mozart scores argues decisively for their inclusion.[92]

The best-known and most controversial example of Serkin's wrestling with the text is his interpretation of the first movement of Beethoven's Piano Sonata Op. 13, the *Pathétique*. The question is whether the Grave introduction to the first movement should be repeated after the Allegro exposition, or whether the Allegro section alone is to be repeated. Serkin was unyielding in his insistence that the movement be repeated from the very beginning.[93] Late twentieth-century scholars and editors come down unanimously on the side of not repeating the Grave,[94] though Charles Rosen writes, "The only musical question is whether or not the structure is more dramatic if one includes the introduction when repeating the exposition, and enhances the parallelism of its return at the opening of the development."[95] Fellow pianists such as Anton Kuerti and Seymour Lipkin prefer Serkin's interpretation. Lipkin calls it less "banal" and "much more powerful." "I have to believe it was Beethoven's idea," he adds.[96] Serkin, of course, grounded his decision to repeat the Grave introduction in his own interpretation of the evidence, but in the end, he wrote, "since the autograph is missing, it is left to each of us to decide."[97]

Similarly, in his interview Dean Elder pointed out the erroneous *ritardando* in measure 226 of the last movement of the *Appassionata* that is included in most editions, instead of the *rinforzando* of the first edition. "Right," admits Serkin. "But I have a hard time giving up the ritard. Some first editions mean a lot and some are unreliable, for Beethoven complains about many misprints. He wrote to Breitkopf: "'You are nothing but a misprint.'"[98]

Serkin's admiration for and collaboration with the German music publisher Günter Henle (1899–1979) stems from this concern for accurate Urtext scores. Henle, an amateur pianist who received occasional lessons from Serkin, had married into the Klöckner coal and steel conglomerate, of which he eventually became the director. According to Serkin, Henle "had resolved that if he survived the war and the German tyranny, he would devote his remaining days to the establishment of a music publishing firm whose purpose would be to turn out the most authentic editions possible."[99] He and Serkin had been in correspondence since 1952, when the latter wrote to express his "pleasure and admiration" for Henle's Beethoven editions.[100] Their relationship developed into a friendship and close collaboration informed by their common interest in one another's work. Henle became an active supporter of Marlboro.[101]

Over the years, Henle asked Serkin's help in resolving dozens of discrepancies among autograph manuscripts, copyists' scores, and early editions so that he could offer the most authentic possible Urtext. Serkin, echoing a criticism that is frequently made of the Henle editions, urged him to explain problematic editorial choices in footnotes.[102] He also tried to persuade Henle to omit fingerings. He told Robert Silverman, "I don't think piano music should be fingered. There are no two hands that are alike. As a matter of fact, I very often change fingering on the spur of the moment. For example, if the acoustics are different, or if one plays upon different pianos, with different sounds and actions, one should always feel ready to change fingerings."[103]

COLLEAGUES

Asked what he looked for in other musicians, Serkin answered "First, personality. It's a vague word, but what other is there?"[104] He was unforgiving in his musical judgments, and musicians whom he felt to have taken the easy way, or to be self-promoting, or to have performed disrespectfully were done and finished, and there was no going back. In this, said one of his children, he was "ruthless." Working with Hans Münch, Felix Weingartner's successor as conductor of the Basel Orchestra and a thorn in Serkin's side for many years, he wrote Irene that "the orchestra plays with contempt, but also contemptibly badly."[105] "Nothing is more strenuous," he wrote in another letter, "than having to hypnotize the conductor and orchestra and pull them along."[106] "It's not that I'm so great," he once said of his colleagues. "It's that they're so terrible." (The almost pathological levels to which Serkin took his self-deprecation is rendered by Claude Frank's paraphrase of Serkin's stance: "He makes it quite plain that to be a musician, to be a pianist, is more than a privilege . . . it is a responsibility, it is a duty, it is something one not only has to be grateful for but something one actually has to suffer for. And we, the people who play the music, are *nothing. Simply nothing.* We are *dwarves.* The players are *dwarves* compared to the masterpieces.")[107]

By the same token, he was seldom happier than when he encountered a kindred spirit, and in his letters to Irene, which are nothing if not candid, negative remarks about colleagues are, in fact, rare. "Reiner is very good, and the [Pittsburgh] orchestra is also good";[108] "Monteux was a true joy";[109] "[Robert] Shaw is an extraordinary musician," he wrote Irene, "I am wildly enthusiastic."[110] The combination of a first-rate conductor and great music inspired in him a deeply felt enthusiasm that was frequently observed by musicians who worked with him. Performing two Mozart concertos in Buffalo with William Steinberg he writes, "Steinberg was *excellent* and it went well with me, too. Too bad that you can't be here, this music is the most beautiful and magnificent that you can imagine."[111]

Of Serkin's contemporaries, Vladimir Horowitz enjoyed a place unto himself in Serkin's esteem and affection, and he always expressed the strongest admiration for Horowitz as a pianist and a musician. (The high regard was reciprocated: it is said that Horowitz spoke badly of all pianists except Serkin and Rachmaninoff.[112] And asked whom he would most like to be if not himself, he said "Serkin."[113]) Serkin later worked fervently to induce Horowitz to come out from his early retirement and was instrumental in bringing him to Japan for the first time in 1983.[114]

When it came to music, he was consistent in his selflessness, but no one could accuse him of sentimentality: "Friendship and music," he once wrote Clara Haskil, "are after all two completely different matters."[115] Friendship, on the other hand, was vulnerable: driving away from Marlboro after an unsatisfactory performance by a colleague and friend of many years, he said, "A performance like that makes me dislike him as a person."

In 1959 he experienced a happy musical encounter with as unlikely a partner as the conductor Leopold Stokowski, famous for his sumptuous transcriptions, with whom he performed the Brahms D minor Concerto. Confirming Serkin's worst fears, Stokowski warned him that he intended to rescore the orchestration. Serkin said later that he was "horrified" and was prepared to leave. But "everything was wonderful—clean, clear. I went to the librarian afterwards and asked—were there any changes? 'No—nothing was touched.'"[116] Stokowski, too, was pleased, and suggested to Serkin that they record the Brahms: "It was

Rudolf Serkin and Eugene Ormandy COURTESY OF PETER SERKIN

in so many ways an unusual performance."[117] (The recording never happened, though they did appear together once again in 1964, performing Beethoven's *Choral Fantasy* at a memorial concert for Pierre Monteux.)

Eugene Ormandy was the conductor with whom Serkin was most closely associated after he came to America, and for years Serkin was virtually the house pianist of the Philadelphia Orchestra. Although their letters frequently assert their mutual love and devotion, one gets the strong impression that Serkin is writing what he thinks Ormandy needs to hear rather than from the heart. But the Serkins had, after all, named their youngest child after Ormandy's second wife, and the two musicians continued their close musical association through the 1970s.

Aside from Ormandy, the conductor he had known the longest and worked with most frequently was George Szell (1897–1970), playing with him in Cleveland (where Szell had been conducting since 1946) almost every year. Szell was widely disliked, Alexander Schneider describing him as a man "with a dry heart and an ungiving attitude towards life."[118] Szell and Serkin had their quarrels,[119] and according to Irene, Szell, who was almost six years older than Serkin, never stopped treating him in a somewhat patronizing manner, as if Serkin were still the kid brother of their Vienna days. Most musicians working with Serkin would defer to him, but not Szell. Seymour Lipkin remembers a 1948 rehearsal of Mozart's E-flat Concerto, K. 482, in which Serkin followed the practice of filling in the long half-notes of the first movement with passage work. Szell objected, and Serkin dropped the runs.

CRITICAL RECEPTION

Few musicians admit to caring about reviews, and Serkin was no exception, though in his case the claim was indisputably genuine. As his daughter Judith remarked, "His harshest critic was always there with him."[120]* Reviews were usually favorable and often enthusiastic, with inevitable exceptions. In the 1940s New York critics enjoyed using the phrase *in the vein*, suggesting a miner working an especially rich vein of ore—and they usually (though not always) found Serkin in the vein. They consistently praised the drive, energy, vitality, and intensity of his playing, his evident seriousness of purpose, his integrity, the quality of his musicianship, and the intelligence, authority, conviction, and ardor that so frequently moved his audiences.

The fault for which critics admonished him most often was his tone, which they would sometimes describe as lacking in color, uniform, unyielding, harsh, loud, even brutal, a judgment that Harold Schonberg dismissed as irrelevant to Serkin's purpose: "The playing was austere. It certainly was not conceived in terms of beautiful sounds. Some phrases came out with a percussive clatter— and neither Mr. Serkin nor his audience could have minded less. What had sound to do with the essence he was trying to extract?"[121] Although Serkin strove for the clearest possible articulation, critics sometimes discerned blurred passages and overpedaling. They could also be irritated by what they described as "nervousness" and by what became almost trademark mannerisms (stamping his feet and humming, or "groaning"), what one critic called his "acrobatics at the keyboard." (European reviewers, especially after the war, tended to be more uniformly enthusiastic than their American counterparts and gentler when they described his playing as wanting; mainly, they were glad to have him back.)

---

* A pianist friend of Serkin's went backstage after one of his recitals. After she had praised his playing, Serkin asked her what she thought of the trills. "I thought they were fine," she said. Serkin: "Then your ears are too slow!"

Serkin himself recognized that performances were bound to be uneven and that it was only rarely that one could expect to feel anything resembling satisfaction. Peter Serkin: "My father's playing was inconsistent, but that inconsistency was part of what made him so interesting. Sometimes I'd hear him sight-reading and it was brilliant and very relaxed. Or if he were playing pieces that he hadn't expected to play that day, that he might not have played in decades, he could show a great suppleness in his approach that was very appealing."[122]

But at times he could be plodding. In a 1973 review Michael Steinberg remembers "intensely compelling, unforgettable performances" of earlier years and admires Serkin's "drive" in fast movements, "the cleanness of his feelings about music," and his "conviction, honesty, and pianistic skill," but adds, "I could not help thinking that there are more different kinds of light and shade, of color and texture, than Serkin let us sense; that slow music need not and should not always be so chaste; that there is more of the bold and unexpected in Beethoven and Brahms than came out in so straight a telling of their stories . . . somehow I don't know what to do with a middle-of-the road *Waldstein* at this point. That is why my affection and respect for Serkin are often mixed with disappointment."[123]

Serkin suffered (and sometimes his playing suffered) from an overwhelming need for pianistic security. He would tell his son Peter that his practicing was intended to ensure that "even if he were awakened at three in the morning and told that he had to go out and play Beethoven's Fourth Piano Concerto, he would have practiced it enough so that he'd be able to go out and do it on the spot." "But," adds Peter, "he also said that in a performance one has to let go of everything that one had thought of back home. He didn't want to solidify a conception of a piece in his head. When it came to actually playing it, he wanted to be open to new possibilities, and I think that's a very positive thing. Many times it would work and be genuinely spontaneous."[124]

Critical reactions to the same works and interpretations, of course, often vary widely. Reviews of Serkin's performance of Schumann's *Carnaval* in his 1965 winter recitals ranged from "singularly harsh and aggressive" (Steinberg, Boston) and "a clangorous pulp" (Felton, Philadelphia) to "melodic radiance" (Rich, New York) and "gorgeously played" (Schonberg, New York). (Of course, it is also possible that he played one way in Boston and Philadelphia and differently in New York.)

Reading over large numbers of reviews, one can't help but be struck as well by the discrepancy in critics' varying perceptions of Serkin's height: some regularly described him as tall and gangly whereas others wrote of him as short and slight, "this mild-mannered, little man, with the manner of Casper Mil-

Rudolf Serkin
PHOTOGRAPH BY
CLEMENS KALISCHER.
REPRODUCED WITH
PERMISSION

quetoast."[125] (The irony of this characterization is that many people who knew Serkin speak of his extraordinarily powerful energy.) In 1936 he was "tall, thin, grave and spectacled" in the *New York Herald Tribune*,[126] while in the next year the *New York Times* refers to his "slightness and the fact that he is not tall."[127] Critics see—and hear—differently. (For the record: he was five feet and ten inches.)[128]

America's only well-known composer-critic was Virgil Thomson, and as a writer and listener he is generally considered to have been in a class by himself, at least in his early years. In 1940, during the first of his fifteen years at the *New York Herald Tribune*, he reviewed Serkin's Carnegie Hall recital (and never another; he prided himself on avoiding the stars of the day): "His pianism is Viennese by schooling, close to the key, unerring in text and weight. He ex-

PERFORMING

Rudolf Serkin PHOTOGRAPHY BY CAMERA ONE, NEW YORK. REPRODUCED WITH PERMISSION

ploits no Parisian gamut of bell and piccolo and trumpet evocation. His tone is the same in all the ranges of its power, rich, smooth and mat, never tinkling, never forced."[129]

Critics invariably noted the contrast between the self-effacing persona (the rushed approach across the stage to the waiting piano and the brief, almost embarrassed bow before getting to the matter at hand, described skeptically by Edward Said as "an act")[130] and the demonstrative expressiveness of his playing. To be sure, Serkin was capable of insincerity, but his stance toward music was no act. His stage manner, however audiences read it, had nothing to do with them and everything to do with the music. His daughter Elisabeth observed, "He mostly seemed to be in a relationship with the music, rather than with the audiences."[131] David Burge wrote that Serkin played "with such fervor and angular abandon that one feared for his survival until intermission."[132] Serkin's bearing was that of a man possessed by music, in anticipation and after the fact.

It was a cliché of Serkin criticism to claim that he was not a "natural pianist." Indeed, Serkin said it of himself. Given his talent, it is hard to know what that means. He mistrusted facility, hated pianistic glibness, and lived and performed by a passionately held conviction that musical truth requires literally infinite effort. In that sense, to say that he was not a "natural pianist" was an unintended endorsement of Serkin's deepest striving. He was, wrote Charles Osborne, not a pianist's pianist, but a musician's pianist.[133] The frequently noted observation that Serkin "fights the piano" was surely a reflection not of his technical capacity but of his struggle with the music.[134] As Serkin got older, he did struggle with a physiological difficulty, namely, very thick fingers, which (as he told his son Peter) eventually became so large that they spilled onto the neighboring keys, "a kind of disability in his later years that he wanted to overcome by assiduous, painstaking, slow practice."[135]

Serkin's long career and multiple recordings of the same piece made it possible for critics to gauge changes in his performances over time. Like most musicians, he slowed down with age, and as an old man he said that for most of his life he had played everything "much too quickly."[136] Having heard his old Prades recording of Bach's *Italian* Concerto years later, Serkin said he was "aghast" and that he had since slowed the tempo from about 146 to the half note to 112.[137] On the other hand, the critic Joachim Kaiser, using an expression that would be much cited in the German press, wrote of Serkin's "wildness of old age": *Alterswildheit*.[138] This was in 1965, and Serkin still had over twenty years of performing ahead of him.

The changes in Serkin's playing from early to full maturity are probingly tracked in an article by Harris Goldsmith, in which he compares Serkin's 1944 recording of Beethoven's Fourth Piano Concerto with Toscanini to his 1964 Ormandy release. Taking a position at odds with received wisdom, Goldsmith credits much of the beauty of the earlier recording to Toscanini: "The fact is that this Beethoven playing, like almost everything Toscanini did, is immensely operatic, freely expressive, and uniquely unconventional . . . Serkin's playing fits beautifully into this order of things." Common to both performances, writes Goldsmith, is a "decidedly unsensuous tone" and a "purist approach to phrasing, dynamics, and textual minutiae." But where the earlier performance is "fresh," "unfettered," and "limpid," in its later iteration it is "more thoughtful" and "reflective": "Passages that the younger Serkin glided over with a nonchalant facility, the older artist illuminates with an introspective penetration." The slower tempos of the later performance, however, "call for a largeness and sheer sustaining power unavailable to the artist. This shortcoming is particularly noticeable in the first-movement cadenza and in the trills in the slow movement, where the leisurely quality simply stretches Serkin's tensile powers beyond capacity, causing the lines to bog down and the phrasing to become brittle and choppy."[139]

A few years later Goldsmith wrote a review of Serkin's 1971 release of Beethoven's *Hammerklavier* Sonata. Comparing it to a 1951 concert performance in the "more impetuous Serkin style of those years," he finds the recording of two decades later "more settled and spacious" but with "a gaunt energy and an excruciating nervous drive." Of Serkin's 1970 performance of the *Hammerklavier*'s slow movement, Goldsmith writes with deep sympathy: "Adherents of Schnabel or Arrau might find Serkin's way a bit tough-skinned and muscular, perhaps even perfunctory. Yet he holds the structure marvelously intact, and even with his severity and limited range of nuance, he suffuses each phrase with a rich humanity."[140]

For many of us, our enduring sense of Serkin's art is shaped primarily by his late career—his musical essence distilled through the otherworldliness of the last Beethoven sonatas. But listening to the recording of a live 1957 performance in Lugano—he was 54 and in magnificent form—one hears a different pianist, obviously younger and less deliberate, but also, liberated from the studio, audibly freer and more spontaneous, in possession of an intensely individual style that is brilliant (in Schubert and Mendelssohn), deeply affecting (in Bach), and with the intellectual, physical, and emotional resources to render an *Appassionata* of inspired lyricism and furious energy. The recording that accompanies this book presents a selection of previously unreleased performances from the late 1940s and 1950, which also reveals Rudolf Serkin at the peak of his power.

A newspaper article by the German musicologist Carl Dahlhaus, written in 1961, accounts for the greatness of Serkin's interpretations of Beethoven's sonatas by showing in precise detail how his musical choices illuminate (and are derived from) the music itself. The slight pause he makes before the recapitulation in the first movement of the Sonata, Op. 31, no. 1, and the straightforward, unexaggerated manner in which he plays it *fortissimo* are based on his mastery of the movement's tempo. His steady, uninterrupted pulse in the *Appassionata,* neither held back nor pushed, gives the sonata the quality of being *one* movement, so that at the end it seems that the listener "can see everything that had happened in one single glance." By playing the theme of the slow movement of the *Appassionata* almost without expression, "instead of like a hymn sung by a men's choir," Serkin allows the variations that follow to emerge as its necessary continuation, rather than merely as a series of paraphrases that are secondary to the theme. Slightly rushing the short allegro section in the introduction to the finale of the *Hammerklavier* Sonata, which seems to have the firm structure of a Bach prelude, Serkin reveals its structural significance as an attempt that is broken off rather than as a beginning. Dahlhaus concludes his article:

> When Serkin played the Adagio [of the *Hammerklavier*], the feeling achieved an intensity at which it stopped being feeling. Nothing could be less correct than to praise the pianist for the "long breath" that carries the music; it wasn't carried, but it was just there. "Adagio sostenuto" become a musical state of being. One thought neither of Beethoven, nor of Serkin. And later, after the concert, one remembered that it is the last step to greatness to become anonymous.[141]

Serkin's musical distinctiveness is cogently characterized by sociologist (and one-time cellist) Richard Sennett:

> The essence of Serkin's art is its intensity. In musical terms, this means that an immense effort is made to make each musical phrase expressive: attacks, ritards, and accents receive great care in his piano playing; the propulsion of the music is built upon the accumulation of these intense musical moments. Rudolf Serkin is not a relaxed pianist, nor is he a sloppy romantic. Rather, he plays like a man in great pain who disciplines himself by focusing on the expressive possibilities of each chord, each melodic fragment under his fingers. It was this way of playing that he communicated to others.[142]

Critics and colleagues have long remarked on the quasi-religious reverence that Serkin accorded to music. The sanctification of art generally and music especially had been a thread running through German culture since the early nineteenth-century Romantics, and it was a keystone for Wagner. Adolf Busch was the most innocent embodiment of this attitude. Concluding a review in 1938, a Swiss critic wrote that to go into more detail about the Serkin-Busch "experience" would almost be "a profanation." "I must only add," he continued, "that each piece became the revelation that had been intended by its creator. Beethoven's spirit wafted through the hall."[143] Virgil Thomson's 1940 review included vocabulary like *transubstantiation* and *sacred flame* without evident irony or criticism. Over time this changed. Placing an absolute value on music, Serkin was an easy target in an age that holds absolutes in suspicion, and even close associates allude with mild sarcasm to "the holy dot" or "the automatic halo" conferred at Marlboro whenever a performer takes a repeat. Once, when Serkin expressed "shock" after Oscar Levant described the coda

*Serkin at
rehearsal*
PHOTOGRAPH
BY PETE
CHECCHIA.
REPRODUCED
WITH
PERMISSION

of Beethoven's Fifth Symphony as "fustian," Levant teased him: "What are you so upset about? You're not even related to Beethoven."[144]

One can also make the argument that Serkin's stance was symptomatic of or even unwittingly contributed to the unhealthy state of classical music in our contemporary life: the ossified repertoire, the star system, declining record sales, audiences that seem to get smaller and older with each concert. The musicologist Joseph Kerman attributes this condition to the "cult status" achieved by classical music: "Temples, priests, vestments, and rites (concert halls, conductors, virtuosos, tails, standing ovations, and so on) promote submission rather than serious reception, repelling the young and many of the elderly too."[145] "An archaic classicist in American concert life" is the label Edward Said gave Serkin.[146] For better or for worse, where music was concerned Serkin was generally not one to think strategically, and to fault him for that is to demand that he be someone other than who he was. His devotion to music was unswerving. If he lacked the charismatic flair of Gould, Richter, and Horowitz, he also lacked their quirkiness, and unlike Rubinstein he was not given to dramatic gestures. But Serkin was passionately steadfast and unsparing of himself like no other musician, and the discipline he practiced was so exacting and so deeply selfless that it is not too much to call him heroic.

Voices

RICHARD GOODE

THOMAS FROST

CLAUDE FRANK

LILIAN KALLIR

Richard Goode
New York, October 7, 2000

Richard Goode, whose many honors include the Young Concert Artist Award, first prize in the Clara Haskil Competition, a Grammy award with clarinetist Richard Stoltzman, and the Avery Fisher Prize, is a leading interpreter of Beethoven. In the 1987–1988 New York season he gave a landmark performance of the complete sonatas and was the first American-born pianist to record them. Since 1999, he has been, along with Mitsuko Uchida, artistic director of the Marlboro Music School and Festival. We talk in his book-lined living room, he on a straightback chair, speaking in a soft tenor voice, his expressive hands punctuating his remarks.

INFLUENCES

I would say that the strongest impressions I had of Serkin as a teacher were when I had several very memorable lessons with him in Philadelphia. Those were the most intense lessons I think I'd ever had with anyone, and along with the Marlboro experience it gave me the idea of just how rigorous and how demanding music was. I remember playing Beethoven Op. 110 for him, in fact, and I remember playing Berg and Schoenberg. The lessons on the Berg Sonata and Schoenberg's *Six Little Piano Pieces* stayed with me particularly, because he had played for both composers and he showed me music that Berg had corrected some notes in, that Schoenberg had marked up, so that I felt in touch with the tradition I'd only read about. Also, from what he said then and later about Schoenberg, it seemed to me that there was something about Schoenberg as he described it, the drastic and absolutely intense and vehement quality about music making with Schoenberg, that seemed to me was very much like *him*.

If he had played Schoenberg's music, he would have played it with the unbelievable energy and intensity, the great drama that he brought to everything he played. He probably would have made a difference to Schoenberg's reputation. But it never happened. I think it's rather interesting how people like Steuermann, who studied with Schoenberg, and Serkin, who was also in that circle, developed so differently. I guess it was once explained to me that he just didn't understand the music and it never did come home to him.

What also interests me about Serkin's musical roots is just how much influence Busch had on him. I sometimes had the feeling that there might have been a dissonance of their personalities, that before he met Busch, Serkin was a different person and a different kind of artist and that Busch's great power and stringency imprinted itself on this young man and formed him in a very, very powerful way for life. I sometimes wondered if certain aspects of the Busch kind of rigor were not native to Serkin, but were learned at that age.

I heard a few of his pre-American recordings, an early recording of the *Appassionata* and many of the ones with Busch. In some way, what I hear in those is even stricter, straighter, and with less personality than he came to have later. My impression—and it's only an impression—is that his playing enlarged, grew, became freer, more imaginative and more colorful afterward. Maybe more romantic or daring.

In some ways I felt that one of the formative things in the Weimar period, a reaction against what was considered excessive romanticism, was very formative in creating Serkin the classicist. It influenced many of the figures of the time, like Busch, and Toscanini also, and the other people who felt that they were removing from the score all the excrescences of previous generations and really revealing it for what it was.

PERSONAL RELATIONSHIP

I was *not* close to him, in the sense that I didn't have an easy relationship to him. I was probably too much in awe of him as a kid. He was always friendly; we had chats; but I must say, no matter how informal he might be on some occasions, I always looked up to him as a master. I didn't call him Rudi. I've never really been able to think of him as Rudi.

From what I hear from other people, his students often had a hard time. I didn't. He was almost never harsh with me. It was always demanding, and there were a few times when he could be harsh, but then for specifically musical reasons. Interestingly enough, that happened when he felt I had played unfeelingly, mechanically, harshly.

He was a very mischievous and witty man, and I had the feeling that he did not want to be pinned down. The part of his world that was absolutely rock solid, like the religious belief of a very religious man, was his devoutness about music, and so much of everything else (it seemed to me) was hard to figure out. Of course, what impressed all his students was this total conviction and total devotion, and as a friend of mine said (and it was very true), he made you feel as if your playing well and your doing the best you could in music, really trying to find the truth in music, was the most important thing. He gave you a sense of the importance of the enterprise as I think very few teachers could have done.

ARTISTIC TEMPERAMENT

I think that, in a certain way, the intellectual side of music was not so important for him, which may have limited him a bit as a teacher. He was a fantastic *model*, a fantastic *temperament*, a fantastic *nature*, as Goethe would call it, but he did not stress the reflective part. I think his very demanding music making was essentially his nature coming through, and I think that other people had more to say about how to think about music, how to distinguish various aspects of music, how to teach people, perhaps, to listen to music.

When I was talking recently to someone in Germany about Serkin and Horszowski, I said that I thought Horszowski was more intellectual than Serkin, and they said, "But that's precisely the opposite of how people feel about them. Horszowski is so romantic." And I said, "Well, you mean that he's more old-fashioned in his approach to the piano, but my sense of it is that when you studied with Horszowski you learned a lot about the way the music was *composed*." Because much of what he said had to do with the composition: he would show you things, the harmony and so forth.

I also had the feeling that Serkin didn't *love* to teach. I think he loved to make music and did inspire and wanted to inspire generations of musicians to take part in music in a deeper way, but I felt that teaching itself did not seem to fill him with joy. And I've known a few whom it did. I think he felt it as a great responsibility.

As you might guess from this, I felt markedly ambivalent about Serkin, even when I was studying with him, and that continued for quite a long time. I think I needed other influences to get away from his very powerful force. I think he tried to counteract his own very powerful force by not putting too much weight in teaching. He would even say he wasn't one of those teachers who called himself a teacher. He would say on occasion, "I'm just a pair of ears." And he didn't want to mark his students, although he couldn't help but mark them nonetheless.

My difficulty with Serkin had to do with this enormous tension that he was under and which his music making exhibited, this fantastic seriousness which could perhaps be inappropriate at times and at times made making music so difficult. I had grave problems with nervousness and would always feel unhappy when I played, and I remember once when I was particularly unhappy, playing the Schumann Concerto in Wyoming, I wrote to him, "What can I do about this terrible ailment? Here I am wanting to be a performer, or at least on the road to be a performer, and whenever I play in public it feels much worse than it does when I rehearse. What can I do about this? Is there anything?"

When I came to the next lesson, he said, "I got your note. I was very touched. You feel better now, don't you?" And I said, "Well yes, I did play." And I waited for him to say something like "I felt that way, too" or maybe give me some advice—"Why don't you take up meditation"—but that was about it. I think he felt, "If you can't stand the heat get out of the kitchen. This is the cross that you bear." After all, Casals had suffered with this all his life, and Serkin, I'm sure, suffered all his life, and he took this as the necessary ordeal that you have to go through if you want to be a performer. He didn't spare himself and I don't think he expected other people to be spared either.

Serkin told me a story once about a monk. He was playing in Japan, I believe, and after a couple of hours of practicing somewhere in a monastery that happened to have a piano, he suddenly became aware that somebody was there. It was a monk, who told him that he had been observing him for two hours and said, "I think I recognize what you do; it seems to be very much like what we do."

What I imbibed from Serkin very much was, first, his tremendous, tremendous devotion to the idea of faithfulness to the text, which of course is a complex notion, but at least that one should do one's best to discover what's there. And the other thing was: somehow I learned from his intensity. But sometimes it was difficult to find yourself in this, because the devotion to the text could lead to literalism, and the intensity could lead to distortion of one's own impulses. So for me Horszowski was a needed kind of counterinfluence, because he was both more analytic in a certain way and more comfortable in another. So it was possible to make music that way, too, somehow, to be more serene than Serkin could be.

EGO AND SELFLESSNESS

It's very hard to analyze the combination of ego and selflessness in a musician. There is the fact that Serkin was tremendously devoted to chamber music, one of the least egotistical kinds of music making, where the ego is folded in.

I read something very surprising in the Busch letters. At one point Adolf says that at any time in the musical world there are only a few musicians who really matter. I think that in some way Serkin may have felt this about himself. He would not put it in such words, but I have the feeling that he thought there were people who were supremely responsible musicians; Szell was one and a few others, but I got the sense that this world was not very large. I think he had a tremendous sense, almost too great, of the distance between even the best performer and a composer, a real composer, but I think in that category of performer he felt he was one of the "not many." I heard him talk with complete approval and admiration of only two pianists, Rachmaninoff and Horowitz, who were obviously a different kind of pianist from himself.

He was very critical of Schnabel. He said an interesting thing about Schnabel and Rubinstein, whom I'd never previously thought of in the same category. He said, "Both of them have a kind of love of self and, as you know, self-love can be very infectious," implying that it was a great thing to have. He didn't say that he didn't have it, but one could infer that. I think he probably felt that it would be a very comfortable thing to have. It was not something that he had and it was not something that he could help his students with. Everything was questioned, a conflict, because you always wanted to do very well, but on the other hand, the admission that you had done well involves a certain kind of conflict, because who am I to say that I have done well compared to what *might* be?

PERFORMANCES

Serkin didn't talk about performing very much, but I think the *act* of performing probably contained a large ingredient of the extreme tension in him. It made a kind of personal drama. Enormous tension came from the music, but it was this *extra* tension that sometimes came from the act of performing. In a performance, it's the sense of occasion, the excitement, nerves, fear—that feeds the tension. The heightening that the whole event produces. It's a kind of greater energy that can go for positive or negative. It can be a thing that enlarges and becomes a kind of resonating chamber, a resonating chamber for your best and worst. You're just hoping to get into the right relation with it.

I think he had a drive to do what he could do so wonderfully well and to keep trying to realize these pieces as well as he could, trying to get them closer to his ideal. I think he would always feel unequal to the task, and for that reason his performances, when they came off, sometimes had an amazing sense of triumph. The pieces that I loved to hear him play were pieces that were triumphant, and so big that they were in some way against the odds: the *Diabelli*; Brahms D minor very much; the *Emperor* (the Fourth is not like that, but in fact his performance of that was amazing); certain aspects of his *Hammer-klavier*; *Waldstein* Sonata very much, and the *Appassionata*, the middle-period Beethoven sonatas—well, many others, but those come to mind: the heroic, triumphant things that I don't think I've ever heard anyone else play with quite that sense of a drama unfolding, a personal drama of coming through and winning a great victory.

One of the most wonderful Serkin performances was the *Wanderer Fantasy*, another great heroic-virtuosic piece. And the A major Schubert Sonata, too, which is different yet again. There were also some tremendously moving pieces that had nothing to do with conflict *whatsoever*, and then you had the sense of someone with a great force not using his force but playing with extreme gentleness, and that was very beautiful, too.

I think his playing in live performances was rarely captured on records. Some of them are marvelous, the Brahms D minor in fact and the *Diabelli* are wonderful, but I don't think that Columbia *seriously* worked out the problem of recording him: he was a very powerful pianist and from too close a vantage point the percussive aspect sometimes becomes too obvious. I think that a slightly more distant recording would have been better. Even so, there are some recordings that really represent him, but the absolute excitement of a live performance could rarely be approximated.

MARLBORO PERFORMANCES

I played a Marlboro tour with Paula Robison and wind players doing a Mozart wind quintet, and I played the Schubert *Variations*, which Serkin had played wonderfully with her. After the Philadelphia performance he came backstage with the gravest of faces, with which he always confronted you when you'd done something ghastly, and said, "You murdered her." And I felt terrible. Apparently I'd played loudly, particularly the bass, and he gave me a little talk about how Schubert's piano had a very light bass and you had to be very careful with a modern instrument. It was pretty bad. Some years later he played the same piece with Paula at the Chamber Music Society and I came backstage. I said, "You murdered her, Mr. Serkin." And then seeing that his face was *really* grave, I bethought myself and said, "You know I'm just joking because you said the same thing to me years ago, and I was just paying you back." And he said, "You did. *With interest.*" You could never get the best of him.

Rehearsing the Bach C major Three-Piano Concerto was the single longest and most involved set of rehearsals I ever had with Serkin. I think it was the only time, except for one small performance, that I ever actually played a work *with* Serkin. And I got an idea of how exacting he was for himself, because he obviously wanted the three pianos to sound just right, which is very difficult anyway. So there were endless rehearsals of balancing, pace, minutest inflection of phrase, and so forth. Very interesting. It went on for a long, long time. The next year we played it with him again, and I remember that when we'd finished the piece that time and people were clapping Serkin said, "Let's play the last movement again." And Sasha Schneider, not to be outdone, said, "Well, let's play the second and third movement." And Serkin, "Let's play the whole thing again!" So we played the whole thing again.

I remember listening to an audition for Marlboro one day at his house and somebody played Mozart's *Duport Variations*. After it was over, Serkin turned to Horszowski and said, "It's strange, you know, why do people play that piece?—it's quite boring." I was heartened by that. So, he thinks a piece of Mozart is boring—that's good. I'd never actually heard Serkin come out and say something like that. It was rather nice.

THE NEXT GENERATION

"Voice," he sometimes said, in talking about pianists, "he has a voice." I told him about Murray Perahia, that I'd heard this really terrific pianist. And then Serkin heard him, and the next time I saw Serkin he said, "But you didn't tell me about him." I said, "Yes, I told you he was terrific." "But you didn't tell me *how* terrific."

I always thought in a way that Peter, being a Serkin, had more right than anyone to Serkin's "mantle," if there was a mantle. I felt that there was a great affinity between Peter and his father, that although they were remarkably un-alike on the superficial level, on some deep level there was a very, very strong relationship in a sort of essential gravity and absolute commitment to every-thing. I have noticed that starting some years back Peter seemed for the first time to be gravitating toward some of the same pieces that his father played, which he plays utterly differently. His father's admiration for Peter was always very evident. I was a little shocked to find that his father didn't encourage Peter at the beginning, since to everybody else who heard him in the early days, the gift was terribly evident. But once his father also made a point of saying to me that he was very impressed with the spiritual quality in his son's playing, that it was very deep and that he admired it very much.

Actually, I always felt that Tony Kuerti, who is really a wonderful pianist, is the person whose playing was closest to Serkin's, in another kind of way. I'm not sure why, but I just think of Serkin most when I hear him, without thinking that he's in any way a copy. I think this is a kind of smooth era—everybody wants to play smooth. Serkin was not a smoothie! And Tony's not a smoothie. Tony's not afraid to be rough, angular, even awkward if the music is served, and puts urgency above any kind of softening qualities; he wants rather to sharpen those qualities, and that reminds me of Serkin. As a friend of mine, a painter, said—meaning it in the best way—of a Serkin performance: "I like Serkin's playing very much, he makes music difficult to listen to."

Perhaps that difficult aspect made for problems, even artistically, because strenuousness is not an unmixed blessing. There was tremendous verve, but almost never a sort of abandon, a light-hearted abandon. With the proviso that it was somehow urgent even in the joy, it was never easy. I don't think he ever felt easy. But there could be tremendous impulse and exuberance.

When my wife met Serkin for the first time, she said, "He's like a light bulb: he lights up." She felt an aura. Unfortunately, she never actually heard him play at his best, because she went only to his later concerts.

I would say that he gave me an idea of exactly that thing that he said was all important: personality. When you talk about somebody you talk about this facet and this facet and this facet, but when you meet them and you know them and also hear them, you also get a sense of a nature, a personality. In his case you felt it most perhaps on certain occasions when he played, that there was this great richness and depth to everything he did.

Talking to you, I have very much a sense of the very serious student that I was and that I missed a great deal of this man because I was too deeply involved in my own stuff. A man with his practical jokes, and his sense of humor, this glinting person.

Thomas Frost
Richmond, Massachusetts, October 5, 1997

A renowned record producer, Thomas Frost was from 1960 to 1980 producer and director of Columbia Masterworks, where he worked with Glenn Gould and Horowitz, as well as with Serkin. More recently he has held a senior position with Sony Classical. The Viennese-born Frost is also a professionally trained violinist who studied composition with Paul Hindemith at Yale. Meeting us in his home in the Berkshires, he is an immaculately neat man of about 70 who speaks with the painstaking care to detail that no doubt contributed to his success as a recording engineer.

FIRST RECORDINGS

The first time I had any connection with Rudolf Serkin was in 1960 when John McClure, who was music director of Columbia's Masterworks department at that time, asked me to do some editing that he didn't have time for. I had been hired just a few months earlier as an associate producer. He had been one of the primary producers during the 1950s, when the industry had not yet expanded to what it was in the 1960s. There were only two other producers at that time: Howard Scott and David Oppenheim. The recording studio was on East 30th Street near Third Avenue; it was known as Thirtieth Street Studio, renowned for great-sounding recordings of Columbia's illustrious roster of classical, jazz, and pop stars.

One of the projects I was asked to edit was the Reger Piano Concerto recorded by Serkin and the Philadelphia Orchestra with Ormandy. The Ormandy recordings were all done in Philadelphia, in what was then known as Town Hall on Broad Street; later it was renamed Scottish Rite Cathedral. The acoustics in the old-fashioned ballroom were outstanding. I had only the score from the sessions that McClure did and almost no other information, as is often the case. The score had a few indications of what the artists liked or didn't like, so I just had to listen to all the takes and construct an edited version.

I did a very careful job, and then Serkin came in to the studio to listen with me. He was very impressed, because he hadn't thought the performance was as good as it actually was. He was always very perfectionistic and worried that his playing wasn't good enough, that it didn't serve the composer well enough. I seem to have made a good impression on him, and during that first year at Columbia it was decided that I would start to handle some of the artists myself:

Serkin, the Philadelphia Orchestra and Ormandy, Bruno Walter, and then various other artists.

The majority of recordings I did with Serkin were from the 1960s. We had done the five Beethoven concertos with Ormandy and with Bernstein. I had produced numbers 1 through 4, because of my new association with Ormandy. And the *Emperor* was produced by McClure, Bernstein's usual producer. In the mid-1970s I planned to record them again, this time with Serkin and the Boston Symphony. But there had been various changes in Columbia's upper management, and this project was suddenly looked at by profit-and-loss accountants and deemed not to be worthwhile. It was a silly way of looking at things, because with major artists in classical music, sales of recordings can only be fairly judged over a couple of decades. But they were interested in the short term, and some of the Serkin recordings had not been overwhelming successes. They were steady sellers, but the people who were in charge then just didn't recognize the significance of this. This project was then taken up by Telarc.

After that, Serkin felt that he was not wanted by Columbia any more, and a relationship with Deutsche Grammophon developed. They were interested in the last three Beethoven sonatas for their video series. What happened was that Serkin agreed to do them with video in live concert. The contract didn't stipulate that they could *not* use them for audio as well, but he didn't realize that. When they put them out on CDs he was very annoyed that they hadn't asked his permission and that he hadn't made the stipulation that it was strictly a video project. Serkin felt that they were satisfactory for video only—if you have the experience of hearing and seeing, the performance is enjoyed by both senses, but when you have audio only, the music stands alone and must satisfy down to the smallest detail.

During the last few years that we were actively involved with him in the 1980s, he had gotten his Vermont barn completely converted to a spacious studio. Its acoustics were adequate for recording purposes, and he had found out that it would be possible for us to set up a recording arrangement whereby he could record himself and just work whenever he felt like it without any particular schedule. He could spontaneously go and record in the middle of the night or whenever. So the Columbia engineers and I installed equipment, and set up microphones, and just left them there. They had devised a system whereby he had a little box on the piano with two or three lights on it. He would just have to push one button, then wait for a green light and start recording. And then when the red light came on, it would mean that he had three or four minutes before the end of the tape, and he'd have to start to think about stopping. After this, he would just have to eject a digital cassette and put another one in. But I don't believe that anything ever done in this way worked out to his satisfaction. We had also done this for Horowitz—maybe he'd heard about it from him. These were the only two artists to have ever received such extraordinary treatment from Columbia. Horowitz wanted to capture his improvisations. He would never do any recording for commercial purposes that way. But since he stayed up late—until 2 or 3 in the morning—and sometimes felt like improvising, he was always curious to hear his own improvisations afterwards and see what he thought of them; while you're playing you have a different impression than later, when you just listen.

WORKING WITH SERKIN

When we recorded with Szell, it was so obvious how different these people were in personality, Szell being an autocrat, very formal and strict, and Serkin very . . . I wouldn't say relaxed, but at least on the surface very warm and unpretentious. A year or so after I was working with him, I called him Rudi like everybody else, and that was that. When we were listening to the first playback in Cleveland and I called him Rudi, I saw Szell cringe.

Serkin had a lightheartedness and childlike quality. During his recording sessions, he would listen to a certain number of playbacks, give me his opinion, and sometimes say he'd want to do something over again. He was very professional and unproblematic. He didn't like to record short sections to patch up something. In that way he was like Horowitz, who also hated that, never doing any little patches, but only larger sections—an exposition, a development section, a recapitulation, or a variation by itself.

The only concerto that he rejected for release in all the years he was with Columbia was the Mozart A major, K. 488, with Ormandy (May 10, 1968), because he felt that the orchestra was too rich, too sumptuous. He felt it was overromanticized and not in a true Mozart style. I tried all kinds of electronic treatments to make it sound leaner—reducing the sound of the orchestra, taking out some of the bass—but I never succeeded, and he never approved it.

Like some other artists, Serkin was never completely satisfied with recorded sound. The fact is that recorded sound is simply not the same as live sound. Not to this day, with digital or surround-sound, it's just not the same. He always felt that the one weakness of recording was the inability to reproduce big climaxes, the big dynamic range from pianissimo to fortissimo.

Repertoire ideas came from him. They were based on the selections he was performing. I don't believe there was any idea that ever came from Columbia.

It was just what he wanted to record. He would call me or Schuyler Chapin, who had become director of Masterworks in 1959. None of his suggestions was ever turned down.

The contractual part of Serkin's recording relationship was rather unusual, because at a certain point in the early 1960s, Serkin's attorney, Victor Leventritt, was negotiating about certain details in the contract and was unable to reach an agreement with Columbia. From then on, Serkin decided that he would continue with what amounted to a handshake agreement under the same terms as the old contract that preceded this negotiation. And he kept his part of the bargain: he didn't record for any other companies, although he could have. He'd had a good relationship with Columbia, particularly with Goddard Lieberson, for so many years. But the financial part was really modest compared to what artists get today: it amounted to a modest advance against royalties. He made much more money from concertizing than from recording. He did have some records that had outstanding sales, such as the Beethoven *Emperor* and the three popular Beethoven sonatas: *Moonlight*, *Appassionata*, and *Pathétique*. But as far as sales were concerned, he was not at the superstar level like Horowitz or Rubinstein.

STRUGGLING

It was impossible to put more work into playing the piano than Serkin did. In every respect—musically, intellectually, physically. Now, there are obviously considerable physiological differences between people. Horowitz, for example, was handed a great physical advantage at birth. Serkin very often looked like he was struggling. I could compare it to a mountain climber struggling to get up those rocks. And he succeeds, because he is so intent on succeeding and conquering the mountain. If some young person who is a naturally born athlete does it, it looks like child's play. It's less interesting, in a way. You don't know whether the person who struggles is going to make it or not. And actually his struggle sometimes made his music making more interesting. It gave it more power, more poignancy. Some of the people who heard him practice at Marlboro thought that it was almost a masochistic ritual, that he could already play these passages, but he would do them over and over and over and over. It was his work ethic.

Claude Frank and Lilian Kallir
New York City, November 10, 1996

Claude Frank, a student of Artur Schnabel who made his debut with Leonard Bernstein and the New York Philharmonic in 1959, has had a distinguished career as soloist and teacher. His RCA Victor recordings of the complete Beethoven sonatas have won wide acclaim. His wife, Lilian Kallir, who studied piano with Hermann Grab, also made her debut with the New York Philharmonic (under Dimitri Mitropoulos) and has enjoyed an outstanding reputation as a musician. Both have long been a part of the Serkin inner circle, and, with their daughter, violinist Pamela Frank, and Peter Serkin now performing and recording together, the family relationship has been passed on to the next generation.

CF: When I was still very young, in Nuremberg, my mother told me that among the very great pianists was Rudolf Serkin; she knew all kinds of things about him: for example, the fact that he sometimes worked on a passage for two months before he thought that he knew how to play it. I reminded Rudi of that thirty years later and he said, "It's not true."

In May 1953 my phone rang at Bennington College, Vermont, where I was teaching. It turned out that Mr. Serkin needed help with coaching and playing chamber music. The scheduled pianist had become unavailable. That is how the friendship began. My luck!

CAREERS

After my first summer in Marlboro, maybe the second summer, he said to me, "Well how do you spend your life?" I said, "I'm teaching at Bennington College." He said, "I know, but is that all you're doing? . . . Why don't you play?" "Because nobody asks me and I don't have a manager." He said, "That has nothing to do with it. How many programs can you play?" And I said, "Well, I do half of the Beethoven sonatas and half of the Schubert sonatas, and Schumann and this . . ." He said, "No, no, no, how many programs *can you play*?" And I had to admit I wasn't really working on programs. So he said, "Why don't you leave Bennington; get ready, really ready—you don't play well enough at this moment—get really professional and the concerts will come." And that's exactly what happened. I left Bennington and really worked very hard. But times have changed. Nowadays it would not be so easy or so automatic, but at that time he really felt the blind faith that the concerts would come.

LK: And he felt that you should not dwell on the horrible peripheral things that you do when you get a manager and a press agent and think only of that, and then the music goes out the window and you're only chasing after publicity and the career. That whole world was anathema to him.

CF: I remember a conversation he had with a Marlboro applicant who was getting into personal things with him and said that her parents didn't want her to study music seriously. (I happened to be there because I was on the Marlboro auditions with him.) She was practically in tears, her parents this, her parents that, and she wanted to be a concert pianist. And Rudi said, "What's that? What is a concert pianist?" And of course, he was so right: there is no such thing as a concert pianist . . . This is one thing he had in common with Schnabel. He quoted Schnabel: *"Der Schnabel hat immer gesagt, Laufbahn ist solch ein hässliches Wort—es sollte Gehbahn heissen.* [Career (literally: runway) is such an ugly word—it should be called progression (literally: walkway).]" And Rudi very much approved of that.

Rudi was not for competitions. Of course, at that time none of us actually were for competitions. In the meantime, you know, if you can't lick 'em, join 'em. One can't do without them any more. Everyone goes in for them, but at that time Rudi thought it was not very musical and that the best people do not necessarily win. And whenever his students asked him "Should I compete?" he'd always say no. And when they did compete, he very often did not particularly want to give them the prize. Altogether Rudi had funny and wonderful ideas about careers.

LK: But that changed for everybody, not just for Rudi. The whole theme now is that when one is very young one plays wherever one can. And in those days one waited, one prepared the debut for years and years. Nowadays they play as soon as they can, because they know it's going to be hard. I do remember a very Serkinesque story about the last Leventritt competition, in 1976. Unfortunately it had been drawn up to beyond musical proportions—not by Mrs. Leventritt, she was already dead—but by publicity, press agents, and there was to be video. It was in Carnegie Hall with five or six finalists, the video cameras were ready, and the deliberations were about to begin, and Serkin left the room. "Where's Rudi?" If the deliberations of the jury were going to be videotaped, he wasn't staying. Even without sound. There should not even be a picture. Some of the jurors said, "Oh, but we have to, we have to." I spoke up and said, "I think Mr. Serkin's presence is more important than the camera's presence.

Between him and the cameras I vote for him." Unfortunately there was no winner that year. Partly because he didn't think anyone was deserving. But he got his way, both ways: no video and no winner.

SUFFERING AND GUILT

LK: I came to the States on the same boat as Hermann Grab, my piano teacher from Prague. He was a very close friend of Richard Robert. So about a year later, since they were such close friends, poor Serkin had to listen to me in Grab's house; from then on I was allowed to play for him once or twice a year. He was really, truly adorable to us. His generosity in giving his time to young people, hearing them play, and talking with them was wonderful. He spent hours and hours with me! But he was hard on himself. He always went to the utmost, to the furthest of the difficulties.

CF: That was one of his credos: We all—all artists—when we have two possibilities of interpretation, we never take the easier one, we always take the better one, even if it's a hundred times harder. If it's equal, most of us take the easiest, other things being equal. Serkin would not only take the harder one when the harder one was better, but also when it was equal. He *chose* to do the harder. And what's behind this is something that he said very often: "We have such a debt to music. Such an enormous debt to music, we have to repay that debt and we have to suffer." The audience feels it and feels he has gone *beyond* where ordinary people go.

   Another instance: in Marlboro he did not particularly like one of the performances by one of the young people, although it was quite good. He said, "Well, she didn't go to the end, and after all, it's the end that hurts!" And what's interesting is that he *praised* hurting, it *must* hurt. And yet it was not the case that the pain eclipsed the joy: there was so much joy, so much humor in his playing. If you think of the last movements of Mozart concertos, you would laugh, almost, because it's so humorous and it was so capricious and so joyful.

LK: But the severity of it and the difficulty of it was always in his mind. Nothing, not even a little minuet, is easy. Everything is equally difficult, on the highest level.

CF: Serkin thought that everything was difficult, of course, because it can never be as good as the music is, as we all know. However, he thought that with enough energy, with enough love, with enough perseverance everything was finally doable. You practice *until* it goes, you see, even if it hurts your fingers, it doesn't matter, *until* it goes. I remember that one of our great friends and colleagues, Eugene Istomin, who was my best man at our wedding, once said to Serkin, "The Schumann Concerto is so beautiful, but it's like a rose surrounded by thorns." And Serkin said, "Practice it and the thorns will disappear." In fact, he felt that it was not only to repay our debt to music that we suffer, he went even further. He thought that you are *guilty* for being allowed to play good music.

LK: One day he paid me a great compliment. He said, "You feel guilty, don't you? We are the champions of guilt. We are the guilt people, the guiltiest people in this place." And that was a compliment. To be full of guilt.

CF: Well, you know, he felt the way Catholics feel about God. We are all born sinners, and we have to do a lot in order to exculpate the guilt.

SERKIN AND SCHNABEL

CF: This *total* lack of compromise, the idea that the music is paramount, that we do it only for the music, we do not do it for the playing, that the editions are important, that the composer's wishes are our guide—actually Schnabel started all that, it is Schnabel's tradition. People said, "Oh, Schnabel is terribly strict, he plays with the right hand what's written for the right hand, he plays with the left hand what's written for the left hand; he will not anticipate a crescendo, he will not do this, he will not do that, he will adhere to the right text, etc." But Schnabel wasn't really as religious about it as Serkin was. In retrospect, when you consider what has happened to this tradition and how it was aggrandized, how it was really exploited and magnified—Schnabel was a Pharisee compared with that. Schnabel now and then allowed the opening of the *Hammerklavier* to be played with two hands. Serkin would never, never play it with two hands.

I told Serkin, "Nine times out of ten I miss it if I have to play it with one hand." He said, "Because you don't concentrate. Whenever I miss it," he said verbatim, "I say to myself *es geschieht dir recht* [it serves you right]." *That* rigorous Schnabel was not. Unfortunately, some of the young people nowadays don't understand; it's all the text, the dots. We call it "the holy dot." You know, the staccato dot which is taken so seriously.

CF: Schnabel's best compliment was "Con amore." When he said that, it was very good.

LK: You know what Serkin did? The kiss of death, when you came out of a concert and he was in the audience, he'd come backstage and he'd say "Beautiful piece." That was really bad.

CF: Once Serkin went backstage after a concert, and the pianist who had just played said, *"Das ist mir gelungen, gel'?* [I did a good job, didn't I?]" Can you imagine? *That* was anathema.

On a personal basis Schnabel and Serkin liked and respected each other tremendously. Schnabel was much older, exactly twenty years older than Serkin. Serkin told me many times, "I really loved and respected Schnabel very much. But," he said, "he was very funny. For example, he would come to my concert, and immediately backstage he would say about a particular phrase, *"Man kann's auch anders 'rum spielen.* [You can play it the other way around, too.] It was a little too soon, a little too soon."

LK: *"Man kann's auch später sagen.* [You can say it a little bit later, too.]"

CF: He didn't appreciate that. Schnabel talked about Serkin once in a while and was actually very complimentary. Of Rubinstein he said, "We expected a lot from him"—that kind of thing. But Serkin, no, with Serkin he was very, very respectful, but with "buts." First of all, he thought he practiced too much. He said, "Nobody can stand practicing that much," and Schnabel claimed that one could hear it. That he played sometimes contritely, driven, and *"verkrampft,"* he actually called it *"verkrampft* [cramped]"; he said it in German: *"Das kommt vom Zuvielüben.* [That comes from too much practice.]"

IRENE

LK: Irene was fabulous. Unbelievable in her own right. She really had some difficult times, I think, with all these wonderful people coming to Marlboro, whom he had invited from all over.

CF: She had to fend them off. And people didn't understand that.

LK: People thought she was this witch, because she could be so unfriendly and would say, "Go away, go away."

CF: One summer Samuel Barber came, of course at Rudi's cordial invitation. And we witnessed this scene. Rudi said, "When can we have Mr. Barber at the house?" Irene said, "Not this afternoon, not this evening, not tomorrow lunch, not tomorrow dinner, not Tuesday lunch, not Tuesday dinner, the only time is tomorrow breakfast!"

AT THE PIANO

CF: Serkin claimed he didn't have a piano hand. Now, I frankly don't know what a piano hand is, but I suppose . . .

LK: It was a little wide, wider than some.

CF: Oh yes, the fingers were so wide that he had trouble getting between the keys.

LK: Well, that is an impediment. They were very stocky, very, very stocky. Thick, thick fingers. But he could do anything with them. There wasn't anything that he couldn't do. That didn't stop him.

CF: Well, no. It was just not a facile hand. And he claimed that that's why he had to practice so much. But that we don't believe. I think he could have done with half the practice. Easily. Mostly it was out of guilt. Yet I don't think he had feelings of inadequacy. In the face of the music he was humble, of course, but he knew very well who he was.

CHAPTER FIVE

Teaching

> *Although I am a pianist, the piano has always*
> *been less interesting to me than music.*
> —RUDOLF SERKIN (1941)

Among the great pianists of his day Rudolf Serkin was unique in the breadth and depth of his commitment to the training of young musicians. Most pianists of Serkin's stature did teach regularly at various points in their lives, but some of them had only a sporadic interest in teaching (Horowitz: "I had pupils because I was bored")[1] and a few (Clara Haskil, Glenn Gould) did not teach at all. But Serkin was known as a "major pedagogue,"[2] and teaching was a constant. From 1939 until 1976 his American teaching career was linked with the Curtis Institute of Music in Philadelphia, where, after nearly three decades as head of its piano faculty, Serkin also served a term as director of the Institute, overseeing the musical education not only of pianists, but of other instrumentalists, vocalists, and conductors. Although it is safe to say that Serkin was not one of those "true teachers" who find their primary fulfillment in the teaching relationship, his teaching was an ever-present dimension in his musical life and reflected that same complicated mix of obligation, devotion, lofty aspiration, and discipline that also characterized his life as an artist.

1915 – 1939

The obligation began in Eger at an early age, when Rudi Serkin was expected to teach piano to his younger sister Maltschi. Almost ninety years later she was still able to imitate the slap he would give her hand when she played badly during her lessons, adding, "He was not very patient."[3] As a youth in Vienna, Serkin taught piano occasionally under the auspices of Eugenie Schwarzwald's schools and summer camps. In 1918 at Topolschitz the 15-year-old Serkin gave piano lessons to the two unmusical children of the Hungarian admiral and later dictator Miklós Horthy. Hearing them eventually confess that they did not like the piano, he made them "vow never again to touch an instrument. Because music, you see, is beautiful!"[4] In the early 1920s Irene Busch also studied piano briefly with her husband-to-be. She remembered that when as a 9-year-old in Darmstadt she once played badly at a lesson, he spat in her face.

During his years in Basel, Serkin established a small studio of regular students, which included Edgar Curtis, a Scottish pianist who had been recommended by Sir Donald Francis Tovey, and the Swiss pianist Felix Witzinger. He also taught the daughter of theologian Karl Barth, Thomas Mann's daughter Elisabeth, and, from 1928 to 1930, the young Hephzibah and Yaltah Menuhin, who had weekly lessons with him while their brother Yehudi studied with Adolf Busch. (According to Menuhin, Serkin considered Yaltah to be the more gifted of the two sisters, although Hephzibah was more disciplined.)[5] By the mid-1930s, he was charging 60 Swiss francs per lesson, close to $225 in current U.S. dollars.[6]

"I am giving quite a few lessons," he wrote to his in-laws in 1935. "Giving lessons makes you rich, but it is exhausting, much more so than practicing. It takes a lot of strength to make these frail and sensitive young souls play a proper *forte*; but in so doing one has done something for eternity."[7] The tone is playful, but suggests the ambivalence that was commingled with Serkin's sense of calling about his role as teacher.

At the invitation of Alphonse Brun, director of the Bern Conservatory, Serkin gave master classes in Bern in 1934 (with thirty students attending) and 1935 (focusing on works of Beethoven, Schubert, and Chopin). Students were required to perform for one another and a small audience of interested spectators in the first week, returning the next week to play their piece a second time, having absorbed Serkin's critique. As always, he set demanding standards and could be quite harsh in these master classes. (In 1958 Serkin was again asked to conduct a master class in Bern, which one observer remembers as "an awkward situation for him, because he did not like to speak in public, and was not particularly comfortable or effective in this role."[8] At its conclusion, he invited three students from the class to study with him in the United States.)

Having thus slowly developed a small coterie of European piano students, Serkin was to find that his teaching career would flourish in America along with his growing fame as a concert soloist. After 1939, he became, along with Artur Schnabel and Rosina Lhévinne, one of the most celebrated teachers of the piano in the United States. It was an invitation to join the piano faculty of Philadelphia's Curtis Institute of Music that set him on this road.

THE CURTIS INSTITUTE OF MUSIC

The Curtis Institute of Music exists in a collection of well-kept, four-story sandstones on Locust Street near Rittenhouse Square in Philadelphia, a neighborhood exuding establishment permanence and conservative elegance. In contrast to the sharp, boxlike surfaces of Juilliard, here an ornately sculptured, arched façade fronts the Institute's entrance. Inside, the walls are wood paneled, adding to a dark, vaultlike feeling, though paintings and Oriental carpets contribute a bit of warmth.

The Institute was founded by Mary Louise Curtis Bok (1877–1970), daughter of Curtis Publishing Company founder Cyrus H. K. Curtis and wife of Dutch-born journalist-turned-publisher Edward Bok. Shortly after her marriage in 1896, she began to channel her interest in music into the activities of the Settlement Music School, adjoined to the Settlement School in South Philadelphia, which had been established to help assimilate and Americanize immigrant families and other "culturally deprived children of the neighborhood."[9]

By 1923 the need to continue to educate the more advanced music students at the Settlement Music School led her to create a separate establishment, the Curtis Institute of Music, for those who intended to pursue careers in music. It was a propitious moment to found a conservatory: during World War I, when travel to Europe had been curtailed, Americans had no alternative but to seek higher education at home. This led to a change in attitude that was further strengthened by the wave of American nativism and cultural self-confidence that followed on the Allies' victory. In addition, America was enjoying a robust economy in the postwar years. The Juilliard School (originally known as the Institute of Musical Art) had been founded in 1919 through Augustus Juilliard's multimillion-dollar bequest, and in 1921 George Eastman had established the Eastman School of Music in Rochester, New York. In 1924 Mrs. Bok put $12.5 million into the Curtis Institute's first endowment, and the school was opened that October.

During the mid-1920s, Mrs. Bok spared no expense to achieve what she thought necessary for a top-flight conservatory. She recruited the finest instructors: in addition to Wanda Landowska and Wilhelm Backhaus, other

Curtis Instititute, Philadelphia. The entrance is under the arched doorways on the left.
PHOTOGRAPH BY GEORGE KRAUSE. REPRODUCED WITH PERMISSION

pianists in the early years included Benno Moiseiwitsch, Abram Chasins, and Moriz Rosenthal. (Few pianists remained long at Curtis, however, as Josef Hofmann, head of the piano faculty, "reportedly . . . tended to give other pianists a hard time.")[10] A string quartet was formed in 1927 (it was originally called the Swastika Quartet after Mrs. Bok's estate, which had been named for the Indian good luck symbol on a suggestion of her friend Rudyard Kipling). Students were able to make use of a collection of excellent instruments owned by the Institute. After 1929, all students were awarded full scholarships on acceptance, a policy that continues today. In the words of Curtis faculty member Carl Flesch, Curtis became "the music student's El Dorado, an institution of which many had dreamt as of an unattainable ideal."[11]

Mrs. Bok's first artistic advisors at Curtis were Philadelphia Orchestra conductor Leopold Stokowski, who developed the Curtis Orchestra as a kind of training grounds for the Philadelphia Orchestra,[12] and the Polish-born pianist Josef Hofmann (1876–1957), a pupil of Anton Rubinstein and one of the greatest pianists of his day. Before joining the piano faculty of the Institute in 1924,

Hofmann had written a column on piano playing for the Curtis Publishing Company's *Ladies Home Journal* (the very fact of such a column is eloquent testimony to the place of classical piano study in middle-class American life in the 1920s). He was appointed Curtis director in 1927.

Mrs. Bok set a tone of graciousness and decorum at Curtis. She was a profoundly modest woman ("All I have done is to give away money my father earned"),[13] but she "wielded absolute control over faculty and staff and closely followed the progress of the students."[14] It is said that she had little windows installed in the practice studios, because she had heard "that the faculty weren't behaving themselves."[15] Mrs. Bok attended auditions as a listener, instituted traditions such as Wednesday afternoon teas and a Christmas dance, and took an intense interest in the well-being of each student. She furthered the careers of extraordinary students such as Samuel Barber and Gian Carlo Menotti, supporting both until her death. According to Curtis cello teacher Orlando Cole, she was in fact "very generous, really too generous. She was much abused in that respect."[16] In the late 1920s department heads received $100/hour for lessons,[17] and Director Hofmann "was being paid a princely salary of $50,000 per year."[18] (In today's dollars, this would have been an annual salary of approximately $500,000.)

Over its first fifteen years, the Curtis Institute had developed into a professional training school with rigorous standards. In 1938, Serkin wrote that "they have only a few good teachers [in America] . . . But students learn to play piano cleanly and elegantly, and that's a big achievement."[19] Indeed, Curtis and the other American music conservatories founded in the 1920s had by then developed to the point that young American musicians no longer felt obliged to seek the best training in Europe but were confident that they could find it at home in America.[20] Today, Curtis continues to be a small, elite conservatory, its enrollment normally fewer than 175 students. Since 1981, its director has been pianist Gary Graffman, who at age 7 had entered Curtis as its youngest student.

1939 – 1968

It was in February 1939 at the Philadelphia home of his friends Samuel Barber and Gian Carlo Menotti that Serkin met with Mary Bok to discuss his forthcoming appointment to the Curtis faculty. Afterward Irene shared the Serkins' delight at the prospect with Mrs. Bok. "We always dreamed over something like this," she wrote in her still rudimentary English, "but never thinking, it could become reality."[21] Throughout March, national newspapers reported the exciting "catch": Rudolf Serkin, the brilliant pianist and subject of so much public

Mary Curtis Bok COURTESY OF THE CURTIS INSTITUTE OF MUSIC

interest in the three years since his debut with Toscanini, had been appointed to the faculty of the Curtis Institute to fill the vacancy in the piano faculty left by Josef Hofmann.

Serkin was delighted to take on his teaching work at the Institute, especially as it guaranteed the kind of security that would offset the increasing precariousness of life in Europe. His contract specified that he would select his own pupils, teach three of them weekly and three of them monthly, as concerts permitted, and would make up for lessons lost while concertizing. Among this first group of pupils was the young Eugene Istomin, who was to become not only a close protégé of the Busches but also one of the most prominent of Serkin's students.

Serkin's salary for this teaching commitment in 1939 was $8,000. Although this initial salary actually represented a decrease from the levels that the Curtis faculty had earned during the 1920s, he wrote to Mrs. Bok that he would be happy to accept these conditions for he understood that "times are very bad for the Institute," which had been squeezed financially by the ongoing effects of the Great Depression. (In 1933 Hofmann had actually found it necessary to issue a statement to the press that the school was not to close, as had been reported.)[22] He was, however, adamant about one thing: "You said that for the present there will be no head of the piano department, but should there be one you will understand that I cannot be assistant. To me personally it would be all the same. I think that one can do one's work well everywhere, but my friends say that it would seriously harm my reputation as concert artist if I did not stand in first place."[23] Serkin's wording reflects the embarrassment and discomfort he seems often to have felt when forced to pursue his own interests.

After two years as a faculty member at the Institute, he was named head of its Piano Department in 1941. His relationship with Mrs. Bok soon grew into a warm friendship. After one of the traditional Christmas dances at Curtis, Mrs. Bok wrote to him playfully: "It was very sweet of you to wire me last evening, but I was very disappointed not to have a dance with you."[24]

During the 1940s Curtis was an especially vibrant place, with its young student "geniuses" such as Leonard Bernstein, Eugene Istomin, Seymour Lipkin, and Ned Rorem. At this time, Serkin's most illustrious colleague on the piano faculty was Isabelle Vengerova (1877–1956), a pupil of Leschetizky and Essipova. She was a formidable presence at Curtis; in his autobiography, Rorem called her "a bejewelled virago who frightened me from across the lobby,"[25] and Gary Graffman described how one Serkin student, on hearing Vengerova approach, "would flatten himself against the nearest wall in the hope of becoming invisible."[26]

During their day, Vengerova and Serkin were considered to be teachers who represented, respectively, the Russian and the Austro-German schools of piano playing. The terms can refer simply to the distinct geographic origins of their traditions of pianism, to choices of repertoire, and to two different styles of playing. The Russian tradition stresses virtuosity (technique, facility, and tone) and a performance convention that might, as Graffman puts it, sometimes allow "emotions to lead the performance away from what the composer wrote";[27]

Isabelle Vengerova
COURTESY OF THE
CURTIS INSTITUTE
OF MUSIC

the Austro-German tradition emphasizes above all else the conceptualization of the music's architectural structure and intellectual design, a subservience of tone and color to that design, and absolute fidelity to the composer's intentions, based whenever possible on consultation with the Urtext.*

Although they are in common use, many of these distinctions grow blurred

---

* In the 1940s Cleveland pianist Eunice Podis experienced these differences in approach first-hand when she studied the *Appassionata* Sonata with both Arthur Rubinstein and Serkin. Where Rubinstein took great liberties with rhythm, as in the syncopated chords on the first page of the sonata, Serkin insisted that everything be played strictly in time. Harvey Sachs, *Arthur Rubinstein* (London: Weidenfeld & Nicolson, 1996), 286.

when examined more closely. Vengerova, for example, who taught in a Russian tradition that focused on the achievement of beautiful sound and legato, had inherited that tradition from her teachers Essipova and Leschetizky, both of whom had also taught Artur Schnabel, a foremost representative of the Austro-German style. If the terms had limited usefulness in midcentury, they are of even less value today, when such national distinctions have all but disappeared. Yet they did signal a common understanding of different musical orientations throughout the twentieth century, so that when the young pianist Peter Orth, for example, after having been trained in the "other" tradition, embraced Serkin's kind of pianism in 1971, he felt that he had left one camp and joined another.[28]

In the 1940s, Serkin and Vengerova divided the most talented Curtis piano students between them, although Ned Rorem, alluding to a generally held belief about the comparative quality of concert grands, observed that "[Vengerova's] students were to Serkin's (in the ken of the cognoscenti) what Baldwin is to Steinway."[29] Each group developed its own esprit de corps, Serkin students often caricaturing Vengerova's method. Anton Kuerti remembers that some made fun of her "spending a whole year on wrist accents" (the carry-through motion of the wrist from above to below the key level and up again, used as motive power and a source of control), although he later came to see that it is "a very essential basic motion of piano playing . . . And certainly those people who learned it ended up with a lot of control and beautiful sound. They could resolve a cadence or appogiatura beautifully."[30]

Gary Graffman, studying with Vengerova at Curtis but also admiring and emulating Serkin, was forced to come to grips with one aspect of their stylistic clash:

I found the secondhand Serkin mannerisms particularly congenial, as they consisted of exactly the opposite of how I had been taught to behave at the piano. While I was barely permitted to move, Serkin students indulged in thrillingly angular arm-flailing, exciting foot-stamping and even occasional humming . . . Vengerova . . . regarded my contortions at the piano with a jaundiced eye, inquiring sardonically, "Do you really believe that the excitement of a Serkin performance and the absolute conviction that he manages to transmit to his listeners are caused solely by his physical gyrations and the stamping of his left foot?"[31]

(Graffman actually had the benefit of both teachers, for in 1952 and 1953 he was a participant at Marlboro, playing chamber music for Serkin nearly every day. He remembers that working with Serkin made him "listen in a different way to what the other musicians were doing, which helped me when I played concertos with orchestra . . . He made me think in terms of orchestral instruments more than of the human voice [which Horowitz had done]: this kind of staccato in the left hand is a bassoon sound; this sound is not violin, it's viola, it's lower, richer somehow.")[32]

Because Serkin's demanding concert schedule did not allow him time to teach regularly, he worked in conjunction with an assistant, at first the brilliant Cuban pianist Jorge Bolet, and then Mieczyslaw Horszowski. Horszowski became Serkin's assistant in 1942, at which time the two had known one another for almost twenty years. Praised for his beauty of sound and loving attention to musical detail, Horszowski had made a sensational debut at the age of 9, had studied (like Vengerova and Schnabel) with Leschetizky in Vienna, concertized with Ravel, Szymanowski, and Casals, and performed not only the traditional repertoire of Mozart and Beethoven but more esoteric works by composers such as Jooans Kokkonen and Donald Francis Tovey. For Ned Rorem, Horszowski's Beethoven was "definitive."[33] His evolution into a beloved presence at the Institute can be inferred from a series of notes to the Serkins from Curtis registrar Jane Hill: in 1942 she refers to Horszowski as "the Polish gentleman . . . (I still cannot spell or pronounce his name)"; two years later he is "little Mr. Horszowski"; and two years after that he has become "sweet little Mr. Horszowski."[34]

Their partnership at Curtis was to last for more than thirty years. Unlike Serkin, Horszowski did not object to being second-in-command to a man ten years his junior, and he never failed to defer to Serkin both at Curtis and at Marlboro. When, for example, Serkin requested that Horszowski, as a new Curtis faculty member, relocate to Philadelphia, he did so, although his memoirs reveal that he felt initially "very lonely, far from his New York friends."[35] Their long personal and musical relationship was characterized by mutual respect and sympathy.

ONE ON ONE

In the more than thirty-five years that he was on the Curtis faculty and in the years up until his death, Serkin's teaching of individual students left an indelible stamp on generations of pianists. At Curtis alone a roster for the years 1939 to 1976 lists seventy-two Serkin students in all, ranging from three to eleven per year. The profound weight of his influence as a pedagogue was centered in this unusually intense life of private instruction.

His relationships to his students and his pedagogical approach were of a

Rudolf Serkin and Arthur Fennimore, Marlboro, ca. 1955. PHOTO BY CLEMENS KALISCHER.
REPRODUCED WITH PERMISSION

piece with the rest of him, that is to say, often characterized by complexity and ambivalence. It could hardly have been otherwise, given the intensity of his drive, the level of his self-discipline, and his uncompromising commitment to the highest possible musical ideals. Add to this the complicated personal inter-actions that often evolve between young musicians and their teachers, espe-cially where so much is at stake: the expectation that the teacher be mentor, role model, protector, parent, career counselor, employment agency, conveyor of secrets to perfect double octaves, and a direct line to Beethoven.

Most of his students agree that his reverent attitude toward music, toward its sacred character, was the overwhelming lesson of their studies. "Serkin," said one of his students, "was a fighter, doing battle for music. What you learned was philosophy. How to make decisions. The virtues of discipline. Never leave a stone unturned. If you think you have it, don't think you have it." This attitude pervaded all aspects of his teaching. Isabelle Vengerova once told an overly casual student in need of chiding, "Mr. Serkin has such reverence for his instrument that he would never even place his hat on it!"[36]

Having started taking lessons at the age of 4—and stopping at 15—Serkin held strong convictions about the stringent timetable required of performing musicians. "I have never seen an accomplished player on the piano or any stringed instrument," he wrote to one would-be pianist, "who hadn't been quite advanced at an age not later than sixteen. I know of none among the outstanding concert pianists who started later than his seventh year. Most of them started when they were four years old."[37] This principle was applied at Curtis. After the 21-year-old Leonard Bernstein auditioned with Serkin there in 1939, he wrote to his parents: "I passed my audition for Serkin but am not studying with him. First he's not yet in the country; second, I seem to be over age (!). They've tentatively allotted him a chap of 16 and a girl of 13, so that he can mold them."[38]

Serkin also believed that there existed an appropriate timetable for the learning of certain repertoire. Lee Luvisi remembers Serkin's vehement objection when, after hearing their shared pupil Peter Serkin play "what seemed an endless succession of works by Bach, Mozart and Beethoven, all assigned by his father, I dared propose to Peter that he should try some Debussy (scandalous!)"[39] Peter Serkin himself remembers:

> When I was 11 or 12 years old, I was listening very enthusiastically to a lot of Schoenberg's string quartets and Webern's music. I listened over and over to many recordings. And my father disapproved. He said—and he said that Schoenberg had said this, too—that you should know all the Haydn, Mozart, and Beethoven string quartets before you listen to this music. I said, "Okay, I'll get all the Haydn, Mozart, and Beethoven string quartets," and that was just great. From his point of view there had to be a progression.[40]

The question of a timetable within a composer's works was not always straightforward. Rorem remembers that Serkin would admonish students "not to attempt this or that masterpiece until they're 'ready,' "[41] but according to Claudette Sorel, Serkin advised her to learn the *Hammerklavier* at a young age: "I thought I was not mature enough to tackle this, but he replied, 'If you do not study it and play it when you are young, you will not have enough years to bring maturity to it.'"[42]

TEACHING

TECHNIQUE AND PRACTICE

"Don't expect too much from any teacher," Serkin counseled one young pianist. "Eventually it is you who are playing and performing. But to express your feelings you need a reliable and thorough technical training."[43] As Serkin used the word, technique is not to be confused with virtuosic facility or sheer speed and power. "Technique," according to Claude Frank, "is the ability to do what you want to do."[44] Other Serkin students define it even more succinctly, as control.

In a 1941 article in *The Etude*, Serkin described the essentials of his approach to technique.[45] Unlike other teachers, such as Vengerova, Serkin put a great emphasis on finger strength as the first step to technique and noted that "there is a vast difference between sure, strong fingers that can also relax and fingers that have acquired nothing but relaxation." To acquire this strength, he recommended to the student the "time-honored system of scales," each scale always to be practiced with a definite purpose behind it. Citing the final thirty-seven measures of the *Appassionata*, he stressed the need for strong fingers, so that the pianist can play with as much speed as volume. "The student must build up a reserve fund of more volume and more speed than he actually needs for the movement," he wrote. "To be able to play just what one needs, and nothing more, is disastrous."

This principle may explain Serkin's response to one student's flawless performance of an extraordinarily demanding Chopin Etude. Serkin had him repeat it immediately, and not only once, but twice, demanding of him more endurance than any real-life situation would ever require. (Anton Kuerti recalls a similar episode, but sees a different motive for Serkin's behavior: "Serkin was particularly cruel to the young people he thought were particularly gifted. When I first played the Schumann Toccata for him, he had me repeat it—the whole thing. When I did that, he asked me to play it a third time for him. He later told someone that he had asked me to do that to be sure that my first playing of it, which had impressed him, was no fluke.")[46]

Again unlike Vengerova, Serkin cannot be described as a teacher with one particular method for developing technique. He articulated his ideas on technique in a kind of pedagogical credo in his interview with Dean Elder. "I don't believe in one approach or technique," he told Elder, "you need a thousand techniques for different composers, even for different works within a single composer. If you apply any single approach, technique, or 'school,' you limit your approach; you are misusing the great works of art."[47]

"I believe in a good system, a good technical upbringing such as Madame

[Rosina] Lhévinne's," he told Elder.* "But from there on out, I believe in find-ing your own way according to the piece you are studying and the way you are constructed. There are no two people alike. There is no end to the acquiring of technique. It goes on all your life . . . If you are really gifted, you can't practice technique too much—your musicality will still come through . . . But what good does it do to feel deeply, if you don't have an even trill in the Beethoven G major Concerto?"[48]

There is no end to it, Serkin said, and he famously required endless practice of his students as he did of himself. "Practice until you feel like you're going to drop," he told Ruth Laredo, "then practice one hour more."[49] To his Swiss stu-dent Felix Witzinger, Serkin recommended eight hours a day: "That's about right. Four hours is the very least to maintain a technique, but to progress you must play about six hours, and then you must sight-read about two hours every day." It was a punishing regimen. Witzinger describes the effect of a twelve-hour practice marathon before his first lesson with Serkin: "My mother left the house, my sister left the house, the cook left the house, and the maid left the house: nobody could stand it any more."[50]

"Just remember the golden rule of practicing," Serkin wrote to a young pianist in 1977, "never repeat a passage or any difficult place in a piece without improving on it right away."[51] Unsurprisingly, for both Serkin and his students, this intense and limitless rigor of practicing was sometimes accompanied by physical pain. To a pianist in California who wrote him in 1961 complaining of what today would be recognized as repetitive motion syndrome, Serkin answered, "If I would tell you of the aches I have suffered while playing, or after playing, or even before playing, it would fill many pages. Trying to over-come it is just part of our profession, and I don't think we can expect help from a doctor."[52] One endures the physical pain because one otherwise has to suffer the much greater emotional pain: the guilt of poor performance.

INDIVIDUALITY

In *The Etude*, Serkin elaborated on the musical purpose behind the hours of practice. "From his earliest and simplest pieces on, the student should form the

---

* This feeling of respect was reciprocated by Lhévinne: when she was hospitalized at the age of 83, she told two visiting students, "If something happens to me and I cannot teach any-more, I would like to send you to Serkin. He is a fine musician." Robert K. Wallace, *A Cen-tury of Music-Making: The Lives of Josef & Rosina Lhévinne* (Bloomington: Indiana Univer-sity Press, 1976), 307.

habit of seeking the musical thought behind the notes," he observed. "What is the score trying to say in any given work? To find out, he must read it for its musical meaning, arriving by himself at his interpretive conclusions. They may be wrong; still there is value in having thought them out for himself. Where ideas exist they can be improved; only a lack of ideas is truly hopeless!"[53]

This emphasis on the individuality of each musician also extended to tone: "I believe that a personal tone exists, and that it is such an eminently personal thing that it is hard to discuss it in a helpful way," he remarked with characteristic reticence in *The Etude*. "The only hint I can offer for the perfection of a fine, singing tone is not to exert too much pressure."[54] For Luis Batlle, Serkin had another specific piece of advice about tone, telling him to study the Chopin Preludes: "It will force you to enlarge your palette. You have five different sounds. You need fifty."[55] Indeed, if the sense of a piece required an ugly tone, so be it. John Browning reports that Serkin once told him, "Sometimes you have to produce an almost ugly sound at the keyboard because life isn't all a series of la, la, la, la, tra, la, la."[56]

Claude Frank observed that what is remarkable about Serkin's students, in fact, is not so much that many of them have gone on to successful concert or teaching careers, but that they all have retained their individual musical styles and predilections, despite having been exposed to Serkin's great personality and influence:

> What all his students have in common is that they don't all play like him, in fact, much less so than Schnabel students play like Schnabel, and for a very good reason: Schnabel demonstrated everything. Once in a while Rudi would demonstrate a phrase, of course, give a hand position, but very little. Therefore none of his students imitated him. But all the students who remained his students have in common that they were all excellent pianists. This cannot be said about other teachers. Not all Schnabel pupils were excellent, not all Steuermann pupils were excellent. Rudi's students, if he kept them, had to be really excellent. That's what he expected.[57]

SERKIN AND HIS STUDENTS

In Serkin's relationships with his own music teachers there had been a critically important nonmusical dimension. Throughout his life he spoke with gratitude of Richard Robert, not only because of his musical understanding, but also because of the warm friendship and concern he and his wife had shown the young student. Replicating this pattern, the Serkins' attention to his piano students extended far beyond the studio, as they would regularly invite them to Thanksgiving dinner, sometimes board students in their own home, and even leave bottles of milk on their doorstep when they were low on cash.

To potential students, as well, Serkin devoted a good deal of time and thought; his files are full of letters from young people, and from their parents, asking for auditions, lessons, lessons with reduced fees, encouragement, advice, help, and tips. Some write confessionally, some send tapes, and some do both, like the Swiss doctor who accompanied his tape with the request that Serkin become his doctor, as music for him was a kind of sickness.[58] Or like the young woman who wrote from Scotland to see whether she might study with him, and noted that she did not think she could accept the restrictions of Serkin's demanding travel schedule. "Would it be possible," she asked, "for me to go with you and would it be expensive?"[59]

Serkin answered a lot of these inquiries, and his response was often more than perfunctory. He was not, however, one to give false encouragement. To a young German refugee who had requested a recommendation in 1941, he replied, "I couldn't in good conscience write you a letter of recommendation since I wasn't able to say much in the way of recommendation when you last played for me. You must understand that I would devalue my other letters of recommendation, if I were to write a letter that would be helpful to you."[60] Wanting to be fair, he would often leave the door open for another audition. "You did not give [the Curtis Board of Examiners] the impression of an outstanding talent," he wrote to one persistent applicant, "and I would be only too glad if you would prove that we are wrong. All I can do for you now is to suggest to play for me again next spring."[61]

Serkin's connection to his students often continued long after they had moved on. Many stayed in touch, and some returned for occasional lessons. Byron Hardin, one of Serkin's first students at Curtis, writes that several times, when Serkin performed in Los Angeles in the 1960s and 1970s, he came to the Hardins' for dinner. "Rudi always insisted that he and I play something for the guests. Always, he would allege that he preferred the old, small Lyon & Healey piano and would require that I play on the Steinway."[62]

Many of Serkin's students remember him with unqualified devotion. This is particularly true of his female students and of those whom he taught later in his life. Cynthia Raim, for example, recalls "a special, loving rapport between the two of us on the musical and personal level."[63] Philippine-born Cecile Licad, whose playing for him as an 11-year-old had moved him to kiss her on the forehead, studied with him for ten years; for her he was like a father.[64]

Yet, as others attest, to be a Serkin student could also be a trial. One student felt that Serkin's high standards made it necessary to be some kind of an ideal self for him, a wearing process. Anton Kuerti wrote that "he did have a talent for making me, and other students as well, feel extremely bad, to put it bluntly … I discussed this with him … He felt that we needed a rude awakening, that this was the only way to save us as artists."[65] Pianist/composer George Walker also expressed ambivalence: "I never felt that he knew how to relate to students. My feelings about him were mixed. No other teacher has ever been as complimentary about my playing as Serkin was; yet, he neither discussed nor recommended anything to me about preparing for a career as a concert pianist. And he never lifted a finger to help me start one."[66]

Indeed, many Serkin students note his reluctance to intercede on their behalf. Serkin was on the jury of nineteen of the Leventritt piano competitions held between 1940 and 1976, for example, but only two were won by his students—Eugene Istomin in 1943 and Anton Kuerti in 1957—in both cases in spite of rather than because of their teacher. In Kuerti's case, Serkin refused to hear him play as he was preparing for the competition, left the hall during the preliminaries, and didn't say a word during the deliberations. When Kuerti emerged as the jury's choice, he recounted, Serkin "finally spoke up, wondering if they were really sure about this."[67] (When Serkin's student Cecile Licad won in 1981, the Leventritt was no longer awarded on the basis of open competition.)[68]

Such reluctance may have stemmed from Serkin's wish to be fair to other teachers' students, but it may also have been due to a rectitude that would regard any intercession as a kind of cheating, or to a purism in championing an absolute dedication to the music itself as the only objective permitted a musician. Unsparing of his students as he was of himself, in his role as teacher, too, he could not but act according to his own character, an element of which—his moral backbone or conscience, what some might call his highly developed superego—dictated a sense of duty in the teaching enterprise, an extraordinary severity of judgment and, for all his very real generosity and inspirational example, a withholding restraint toward his students.

DIRECTORSHIP

When Director Josef Hofmann left the Curtis Institute in 1938,* it was expected that any future director would also be an established, prominent musician. The

---

* According to Wilbert Davis, Hofmann had resigned because he felt that budget cuts "would threaten the quality of instruction," but personal reasons (problems with his marriage and with alcohol) also played a role in his departure. "Editorially Speaking," *The Curtis Institute of Music Alumni Association Newsletter* (winter 1977): 3.

composer Randall Thompson followed Hofmann, serving a short term as director until the appointment of Efrem Zimbalist in 1941. Zimbalist, a Russian-born violinist and pupil of Leopold Auer who had taught at the school since 1928, became Mrs. Bok's second husband two years after his appointment as director. He insisted thereafter that she not interfere in his running of the school. (According to Philadelphia bassoonist Sol Schoenbach, Mrs. Bok "would complain to me about him, but she would never do anything about it—she was too lady-like.")[69] He was to remain as director for twenty-seven years.

When Zimbalist retired in 1968, the Curtis Board of Directors saw in Rudolf Serkin a natural choice as his successor. For Serkin himself the Curtis offer represented an opportunity to broaden his musical influence. His decision to accept it was also motivated, according to Irene, by the sense that at 65 years of age he might do well to cut back a bit on his touring schedule. Furthermore, it was her belief that Serkin's hearing was deteriorating, something that might ultimately threaten his performing life. To the press, Serkin offered another explanation: "I think I am the only head of a major conservatory who is an active performing artist. I feel that it is important for me to bring to the students the experience of the concert stage."[70]

An announcement came on January 31, 1968. Serkin wrote to his friend Supreme Court Justice (and amateur violinist) Abe Fortas about the challenge of his new position: "In Philadelphia much dust has accumulated, I shall blow hard, but how strong are my lungs? At least there will be a big cloud and a mess."[71] Others confirm Serkin's impression of a dusty institution: Orlando Cole remembers that "Curtis under Zimbalist went through a period of quietude . . . If we went to New York people would ask, 'Is Curtis still open?'"[72]

When questioned by the *New York Times* about his directorial intentions, Serkin cautiously declared "that it was too soon to talk of his 'ideals and dreams,' but that his aim would be 'to make music.'"[73] Although he would downplay his own leadership to the press, Serkin quickly began to move the Institute toward a dramatic growth and deepening of its educational goals. In retrospect, his was a wide-ranging vision for transforming the Institute into a state-of-the-art academy for the training of well-rounded classical musicians. It was no exaggeration to say, as Martin Mayer phrased it in the *Times*, that Serkin "turned the store upside down."[74]

As he addressed the Curtis curriculum, Serkin focused on initiatives in four distinct areas. First, he vastly expanded the program in music theory, insisting that candidates for the bachelor's degree pass no fewer than thirteen theory courses, and hiring three new theory teachers (Robert Levin, Mary Anthony

Cox, Louis Martin) trained by the great French pedagogue Nadia Boulanger. Rosario Scalero had taught music theory at Curtis from 1924 to 1946, it is true, and numbered among his pupils Gian Carlo Menotti, Ned Rorem, and Samuel Barber. Courses had not been required of instrumentalists and vocalists, however, and by requiring the study of theory of all students Serkin immediately changed the shape of the Curtis curriculum.

Second, Serkin made significant changes in the orchestra department, which had been in a state of decline. The relationship between Curtis and Stokowski's Philadelphia Orchestra had been close during the 1920s; under Fritz Reiner, who came in 1931 and remained for ten years, the collaboration had continued, and Curtis student orchestra concerts would regularly take place at the Academy of Music. But more recently there had been problems in the program. As director, Serkin was able to forge a renewed close connection between Curtis and the Philadelphia Orchestra due to his friendship with Eugene Ormandy, who began to lead Saturday morning rehearsals of the Curtis orchestra.

"I feel it is very important for every instrumentalist to play in the orchestra," Serkin told the *Philadelphia Inquirer*. "We want our people to become soloists, but who can tell? There are hundreds of excellent players for every one who becomes a solo artist. Is it personality? I don't know. Playing in the orchestra gives them a feeling for playing with others and that is important."[75] Ormandy also persuaded visiting conductors of the Philadelphia Orchestra to conduct the Curtis orchestra when they were in town. "Playing in the orchestra used to be a chore for the kids," Sol Schoenbach was quoted as saying. "Now you can't imagine how excited they are."[76]

Third, and especially significant as a real departure from Curtis tradition, was a new emphasis on chamber music. Chamber music had not had a very prominent place at Curtis, Zimbalist regarding it as "something one did in retirement."[77] Drawing on the community he had created at Marlboro, Serkin brought chamber music colleagues such as Felix Galimir, Mischa Schneider, and the Guarneri Quartet, three of whose members were Curtis graduates, to coach chamber music at Curtis. Serkin colleagues Jaime Laredo and Isidore Cohen, both with strong chamber music backgrounds, also joined the faculty. "Chamber music is really the center of Curtis," Serkin told the *Inquirer*. To be sure, Serkin did not advocate the centrality of chamber music to the extent of neglecting the soloist's needs. Rather, as he told the *New York Times*, his hope was "to establish a vital chamber tradition at the school without losing the intense concentration and long practice hours required by a solo career."[78] Curtis Director Gary Graffman confirms that this was Serkin's most fundamental innovation and most lasting influence on the preparation of musicians at Curtis. "There surely was chamber music before and the students theoretically had to take it and played it very well, but it was not stressed at all," he remembers, going on to add, "Now it's stressed more than ever."[79]

But none of these three changes to the Curtis educational program received as much public attention as did a fourth: the expansion of the opera program. Due simply to its larger-than-life nature and cost, opera was to become both the most visible sign of Serkin's artistic leadership in the Philadelphia music scene as well as the most intractable source of his conflict with the Curtis Board of Directors.

Curtis had produced operas since 1929, when Mrs. Bok became chair of the board of the Philadelphia Grand Opera Company, which then affiliated with Curtis. Their first full-scale opera, a student production of Eugène D'Albert's *Tiefland* under conductor Artur Rodzinski, was performed on May 12, 1929. Two years later Curtis enjoyed an exceptional triumph when, on March 19, 1931, it offered the American premiere of Alban Berg's *Wozzeck*, a production launched with a $40,000 start-up gift from Mrs. Bok.[80] In 1941, the Philadelphia Opera Company gave the first English-language U.S. production of Debussy's *Pelléas et Mélisande*, with Curtis students in the orchestra.

Since those days, however, the opera program had been in decline. Serkin sought to restore opera to its former level by bringing an old friend, Max Rudolf (1902–1995), to join him at Curtis. The German-born Rudolf had held posts in opera houses in Freiburg and Darmstadt before moving to Prague in 1929, where he worked for six years with George Szell. Rudolf had most recently been music director of the Cincinnati Symphony Orchestra, following a term as artistic administrator of the Metropolitan Opera under Rudolf Bing. His plans for the opera program included giving each singer at least four hours of personal coaching per week in addition to rehearsals, acting lessons, and other elements of opera singing. To Serkin's delight, scenic designer Dino Yannopoulos agreed to join Rudolf in the opera department, and later became its director.

Under Serkin, the Curtis opera department tended to produce lesser-known works rather than warhorses, a policy instituted in part to ensure that Curtis students would not be compared with more famous singers in familiar roles. Max Rudolf's first full production was Wolf-Ferrari's *The School for Fathers* in 1971, and during Serkin's tenure as director Curtis also offered full orchestra productions of Cimarosa's *Il Matrimonio Segreto*, Stravinsky's *The Rake's Progress*, Wolff-Ferrari's *I Quattro Rusteghi*, Hindemith's *Hin und Zurück*, and Benjamin Britten's *The Rape of Lucretia*. When more familiar operas were produced, the use of scholarly texts gave them new interest: music critics praised a 1974 production of the *Barber of Seville* for erasing decades of editors' whims.[81]

These productions were welcomed not only for their intrinsic merit, but also because through them Curtis had "sallied out of its hallowed walls to present opera in public."[82] Nor was it only in opera productions that Serkin opened Curtis's doors to the general community, but also in orchestra concerts and student recitals, so that by 1974 Samuel Singer would write that "some of the best concerts outside the Academy of Music are at the Curtis Institute of Music, not only by distinguished faculty members such as Rudolf Serkin, but by the students."[83]

THE SERKIN TONE

Serkin's vision for Curtis included other proposed changes. In 1969 he oversaw the purchase of an adjacent building to contain the Curtis library and equipped it with facilities to make the collection more accessible. At one point he entertained the idea of introducing "a department for piano technicians,"[84] and in a 1972 memo he describes plans for listening facilities and language laboratories. There was also the vexing question of composition: "Our composition department is a problem," Serkin told the *Philadelphia Inquirer* in 1968. "We are, after all, a school for performers, and I don't know how far we want to go with composition."[85] By 1975 this had not changed: "It is a weakness," Serkin conceded in an interview with Daniel Webster.[86]

Serkin's wish to be surrounded by people who shared his musical judgment extended not only to colleagues on his faculty, such as Ormandy and Rudolf, but also to administrators, most of whom had Marlboro associations. Bassoonist and Marlboro administrator Anthony Checchia became his administrative assistant, running Curtis's day-to-day operations; Sol Schoenbach's son Peter (also a bassoonist) became academic dean. Serkin invited close friends to be commencement speakers: psychiatrist Richard Sterba in 1969, architect Willo von Moltke in 1972, and Ernst Gombrich in 1973.*

He sought to attract the foremost artists to visit Curtis, to inspire and per-

---

* In his commencement address, Gombrich recalled meeting Serkin as a youth in Vienna. When the younger Gombrich first "looked up to him in awe it was, I think, for an incredible trick he had of putting a nut on the floor and cracking it with his head, but I soon found out that he could do other things as well." Ernst H. Gombrich, Commencement Address, Curtis Institute of Music, Philadelphia, May 12, 1973, p. 1.

haps to be inspired. An invitation was extended to Maria Callas, who paid a visit to Curtis in February 1971. Having arrived for a two-week master class, she found "eighteen students, none of them remotely ready for the advanced work which interested her."[87] As part of a fiftieth anniversary celebration in 1974, Leonid Kogan and Paul Badura-Skoda participated in a series of master classes, as did Mstislav Rostropovich in March 1975.

As director, Serkin displayed the same traits that had been serving him so well as artistic director of Marlboro: ironclad conviction blended with a casual and friendly, open manner. He had a laissez-faire attitude about hierarchy; once, for example, he overruled a faculty member who wanted to expel a student for hurling an obscenity at him. Peter Schoenbach remembers that "he would often take no action rather than take an action, because he'd learned that many problems, if left unaddressed, will simply go away. He would never hold a grudge. He was a very sweet person, but he also had very strong opinions and a temper. When he was really annoyed, he let you know. When that happened to me a couple of times, my father would say, 'You've been Serkincized!' "[88]

Irene Serkin, for her part, also played an important supportive role at Curtis, upholding the traditions of the Institute, such as its Wednesday afternoon teas, while trying to create a less stuffy social atmosphere, sometimes bringing her dogs along to the teas. She showed a motherly concern for sick faculty members and tried to nurture the students, many of whom were far away from home at a very young age. She kept a watchful eye on the physical plant and attended (as did her husband, if he was not on tour) every one of Curtis's numerous student recitals.

LEAVING CURTIS

The final chapter in Serkin's relationship to the Curtis Institute of Music was a bitter one, and bitter it would remain. Although the Serkins' departure from Curtis in 1976 in no way affected his stature in the musical world, they were deeply wounded by the circumstances of his leaving; for the rest of her life, Irene Serkin refused to return to Philadelphia.

Almost from the start, the exciting growth and change at Curtis had been accompanied by behind-the-scenes tension and concern. In addition to discontent about the time demands of orchestral participation, there were students and veteran teachers who resented the new insistence on theory classes, and the faculty members brought in to teach those classes had no job security. Serkin was never fully aware of the students' resistance to these classes nor of the eroding atmosphere in them. "I saw this happening and warned him indirectly," Sol Schoenbach remembered, "but he was so convinced that all these people were his friends and would cooperate."[89] According to the official history of the Institute, Serkin's changes gave rise to a desire "for a greater sense of structure within the school and for a more even-handed balance between departments."[90] Many of the "old guard" felt eclipsed by the addition of so many of Serkin's protégés, the "Marlboro Mafia." As one faculty member put it, "Under Serkin, the atmosphere got a little 'thick.'"

In addition to internal dissatisfaction with curricular and personnel changes, financial matters were a major focus of concern for the Curtis Board, which questioned whether the large budgetary demands of an opera program could be sustained by a conservatory the size of Curtis. With Mrs. Bok's death in January 1970, Serkin lost his most generous backer. Even in 1969, her son Cary Bok, who had assumed most of his mother's responsibilities, had expressed financial worries, suggesting that prospective students of marginal ability be rejected to reduce the student body by as many as twenty. The academic program was approved based on a reduction in costs and the release of certain faculty members.

Certainly, in late 1973 the entire country was experiencing the worst economy since the end of World War II. Due to substantial losses of endowment income, many other schools were also forced to reduce faculty size, as the heady expansion of educational institutions that had characterized the 1960s came to an end. But Serkin rejected the notion that the expansion of Curtis, especially its orchestral and opera programs, had been excessive. He affirmed that he had "always accepted any students only on their merits, never in connection with thoughts or plans of building up orchestra or opera," pointing out that the integrity of Curtis's most illustrious violin teacher, Ivan Galamian, and Serkin's own presence at auditions guaranteed this. He attributed the reason for growth to the simple fact that the "number of applicants for strings increased" and reminded the Board of Directors that "Mr. Cary Bok realized that to bring back the institute to the original ideals and purpose would be very expensive, and he enthusiastically supported this effort."

But the weight of the alliance between conservative faculty members with curricular complaints and those Board members with financial concerns could not be overcome. The Board informed Serkin that his contract would not be renewed. Sol Schoenbach claimed that Serkin "came up to our apartment on Rittenhouse Square and just sat there and cried."[91] By December 1974, Serkin had written to M. Todd Cooke of the Board of Directors, expressing his ostensible desire to leave "to devote more time to studying and to concertizing."[92]

Whatever the merits of the argument that Serkin had been less than cautious with the Institute's budget and less than diplomatic in effecting too much change too quickly, his defenders regarded this dismissal by the Board as shabby. Ormandy commented that "the way Serkin had been treated by Curtis was shameful and a disgrace."[93] In Philadelphia's *Sunday Bulletin*, James Felton asserted that the triumph of the conservative Board members would "lead back to the dark ages at Curtis and ultimately crush the hopes for a performing arts–oriented school built so tangibly and brilliantly by Serkin and his associates in eight shining years."[94]

To the outside world Serkin explained his resignation as due to time pressures: "We moved back to Vermont from Philadelphia, and I have resigned from Curtis because I felt it increasingly difficult to combine the directorship of Curtis with my concert activities," he wrote in 1976.[95] However, to Jonathan Sternberg, a colleague at Temple University, he went a bit deeper into the truth: "My contract with the Curtis Institute was terminated three years ago by the Board of Directors, and I served only later to help the school out until they had decided on a successor to me."[96]

Inevitably, Serkin's colleagues thought about the future of the Institute even as they commiserated with him about what had come to pass. Ivan Galamian wrote of his sorrow on learning that Serkin would resign as of June 1, adding, "Do you think the Board of Directors of Curtis would consider Felix Galimir as the future Director? I have the same high regards for him as you have."[97] In March 1976 plans to find a successor for the position included talks with Isaac Stern and George Rochberg. Mieczyslaw Horszowski suggested Alberto Ginastera and Yehudi Menuhin as possible directors.[98]

In January 1977 M. Todd Cooke and three other Serkin defenders resigned from the Board in a dispute over continuing the public performance program instituted by Serkin. Curtis oboist John de Lancie eventually succeeded Serkin as director. When Serkin left, or soon thereafter, many of those close to him, such as Ormandy, Schoenbach, and Checchia, demonstrated their support for him and their chagrin at his dismissal by resigning from Curtis as well. The stress and disappointment of his dismissal from Curtis must surely have contributed to the extended bout of ill health that Serkin suffered following his departure. In the early months of 1976 he had to spend a month in the hospital with a flu; after the Marlboro season of that same year he was prevented by his doctor from making a tour of Japan to which he had been looking forward.

Six years later, in September 1982, Cary Bok's wife wrote to Serkin, expressing the desire of the Board of Directors to demonstrate their love and devotion by conferring on Serkin the title of Director Emeritus and naming a room at Curtis for him on the occasion of his eightieth birthday. Serkin responded, expressing gratitude for the idea (which some considered more of an insult than an honor, given what had happened), but explaining why he could not accept their proposal:

> When Cary asked me to become Director I took it as a mandate to bring the Institute back as close as possible to the original intentions of the beloved founder of the school. When, five years later, I was informed that my contract would be terminated, I took this for an expression of dissatisfaction with my intentions and my service, as expressed earlier by some members of the Board. Unable and unwilling to make compromises, I accepted this solution with great sadness.[99]

Attributing the direction his leadership had taken to "the original intentions" of Mrs. Bok, Serkin once again deferred to her vision, thereby legitimating his actions as a reflection of her will. Perhaps, in a life that still included a demanding concert schedule as well as the leadership of Marlboro, Serkin had, quite simply, been overextended at Curtis. Without question, his leadership had been based on his exemplary artistic achievement and a strong vision, but the qualities that had led to splendid results at Marlboro were stymied at Curtis by the complexities of an established conservatory with its own traditions and mores. Nonetheless, despite the discrepancy between his original visions for the Institute and their incomplete fulfillment, and despite the crushing disappointment of his departure, Serkin's years at Curtis had pushed the Institute toward a new vitality, so that for many observers the period of his directorship had restored its early luster and given it a second golden age.

THE INSTITUTE FOR YOUNG PERFORMING MUSICIANS

After leaving Curtis in June 1976, Serkin was invited to join the faculty of other music schools, Juilliard and Indiana University's among them. Serkin declined these offers, writing that he did not wish to add to his work schedule. Indeed, for a 73-year-old, his professional life of concerts and the directorship of Marlboro was extraordinarily full by any measure. But his desire to keep working with young people, and perhaps a need to make good the recent disappointment at Curtis, were still motivating factors for the future. By 1978, he had a plan for a school of his own, the Institute for Young Performing Musicians in Guilford, Vermont, which was to provide talented pianists with optimal conditions for a period of intensive study, from a few months to several years.

Using money awarded by a prize from Siemens, the German electrical conglomerate, Serkin purchased a house large enough for two students a few miles from his own and persuaded the pianist Luis Batlle to share the coaching and teaching. Israeli pianist Yefim Bronfman and Juilliard graduate Stephanie Brown were the Institute's first two students. They were followed by Cecile Licad and Peter Orth, who were to be the Institute's last students.

Stephanie Brown remembers that Serkin "had a very clear philosophical and artistic vision of students being in the country, away from the distractions of the city, being able to practice as much as they wanted to, and being able to study not only piano and music, but also philosophy and art and all the other disciplines that he believed made a well-rounded musician and person."[100] Serkin also saw the Institute as a structure that could bridge the necessary transitional period in a performer's career between conservatory and full-fledged concertizing. "Many extraordinarily gifted musicians after they have finished their formal studies and musical training find themselves in need of further guidance, new artistic directions and often assistance to continue such advanced studies, developing as performers," he wrote. "The Institute for Young Performing Musicians has been founded in the hope to help such artists."[101] He described how the Institute could accomplish this goal by arranging small concerts at various New England sites. As he told Robert Silverman, "We will start small, but I hope we will grow." Chastened perhaps by his Curtis experience, he added, "Not too large, so that we do not lose control."[102]

Peter Orth describes his two years as a student at the Institute as intense and memorable, if somewhat more spontaneous in reality than on paper: "We didn't have regular piano lessons once a week. We never knew when Rudi would call. When he was in the mood, he'd call and say, 'Come on up at 2:00.' Sometimes he'd see us two at a time. In wintertime, after lessons, [Serkin's daughter] Margie and I would go tobogganing down the side of the hill. We'd come back in wonderful humor, and he would look at us and smile. And Irene would make hot chocolate."[103]

The experiment was short lived. The full range of educational and professional opportunities that he had envisioned for his students never materialized. The Institute's isolated living situation became a trial for the students, Bronfman and Brown leaving after only a few months. Orth, who had won the Naumberg International Piano Competition in 1979, remained in Vermont, and Licad, having been awarded the Leventritt Prize, began a busy concert schedule, performing with major orchestras around the country. And Serkin, at the end of a teaching life of nearly seventy years, turned increasingly to his performing and recording commitments. If he felt any lingering disappointment at the abandoned idea of his own institute, it was more than offset, as we shall see, by his fulfilling life at the Marlboro Music School and Festival.

Voices

EUGENE ISTOMIN

SEYMOUR LIPKIN

LEE LUVISI

RUTH LAREDO

Eugene Istomin
Washington, D.C., December 21, 1996

Eugene Istomin was born in 1925. The most prominent of Serkin's first group of Curtis students, he also became especially close to Adolf and Frieda Busch. At the beginning of his spectacular early career, he won both the Leventritt and the Philadelphia Orchestra Youth awards. He was the youngest participant at the first Prades Festival, performed in the Stern-Rose-Istomin Trio, which won a Grammy in 1971, and has made solo recital tours throughout North America, the Far East, Europe, and Australia. Married to Marta Casals Istomin, he speaks with us in his grand apartment in Washington, D.C.

THE CURTIS YEARS

I first heard Serkin play in a concert with Toscanini in 1936, but I didn't lay eyes on him as my formal teacher until October 1939, when I was thirteen. The war in Europe had just started. I found him a mixture of incredible sweetness and devastating severity. When I was fourteen or fifteen, and he had scolded me about something, I would say, "You shouldn't expect me to play as well as you." He answered, "What do you mean? I expect you to play better! You should play better! You're more gifted than I am! " Was he joking? Or wasn't he? In some ways he wasn't joking. He was enormously powerful, and he had a way of looking small, so that in talking with him, you felt a sort of self-effacing, nervous, reticent person. But actually, physically, he was very compelling: he was tall, and he had these enormous, enormous hands and tremendous power.

An illustration of his rigorousness: I'd been to the Philharmonic to hear him play the Brahms First Piano Concerto with Barbirolli and basking in the pride of now being his pupil decided to learn it for myself. When I came to him for the first lesson with the opening movement more or less "ready," there were a lot of mislearned notes. He picked up a chair and held it up as if to smash it over my head, because he was so outraged with some of the things that I did.

We once had a confrontation about the way to play the first movement of Beethoven's piano sonata Opus 54. I was at that time enamoured of Schnabel's way of playing across the bar line—Schnabel played in long curves, so to speak, and I was doing a lot of that as very impressionable youngsters do. Serkin said, "Well if you insist on playing these passages out of time, it's better not to play that sonata." And I said, "Well then I won't!" And that was the end of that class. Far from being crushed, I simply went underground with my Schnabelian curved time.

SERKIN PERFORMS

Serkin could give concerts of very difficult programs that were practically flawless. They weren't always things that you would necessarily agree with entirely. You have only to listen to that recording, for half a century a collector's item, of the Beethoven Fourth with Toscanini (every one with Toscanini had a special glamour). I was present at studio 8H, dry and infamous as it was acoustically, to see and hear that performance. Fast, fluid, straight as an arrow, "flawless." The era seemed to require a response to the terrible tension of the pre-war years. The orchestras tuned to 445 or even 450 rather than 430 or less of the previous times. In defiance of his pianistic limitations, Serkin succeeded in surpassing the greatest virtuosos in this performance and others at the time. Such was his will and determination under that sweet, shy, reticent smile.

He played Schubert beautifully, and yet, there is a vernacular Viennese "charm" that he knew how to put in his personal comportment that did not reach his fingers. To my mind, the ideal romantic players are the ones who exploit the innate qualities of the instrument but do not go beyond them. Arthur Rubinstein was one. Rachmaninoff was another as well as Schnabel and Cortot. Each different from the other, but equally loath to force from the piano a "harsh" sound. Now there is a lot of Beethoven that demands more from the instruments than they can give, which certainly delighted the composer but which frustrated the "romantic" pianist. Therefore what is deemed "unplayable" in this sense Rubinstein and Rachmaninoff and Horowitz simply did not play, because it required something extra-instrumental. And this was a quality that Serkin had in unique supply. However, it did not lend itself terribly well to recording, which is why Serkin's records, though many are magnificent, don't quite do him justice. His main essence, which is beyond sound, was missed. Schnabel did much better in this sense. Horowitz and Rubinstein were totally focused on the quality of their personal "sound." As for Rachmaninoff, to this day the tone of his recordings comes through the now archaic medium with a vivid, limpid "golden" beauty that to me proves that there *is* such a thing as "tone" and the "perfectly turned phrase." But in Serkin, there was an awkwardness that suggests a modesty (as in fig leaf) about turning the "perfect phrase." If it's true, if it's pure, it has to not quite succeed. Suffering to attain something is what it's about. There is no elegant way of being born or dying, or thinking about first causes. That was Beethoven's credo—and it was Serkin's, too.

As time went on, over the years, Serkin gave more of himself by far to his students than the others, harsh as his judgment may have seemed sometimes. As a pedagogue, only Schnabel was comparable in influence, but I think he projected an erudite sovereignty, while Serkin projected humility. And certain aspects of his personality in certain repertoire are absolutely incomparable. A lot of music is extremely beautiful when it's superficial, but he could never be superficial. That was when he was least convincing, when he had to take advantage of effect. But in that central European repertoire, when that was not the strong point of the music, then he was the greatest. I really think Beethoven suited him best of all, although he was wonderful in Mozart, he was wonderful in Bach, he gave me the most beautiful performance of the *Goldbergs* I have ever heard.

Mystical would be a word I'd use in the sense of possessed, the quality of possession. This curious quality, a certain peasant quality that he had, a certain purposeful awkwardness that he had adopted, mixed with the total sense of mission. And at moments of his best, most beautiful playing, it was that quality that the saints also had—willingness to "burn at the stake," that quality of complete ecstasy and asceticism stripped of any element of effect so that in the end, the no-effect became the effect. Finally, let us remember that he influenced the greatest generation of American pianists in the second half of the twentieth century. Not a single one is untouched by his integrity.

Seymour Lipkin
New York, December 14, 1996

Seymour Lipkin, born in 1928 in Detroit, has had a career as both conductor and pianist. After studying with Koussevitsky, he was George Szell's assistant in Cleveland for six years, Leonard Bernstein's assistant at the New York Philharmonic, and for twenty years conductor of the Long Island Symphony Orchestra. As a pianist he has performed more recently with the Chamber Music Society of Lincoln Center and is on the faculty of both the Curtis Institute and the Juilliard School of Music. On the walls of his Upper West Side apartment are photographs of Serkin and Toscanini.

STARTING OUT AT CURTIS

The six years that I studied with Serkin were a major, major time of my development. He was the single most decisive influence on my musical life. I was 11 when I went to Curtis. My father couldn't just pick up and move his [medical] practice [from Detroit]. My mother came for the first year, but then she left. So I was on my own. That may have been a reason Serkin felt empathetic with me, since as a boy he had done the same thing.

Even before I met Mr. Serkin, there was an air of great deference and great respect associated with him — you don't fool with him. I had to audition a second time for him, and then he accepted me. I played a Beethoven sonata, Op. 22. I'm not too sure what else I played, but I remember that very well because another of his students, who was a few years older, had told me, "You want to impress Mr. Serkin? Go like this with your hands, throw up your hands." So I thought, "Well, why not?" And I did. At that time Serkin was like a jack-in-the box [at the piano], he was just wound up, he would stamp his feet. In later years he pulled it down.

LESSONS WITH SERKIN

When I had my first lesson with him, I was 14, a kid, so I started to take off my jacket, and he said, "No, no, leave your jacket on, out of respect for the composer." Good grief! The composer wasn't there! Of course, he really meant that I should show respect for *him*, but he would never say that. Insofar as he represented the composers, it was an oblique way of demanding respect for himself, in my opinion, although not for himself in his own person.

Studying with him was really a tremendous tonic for me, because I was a little bit all over the place at the time, rather on the wild side, no one could get me to buckle down. I wasn't too solid in my scholarship at the school and was in danger [of failing]. He didn't have to say anything, but you just knew that there would be no getting away with anything. One can be severe in destructive ways or severe in supportive ways, and although I gather this was not the case for everybody, for me he was very supportive. I knew he was in my corner, no matter how strict he was.

One of the great pieces of luck of my life is that I didn't study with Vengerova. Leonard Bernstein came when I was 12, in 1939, and studied with Vengerova. Bernstein could handle anybody; you couldn't have put Bernstein down with a fire truck, but I would not have survived her because she was destructive. She was very critical and had very high standards, but in a destructive way. People simply were destroyed by her. She would erode their confidence. Serkin always built my confidence, even when he didn't like what I had played. What he conveyed was not that you were no good, but that you had failed to live up to a standard, and the implication was that you could live up to the standard if you worked hard enough. Also, he clearly liked me, and that helped. I had a kind of intensity that seemed to appeal to him. He let me develop my own way. If I had had the kind of teacher who imposes his ideas, I would have simply resisted, given how I was, and we would have locked horns.

As a teacher, he was not really someone who could explain what you had to do to get the results that were needed. Perhaps he wasn't quite sure himself— but what he did do was create an overwhelming necessity that you had to do it well. I don't remember what the words were, but you felt you just had to go home and knock your head against a wall until you figured out a way to do it. The important thing about studying with him was the idealism of it, the sense that you and he and all of us simply had to knock ourselves out to do everything possible to fulfill our responsibility to the great music that we were playing. You can't ask for more than that.

Certain principles of interpretation would emerge from his teaching. He was very much for keeping the same tempo all the time, but he would just say, "No, no, no, don't slow down." So you'd have to go home and think about it to extract the principle.

Serkin was relentless in going after technical exactitude and cleanliness down the line. He wouldn't tolerate sloppiness of any kind. For Serkin it had to be immaculate, even if he had to go over it 4,000 times. He never described to us how to practice. I gather he was ruthless with himself, practiced hours and hours, over and over. The more I thought about it over the years, the odder it seemed: I don't understand why he didn't talk to us about how to practice, what to practice.

I wonder whether there was something about the way he worked that he didn't want to divulge, whether it was because he was a little ashamed of it, that he had to do so much, or whether it had a certain self-punitive quality about it that applied to him but not necessarily to other people. It's hard for me to believe that he didn't really want to tell his secrets. That doesn't fit. It's almost as if he were unhappy with what he had to do to himself and that he didn't think that it was appropriate. It was very striking.

Serkin would never say to you that you had to study the form of a certain piece and understand its structure. That I learned later. His approach was a little bit mystical. You put in the time and somehow or another you got to your goal. And I'd go home and think, "Ayyy, help!" The message was that you just keep at it until you get it. His influence was in conveying the need to realize that you're not such hot stuff. It was the need to devote yourself to something bigger than you are, the necessity to do it. And the fact that it's not so impressive if you are hot stuff, it's not very interesting in the long run. That was the big lesson: Shape up.

I had a long history with him with the *Emperor* Concerto, because I studied it with him. I remember very well that when I played it I was banging the hell out of it, and he complained how harsh it was. So I thought I had better pull it back. When I came back with it the next time, he said (these days you probably wouldn't say it), "It sounds like a girl." I thought, "Oh well, you can't win."

He was not very interested in the sound of the instrument. That was incidental. He was after the intensity of the feeling, the responsibility and the power of the music, and if the piano didn't want to do it—well, I don't want to say he hit it, but he subdued it. It was very different from Mr. Horszowski, for instance. Mr. Horszowski had this wonderful warm sound that he seemed to carry from one instrument to another. I don't remember whether he told me—after years go by you're not sure—but I believe he said, "Well you know, I make friends with the piano." I think Mr. Serkin and the piano didn't make friends—the piano was an antagonist to be subdued, mastered.

So in the early years he didn't care if the playing was awful: he said, "Do it!" He did complain when I got too brutal, but we never heard about the beauty of sound or about color, phrasing, or anything like that. Toscanini, on the other hand, was obsessed with achieving a singing sound from the orchestra. He'd scream bloody murder, "Cantare, cantare, sostenere!" You could just watch it in the beat, it just soared through a *legato* all the time. Toscanini had a singing line like nobody else. Serkin did not. The driving rhythm, yes, but the *cantabile*, no.

DOING IT YOUR WAY

I don't remember his demonstrating, ever; I think he may have played one chord once, but he almost never demonstrated anything on the piano. For me it was wonderful, because I sensed that he did not want you to do what he did. I began to realize that what he really wanted from you was to come with a strong point of view. When I came with an idea that I had worked out, he wouldn't say anything. I'm sure it couldn't have been the same idea as his, but he would leave you alone. When you were wishy-washy, then he would say it should be this way or that way. So I was very sure to have my ideas set before I went in.

He always advised us, "Don't listen to other people's recordings when you're working on things." He didn't want you to take the easy way out, and certainly not by imitating him. I think that that is absolutely right. Because otherwise it results in the famous impersonal performances that you hear all the time. You say, "Oh Horowitz played it like that, I remember," but there's no personal conviction behind it.

PERSONAL QUALITIES

The very problematic thing about him was his insistence on a kind of personal humility which I often felt was a cover, because when you scratched it, he was there like iron. He seemed all deference and sweetness and light, but if you touched him there was no way he was going to budge.

He was very, very chary with praise, but you would hear about it occasionally from other people. When I won the Rachmaninoff Competition, I made my debut playing the First Tchaikovsky Piano Concerto with the Boston Symphony at Tanglewood, and he came all the way down from Vermont to hear me. I don't remember that he said anything particular to me—he was very nice—but someone else told me that he had said, "I didn't know that concerto could sound so noble." But he wouldn't say it to me.

When I was conducting the Long Island Symphony, it must have been in the late 1960s, I wanted to have Mr. Serkin play with the orchestra. I said, "Mr. Serkin, would you consider coming and playing a benefit for the orchestra, to be shared with Marlboro?" But he said, "Oh no, I'll play the benefit for your orchestra alone." That was very characteristic. We played the *Emperor* Concerto and the *Choral Fantasy*. We rehearsed like anything and I said to him, "We'll only need you for one rehearsal. Because we're going to rehearse the hell out of it beforehand." And he said, "Look, I'll come more times if you want me." That's how he was. He came and everybody just loved it. There was a little reception afterwards, and Mrs. Serkin was there; she came over to him and said to him in German, *"Du hast schön gespielt* [You played beautifully]." I thought that was terrific, because for her it was the *Emperor* Concerto no. 77.

TEACHING AT CURTIS

In 1969 Mr. Serkin asked me to come and teach at Curtis. I was scared to death, because I had never taught anybody in my life! That was a really terrific thing about him: he decided whom he had confidence in and he went down the line, whether it was the boys in the Guarneri Quartet or opera at the Curtis. Everything that happened in that school was a result of his vision.

He instituted a kind of jury at the Curtis. The way he put it was so characteristic. He said, "I think all our students should play for all of us; my students should play for you, and yours for me." I thought, "Oh sure, yeah, right." I mean, everyone was scared to death: it was an audition for him, of course. But he persisted in that fiction.

The first of my students who played was a fine pianist who is now in California. I was petrified. I worked with her very hard before she played the audition. I think it was Beethoven Op. 31, no. 1. She finished, and Horszowski turned to me and said, "Congratulations"—as if there had been any question of whose audition that was. It was so funny, because it was so transparent, but the fiction was that it was her audition.

So I passed, and he was very supportive. Interesting, with all of the force of his leadership, that he did not try to take over any individual's decision making. I decided who should stay and who should leave, despite the fact that he had forty times the qualifications that I had. I didn't know anything about teaching. I made some mistakes and kept people there who probably should have gone. But he didn't interfere.

I remember once someone who came in to audition had something in his back pocket that looked to me like a knife—it could have been a comb, but it looked like a knife. He couldn't play at all: it was a disaster, and he seemed rather aggressive and dressed in a street way. I grew really very frightened, because here was Mr. Horszowski sitting there, about three feet tall. I thought this guy was a dangerous character, especially because his playing was disastrous. Well, Mr. Serkin got up and walked over to him, put his arm on his shoulder, reassured him, calmed him down, thanked him for coming, and helped him out of the room. I thought that was just terrific! Because he handled the situation so beautifully, with a kind of sympathy for this poor kid . . . It was quite wonderful.

I called him when he left the Curtis to ask if I should leave, too, and he said, "Are you kidding? Of course you can continue." And I'm still teaching there, over twenty years later.

Lee Luvisi
New York, November 10, 1996

Lee Luvisi, born in Louisville, Kentucky, was in 1957 the youngest instructor ever to join the Curtis faculty. He was an early teacher of Peter Serkin. He has performed throughout the world as a soloist and has collaborated with the Guarneri Quartet and numerous other chamber musicians. He has been artist-in-residence at the University of Louisville School of Music since 1963 and is an Artist Member of the Chamber Music Society of Lincoln Center. It is there that we meet him, courtly and silver-haired, shortly before one of his Sunday afternoon concerts.

AMBIVALENT STUDENT

In the early summer of 1952, when I was 14, I went with my parents to the farm in Guilford to play for Mr. Serkin. It was a wonderful experience. We met the whole family. My father took movies, which I still have, of Mr. Serkin holding Peter, who was then only about 4 years old, on his arm. In the background one can see Adolf Busch. It was only five or six days after we returned home that we learned of Mr. Busch's death. Serkin accepted me at Curtis, a tremendous honor, of course, and the following autumn I began my five years of study with him.

I'm sure that any of his former students would tell you they are still ambivalent about their years with him. First of all, his was an overwhelming personality. For me, to come under so powerful an influence at age 14 was difficult. He became a father figure whom I both loved and feared at the same time. Just as a friend he was always extremely warm and generous. In the teaching studio, however, where music was his serious and sacred concern, he could at times border on what seemed to me at that age like cruelty, although in retrospect I know he hadn't a malicious bone in his body.

During my first year at Curtis, I played for him only twice; most of my lessons were with Horszowski. Serkin first heard me shortly after school began in September, and I played a Beethoven Sonata, Op. 27, no. 1, at the end of which he shook his head and looked at me rather pathetically. "You know, when I accepted you, I thought you had talent. Now I'm not so sure." I was devastated. I'm certain it never occurred to him just how hurtful that was to me, but it absolutely colored most of my first year at Curtis. I felt like a failure and that I had no business being there.

The next time he heard me, in March or April, I played two French works, Franck and Fauré, that I was about to perform with the Chicago Symphony at a Young People's Concert. When I finished, he walked over, hugged me, and said, "Beautiful! Marvelous! You are an artist. I have nothing whatsoever to say to you about them." I felt like a tennis ball that had been whacked from one end of the emotional court to the other. I really didn't understand where I stood at that point. Things were never again quite that bewildering, but it was a rough beginning.

As best I can recall, his tendency was to be rather extreme one way or the other. If he liked the way you played—and that was not often—he would be very generous in his praise. He'd say a few words: "A little thing here or there, but it's very good, wonderful." And if he was unhappy with what you had done, he could be quite harsh and dismissive. I remember one particular lesson at which I played a Mozart concerto for him, one of the longest, K. 482. He let me play it from beginning to end, all forty minutes. When I stopped there was a deafening silence. He sat hunched over in the corner as he was wont to do, and I thought "Oh my god, what's coming?" Finally he got up, came over to me, and with real anger in his voice said, "How can you do that to Mozart? It was so painful. I can't talk about it. Go home." And that was the end of the lesson. Looking back, I'm sure I did play it miserably.

I think I was something of a challenge to him. Not that I was outwardly a rebel, but my whole training, good as it was, and my sense of what music was all about, were quite different from what he was offering me. I suppose I did rebel inwardly to some extent, though. I'm half Italian; I grew up surrounded by Italian operatic recordings, things of a highly lyric, emotional nature. I remain very much of that particular aspect of music, with no apologies. But Mr. Serkin thought, rightly, that there were far more important things for me to consider. He had a vision of the total edifice of a piece of music. I had always tended to think in smaller terms and it was a difficult adjustment for me to begin seeing music in a big, whole way. My reluctance then, too, to tackle works

that were really technically demanding prompted him to dub me affectionately—and sometimes not so affectionately—his "adagio player."

Mr. Serkin was not a teacher of technique, although he often claimed that
one could never have enough of it. He rarely talked about the piano or how
to play it. What you learned you learned mostly from observation of those
incredible hands of his. They were like truck drivers' hands or thick sausages,
not what you would expect of an artist. The skin was so stretched from hundred of thousands of hours of practicing that his joints simply didn't show.
Rather like snakeskin. While he would never actually sit down and play anything at a lesson, he did lean over you to demonstrate certain things. And if
you had any awareness at all of what was happening, your approach to the keyboard was forever changed. For instance, how he would keep his hands so close
to the keys. That became an object lesson for all of us. Not to waste motion.

He said so many memorable things to me that I continue to pass on to my
students. A few examples: "The worst crime you can commit as an artist is to
bore your listeners"; for another, "People who come to hear you are entitled to
hear all the right notes, don't you think?"; also, "You can't play Mozart beautifully unless you can play Tchaikovsky well . . . And vice versa." That last one
made no sense to me at the time; now I understand precisely what he meant
by it.

Outside the studio, he was really a father to me. As I said before, he could
be very warm and generous. He would give Christmas gifts of scores, touchingly inscribed, which I treasure to this day. And his sense of humor! Whenever he telephoned me it was with a disguised voice: "Hallo, this is Pablo Casals"
or "This is Jascha Heifetz." There was always a kind of banter that existed
between us.

The Serkin house was always open to his students. I remember one evening
a few of us were asked over for dinner, and afterwards Mr. Serkin said, "I have
something very special I want to show you." He disappeared for a moment and
came back down the stairs with a large folder. "First of all, before I open this,
please stand back from the piano." He then uncovered the manuscript of the
Brahms A major Piano Quartet. What a thrill that was! Especially for me, as I
was studying it at the time. He showed us one page where Brahms had originally conceived the opening of the slow movement without the piano, only the
strings. It was so beautiful to see! Serkin was wonderful about sharing with us
the many treasures he kept in his home—first editions, composers' letters, etc.
I remember that with the greatest gratitude.

PRACTICING

In a relaxed moment at Marlboro, I once asked him, "Mr. Serkin, why, after the life you have had in music, the years you have devoted to hard work, do you still find it necessary to practice the incredible hours you do?" He responded, very forthrightly, "You know, I'm not a natural pianist. I never was. It always came very hard to me. If I don't work hard I can't play. I'm no different from most musicians; I don't always feel like going out there and playing. But I want to be ready when that happens so it's still above average. And I can't count on inspiration; that's a gift from God. But when it comes, I want to be ready." I never forgot that. I thought it such a beautiful statement, one that every musician should hear.

I was often at the Serkins' for lunch, after which he would usually excuse himself to go practice. A couple of times I asked Mrs. Serkin if I might quietly sit downstairs and listen. I would then hear him go on for hours, sometimes playing only scales and arpeggios. *Prestissimo, fortissimo,* hands crossed, thirds, sixths, two keys at once, anything you can imagine, all the while stomping on the pedals and singing like a man utterly possessed. But this was his way of life. I heard him work like this many times at Marlboro, too, where he would slip into the nearest empty studio, even if there was only an upright, and go at it furiously for hours at a time. It was natural enough, I suppose, that some of his students felt the compulsion to do likewise. He had to practice that hard, and the assumption was that we should do the same. Besides, he expected it of us.

When I was very young I was, I believe, one of those "natural" pianists. I had facility like a lot of youngsters when they're 8, 10, 12, and don't have to think about it. That feeling of naturalness began to disappear, however, when I started my studies with Mr. Serkin, primarily because of his insistence on an ever bigger and bigger tone. The word he used with me more than any other in his teaching was "More, more, more." I could never give enough sound to please him. I would play until my fingers almost bled and still he would plead, "More, more, you play like a baby; you will never be heard with an orchestra." Well, I don't pretend to have ever achieved one half the strength that man had at the piano, but I have seldom been criticized for being unheard with an orchestra. So I'm not convinced that that degree of power is necessarily a requisite for successful performance. But he believed it very strongly. It was simply his way, and, needless to say, it worked magnificently for him. As for myself, I developed some serious arm problems in later years as a result of that approach and had to drastically alter both my work habits and certain basic ways of dealing with the instrument. The naturalness largely returned.

M A R L B O R O

I went to Marlboro for maybe eight, nine summers at an early age. It was, and remains, an extraordinary place. I heard music making there I shall never forget. It was there that I first heard, among countless other great works, the Schubert Octet, one of my favorite things in all of music. It was two o'clock in the morning; I was standing in a light mist, peering through the window of a studio at the corner of the campus. I remember there were Felix Galimir, Sasha Schneider, Herman Busch, and others all legendary to me now, some of them in quite a state of inebriation at that hour of the morning. Sasha particularly. But playing like gods! Especially, I remember Sasha and Herman Busch having an argument over the tempo of the fourth movement Andante. Sasha was really quite gone at this point. He got up and took Mr. Busch by the arm, and said, "Come, Herman, didn't you ever take a beautiful woman for a walk in the park?" And as they strolled around the room, arm in arm, the others proceeded to play the movement at the most beautifully seductive tempo imaginable. I can't hear that movement today without feeling that tempo. I criticize every group that plays it faster—and every one does.

One evening, when I had brought his daughter Liz home after a date and was sitting in the car with her on the driveway at the farm around 10:30, Serkin came out to investigate. Now, any other father would have said to his daughter, "You have to come in, it's late." But instead he said to me, "You have to go home now so you can get up early and practice."

I felt I heard Mr. Serkin play his best at Marlboro. He was more relaxed, if you could ever have called him relaxed, more himself at Marlboro than anywhere else. He came closest to playing truly beautifully there. Beauty of sound was, in my opinion, never paramount in Serkin's music making. Rather, it was how he thought about the music that was most important. Sound was just an incidental part of it all. And yet I can recall so many instances at Marlboro, a turn of phrase here, a concept there, inspired moments that were just exquisitely beautiful in a way I didn't always hear from him at more formal concerts in New York or Philadelphia.

C O U R A G E

Back in the 1970s I gave a recital at Curtis at Mr. Serkin's invitation. I was playing the *Hammerklavier* in those years. Why, in my right mind . . . I should never have . . . but I did. There, sitting in the front row, was Serkin. Now, that was tantamount to suicide to walk out and play the *Hammerklavier* with

Rudolf Serkin right under your nose. Somehow I got through it. In all my previous performances of the sonata I'd played the opening with two hands, as almost every pianist in the world does. I hadn't wanted to make a mess of it at the very beginning. Moments before going on stage I had a fit of conscience. "My god, Serkin's sitting there; if he sees me play that with two hands, he'll never forgive me. He won't speak to me the rest of my life." I had never even practiced it with one hand. But, I knew, it had to be all or nothing. Da-dum! And for the only time in my life I hit it absolutely perfectly. Every performance thereafter, when I attempted it with one hand, I made a god-awful mess. He was so proud of me afterwards. "Wonderful, with one hand! Courageous of you! Wonderful." "Thank you, Mr. Serkin, I do it all the time."

When I was 19 years old I joined Columbia Artists in New York. It was my first management and a momentous event in my life. All of a sudden here I was, part of what was perceived to be one of the most prestigious such organizations in the country. It was big time and I had many apprehensions about it. I went to Mr. Serkin for advice about it. I told him, "Mr. Serkin, I've just signed with Columbia. I don't know these people, I don't know how to deal with them. Can you help me?" He just dismissed me, saying, "Don't worry about those things. They're unimportant. Just love your music, that's all. Don't think about anything else, just love your music." I came away so irritated, so angry with him. How could he give me this naïve, simplistic answer? I needed help, I wanted some practical advice. I remained angry with him for a long time. I thought he just hadn't heard me or didn't care. But, you know, I came to realize that that *was* the only answer. Because one is powerless, really, to deal with a lot of those other things. Really quite powerless. The only thing you can do is try to play as beautifully as possible, be true to the music, true to yourself, do the very best you can, be ready, love your music. He was right. In time, you always realized he had given you precisely what you needed to hear.

Ruth Laredo
New York, January 12, 1997

Ruth Laredo, born in Detroit, has been a soloist and chamber musician since her studies with Serkin at the Curtis Institute from 1959 to 1964. She was the first pianist ever to record the complete solo works of Rachmaninoff and has also stimulated a revival of interest in the music of Scriabin. She has been on the faculty at Yale and Curtis, and in addition to her many master classes performs regularly at the Metropolitan Museum Concert Series. Two Steinway parlor grands line a wall in the studio of her sunny Upper West Side apartment.

There are many layers of truth when it comes to Rudi, as you've probably heard. I think he may have been one of the deepest and most complicated people I've ever met. I probably understand more about him now from this perspective, at my current stage of life and after he's been dead for some years, than when I was studying with him.

TEACHING STYLE

I remember bringing a pencil to my first lesson with him. After he made a comment about Bach and as I was writing it down, he said, "What are you doing? Put that away." I was puzzled. He said, "Either you're going to remember this or you're not. Put your pencil away." This philosophy also applied to markings on music. There's not a single mark that I got from him in any of my music. I think that attitude is very, very smart. Everything has to be up here, in the head. So it became a habit with us to pay attention.

He'd sit in the corner and listen to us play. He was probably the greatest listener I have ever encountered. He absorbed what you were playing. It was something to behold. Nothing else entered his consciousness, you knew that just by looking at him. If you saw him at a concert or at an informal event where music was played, he was so completely involved in the listening experience that nothing, absolutely nothing, would distract him. And when you have a teacher who listens to you with that kind of intensity, you learn to listen at a different level from what you had been doing.

Once in a while I was asked to come and have my lesson at his house, which was just a few blocks away from the Curtis Institute. He had a beautiful studio upstairs on the second floor. The piano was covered with a great big blanket: he believed in handicaps. This was one of his quirks—he imposed it on all of us and we're all stuck with it now. He did not want you to play on a good piano with the lid up. You were to play on a crummy piano with a blanket covering it, so that you would have to struggle. I understand why he did that. It is extremely pleasant if you have the opportunity to play on a good piano, but most of the time that's not what happens. So it was good training for us, although we complained about it. And these were conditions that he also imposed on himself. It was part of his way of life.

What the composer had written was supreme, and you were never to say anything against a composer. That was one of the laws. I remember talking with some friends in front of the dining hall at Marlboro about the Tchaikovsky Trio. It's an extraordinarily long trio, and in the last movement musicians traditionally take an immense cut that is indicated, I think, by the composer. You are supposed to go from one sign to another sign and leave out everything in the middle. Not knowing that Rudi was around, I said, "I'd better not take that cut with Rudi looking over my shoulder." But in fact, he had been listening to us and he jumped right into the conversation at that point and said, "Well, I wouldn't take that cut because I wouldn't want Tchaikovsky looking over my shoulder." He always felt that the composer was looking over his shoulder all the time, and he had total identification with the music.

At Marlboro Rudi made it clear that he wanted us to attend Casals's master classes whether we were string players or not. I was often the pianist who played for the string players in those classes, and gained enormously from that experience, hearing Casals talk and listening when he objected to the precepts I'd been taught. Rudi wanted us to do exactly what the composer had written, to the letter. But Casals would tell the string players, "If you have to change your bow, if you have to do this, or that, you've got to make it easier and use more bow. It doesn't matter what the music says." And that was really interesting to us, very stimulating. I think that was one of the great strengths about Marlboro: you could hear different points of view, and after you heard them, you decided what you wanted to do.

My attitude toward music was very much formed by Rudi. I know that I have internalized certain things that won't go away. It's rather like having parents: you don't know exactly what they said to you, you didn't write any of it down, but you know that you are the living proof of what they educated you to be. And I think that's the way it is with Serkin. And that's the best kind of teacher.

Rudi was very, very busy in those early years. He would be away on tour for a very long time, and he wanted us to play for someone in his absence. He thought I should play for Mr. Horszowski. I liked Mr. Serkin's energy and drive. I also admired Mr. Horszowski as a musician and looked up to him when I heard him play, but he was not the teacher for me. I don't know how Serkin realized it, because I certainly wasn't about to tell him. But I know that he became aware of it, because he said, "You're not going to have any more lessons with Mr. Horszowski."

I learned a lot from the Vengerova students. They had a piano method, which we never had. Rudi never taught technique, he never taught how to play the piano: he taught us music. If you couldn't play very well, you'd fall behind. I know that not everybody was suited to study with him—at that point, anyway. He only took people who were already formed in some way, as young artists. So it was helpful for me to pal around with these students of Vengerova, who had a pedagogical method of how to approach the keyboard.

SERKIN THE MUSICIAN

One thinks of him in association with Beethoven, Schubert, Mozart, Brahms. I played those composers for him, he insisted on that, but he also knew about any other music you'd care to play for him. After I graduated from Curtis I was involved in a recording of the Scriabin piano sonatas. I wanted some guidance in this music, because I had never played it. I went to see him in Philadelphia. He was very kind, and I played a lot of the music for him. He was very helpful, very insightful, although this was Scriabin I was playing, not one of the composers associated with him. But if you asked him, he knew. He was like the Wizard of Oz: he really did know.

There was no show biz about him, that was absolutely true. When he walked onto the stage, he looked almost as if he were being hunted. Nothing like Arthur Rubinstein, who would walk out as if he were pleased to be there, or like Horowitz, who was very gracious and welcoming. Rudi's hands would be rolled up, like fists. You sensed a terrible conflict. He was extremely nervous every time he played. This can be very hard to understand if you think of how great a musician he was, his experience, his reputation, and all of the other elements that go to make up an international career like his. And yet, that didn't mean anything to him. At that moment he was simply a soul who was faced with the task of presenting us with this Brahms Concerto and he felt that it was too much for him: he did not know if he could do it.

He often played many wrong notes at a performance. I'm sure it hurt him almost physically to play wrong notes, but it was part of a Serkin performance, and you left it feeling elevated, enlightened. It was such an incredibly spiritual thing to hear him play. I don't know who does that today. I can't think of anyone. He was completely unique in that way.

CHAPTER SIX

Marlboro

Please do remember that Marlboro is the real world, the rest is only a nightmare.
—RUDOLF SERKIN (1972)

Bassoonist Sol Schoenbach remembered the day when Rudolf Serkin showed him the site of Marlboro for the first time: "We drove through all kinds of backroads—we didn't know where we were—until we suddenly emerged and saw a building and a dirt road. Rudi said, 'This is the place.' I thought he must be crazy. 'How are people ever going to find this place?' I asked. 'Well,' he said, 'they'll find it, you'll see. Give me good music and some good musicians, and they'll find us.'"[1]

Serkin's words were prophetic: the Marlboro Music School and Festival, located on the secluded hilltop campus of Marlboro College in southeastern Vermont, has not only found its audience for more than fifty years, it has inspired the founding of respected string quartets, including the Cleveland, Guarneri, Orion, and Vermeer; it has contributed players to a host of chamber music ensembles and countless symphony orchestra desks; and it has been emulated by chamber music organizations and festivals in America and Europe. An extraordinarily successful and influential enterprise, Marlboro is now also a fabled name with a fabled history. The driving force behind Marlboro was Rudolf Serkin, and for forty years his work as its artistic director was a third ever-present dimension in his already strenuous life of performing and teaching. As Marlboro's remarkable history is inextricably linked to Rudolf Serkin's life, so the inner laws and impulses of his intense and complex character are mirrored in Marlboro itself.

THE ORIGIN

The "prehistory" of Serkin's life at Marlboro grew out of the neighborly relationships in his Vermont community. One of his neighbors, Dr. Walter Hendricks, whom he had met shortly after World War II, had decided to found a small college on his Vermont property about 8 miles west of the town of Brattleboro. In 1946, Irene recalled, Hendricks "asked my father and my husband to give concerts for the benefit of the College, and announced them in the papers, even before they could answer."[2] The first such concert took place in Brattleboro in December 1946 and raised $3,600.

A few years later, in the fall of 1949, Serkin heard about the plight of three musical colleagues from the time of the Busch ensemble in Europe: flutist Marcel Moyse, his son Louis (a flutist and pianist), and daughter-in-law Blanche Honegger Moyse (a violinist and Busch protégée) were stranded in Argentina and desperate to get out. As he had had to do so often over the previous decade, he looked for a way to help these emigrés and approached Hendricks about the possibility of the Moyses teaching music at Marlboro College. The president was eager to secure such a fine faculty, and the Moyses came to Vermont.

Meanwhile, Adolf Busch was attempting to recover from the breakdown in his career and health. Rosalie Leventritt wrote to Serkin of her concern: "I have the idea that Adolf feels now that he must put himself in order quite by himself and that even if we do lend him a little of our strength, he must not be made to realize this . . . The wounds are deep and I cannot judge if he will hold at this present status."[3] Those who loved him sought a way to help him out of his crisis, and one was proposed: "something for Adolf," a summer music school at Marlboro College near the Serkins' home in Vermont. Serkin did not originally intend to participate in Marlboro as actively as would his father-in-law. The day-to-day work would be done by Adolf, the Moyses, and the other Marlboro cofounder, cellist Herman Busch.

In 1950, Marlboro College announced the opening of its Music School with a summer session from July 1 through August 13, to be directed by Marcel Moyse with Rudolf Serkin as head of the Advisory Board. Principles that were to become the hallmarks of Marlboro date to this early beginning: participants were asked to submit their own requests for works to be studied during the summer, and scholarships were already in place to enable any gifted performer to participate regardless of financial resources. In that initial summer there were almost no resident students, except for violinist Philipp Naegele. Al-though Irene always insisted firmly that 1950 was really the first year of Marl-boro, it was only in the following summer that it was incorporated as a sepa-rate institution, while continuing to rent the Marlboro College campus. The first official season of the Marlboro School of Music was held from July 1 to August 18, 1951; when it attracted fifty-four participants, its future as a contin-uing venture seemed plausible. (Enrollment increased rapidly thereafter, to its current average of seventy to eighty musicians.)

Just as the musicians were preparing for their 1952 summer season, how-ever, Adolf Busch's death forced a change in Serkin's plans for his work at Marl-boro, as Irene described to Agnes Meyer: "A great part of the burden of the music school lies now on his shoulders. And we feel that the school in a way founded for Papi and his musical influence should now try to carry on as best as possible, so that what he wanted to teach and give to young musicians might still be handed on. But it is difficult."[4] Serkin, who had had absolutely no ex-perience in such a role and, given his complex temperament, may not have been especially suited to it, was called on to assume major responsibility for the administration of Marlboro. By taking up this work he was ensuring that what was intended to be a new phase of Busch's musical life would continue as a musical tribute to that life. Nearly twenty-five years later, his sense of mission had not changed: "Of course Marlboro itself is a memorial to Adolf Busch, who founded it," Serkin wrote in 1976, "and I try to continue as well as I can in his spirit."[5]

CHAMBER MUSIC AND
THE AMERICAN MOMENT

Serkin defined Marlboro as succinctly as possible in a letter of 1961: "You will see that Marlboro is not a camp nor exactly a school, but rather a gathering of professional musicians for the purpose of studying chamber music."[6] Before the 1950s, a general understanding or appreciation of chamber music in Amer-ican music had been rare. At a public lecture in Chicago in 1945, for example, Artur Schnabel observed that "the chamber music literature is being forgotten. To the young generation most of its works are unknown."[7] Classical music was dominated by European "stars," the larger-than-life orchestral conductors (Toscanini, Stokowski) and soloists (Heifetz, Rubinstein, indeed Serkin him-self). Furthermore, because chamber music requires a particular attitude and approach, a musician who had grown used to the solo spotlight might not nec-essarily be comfortable in the diffused light of collaboration.

To be sure, there had been a few isolated venues for chamber music before the 1950s. In 1918, Elizabeth Sprague Coolidge initiated the Berkshire Festivals of chamber music, and sponsored prize competitions, commissions, and radio broadcasts. In 1925 she established the Elizabeth Sprague Coolidge Foundation in Washington, D.C., which focused primarily on contemporary music. And chamber music concerts were held under the auspices of Ira Hirschmann's New Friends of Music in New York and the Gertrude Clarke Whittall Foundation in Washington, D.C. Significant as these efforts were, however, their impact was essentially confined to a small circle of Easterners. In the 1930s and 1940s most American concert halls were too large for the intimacy of chamber music, and there were only a handful of string quartets, like the Curtis Quartet, whose cellist Orlando Cole remembers that "audiences were very unsophisticated . . . Performing the last quartets of Beethoven was like playing Bartók quartets today." The desire to hear chamber music could not be assumed even in educated audiences throughout the United States.

Adolf Busch had long cherished the wish to play chamber music in "a relatively small community of professional musicians from throughout the world, of widely diverse ages and backgrounds"[8]—an ideal similar to what Serkin had encountered during his days in Vienna, where both Schoenberg's Society for the Private Performance of New Music as well as Eugenie Schwarzwald's summer communities (which Serkin frequently cited as an inspiration for Marlboro) had, in their distinct ways, provided him with models. It was not only the recollection of these European prototypes that influenced the concept of Marlboro, however; at just this time in postwar America, educational institutions in general were undergoing change. David Riesman, noted University of Chicago sociologist and Vermont resident, described the newly formed Marlboro College in Vermont as one example of this latest, egalitarian educational trend, a trend that sought

to diminish the barriers that existed even a few years ago between most students and their teachers. The emphasis at Marlboro . . . on the joint enterprise of faculty and students only makes more articulate and full-grown a pattern which is becoming widespread. It can be seen in the shape of the classroom, where the elevated dais is on its way out, to be replaced by the seminar table . . . Much as parents are no longer forbidding and awesome "governors" to their children, so college professors are no longer either remote figures of fun or remote figures of worship and fear.[9]

The central idea of Serkin's Marlboro shares much with this concept. The initial notion of teachers and pupils soon gave way to a more egalitarian mixing of seasoned musicians and talented young professionals. Experienced musicians would not dictate to younger ones, but all would play together in a spirit of shared discovery and reach a joint interpretation of the music at hand. That Serkin embraced this approach, so antithetical to the authoritarian style of most European teaching, testified "to what an extent a pianist from the heart of old Europe had become an American."[10]

Serkin, who, despite being counted among America's cultural elite, always remained in a certain sense the grateful immigrant, agreed with this assessment of the quintessentially American nature of the Marlboro concept: "Only in America," he once observed, "could Marlboro have happened. Nowhere else will you find this complete lack of selfishness, this coming together of musicians from all countries and all backgrounds, this dedication to the composer and his music rather than to the performer's glory."[11] The other founders of the Music School would surely have echoed these sentiments. One of Marlboro's early supporters, Serkin friend and author Dorothy Canfield Fisher, believed that the founders, as European emigrés, not only rejoiced in American openness but also enriched American values in the mid-1950s: "They had all become Americans. To give our country, their country, the especial service for which their lives had prepared them, they began this summer teaching and making of music . . . on faith in the idea that more and better music will make our materially prosperous American life more deeply worth living."[12]

THE MARLBORO CULTURE

If Marlboro was influenced by its time, it was and has remained a unique institution with its own unique culture. According to Busch's original notion, musicians would congregate without pay at a summer retreat to study chamber music together in a relaxed setting. Performances would occur only as a byproduct of study. This was the vision that Serkin pursued, and despite all the changes at Marlboro, much of this spirit characterizes it even today.

Although Serkin liked to allude to an often-quoted aphorism of Robert Schumann and describe Marlboro as "a republic of equals," *family* is probably a more accurate metaphor—and a very traditional, 1950s-style family at that, with Serkin as the father, and a strong one, indisputably in charge. As in most families, procedures and rules were often unspoken and sometimes mysterious, driven by inherited (sometimes barely conscious) traditions and evolving

Peter Serkin and Mieczyslaw Horszowski, with Peter's oldest daughter, Karina
PHOTOGRAPH BY GEORGE DIMOCK. REPRODUCED WITH PERMISSION

experiences rather than by a more explicit and formal codification of agreed-upon principles.

Marlboro was, of course, founded quite literally by two families, and within the "marriage" that produced it, the Moyses and the Busch-Serkins often seemed like "in-laws,"* their interactions sometimes taking on a charged quality when their distinct Francophone and German backgrounds, their egos, and their musical predilections and ambitions clashed. And those who constitute Marlboro—the musicians, but also the staff, the relatives of participants, and a few old-time supporters—continue to be known among themselves as "the Marlboro family." Given all the strains to which families are subjected, it has to be said that the Marlboro family has been on the whole a remarkably happy one.

Central, too, and distinguishing Marlboro from other summer institutions

---

* With the marriage of Marcel Moyse's daughter Marguerite to Björn Andreasson, son of the second violinist of the Busch Quartet and a kind of "younger brother" to Irene, the two families became something very like literal in-laws.

such as Tanglewood and Ravinia, has been the notion that Marlboro is to be more of a school than a festival, a concept that Serkin was fierce in defending. In declining a 1961 invitation from Ravinia's artistic director to bring Marlboro to Ravinia for a week, Serkin wrote, "What we are trying to do in Marlboro might be unfavorably influenced by publicity and too much spotlight. We really dedicate those seven weeks at Marlboro to serious and intensive studies of chamber music, and the concerts are just a by-product of those studies."[13] Nearly twenty years later, Serkin reiterated this fundamental tenet: "In advertising Marlboro this summer, the fact of the Festival is stressed too much. After all, it is a school of learning and listening, and I am afraid we might end up with only the Festival in the near future."[14]

In Serkin's day, this concern for preservation of its particular culture could also be seen in the austere, almost Quaker-like plainness of Marlboro's self-presentation. Such an insistence on understatement can, of course, be a profound form of elitism, but the culture of Marlboro was in fact very much like Serkin himself, a man whose contradictory nature was both elitist and egalitarian, exclusive and inclusive, demanding and generous, controlling and liberating.

THE 1950S

In the early years of Marlboro, Serkin was still unsure of the ultimate shape the school would take. In 1951 he even contemplated the possibility that it might one day evolve into a year-round music school.[15] Early programs in the dining hall, which served as a concert space, had often included solo works or entire solo recitals. (These were helpful in boosting ticket sales, particularly when the soloist was Serkin.) Structures were casual and the atmosphere spontaneous. "It grew on its own," Serkin told the makers of a 1957 German documentary.

As the decade progressed, it fell to Serkin as artistic director to develop the financial, administrative, and creative leadership that would stabilize the institution. At first, he financed the summer program largely out of his own pocket, but despite his great reluctance to ask for money he was soon forced to look for outside support, turning to those affluent music lovers such as Dannie and Hettie Heinemann, Rosalie Leventritt, and Eugene and Agnes Meyer who had supported him since the 1930s and had become his friends. Mrs. Leventritt, whose son Victor and son-in-law T. Roland Berner served as legal advisors to the Serkins during the founding of Marlboro, suggested after a deficit following the 1951 season that Serkin establish a small executive committee "if you are seriously considering continuing."[16] Although Agnes Meyer had not expected

Bach's Fourth Brandenburg Concerto, *Marlboro, August 23, 1953. Marcel Moyse and Louis Moyse, flutes* PHOTOGRAPH BY CLEMENS KALISCHER. REPRODUCED WITH PERMISSION

to be a major contributor initially, writing to Serkin that "all of my efforts now have to go into social work to strengthen the civil defense of our nation here at home,"[17] she soon assured Serkin that she would come to his assistance.

While these Washington and New York families were supporting Marlboro from the outside, Serkin also found support from his civic-minded neighbors in Vermont. The attorney Paul Olson had been key to the incorporation process,[18] and the financial side of Marlboro in Vermont was handled until his retirement by Henry Z. "Zee" Persons (1892–1978) at the Brattleboro Trust Company, who had rented the Serkins their first Vermont house on Ames Hill in West Brattleboro and for whom Marlboro's Persons Auditorium was named when it was completed in 1962.

Although Serkin regularly donated to Marlboro his income from occasional summer concerts at Tanglewood or in New York, until 1960 every season was still ending up in the red. But with characteristic tenacity in holding to his ideals, Serkin would not entertain the idea of reducing the debt by making the school more commercial or relocating it. "If anything," he told *Time* magazine, "we will be more selective in the future."[19] (Furthermore, putting the situation in perspective, Serkin wrote to Irene in 1958 of their friend Gian Carlo Menotti's financial problems with his Spoleto Festival, telling her that "he's sold everything he owns. You see, there are worse things than Marlboro.")[20] Serkin's network of friends again supplied what was needed when George Szell recommended that Frank Taplin, the former president of the Cleveland Orchestra, organize Marlboro's finances. Taplin established an annual fund and an endowment fund, major steps in placing Marlboro on a firmer financial footing.

In 1956 Serkin invited Harvey Olnick, a respected musicologist from Toronto who had met Serkin through the Leventritts, to organize Marlboro administratively, much as Taplin had organized it financially. Olnick developed general procedures, establishing a chamber music library and a legendarily complicated but effective system of scheduling rehearsals, improving fund-raising solicitation, and raising faculty salaries (to $100/week, though the practice of giving salaries was discontinued in the early 1960s).

"I thought Marlboro should aspire to be something like the Institute for Advanced Study at Princeton," Olnick recalls.[21] To raise public recognition, he invited journalists to Marlboro; one of the results was a pivotal *New York Times* article in 1956, whose author, Howard Taubman, wrote about his visit as if he had discovered Shangri-La, enthusiastically hailing the work at Marlboro as "music-making in its finest and most joyous state."[22] Serkin was largely pleased by Olnick's aggressive plans for Marlboro and liked him personally, but Olnick had bruised some egos along the way and left Marlboro in 1957.

In November 1958 bassoonist Anthony Checchia took over as business manager (he is now also artistic director of the Philadelphia Chamber Music Society), and in 1960 concert manager and artists' representative Frank Salomon also joined the Marlboro staff. Working as a team, Checchia and Salomon directed Marlboro's activities from then on and continue to do so today, having returned to Serkin in kind the same sort of constancy that he himself showed in his many professional and personal relationships. Both of these men, so close to Serkin for so many years, have absorbed his values completely and demonstrate those traits of familylike regard, tact, and intense loyalty that are so characteristic of Marlboro and were so important to Serkin in particular.

Even more critical than securing financial and administrative support, however, was Serkin's oversight in establishing Marlboro's musical community. The expertise of the original cofounders covered piano, woodwinds, and most of the strings. After Busch's death in 1952, however, there was a clear need for a mentor to the violinists. Serkin turned to Felix Galimir (1910–1999), who, as a young man, had heard Serkin in Vienna and who first met him at the home of the Leventritts while a member of the NBC Symphony in New York. His Galimir Quartet (consisting of Felix and his three sisters) had been closely associated with the Second Viennese School in post–World War I Vienna, and Galimir could bring an intimate knowledge of this music to Marlboro. After 1954 he remained an influential and beloved "senior" at Marlboro for forty-six years and was especially valued for his assessment of potential string players.

In 1956, two years after Galimir's arrival, Serkin invited another violinist to Marlboro whose impact was at least as great. Alexander (Sasha) Schneider, his close friend, was to become a member of Marlboro's inner circle (a photo of the two men laughing together, their lined faces full of mischief and merriment, is inscribed by Sasha to Rudi: "From one goi to another goi, with all my thanks for an unforgettable week of Mozart"). A mercurial, earthy man, Schneider had an especially powerful effect on young musicians and a passionate interest in mentoring their musical development. "Marlboro is very important for *young* musicians who are extraordinary talents," he told Isaac Stern in a televised interview, "who play beautifully their instruments, but who have no idea about music." Accounts differ as to the reasons for his departure in 1977 (a rebuke about his high-handed coaching style? his exploiting Marlboro as a warm-up for New York concerts? a disparaging remark about Adolf Busch's violin playing in front of Irene?). For his part, Serkin regretted the rift, writing in a letter to Frank Salomon in 1980: "You know how much I miss Sasha and I am not certain that he knows."[23] It was Schneider who conducted Mozart's G major Piano Concerto (K. 453) at Marlboro in 1991 with Peter Serkin as soloist to honor Serkin's memory in the first Marlboro season after his death.

Serkin's musical leadership was also focused on constituting the group of younger participants. He looked not only for musical talent and the recommendation of a sponsor, but also for the right "personality, which, of course, should fit into the Marlboro family."[24] In later years he even thought of instituting an interview at auditions to ensure the fit.* Sometimes family connections themselves seemed to weigh heavily. In 1955, for example, after a disgruntled Felix Wolfes complained to Metropolitan Opera baritone (and Fritz Busch son-in-law) Martial Singher about their working relationship the previous summer, he concluded (correctly) that "if only one of us two should work

---

* When he discussed this idea with one of his children it was pointed out to him that great musicians could sometimes be "assholes." Serkin challenged, "Name one!" "You!" came the reply. Whereupon Serkin shot back, "Oh, but I'm not a great musician!"

Alexander Schneider and Rudolf Serkin PHOTOGRAPH BY WOODROW LEUNG.
REPRODUCED WITH PERMISSION

in Marlboro again, it will of course be you, since you are part of the 'family' there."[25]

Serkin established a ratio of one to six between senior and junior partici-pants (today it is closer to one to two). Stemming from his pedagogical belief that it was critical to form a talent before too much time had passed in estab-lishing bad habits, he also instituted an age limit of 25 for younger partici-pants, a guideline not always strictly enforced. Some lines in a 1960 letter to Serkin from pianist John Browning may serve as a summary of what Marl-boro had been able to achieve for its musicians during its first ten years: "I cannot tell you in adequate words how much Marlboro meant as a clarifica-tion of musical ideas, a source of wonderful friends, and a place where one's idealism about music is restored and strengthened . . . It was as if many things came to life."[26]

By the end of the 1950s Serkin had instituted significant changes. For Ver-monters, many of whom had become accustomed to enjoying the music infor-mally, sitting on the grass outside the dining hall, tickets were now required. Furthermore, with Marlboro now engaged in heightened fund-raising, blocks of season tickets were set aside for donors, leaving fewer for local residents. In spite of Irene's best efforts, the intimate local atmosphere was giving way as the institution developed.

Even more than in its ambience, however, the critical changes at Marlboro concerned the quality of the music making. Initially Marlboro had included among its participants enthusiastic amateurs, whose fees had helped to fund the more gifted professional musicians (similar to the policy in Schoenberg's classes in Vienna). But by the end of the 1950s, this practice of mixing amateurs in among the professionals had dwindled and then ceased. Serkin attributed this critical change toward greater professionalism to the advice of Isaac Stern, who visited Marlboro in 1959.[27] Harvey Olnick, too, tried to persuade Serkin that his time should not be wasted with amateurs. But according to Felix Galimir, the increasing professionalization of Marlboro in the late 1950s was directly Serkin's doing, an outgrowth of his high expectations: "Let's be honest . . . he could not stand a bad performance. He was very unhappy if something was not up to his standards. So [the professionalization of Marlboro] is all his fault."[28] Galimir's view has the ring of truth. This crucial juncture at Marlboro, which determined its future identity and future renown, also reveals Serkin in his characteristic modus operandi, deferring to another authority when making a problematic decision and creating a certain opacity around the exercise of his power.

THE MUSIC AT MARLBORO

Over the forty years of Serkin's presence there, the musical repertoire at Marlboro was remarkably consistent, dominated by the Austro-German canon of chamber works. The music of Bach, Mozart, and Beethoven was performed nearly twice as frequently as that of the other great German composers, Brahms, Schubert, Haydn, Schumann, and Mendelssohn, who were also well represented. Serkin and other "elders" determined the programs for Friday, Saturday, and Sunday concerts as well as informal Wednesday evening concerts only days in advance, so audiences attended without knowing what they would be hearing. Certain seasons produced their own particular emphases: in 1955 scenes from Mozart operas; in 1958 and 1959 an ambitious series of Bach cantata programs under Blanche Moyse; in 1963 a brass quintet; in 1964 a series of madrigals. To honor Adolf Busch, at least one of his compositions was included nearly every summer, with Irene Serkin often taking part in the performances.

Beyond studying the canonical works of chamber music, Marlboro also explored and resurrected more obscure examples of eighteenth- and nineteenth-century music, as well as providing a platform for twentieth-century chamber music.* In the very first season, the Moyse Trio performed music by Florent Schmitt (1870–1958) and Bohuslav Martinů. In 1959 Serkin made a concerted effort to invite contemporary American composers such as Walter Piston, Aaron Copland, and Roger Sessions to Marlboro to hear their works performed. Sessions's visit to Marlboro included two hours spent discussing his string quintet with the musicians, who then performed it, moving him to write later that he could "really not imagine a better performance."[29] This effort to include the exploration of contemporary music at Marlboro received a boost from the Fromm Music Foundation in 1960 and from a Rockefeller grant in 1963, which made it possible for an impressive list of contemporary composers to spend time at Marlboro. Serkin's friend Leon Kirchner, eminent composer and professor of music at Harvard, was named to guide the program and did so for ten years.**

Felix Galimir remembered that Serkin "wanted us to play Schoenberg. He didn't really like the music, but he thought Marlboro was a place where Schoenberg should be played."[30] Kirchner thought of Serkin as a kind of King Arthur, glad to send his "knights" out to have their musical adventures. Some, however, felt that Marlboro's involvement in contemporary music was half-hearted in comparison with the overwhelming dominance of canonical chamber works in the daily music making.

Over the years, some critics claimed to have identified a "Marlboro style," characterizing it as a "blend of young fire with searching musicianship,"[31] a

---

* A representative two weeks during the 1976 season included works in rehearsal by the following composers: Allanbrook, Amram, C. P. Bach, Bartók, Beethoven, Berg, Bliss, Boccherini, Brahms, Britten, Bruch, Busch, Buxtehude, Colgrass, Danzi, Debussy, DeFalla, Durey, Dvořák, Erlich, Gastyne, Glazunov, Glinka, Gounod, Haydn, Hindemith, Hummel, Husa, Ives, Janáček, Keldorfer, Kodaly, Martinů, Mendelssohn, Milhaud, Mozart, Petzold, Poulenc, Prokofiev, Rachmaninoff, Ravel, Reger, Riegger, Rossini, Rust, Schoenberg, Clara Schumann, Robert Schumann, Sessions, Sibelius, Spohr, Stravinsky, Thuille, Villa-Lobos, Vivaldi, and Kurt Weill.

** Felix Galimir, Siegfried Palm, and Schoenberg's son-in-law Rudolf Kolisch were the senior musicians especially involved with this program. Composers who visited Marlboro in its first thirty years included John Adams, David Amram, Samuel Barber, Howard Boatwright, Elliott Carter, Paul Chihara, Aaron Copland, George Crumb, Luigi Dallapiccola, David Del Tredici, David Diamond, Lukas Foss, Jeffrey Jones, Tonu Kalam, Earl Kim, Barbara Kolb, Christopher Lanta, Fred Lerdahl, Marc Neikrug, and Walter Piston.

"sweetness of tone and richness of feeling,"[32] or the "delicate refinement of every detail, precise articulation and playing with the greatest possible vibrancy while making room for each separate voice."[33] For some this refinement could be excessive: in a letter of 1963, Samuel Barber took issue with the Marlboro tradition of what he considered to be exaggerated phrasing,[34] and in 1967 critic Michael Steinberg also described how, to a fault, Marlboro "players italicize every upbeat, every downbeat, every change of harmony, every phrase ending, every phrase beginning, every melodic contour, every change of texture."[35]

Not only the artistic director but also a fully engaged participant, Serkin set Marlboro's musical standard most of all by his own music making. Although his summer season at Marlboro meant weeks of responsibility and very hard work rather than recuperation, it also meant a chance for Serkin to be more relaxed as a musician, to play for the joy of playing without the extrinsic demands of the professional music world, to share his "deepest self"[36] with others.

In the 1950s Serkin's performances at Marlboro included solo works such as Beethoven piano sonatas or Bach's *Italian* Concerto, and unexpected collaborations, such as a *Schöne Müllerin* with Martial Singher in 1955 or Fauré's Quartet in C minor with Blanche Moyse, Leslie Malowany, and Herman Busch in 1957. In 1956, the two-hundredth anniversary of Mozart's birth, Serkin performed four Mozart piano concertos with Alexander Schneider conducting the Marlboro Orchestra. In the same year, which was also the hundredth anniversary of Robert Schumann's death, a program was also devoted to that composer's music, with Serkin playing *Carnaval* and the Trio in G minor, Op. 110.

In 1959, enjoying the collaboration of Harold Wright, Myron Bloom, and Benita Valente, Serkin played in (and made a famously lovely recording of) Schubert's *Der Hirt auf dem Felsen* and *Auf dem Strom*, giving three further performances of these pieces in the 1960s. He also performed the *Trout* Quintet four times in the 1950s and 1960s, but after 1969 performed no other work by Schubert at Marlboro. Five times over his forty years there he participated in performances of Bach's Fifth *Brandenburg* Concerto. Over the years Serkin also liked to play Dvořák and Smetana and works by those composers with whom he had a personal tie: Busch, Reger, Busoni, and Martinů. (Serkin's musical participation at Marlboro after 1964, when performances began to be systematically taped, is covered in detail in the discography.)

Not all of Serkin's music making at Marlboro necessarily ended with a performance. Representative is the 1976 season when, over the course of the seven weeks of the summer, the 73-year-old Serkin rehearsed eleven different works, four of which (Mozart's *Kegelstatt* Trio, Bach's Third *Brandenburg* Concerto, Schubert's *Der Hirt auf dem Felsen*, and Reger's Clarinet Sonata) were not performed, but seven of which did see a performance: Bach's 14 Canons on the First Eight Bass Notes of the Aria Ground from the *Goldberg Variations*, the Fifth *Brandenburg* Concerto, Concerto for 3 Pianos in C major; Mozart's Woodwind Quintet in E-flat major, K. 452 and Sonata in D major, 4 hands, K. 381; the Busch Quintet, Op. 35; and the Beethoven *Choral Fantasy*, Op. 80.

The *Choral Fantasy* had been on his schedule every single year since 1957. Written in 1808–1809 and scored for vocal soloists, piano, and orchestra, it anticipates Beethoven's Ninth Symphony both in its form and in its dramatic power. Serkin recognized that this piece would be a fitting conclusion to the summer: because even the other pianists, extra woodwinds, and members of the extended Marlboro family could be onstage in the chorus and celebrate the past season with one another, it was truly a piece for the entire community. (Of course, it also has a wonderful part for piano solo!) It became a Marlboro tradition. Although Serkin tried to call a halt to it on more than one occasion, participants insisted that it continue. It was their way of honoring him, and eventually became a quasi-sacred event: "There was the great man counting time with pursed lips, holding a difficult trill for its full six beats, in a work he had performed over a hundred times," Joseph Roddy wrote in 1985. "The sight of their old idol still so unvain in his art . . . set off unashamed tears on stage and some out front."[37]

THE 1960s

During the 1960s, when Marlboro's fame—and Serkin's—were at their peak, Serkin's presence at Marlboro had a profound influence on American attitudes toward chamber music. "For a renowned soloist to commit an entire three months to chamber music was rare," Arnold Steinhardt writes. "With this act [Serkin] put an official stamp of approval on the genre and served notice to music lovers, managers, and the musicians themselves that it was all right for soloists to associate with chamber music—even to *be* chamber musicians."[38] A new generation of musicians, wary of careerism and bourgeois tastes (including the taste for virtuosic star soloists), began to eschew "the Horowitz-Heifetz-Toscanini pressure cooker"[39] and embrace a chamber music ideal that called for depth and intensity, mutual listening, a communal approach to the music.[40]

Contributing to the changes at Marlboro that enabled it to be so influen-

Beethoven's Choral Fantasy, *Marlboro* PHOTOGRAPHY BY GEORGE DIMOCK.
REPRODUCED WITH PERMISSION

tial in the 1960s was the completion of the festival auditorium in 1962. For
many people, the "handsome wooden structure resembling a Norse banquet
hall,"[41] with its larger audiences, became a symbol for the new era and for the
irretrievable loss of the old, intimate Marlboro. Serkin was aware of the consequences of change and ever mindful of the delicate balancing act required to
retain Marlboro's distinctive character: "I would like to see the Marlboro idea
expand, in that with more money we could bring people here whether or not
they can afford it," he told Alan Rich when the new hall was opened. "But ours
is a very fragile idea. Already I think we have too many participants here, or at
least enough. With more people we might begin to think about more popular
programs, and this would be too bad. Audiences are good, because they help
the acoustics of the hall. But only if they let us do what we want to do."[42] Tony
Checchia remembers: "Things were in a constant state of flux, but in a good
way, because nothing was fixed in stone. Formulas were the last thing that he
was interested in! We took it year by year, learning what makes most sense for
the total operation . . . He tried to find people who were generous in spirit, generous with what they had to offer."[43]

By the sheer force of his artistry and personality, Serkin acted as a kind of magnet to the many generous people who were drawn to Marlboro, but throughout the 1960s he was also actively engaged in finding them. He solicited a Music Advisory Committee for the School; agreeing to their titular role on it were friends such as Eugene Ormandy, Samuel Barber, Gian Carlo Menotti (who accepted the invitation hoping that Serkin would in turn figure in his Spoleto chamber music series), Myra Hess, Fritz Reiner, Aaron Copland, Leonard Bernstein, Robert Shaw, and George Szell (whose reply to Serkin included a P.S.: "Pussi!"—Viennese slang for a kiss).

Serkin was also liberal in extending invitations to other renowned pianists. In 1962 Sviatoslav Richter wrote of his regret that, although he would like to know the chamber music repertoire better, he could not accept Serkin's invitation to come to Marlboro.[44] As early as 1956 Glenn Gould had offered to send one of his compositions, a string quartet, to Marlboro for performance and had thought of being an informal participant.[45] He did visit Marlboro in 1973, in fact, to record a program on Casals for the CBC.[46] Serkin also tried to lure his good friend Vladimir Horowitz to join him in a recital of the four-hand Schubert F minor Fantasy during the 1975 Marlboro season, but the visit never materialized.[47]

The luminary who did accept Serkin's invitation, however, and set his mark on Marlboro from 1960 to 1973, was Pablo Casals: his presence at Marlboro during the 1960s became the defining feature of its completed evolution from a "backwoods outpost"[48] into a chamber music shrine known the world over. The idea of bringing him to Marlboro required a greater financial commitment than had been normal at the school. Agnes Meyer in particular supported the plan by sending Serkin a check for $3,000 in 1959 and promising to send an additional $3,000 the following year.[49] Serkin was soon able to write her that Casals had accepted his invitation, adding that "without your encouragement I don't think I would have asked him. But you made me feel almost like a special ambassador, and with that feeling of an important mission I could even talk about 'arrangements' (though very blushing)."[50]

Casals stayed for two weeks. After the summer, Serkin wrote to Agnes Meyer of the impact his visit had made:

> He is our only link with a great past; his accumulated knowledge and wisdom, his genius for his instrument, and his genius for music, combined with an incredible gift to teach and say in very *simple* words the results of a lifetime of studies—all this is a feeble attempt to describe the inspiring, and with many of the students transforming effect his visit has made . . . His playing and teaching gave courage

to so many of the listeners and participants, who (although technical experts on their instruments) are afraid to show feeling in their playing, and Casals shows that being emotional does not mean being sentimental. This seems to me the main message he has to give to this generation.[51]

Beginning in 1962, Casals regularly remained for the entire Marlboro season, conducting concerts with the Festival Orchestra and holding a series of master classes each year. He and his wife, Marta, occupied a renovated farmhouse with a great sugar maple in the front yard and a stone terrace in the back, abutting a rolling meadow. In his autobiographical reflections, he described his appreciation of Marlboro's special mix of nature and music, calling it "a veritable Arcady of music."[52]

Participants in the main were thrilled to be able to be so close to Casals. Yo-Yo Ma stated: "I'll never forget the way his mind and body would radiate vitality the moment he raised his baton. That was an inspiration for a lifetime."[53] Arnold Steinhardt, who recorded Bach's *Brandenburg* Concertos and Mozart and Beethoven symphonies with Casals, remembered that under his baton there was "an energy and suppleness that is rarely heard in an orchestra usually weighed down by the demands of good ensemble."[54]

After a while, however, Casals's presence created a delicate situation that taxed Serkin's diplomatic skills, for it shifted the balances at Marlboro: rules were bent to accommodate him, and his orchestral concerts, which some thought to be of questionable value in proportion to the time they demanded, had become a large part of the program. (The exception that was made for Casals of emphasizing orchestral works ceased after his death.) Some were disturbed by what they considered the cult of personality that centered on him.

Despite these internal tensions, and perhaps even adding to them, Serkin, the only undisputed authority at Marlboro, never abandoned his self-effacing, respectful attitude toward Casals. He felt, clearly, that the Spanish cellist presented the Marlboro musicians, especially the younger ones, with the most precious gift possible: close exposure to great musicianship tested by life and history. Less beneficial to the Marlboro spirit was Casals's extremely conservative musical taste: he refused to attend rehearsals or performances of music written in a post-nineteenth-century idiom. Casals's presence at Marlboro sealed the changes that had occurred since the beginning of the decade. Serkin, who believed in the value of change, seems to have been pleased with the direction things took during these years, though many felt that the loss was great and the price paid, heavy.

Marcel Moyse (1889–1984), particularly, felt eclipsed by Casals and directed

Pablo Casals. Facing him are Alexander Schneider, Jaime Laredo, and Pina Carmirelli
PHOTOGRAPH BY J. M. SNYDER. REPRODUCED WITH PERMISSION

his anger at Serkin. A master of the French tradition, the former first flutist of the Opéra Comique was a "superbly instinctive musician with an unfailing sense of form and vision,"[55] a great colorist and also a vivid teacher, who would, for example, compare the lush low register of the flute to rich homemade mayonnaise spooned up from the bottom of the bowl.[56] As word of his teaching spread in the 1950s, the woodwind population at Marlboro increased. To assuage his hurt feelings in light of Casals's dominance and to enable him to continue to offer his special gifts, Serkin and Checchia arranged for him to teach new week-long woodwind "seminars" before the Marlboro season opened.

Although these seminars were in great demand, and although Serkin indicated his respect for Moyse by encouraging all instrumentalists, not only woodwind players, to attend these classes, in 1966 Moyse decided that he would not return to Marlboro.[57] One year after Casals's death in 1974, however, reconciled by Serkin's backstage congratulations at a concert celebrating his eighty-fifth birthday, he did in fact return, directing the Mozart Serenade in B-flat, K. 361 for the seventh time (seated in an overstuffed armchair).[58] Serkin was gratified: in encapsulating the 1977 summer season, he wrote admiringly that "best of all Marcel Moyse, though physically weak, is full of fire and inspiration."[59] Moyse continued to teach at Marlboro until his death in 1984.

In the 1960s Marlboro was often invaded by guests who made the journey for Casals's sake alone. The 85-year-old Queen Elisabeth of Belgium visited the festival for the first time in 1962, adding a certain uncharacteristic glamour to Marlboro's image, as the *New York Times* reported: "Gesturing at the white buildings scattered on the hilly campus with music pouring from every window, she said: 'This is the first music school of the world.'"[60] In 1967, at the height of the Vietnam War, Serkin received a more controversial visitor, one who had helped to trigger the generational conflict characterizing so much of American society during those years and from which Marlboro was not immune. Vice President Hubert Humphrey had known Serkin since 1947, when, as mayor of Minneapolis, he had met Serkin after a concert there. For the older Serkins Humphrey's visit was to be simply that of another music-loving friend with whom they wished to share their wonderful institution, but for many of the young participants passionately opposed to the war, he was the symbol of an immoral government.

In July 1967, FBI helicopters filled with security men descended on the secluded slopes of Marlboro, interrupting Pablo Casals's orchestra rehearsal and evoking outrage among the musicians. "Those times were just unbelievable," Sol Schoenbach remembered. "Serkin didn't know what to do. He was ready to destroy the whole festival, and said, 'If you insult my friends, I'm leaving.' We finally worked out a compromise: the angry students wrote letters of protest and Serkin promised to give all the letters to Humphrey. And he did just that: he handed him about seventy letters, which I'm sure Humphrey never read."[61]

Disruptions such as these were secondary, however, and peripheral to the central purpose of the institution: "Marlboro isn't about the famous people," Irene once observed, "but about the young people." For the young participants especially, their time in the highly charged atmosphere of Marlboro loomed in the memory as a formative experience sine qua non. Pianist Murray Perahia called his first year at Marlboro "a kind of revelation."[62] For Richard Goode it was "perhaps the most important part of my musical education."[63] Yo-Yo Ma, who participated for four years in the early 1970s, remarked that "the sense of fun, camaraderie, and common culture found at Marlboro remain with me as the essential elements of good music making."[64]

TOURS AND RECORDINGS

By 1965, Marlboro was launched on various initiatives to bring its music to a wider audience. As Harold Schonberg put it, Marlboro was "beginning to assume the characteristics of a major national industry."[65] Serkin's attitude toward one of these initiatives, Music from Marlboro, the touring offshoot of the summer's work, reflected his ambivalence about the price of Marlboro's success. The first full-fledged Music from Marlboro season began in a spectacular way in 1965, when Serkin and a group of thirty-eight participants embarked on a four-and-a-half-week tour of Europe and the Near East under the auspices of the U.S. Department of State. After this launch, three different ensembles toured East Coast cities, each group playing one program approximately a dozen times. Later, a fourth group was added, and ultimately groups would perform in three hundred communities around the country. Seniors like Galimir and violinist Pina Carmirelli advised Serkin about the constitution of the various groups, and Frank Salomon acted as agent, but although Serkin did not himself perform on these tours, he made the preliminary—and ultimate —decisions about performers and programs.

In the first season the touring programs were characterized by a variety of ensembles and periods: one program featured Mozart's C major Trio, K. 548, Irving Fine's *Fantasia for String Trio*, Brahms's songs with viola, and Dvořák's E-flat Piano Quartet, Op. 87. The *Boston Globe* critic Michael Steinberg praised the "succession of contrasted but related timbres and fabrics" in the sequence of the program, although he was critical of most of the performers.[66]

One of those performers, cellist Madeline Foley, unhappy with the experience, wrote to Serkin of her dismay: "I felt so much of the music was trampled on and kicked around—mostly due to too fast tempi and roughneck playing."[67] But flutist Paula Robison has speculated that such conflicts of approach may not have been entirely unanticipated: "Although Mr. Serkin, I believe, tried to put together ensembles that were congenial musically and personally, I think he also purposely did the opposite on occasion. It made it necessary for us to get along, to adjust and cooperate."[68] At Marlboro, the side of Serkin that liked to keep things lively, to destabilize and provoke change, could prevail more easily than had been possible at Curtis.

Eventually, Serkin came to worry that the tour might eclipse the fundamental focus of the Music School. "I am really getting scared that sooner or later Marlboro will be mostly preparing for tours," Serkin wrote to Salomon in 1977,[69] and again in 1980: "I am really deeply worried and disturbed by the problems this great success of 'Music from Marlboro' poses."[70] Despite the fact that the program provided performing opportunities for the senior musicians and professional seasoning for the newcomers, despite the fact that it enabled Marlboro to build and educate chamber music audiences throughout the United States (as did the Music from Marlboro broadcasts: ten different thirteen-week series of 60- or 90-minute radio programs, beginning in 1968), these benefits could not entirely offset Serkin's fear of distorting the pure focus of the summer's work.

Less fraught was Serkin's project to issue the music of Marlboro on recordings. Columbia Records' first releases from Marlboro were two Mozart concertos in 1956, followed in 1957 by the Beethoven Octet in E-flat major, led by Marcel Moyse, and the Dvořák Serenade, Op. 44, directed by Louis Moyse. Serkin also saw the value of producing recordings of chamber music by composers who might not be marketable enough for Columbia but would find an audience among Festival attendees and other chamber music aficionados. The Marlboro Recording Society was established in 1969, funded by Dr. and Mrs. André Aisenstadt, with cellist Mischa Schneider serving as artistic director and Paola Saffiotti as administrative coordinator. As in every other aspect of Marlboro activity, Serkin's personal attention to the production of these releases was detailed and deep. Twenty recordings have been issued in this series, originally available only through the Marlboro organization.

THE ARTISTIC DIRECTOR

In the evolution of Marlboro, among its "family members" and in the various forms of its musical life, Serkin was always at the center. Even the one summer when he was away from Marlboro, in Switzerland in 1979, Serkin's unseen presence was palpable. As oboist Neil Black described it, "He is to be met with every day, everywhere: in those lingering conversations between musicians in their off-duty moments, and he is constantly the point of reference . . . It is curious to know, to respect, even to feel an affection for a man whom one has never met face to face, but this is how it is."[71] Serkin served as the ultimate musical arbiter and advisor, about individual interpretations of specific works and wider questions requiring his "musical wisdom." At times, "when approached by young musicians wanting to find answers to musical queries," pianist András Schiff recalls, "he could be elusive. This wasn't unkind or rude but the wisdom of someone who knew that there weren't any easy answers or short cuts."[72]

Despite his genuine, unaffected modesty and his gestures toward egalitarianism, whether deciding concert programs by committee or helping out in the

Lee Luvisi, Cesar Saerchinger, Rudolf Serkin, James Levine, Anton Kuerti, Claude Frank
COURTESY OF PETER SERKIN

dining hall, Serkin remained in a position of absolute authority and would protect that authority if he felt it necessary. When the administration once proceeded without his approval to award two summer fellowships, he wrote, "Even though I agree with the choices . . . I wonder who was consulted about them? In any case, I strongly feel that the Artistic Director, whoever it may be, has to be consulted first."[73] This special status was sometimes evident in little ways. Richard Goode remembers: "One noticed at Marlboro that Felix Galimir was 'Felix' and Madeline Foley was 'Madeline' and Sasha Schneider was 'Sasha,' but for most people, it was 'Mr. Serkin.'"[74] And it was Mr. Serkin's opinion that counted above all others: "If you disagreed with him, well, you had to leave," Felix Galimir remembered. "He would cool; the relationship would cool off."[75]

Fulfilling his obligations as artistic director required of Serkin a phenomenal commitment of time and energy, coming as it did after the stresses of a year's touring and teaching. Cellist Siegfried Palm observed that it was "very exhausting for the seniors who may no longer be so young to work for six hours a day sometimes, on three different pieces, rehearsing and playing them

Kim Kashkashian and Rudolf Serkin PHOTO BY ANNA BUCHTHAL.
REPRODUCED WITH PERMISSION

themselves,"[76] and here too, Serkin set the standard. During the Marlboro weeks, Irene remembered, he would often come home at one o'clock in the morning, get up and be back at the school by nine o'clock. In addition, there were always guests at meals and on the farm. Once each summer, the Serkins would host two hundred people at a picnic on the Guilford lawn during the last week at Marlboro.

According to Irene, Serkin was an effective leader in part because he had the traits of a good politician: he could easily mingle with people at receptions but, she added, be mentally absent at the same time. (He also had a politician's gift for remembering names, even after great amounts of time had passed.) Tony Checchia, too, remembers Serkin's interpersonal skill: "He was extremely good with people. He understood their motives, whether good or bad. He was very quick and unusual in that way. He was also very capable of seeing the third and fourth ramifications of everything we would do. He would anticipate like a great chess player."[77]

Frank Salomon describes the power of Serkin's leadership: "Mr. Serkin's policy changes were attempts to constantly improve the Marlboro experience.

For example, when Mr. Serkin noticed that having many of the same people return each summer made things a bit inbred and stagnant, he introduced the policy of accepting new participants on a one-year basis. A second year was a possibility, even a third. But then it was time to give others the opportunity. This was one of the most important actions Mr. Serkin ever took, since it has meant that each summer at least a third of the seventy-five participants are attending for the first time with their enthusiasm, talent and sense of discovery energizing the whole community."[78]*

"Mr. Serkin had specific ideas about how Marlboro should be presented," Checchia recalls. "He liked everything to be very plain, nothing fancy, nothing that even hinted at commercialism or sales."[79] His attention also took in the smallest details of language in written presentations of the enterprise, such as fund-raising efforts. In one document, for example, he circled the phrase "It is vital to the success of Marlboro that its participating artists . . ." and wrote a question mark next to the word "success," indicating that in this, as in everything, any suggestion of easy self-satisfaction was anathema to him.

Nevertheless, he was aware of the public relations aspect of the undertaking and supported it if it met his conception of the reality of Marlboro. Although he rejected a request to make a documentary about Marlboro because of his "fear that it might do something to the special atmosphere and so, naturally, it could not be an accurate documentary,"[80] he was scrupulously exhaustive in his insistence that the collection of 25 years of Marlboro programs known as the Red Book be distributed to everyone associated with Marlboro, primarily for its historical value, perhaps, but also because it was in his view an appropriate kind of publicity.

Though not necessarily by calculation, he was also adept at presenting the harmonious and uplifting side of Marlboro to the many journalists who came for the Marlboro story. When told about one participant's claim that "At every concert . . . there are 70 jealous musicians in the audience," Serkin responded: "Not everyone can come with a pure heart. But we welcome those who can't and hope that Marlboro is the medicine to cure them . . . If you scratch a person, his goodness comes out."[81] Of course, Serkin could be devilish, too: feeling that the performers at a particular rehearsal needed privacy, he had an associate discreetly ask all auditors to leave the room. After everyone else had left and the last visiting critic was on his way out, Serkin went up to him and asked, as if shocked, "What?! You're leaving?!"

---

* This policy does not apply to "seniors."

Serkin oversaw everything at Marlboro without seeming to, making his intentions clear but always indirectly. His good friend Luis Batlle observed that "very often, when he had a problem that he wanted to communicate, the link was Irene. It wasn't that he would send her, exactly, but he would have talked to her about it, of course, and she sensed that he needed someone else to deliver the message."[82] This characteristic indirectness could border at times on insincerity. It could also have an unkind aspect:

> One summer, a well-known musician was apparently not greatly admired by Rudi. Near the end of the summer, he and Rudi were sitting together outside somewhere, and he said he'd love to come back the following summer and play this and that, and Rudi remained silent. The musician noticed that and said, "You *would* like me to come back, wouldn't you?" And Rudi said, "What a question!" That's a reasonable way of dealing with the situation, but what was less nice was that he repeated this story. It circulated. He prided himself on it.[83]

In fact, Serkin had to field countless requests to attend Marlboro. In the 1970s and 1980s it attracted many musicians who saw it, perhaps inevitably, as "a certifying agency" for a chamber music career, a private club where one could establish important contacts. "Most [students] come up through the major eastern conservatories where they know a Marlboro elder who will push for their admission," one participant observed. "That's the way it is in the music profession and Marlboro epitomizes that situation."[84] Just as Marlboro had not been immune from the political pressures of the 1960s, so it could not remain untouched by the intensifying pressures of the classical music world. (It has made efforts to resist these pressures, as, for example, in its practice of not charging audition fees.)

Serkin's leadership role extended to the Marlboro tradition of madcap practical jokes, which past participants like especially to remember. His lifelong love of practical jokes was no doubt an ingrained part of Serkin's nature, perhaps a compensatory release from the enormous discipline of his life, but at Marlboro it also served the strategic purpose of diffusing the tension of the younger participants, who knew that they were always being judged. Legend has it that Serkin was the first to throw a wadded-up napkin (directed at his daughter Judith) in the dining hall after the first dinner, starting a tradition of napkin throwing that has continued after his death. (Even Casals and Queen Elisabeth were forced to take refuge under an umbrella.)

The charged high spirits also extended to romance, and Marlboro acquired a reputation for sexual liberation. Serkin, no prude, did not discourage this

The Serkins at their annual picnic for the Marlboro musicians, Guilford, Vermont
PHOTOGRAPH BY CLEMENS KALISCHER. REPRODUCED WITH PERMISSION

side of Marlboro; it is said that when an elderly lady once rebuked him about the free atmosphere, he replied, "That's the way we like it." Over the years, Marlboro summers have resulted in countless marriages (including those of Anthony Checchia to Benita Valente and Judith Serkin to Rudolph Vrbsky). Of course, when Marlboro's robust heterosexuality was heightened—as sometimes happened—to the point of outright machismo, participants who did not share in it could well feel alienated.

Ultimately, however, for all the real tension behind the idyllic image of Marlboro, and for all the sometimes frustrating indirectness of his leadership, Serkin's standards at Marlboro were admired far more than his displeasure was feared. The greatest skeptics were usually won over by his genuine devotion to music, and as the very embodiment of Marlboro and all it represented, he inspired what can only be called love.

Rudolf Serkin in the Marlboro dining hall, Tony Checchia behind him on his right
PHOTOGRAPH BY WOODROW LEUNG. REPRODUCED WITH PERMISSION

THE MARLBORO LEGACY

If Busch's spirit hovered over Marlboro as it began to evolve, by the time of Serkin's own death in 1991 he himself had become so overwhelmingly identified with Marlboro that some people actually doubted whether it could in fact go on without him. Although it would be a strange irony if an institution devoted to communal enterprise were so dependent on one man for its existence, the fact remains that at his death Marlboro had become Serkin's institution absolutely.

Reporting on the memorial service held for him in Carnegie Hall, the *New York Times* observed that "to a great degree, it was not Serkin's pianism that was celebrated so much as his Marlboro persona, his role as a teacher and as an advocate of the notion that chamber music represents an ideal toward which soloists must strive."[85] Upholding that ideal, Marlboro today continues in a sense as Serkin's own living legacy, just as it once was Adolf Busch's. With typical tact and family feeling, it was only after Irene Serkin's death in 1998 that Marlboro announced its new artistic directors. The selection of pianists Richard Goode and Mitsuko Uchida ensured that the high musicianship and integrity characteristic of Rudolf Serkin would continue to inform the next generation of Marlboro leadership.

Speaking with a visitor who had attended a first concert there after Serkin's death, Irene reflected on the fact that in their forty years at Marlboro she and Rudi had never missed a season but once, during his sabbatical year when they went to the Engadine. Otherwise they had been at every Wednesday evening informal concert, every Friday, Saturday, and Sunday concert. Looking around at the simple, shedlike auditorium and the green hills surrounding it, at the relaxed mix of musicians and audience members milling about, still caught up in the music, she added: "Do you understand now what Rudi was?"

Voices

PHILIPP NAEGELE

BLANCHE MOYSE

ARNOLD STEINHARDT

Philipp Naegele

Marlboro, Vermont, October 4, 1997

Philipp Naegele, a violist, is William R. Kenan Professor of Music (Emeritus) at Smith College. Born in Germany, he received his Ph.D. from Princeton University and studied under a Fulbright at the Vienna Academy of Music. He has also served on the faculty of Amherst College. We meet Mr. Naegele, a trim and slightly formal man in his sixties, in his summer house in Marlboro, which formerly belonged to the Serkins.

---

1 9 5 0

When I was in graduate school I saw an announcement that Rudolf Serkin, Adolf Busch, Marcel Moyse, and some others were giving lessons in chamber music at Marlboro College in the summer of 1950. Since their names were household words and revered, I wrote to Marlboro College, but received no reply. Therefore I wrote to my parents, who knew someone who knew Herman Busch. Herman called Adolf, and Adolf said, "Well, he should come." And I got a letter saying, "You're accepted!" So I arrived by train in Brattleboro and got out to Marlboro College and went up to the dining hall. Marcel Moyse and Blanche, who was pregnant, and Louis [Moyse], who was smoking his pipe, were sitting there, and Herman was deep into his beer. I looked around and saw nobody else and asked what was going on. They said, "Well, a number of people have driven up and taken a look and gone away again, but you *stay!* Adolf will be here tomorrow, we'll work something out."

I couldn't leave anyway, because I'd come by train, and there was no train back till the next day. Adolf did show up the next day and put his hand on my shoulders and said, "You're staying! We are going to be playing some good music. I'm very happy you're here, we'll see what we can do. It'll be a good summer." The result was that two or three times a week I'd drive in an old Ford over to Guilford where we would play chamber music in Adolf's studio. The people available were the Busch Quartet minus the violist. And there was Irene. And there was Rudolf Serkin. And me. And we'd play quartets and quintets. All summer long. And then I'd go back to Marlboro, and practice—nobody else around except two pianists and one flutist, that's all.

There would be Sunday afternoon concerts, because Adolf would come over and play Bach solo sonatas in the dining hall for an audience. And the Busch-Serkin Trio would play. And the Moyse Trio would do a lot of Martinů. It was great, great music making, with a chamber orchestra recruited from the neighborhood and as far away as New York City, Bennington, or Boston. The audience was the neighborhood, as it is still on Wednesday nights: friends and neighbors.

BUSCH AND SERKIN

The second summer (now officially the first), there were more people. Afterwards Busch came over and said, "My wife thinks you don't look so well, you need some rest and feeding, so why don't you live with us for a while?" So I went over to Guilford and lived in that little shed next to what is now Judith Serkin's house and got some lessons and good food.

This was typical for Adolf, by the way. In the fall of 1951, they needed a violist for a concert at the Southern Vermont Arts Center in Manchester. It was to be the standard Busch Quartet minus the regular violist, who was ailing. He said to me, "Why don't you play?" "I don't have a viola." "Oh, that's not a problem, I'll get you one." He brought me a viola made by his father. A real box. He's playing on a Stradivarius, and I'm playing on this red box. I said, "I can't do this." "All right, go to New York and we'll borrow one from my friend Karl Berger, a Swiss violin maker." So I did get a viola from him. And then we had three rehearsals. And I had to survive Beethoven, Op. 59, no. 1 and Haydn Op. 76 without rocking the boat. But that was his attitude.

So I stayed. And it changed everything. "You're going to become a musician. Why don't you stop going to Princeton Graduate School and live with me?" The way to get a doctorate was to get an honorary doctorate. That was his message: Don't write a thesis, don't do all that. Play! Practice! And then get your degree on the basis of merit, as Sir Donald Tovey had secured one for Adolf in Edinburgh. But I kept going to graduate school, because I had a scholarship and I thought I might need the security of a degree later on.

Adolf's attitude toward music history was that it was nothing but a bunch of anecdotes and gossip. And yet his studio was lined with complete editions that were turned out by musicologists, who did a lot of heavy lifting in order to prepare those editions of Schütz and Bach, Mozart and Brahms, which he was perfectly happy to consult. He did make this connection, all right, and they respected me for my academic background. Serkin would ask me things, and if I didn't know the answer to their questions, he would say, *"Wozu habe ich dich studieren lassen* [What did I have you study for]?" As if to say, *"We* didn't study, why should we know?" And yet, more often than not, they knew an answer, I think probably out of their dedicated intellectual curiosity, because they were totally self-educated, and very profoundly so, as it turns out.

There was also an admiration for the academy. They were good friends with Sir Donald Francis Tovey, who was the quintessential scholar-musician, and they had no problems with that. I think they just objected to academic pursuits becoming a substitute for general musical ability. I think they probably would have preferred the last second violinist sitting in an orchestra to the last Ph.D. teaching music appreciation. They had a home-grown, practical, hands-on, craftsmanlike attitude.

Adolf was the unquestioned elder statesman of the two. Nothing that Adolf could say or do was going to be a problem for Serkin. It wasn't that he took orders from him, it was simply deference. I always found it particularly moving, because in those years Serkin was the great virtuoso and practiced and practiced and practiced, while Adolf was a composer and chamber musician, and because he had other interests in his later years did not maintain his technique in the same way that Rudolf Serkin did, with the same relentless dedication through many, many hours of practice. And yet Serkin would never ever question Adolf's preeminence. He was thinking about technique, and about how he could adapt his massive hands to the limits of the narrow keys of the piano. He was thinking *all* the time about how to get just the right attack to start the Beethoven Fourth Piano Concerto and would work relentlessly on it. And yet he never would have conducted, he would never tell anybody else how it should go.

If you asked him what tempo something should be in, he wouldn't tell you. But after you took a tempo he would say, "It's too fast." He would never say, "Listen to me." He would never demonstrate. He said that he had found his own way and, given the right attitude, habits, and talent, you will find yours. But there was no law, except integrity and seeking out the composer's intent.

Casals thought in terms of laws, and he considered himself the executor of them and made no bones about saying so. There were laws, such as variety, that art is like nature, that no maple leaf is exactly like any other maple leaf, and no note is the same as any other note, there must be a constant up and down— which is all very well, but in the hands of lesser artists it boils down to very little. Serkin would never talk about that . . . He'd never *talk* [laughter]. And when you rehearsed a piece, he'd just say, "Do it again. Play it over." At the most he'd say, "I think you should come in a little earlier." But no adjectives. No descriptive paragraphs about what this piece is about.

And yet he'd be highly critical if your playing didn't reflect a vision, similar to his at least, of the significance of that particular piece. And that's why he was so worried about certain works, was very protective of them, and actually tried to keep them from being played by most people at Marlboro, they were so precious to him. Smetana's Piano Trio, for example, was holy to him, the Mozart Clarinet Trio, the Dvořák Piano Quartet in D and the Piano Quintet.

He must have had some kind of feeling that if pieces are not played right, they actually hurt, that they're not immune to what we do to them. And that must be behind this extreme sensitivity to everything that goes into a performance, the motivation of the artist (is it self-serving?), the depth of the artist's conception, the reception of the work, the demeanor of the person on the stage—everything that goes into an intelligent performance of the piece affects the piece. I think he must have been in great agony listening, more often than not. His presence was the presence of the Great Conscience.

After Busch's death, Serkin tried to limp along. All of Marlboro was in a sense an Ersatz for Adolf Busch. The only way he could replace Adolf was through a very large number of people at the same time. Yet Rudi was not a different man after Adolf died. I don't really remember his grieving, although he would often have a serious look on his face, intent on preserving Adolf's values in founding Marlboro.

MARLBORO IN THE SIXTIES

Serkin was the kind of man who needed someone out in front. He was a force in himself, but he always preferred another person as his executor. So after Busch's death, he began to defer to Sasha Schneider. And then he deferred to Casals, and finally he deferred to the public relations flurry that came along with Casals.

Serkin was ambivalent about the circus around Casals. Casals at Marlboro played the role of the master, the authority figure. And this was totally opposite to the ethos of the place. Serkin would go to every rehearsal that Casals conducted, to every master class, for *hours*. Casals was trying to get the Marlboro orchestra to play the opening of a Bach Suite in a certain way and went over it hundreds of times. Undoubtedly, many people began to wonder why, but Serkin was sitting out there, even though everyone would have accepted it if he had been practicing instead. He preserved our sense of community in this way.

In private, Serkin might say, "I'm not so sure I really like the way he plays

Bach." But when he and Casals played together Rudi was incredibly good at accommodating to Casals without compromising himself. He let Casals have an orchestra, even though it was against the Marlboro practice. No conductors! Of course, there had been a chamber orchestra all the time, with leadership from the violin, but this was a concession to Casals.

Marcel Moyse had wonderful pedagogical principles that he communicated, despite his use of alcohol and his tendency to self-aggrandizement. He was a great raconteur and his house was always open to large groups for fondue. When Casals died, he became the Old Man in Residence at Marlboro. Then Horszowski became the Old Man, but he was too modest a person to carry off the role.

No one would have predicted that Serkin would live so long, because he put himself out so much and did not spare himself. He had a unique combination of greatness and modesty. Rudi was the only person I know whom you could put on a pedestal and after looking all around in the world, still keep up there. He never made any claims other than being totally dedicated to his craft. Just to be taken seriously by Rudi was wonderful approbation. It meant more than anything else to me and always will.

Blanche Moyse
Brattleboro, Vermont, June 3, 1995

Violinist Blanche Honegger Moyse, born in 1909 in Geneva, studied violin with Adolf Busch and made her debut with L'Orchestre de la Suisse Romande. For many years a member of the Moyse Trio with her father-in-law Marcel Moyse and his son Louis, after 1949 she served as chair of Marlboro College's music department for twenty-five years. She established the Brattleboro Music Center in 1949, and since retiring as a violinist in 1966 has dedicated the majority of her time to the study and performance of the choral works of Bach. When we speak with her she is vigorous and direct at the age of 86.

COMING TO MARLBORO

After World War II my family went to Argentina, which had become pro-Nazi, although we did not know this, only to find that Perón had taken over the government and that it was no longer safe for French people. When Busch and Serkin heard about our situation, they recommended us to the president of

Marlboro College, and after about one year, our whole family, including my in-laws and three children, came to this county.

In 1949, right after we arrived, I founded the Brattleboro Music Center, hoping to give us a professional activity in the winters in addition to teaching. Then the next year, Busch and Serkin said to us, "Why don't we do what we have always dreamt of and start a music school? We are a very good group. We can do that." And we did. But for several years, Marlboro College was on the verge of default; they couldn't pay our salaries; and one of us (my husband or I or one of my in-laws) always wanted to leave. I remember, though, in the early years Rudi would say to me, "Look, if you're not happy here, tell me, and I'll recommend you to another college." But whenever I thought about really leaving, I'd tell myself, "No, you can stay." Then, one day about ten years later, when I said to Rudi, "I think that now I really *would* like to change," he responded, "Ah no, not after all you have created here! No, no. You must not change any more!" As we continued to collaborate in Vermont, I came to be close to Serkin, but we were never really intimate—not that it would be easy to be intimate with him.

Most of my contact with Rudi, naturally, was at the Marlboro Festival, and if Adolf had not died so soon, I'm sure the Festival would have remained a school because he loved teaching so much—to involve everyone in music making. It was really his joy, and he wanted everyone to become good. Adolf was not afraid of bringing musicians to Marlboro who were not that good and helping them to become better. But Rudi was not like that; he couldn't *stand* mediocrity. He just wanted to bring in first-class people to begin with and then try to have them become better. He wanted everything to be at the highest professional level.

So, after Adolf's death in 1952, the character of the Marlboro Festival changed, little by little. For many years we did not know whether it was going to survive or not because it was very difficult to find money. In fact, I believe that for quite some years Rudi personally supported the Festival. But he didn't want that to go on forever, and it took many years for the Marlboro School and Festival to establish itself.

CHANGES AT MARLBORO

After Adolf died, Gösta Andreasson, then second violin in the Busch Quartet, was invited to Marlboro, but Gösta stayed for only one season because he didn't feel at ease there. Felix Galimir then came to Marlboro to replace Gösta, but some years later Serkin also invited Sasha Schneider, at which point a lot changed. Rudi gave him complete authority, which Sasha accepted very easily. Of course, his authority was not official, but Sasha didn't need a title. He was quite a presence. He loved life. He loved women. He loved to have fun. He rarely deferred to anyone. And he had a kind of royalty about him that made an official title unnecessary. Sasha was also a wonderful musician, although not very refined; for example, he didn't like the last Beethoven quartets because they were too serious. That was not Rudi's attitude at all, of course, who, deep down, had a diamondlike devotion to music, a reverence for its greatness. Still, Sasha could be respected for other qualities, such as his joy of life and of making music, and there were many benefits to having him at Marlboro, because he always had lots of young people around him, whom he brought with him. So, over the years, more and more young people came to Marlboro to benefit from contact with both of these artists, each of whom had a kind of glamour and following of his own. And I remember this as a very successful period for Marlboro in general, although not so much for my family.

As cofounders we were a part of the Festival, of course. In fact, my father-in-law had his own court of wind players and many singers (in fact, Tony Checchia also came to many of his classes), and I did my work kind of on the side. Clearly, it was Schneider who was the fashionable "up-front" star; so in many ways there were two trends going on at once. But even though Sasha was the boisterous bon vivant at Marlboro, it was truly and fully Serkin's operation. He could also depend on Tony Checchia and Frank Salomon, both very loyal and good diplomats, to arrange what needed arranging when so many people need to get along with one another for several weeks. In his very last years, however, I do remember Serkin said to me that he was not always happy with what went on at Marlboro because he thought people were starting to make decisions without consulting him. And he was disappointed with the music making, feeling that there was too much politics and more interest in giving concerts than in learning more about playing better, just for the love of it.

CHARACTER

If one wanted to make a psychological study of Rudolf Serkin, it would be incredibly interesting, because his was a very, very complex character, unlike Busch. Busch was simple, all in one piece, and it was rather easy to see all of him. He wasn't very subtle, and he could be rude and mean if he was angry, but you always knew where you stood. But that wasn't true of Rudi, who was unpredictable, full of surprises. He could be adorable—and not only because it served some ulterior purpose (though he could do that extremely well), but also just because he wanted to be. And he could be very generous. At the same time, Rudi could be incredibly mean or fickle. It was always so disconcerting to me, because you never quite knew where you stood with him. My own theory is that his parents had never told him "Don't do this" or "Don't say that." And I think that from the very beginning, Serkin was looked upon as a prodigy, not only as a child, but also as a man. He was a great, great artist, and very often, to great artists everything is offered as if they were kings. In fact, he sometimes had a difficult time working even with people he respected very much because it was not easy for him to accommodate others in his space. I also think that because he was spoiled by those around him, he could act somewhat childlike: nice when he wanted to be, not nice when he didn't feel nice, and sometimes manipulative to get what he wanted.

For example, one summer Rudi asked me to organize the season. He wanted to play a Mozart concerto in August, and I knew it would be difficult to get an orchestra together. So at the beginning of the summer, I said to him, "I have to know now who you want. I will need bassoons and I really should get them soon." But Rudi answered, "Oh, we have plenty of time." Still, I insisted, "But I need to have the money beforehand." "No," he answered. So the weeks went by, and then two weeks before the concert, I could not find a bassoonist! With much effort I finally located one in Washington, who agreed to come—but only if we agreed to pay his wife's expenses as well! Of course I had no choice, and so we did agree. When I told Serkin about it, he asked me, "Why didn't you hire the bassoonist before now?" I replied, "Because you told me not to." And then he said to me, "Why did you listen to me?" These kinds of exchanges were not so untypical, and so over the years we had some difficult moments. I remember once saying to Irene, "An artist should also be a good human being," to which she replied, "Oh! You're asking much too much!"

So, I remember wonderful things about my relationship with Rudi and some very hurtful ones too—lots of them—but that does not diminish my affection for him, of course, or my admiration. I think he was a great artist and basically a wonderful man—perhaps with too much freedom to be the way he felt at any given moment, without concern for others. At the same time, he could also go very much out of his way to be kind. When we first came to Vermont, for example, we were suddenly expelled from the States, so Rudi drove us to Canada, lent us money, and arranged with friends in Washington to make our return possible. I also remember his moral outrage when we were billed for services that Rudi thought should have been rendered without charge. So he was also capable of doing fantastic things for others.

There is no doubt that Rudi was one of the great people in my life, although

I will never really understand how he could be so affectionate and loving at some times and then at others, say things that seemed intent on destroying. I adored Adolf Busch because he was completely open, and I would like to have been able to love Rudi in the same way, but he did not make it possible, especially after Adolf's death, when Rudi changed a lot. They say that a man can only become the man he is after his father has died. Certainly, Rudi was like a son to Adolf, so while it seems terrible, I think there is some truth to it. There may be heartbreak, but there is also something that makes the son continue forward on his own wings.

Arnold Steinhardt
Philadelphia, December 9, 1996

Arnold Steinhardt, a pupil of Ivan Galamian at Curtis and Joseph Szigeti, won the 1958 Leventritt Award and was Bronze Medalist in the Queen Elisabeth Competition in 1963. Since 1964 he has been first violinist of the Guarneri Quartet and has appeared throughout America and Europe as a recitalist and soloist. At our meeting at Curtis, where he is on the faculty, Steinhardt is very cordial despite his busy schedule, with a certain cool quality about him.

I first came up to Marlboro at the end of 1958. Then in 1960 I was in the service and had a two-week furlough, so with my army clothes and my hair shaved off I went to Marlboro where they allowed me to stay for two weeks. I heard the last concert. Then I couldn't keep away. I was there every year, year after year, and after that parts of years. It was great.

SERKIN MAKING MUSIC

I don't think Rudi was an easy man to understand. The man was driven, driven to work, and he was completely obsessed and overtaken by music. Some of this is intuitive, I don't have hard evidence, but if you place any kind of value on the way a person's face looks, you could see a deep suffering in Rudi's face. I suspect that he was a man who had experienced grief and personal difficulty at a very deep level. Maybe that was one of the reasons for his high-jinks humor: the other side of him was to just let all hell break loose and to behave like a 13-year-old. Serkin was such a wonderful combination.

It may be a corny cliché to talk about an artist having to suffer, but that was certainly a component in his greatness as an artist. He not only had to over-come the darker things in order to be a musician, but he also had to struggle with the difficulties of becoming an outstanding pianist, as well as with the dif-ficulties that he perceived in the music itself. None of these things were easy for him.

For example, the way that he dealt with music was hard to pin down. He never made obvious choices for musical problems, I feel, and that was his greatness and sometimes that was his weakness. Because not all Serkin per-formances were equally great. There was a great variety. Not that that's not true of all artists, but I thought that was especially true of Rudi. Sometimes, where anyone else would have decided, "Well, in this part of the Schubert Sonata you have to go in this particular direction, otherwise it's not going to work" (and he was a very smart man, he knew that), he said, "That's too easy. I'm not going to take the easy route. I'm suspicious of easy routes. This is too great a piece to be easy. So I'm going to look at other avenues and see where they lead me." And often they led him into his greatness—sometimes they didn't.

Sometimes you wondered, "Why is he torturing himself about this? Just let him play it beautifully and naturally and freely." When it wouldn't work, when it was unsuccessful, you would ask yourself that question as a listener. But then when it worked—and many, many times it did work—it wasn't just excellent music making, it was an event. It was a major emotional event. On all levels, even visually, you know, to see him triumph over himself. Literally. It was amazing.

I remember during one of the summers I was at Marlboro, I lived in Mather House, just to the right of the dining hall, and next to it there was an extra lit-tle studio, a converted garage where a pianist would practice every morning and basically wake me up. I heard the pianist practicing scales painfully slowly, and I thought, "Who is this person who's playing here? It's obviously not a par-ticipant, it's somebody at an intermediate level playing scales very, very slowly." I thought, "Why do they let such a person who plays at this level in here?" And then the scales would slowly get faster and faster and in the stupor of my sleep I would think, "Well, it is getting better." You know? And by the time I was awake, the guy or the girl was playing at full speed and it was very good. But the process from slow to fast was very, very slow, painfully slow. And then, the next morning, it was the same guy or gal doing the same thing. Slow, slow. And I would ask myself again, "How did this person get this special dispensation to practice here?"

Then one day I got up early and went around back on the way to the din-ing hall, and bumped into Rudi, who was coming out of this room! And I put it all together, and I said, "Oh my God! It's him! It's the great man himself!" That's the way he did it.

MARLBORO EXPERIENCES

Rudi could be wicked. He would smile at you very sweetly and then, still with that sweet smile on his face, he would say something terrible to you. It was very funny. When we first performed the Dvořák Piano Quintet with Peter Serkin, we were all young. We were older than Peter, but very young and imbued with ideas of musical analysis of phrases, rather self-consciously in those early years, as most young musicians are. You know, you play intuitively up to a certain point, and then you start to think. Once you start to think, it's kind of danger-ous at times. We were thinking a great deal of enlarging the scope of that Dvořák Quintet and getting the most out of it, the phrasing, the dynamics, the ritards, and the accelerandos.

Before we played it in Nantucket we played it at Marlboro, a really high-powered performance. After the concert I walked around to the front of the hall and bumped into Rudi. And he smiled at me and didn't say anything. He had obviously just been to the concert. I said, "Well Rudi, what did you think of our performance?" He said, "Well, you know, they used to play like that in Vienna, when I lived there as a young man"—there was a long silence—"that's why I left." That was it. Oh, it was mean, but he said it with a grin on his face, and I wasn't crushed by it. He had made his point, and it was a very important point: we'd exaggerated too much, it was overkill, over the top. You know, maybe it was a very hormonal performance. You can forgive young people for having too many hormones.

Once, before I went to have dinner with him up in Guilford, already having a long history with him of reciprocal practical jokes, I bought a rubber fishing worm at Sam's Army and Navy Store in Brattleboro and when he wasn't look-ing I put it in his spaghetti. And he kept on talking. (This was also Serkin's humor, never to acknowledge a joke. Never ever.) And so I became impatient —"Why isn't he recognizing this?"— and he kept on eating, I kept on watch-ing, and nothing happened. After two or three moments somebody asked me something, and I turned away to someone else at the table, and when I turned back the worm was hanging out of his nose.

He put a cherry bomb in my car. He did do that. He had bought a cherry bomb, which you attach somewhere in the ignition, and had someone open the hood and attach it. I turned the car on and the motor seemed to be explod-ing. I thought it was the end of my car.

SERKIN'S TONE

I don't think Serkin was the kind of person who said, "This is what I want you to do in my camp, in my festival." He led by example. He was such a powerful example musically, he was so tough on himself in terms of the music. And so his example led to an incredible seriousness, a musical seriousness in the camp, because the specter of Rudi hovered over us all. But by the same token, there was the specter of Rudi the practical joker and there were all these gags going on, even when he was far away, all kinds of practical jokes taking place. He was responsible for the music and also for the humor in some kind of extended sense. He really set the tone.

People responded to him on a personal level, people from the audience, his fans, or his students. He made you feel as if he cared about you and he made you feel very special. He was a magnet: people were drawn to him socially, partially because of what he was on the stage, but also partially because of this aura around him when he spoke, because of who he was as a human being. That was really amazing.

And that was also an incredible gift for a person who is running something. Everybody left feeling "Rudi is my friend, you know, he really is my friend." I think that he needed that. A person who is inwardly absolutely resolved and quiet and peaceful could say, "I'll be friendly to *you*, I'll be not so friendly to *you*, *you* I don't like at all." But Rudi fed off all relationships to various degrees, and human contact had a really high value for him. And that might also have helped him in attracting new people to the camp.

You know, Marlboro, like any organization, is an organism and it evolves. In the 1950s you had a few incredible people and then there were some locals. Marlboro was nothing at all like what it was during the time I was there, when a slew of great, high-powered instrumentalists, like Leslie Parnas and Jaime Laredo and Shmuel Ashkenasi and Michael Tree and John Dalley and Dave Soyer, all arrived, wanting to play chamber music together. That was a golden period. It wasn't that way in the 1950s. And so it grows and changes like an organism, and then it changes again. Even when I was there, there were people who were incredible and there were people who were not so good. Nowadays, "not so good" doesn't do it. People are so anxious to go there that unless you're at the very highest rung of the ladder your chances are nil, forget it. The standards are incredibly high, so it's changed once again. I don't know whether musically it hasn't changed in another direction. Maybe the performances aren't as spirited, or spirited in a different way, but it's changed. And if it goes on for another decade it will change: it's just inevitable.

There's no stopping it, either. But certainly when I was there I had the feeling that it was bathed in a golden light. It was the most amazing, amazing experience. Part of it was a product of my own age: I was in my twenties and in a way I was like an empty blackboard just ready to be written on. There were so many experiences that were meaningful. Learning all that repertoire, most of it for the very first time, and acquiring all those ideas for the very first time from people like Serkin and Moyse and Sasha Schneider, Felix Galimir, these people who were my mentors. It was a great, great experience for me, and I think for many others.

And ultimately, it was Serkin's camp. The power was there, he was the one who was sitting on the throne. And he still does now, even though he's gone several years. You know, his spirit is there, hovering.

Serkin, his six children and their families, 1980. Upper right, standing: John Serkin. Seated: Elisabeth Serkin, Marguerite Serkin, Peter Serkin, Ursula Serkin. Lower left: Judith Serkin. PHOTO BY DOROTHEA VON HAEFTEN. REPRODUCED WITH PERMISSION

Serkin's life was music, and only illness and age could slow him down. When asked at the age of 71 about retiring, he replied with another question: "Retire from what? I am a musician."[1] In the late 1970s, he began to schedule fewer performances and to cancel more often. Canceling a concert in 1977, he had to reimburse the local arrangers $389 for their out-of-pocket expenses. "Don't try to play from memory any longer," advised Sasha Schneider in 1985, "and play only concerts with orchestras. Recitals are too hard on the *tuches*."[2] His final Carnegie Hall recital, in which he played the last three Beethoven sonatas, was held on April 8, 1987, fifty years after his debut recital in that hall. (As it happened, Peter Serkin had played his *first* recital in Carnegie Hall five days earlier, performing Wolpe, Takemitsu, and Messiaen, in addition to Bach and Beethoven's *Diabelli Variations*.) By the end he was playing only at gala season openings of major orchestras. He held his last concerts on September 28, 1988 in Chicago and on October 2 in Cleveland, playing the *Emperor* Concerto on both occasions. His manager, Mary Lynn Fixler, flew out from New York to be with him and thought he looked so exhausted that she wondered whether he would collapse.[3]

Now well over 80, he had survived many of his friends and all but one of his siblings. In the spring of 1989 he wrote a German acquaintance, "There is so much to write, to explain, but I was not, am not, healthy, little energy, canceling concerts is depressing, so forgive me!"[4] He canceled the few concerts he had scheduled for the 1989–1990 season (including the Reger Concerto, which was to have been recorded, in San Francisco). Playing Beethoven's *Choral Fantasy*, he performed for the last time in public at Marlboro's final concert of the summer, on August 13, 1989.

Serkin's illness, an intestinal cancer that had spread to the liver, was diagnosed in August 1990. Returning to the house for lunch one day after having gone to the studio to try to play, he told his son John: "I just sat there for three

The Gombrich family and Rudolf Serkin, London, probably early 1980s PHOTOGRAPH BY
CHRISTOPH LEHMANN. REPRODUCED WITH PERMISSION

hours. I just can't play anymore, so I study the scores. It sounds better that way
anyway."[5] It was "unthinkable," said Peter. "For the very first time in all the
time I knew him he no longer had it in him to play."[6] His friend and associate
Luis Batlle remembered bringing the score of the *Goldberg Variations* to Serkin's hospital bed. "Poor Rudi! He wanted to record them. He didn't know he
was dying."[7] When he was no longer able to speak, his fingers, moving on the
bed, showed that he was still working the piano in his head. Peter: "You could
see he was playing the *Goldberg Variations*. I just sat, quiet, and watched him
play. He went through the whole sixteenth variation, finished that one, then
the next, the seventeenth variation, and on."[8]

On March 28, 1991, he turned 88. He died at home on May 8. (Some press
reports had it that he died in a hospice, upsetting Irene, who had looked after
him to the end.) Condolence letters arrived in Guilford by the hundreds. Wrote
Max Rudolf, "I will never forget Rudi's power to express and give form to
music, his quintessentially musical nature [*sein urmusikalisches Temperament*],
and above all his incorruptability. When it came to artistic decisions, he knew
no compromise."[9] He was buried on May 31, the fifty-sixth anniversary of his
and Irene's wedding, in the presence of their children and grandchildren.

EPILOGUE

All over the world pianists and orchestras dedicated performances to his memory, at Marlboro that summer repeatedly. On the morning of September 23, Peter Serkin opened a memorial concert at Carnegie Hall with the Aria from the *Goldberg Variations*. With Judith Serkin playing one of the cellos, the program closed with the Adagio from Schubert's C major Quintet.

Irene said she didn't want to reign over Marlboro like a Cosima Wagner, but she remained feisty. Her health, which had not been good for some time, continued to decline, and having chosen her gravestone and seen to its wording—all that was missing, she said, was the date—she died on December 1, 1998, in the same house as her husband. The graves of Adolf and Frieda Busch and Susan, Irene, and Rudolf Serkin lie in a row on the far side of a churchyard in Guilford, Vermont, under lilac and rose bushes.

CARNEGIE HALL RECITALS, 1937–1987

11-Jan-37	Mendelssohn:	Rondo capriccioso, Op. 14
	Beethoven:	Sonata No. 21 in C major, Op. 53, "Waldstein"
	Reger:	Variations on a Theme by J. S. Bach, op. 81
	Schubert:	Drei Klavierstücke, D. 946
		No. 1 in E-flat minor
	Schubert:	Impromptus, Op. 142, D. 935
		No. 4 in F minor
	Chopin:	Four Etudes, Op. 25
		No. 2 in F minor
		No. 10 in B minor
		No. 6 in G-sharp minor
		No. 11 in A minor
31-Jan-38	Mozart:	Fantasy in C minor, K. 396
	Mozart:	Minuet in D, K. 355
	Mozart:	Gigue in G, K. 574
	Beethoven:	Sonata No. 29 in B-flat major, Op. 106, "Hammerklavier"
	Schumann:	Abegg Variations, Op. 1
	Chopin:	Polonaise in F-sharp minor, Op. 44
		Scherzo in B minor, Op. 20
10-Jan-39	Bach:	English Suite in G minor, BWV 808
	Beethoven:	Sonata No. 26 in E-flat major, Op. 81a, "Les Adieux"
	Schubert:	Fantasia in C major, D. 760, "Wanderer"
	Mendelssohn:	Songs without Words
		A minor, Op. 38, No. 5 (?)
		G major, Op. 62, No. 1, "May Breezes"
		C major, Op. 67, No. 4, "Spinning Song"
	Mendelssohn:	Fantaisies, Op. 16
		No. 2, Scherzo in E minor
	Liszt:	Etudes d'exécution transcendante d'après Paganini
		No. 5 in E major, "La Chasse"
		No. 6 in A minor
17-Nov-39	Bach:	Capriccio on the Departure of His Beloved Brother, BWV 992
	Beethoven:	Sonata No. 24 in F-sharp minor, Op. 78
	Brahms:	Variations and Fugue on a Theme by Handel, Op. 24
	Chopin:	Etudes, Op. 25

15-Nov-40	Mozart:	Prelude and Fugue in C major, K. 394
	Mozart:	Sonata No. 5 in G major, K. 283
	Beethoven:	Sonata No. 23 in F minor, Op. 57, "Appassionata"
	Reger:	Variations and Fugue on a Theme by Telemann, Op. 134
1-Dec-41	Bach:	Toccata in E minor, BWV 914
	Beethoven:	Sonata No. 14 in C-sharp minor, Op. 27, No. 2, "Moonlight"
	Schumann:	Etudes Symphoniques, Op. 13
	Reger:	Aus meinem Tagebuch, Op. 82
		Allegro in D minor
		Andantino in A minor
		Vivace in D major
	Smetana:	Three Czech Dances, T. 112
		Polka in F-sharp minor
		Polka in A minor
		Polka in F major
	Chopin:	Barcarolle, Op. 60
	Chopin:	Polonaise in A-flat major, Op. 53
1-Dec-42	Beethoven:	Sonata No. 26 in E-flat major, Op. 81a, "Les Adieux"
	Schubert:	Sonata in A major, D. 959
	Chopin:	Polonaise in F-sharp minor, Op. 44
	Mendelssohn:	Scherzo a capriccio in F-sharp minor
	Rachmaninoff:	Preludes, Op. 32
		No. 6 in F minor
		No. 11 in B major
		No. 8 in A minor
	Liszt:	Etudes d'exécution transcendante d'après Paganini
		No. 6 in A minor
7-Dec-43	Mozart:	Ten Variations on a Theme by Gluck, K. 455
	Beethoven:	Sonata No. 24 in F-sharp major, Op. 78
	Schumann:	Carnaval, Op. 9
	Schubert:	Impromptus
		No. 3 in G-flat major, Op. 90, D. 899
		No. 4 in F minor, Op. 142
	Ravel:	Miroirs
		Une barque sur l'océan
		Alborada del gracioso
	Chopin:	Three Etudes, Op. 25
		No. 10 in B minor
		No. 2 in F minor
		No. 11 in A minor
15-Jan-45	Beethoven:	Sonata No. 8 in C minor, Op. 13, "Pathétique"
	Reger:	Bach Variations, Op. 81
	Brahms:	Klavierstücke, Op. 119
	Chopin:	Impromptu in F-sharp major, Op. 36
	Chopin	Scherzo in B minor, Op. 20
	Smetana:	Four Czech Dances, T. 112
		Furiant, vol. II, no. 1
		Polka in F-sharp minor

		Medved ("The Bear")
		Polka in F major
4-Dec-45	Beethoven:	Fantasia in G minor/B-flat major, Op. 77
	Beethoven:	Polonaise for Piano in C major, op. 89
	Schubert:	Fantasia in C major, D. 760, "Wanderer"
	Mendelssohn:	Fantasies, Op. 16
	Schumann:	Abegg Variations, Op. 1
	Debussy:	Four Preludes, Book I
		Danseuses de Delphes
		Ce que'a vu le vent d'Ouest
		Les sons et les parfums tournent dans l'air du soir
		Les collines d'Anacapri
	Chopin:	Barcarolle, Op. 60
	Chopin:	Bolero, Op. 19
4-March-47	Bach:	Capriccio on the Departure of His Beloved Brother, BWV 992
	Beethoven:	Sonata No. 29 in B-flat major, Op. 106, "Hammerklavier"
	Chopin:	Etudes, Op. 25
12-April-48	Mozart:	Fantasia in D minor, K. 397
	Beethoven:	Sonata No. 24 in F-sharp major, Op. 78
	Brahms:	Handel Variations, Op. 34
	Chopin:	Preludes, Op. 28
26-March-49	Bach:	Italian Concerto, BWV 971
	Mozart:	Rondo in A minor, K. 511
	Beethoven:	Sonata No. 30 in E major, Op. 109
	Schumann:	Romances, Op. 28
		No. 1 in B-flat minor
		No. 2 in F-sharp major
	Schubert:	Impromptu No. 4 in F minor, Op. 142, D. 935
	Debussy:	5 Etudes, Book 2
		Pour les degrés chromatiques
		Pour les degrés agréments
		Pour les notes répétées
		Pour les arpèges composés
		Pour les accords
	Chopin:	Tarantella, Op. 43
2-Dec-49	Haydn:	Sonata in E-flat major, Hob. XVI: 52
	Bach:	French Suite No. 5 in G major, BWV 816
	Beethoven:	Sonata No. 21 in C major, Op. 53, "Waldstein"
	Schumann:	Symphonic Etudes, Op. 13
1-Dec-50	Bach:	Chromatic Fantasy and Fugue, BWV 903
	Beethoven:	Sonata No. 26 in E-flat major, Op. 81a, "Les Adieux"
	Schubert:	Sonata in B-flat major, D. 960
	Brahms:	Rhapsody in E-flat major, Op. 119, No. 4
	Schumann:	Abegg Variations, Op. 1
	Chopin:	Ballade in A-flat major, Op. 47
	Chopin:	Bolero, Op. 19

7-Dec-51	Bach:	Prelude and Fugue in A minor, BWV 894
	Brahms:	Variations on a Theme by Robert Schumann, Op. 9
	Beethoven:	Sonata No. 23 in F minor, Op. 57, "Appassionata"
	Weber:	Invitation to the Dance, Op. 65
	Busoni:	Berceuse (1909)
	Busoni:	Perpetuum Mobile (1922)
	Chopin:	Barcarolle, Op. 60
	Chopin:	Polonaise in A-flat major, Op. 53

5-Dec-52	Haydn:	Sonata in C major, Hob. XVI: 50
	Busch:	Sonata in C minor, Op. 25
	Schubert:	Moments Musicaux, D. 780
		No. 1 in C major
		No. 2 in A-flat major
		No. 3 in F minor
	Beethoven:	Sonata No. 21 in C, Op. 53, "Waldstein"

23-March-54	Beethoven:	Sonata No. 8 in C minor, Op. 13, "Pathétique"
	Beethoven:	Sonata No. 28 in A major, Op. 101
	Beethoven:	33 Variations on a Waltz by Diabelli in C major, Op. 120

23-March-55	Bach:	Fugue in A minor, BWV 904
	Schubert:	Sonata in C major, D. 840, "Unfinished"
	Beethoven:	Sonata No. 23 in F minor, Op. 57, "Appassionata"
	Brahms:	Handel Variations, Op. 24

4-Dec-57	Martinů:	Sonata (1954)
	Bach:	Italian Concerto, BWV 971
	Schubert:	Impromptus, D. 935
		No. 2 in A-flat major
		No. 4 in F minor
	Beethoven:	Sonata No. 29 in B-flat major, Op. 106, "Hammerklavier"

9-Dec-58	Mendelssohn:	Variations sérieuses in D minor, Op. 54
	Mozart:	Rondo in A minor, K. 511
	Beethoven:	Sonata No. 31 in A-flat major, Op. 110
	Chopin:	Etudes, Op. 25

8-Dec-59	Haydn:	Sonata in E-flat major, Hob. XVI: 52
	Beethoven:	Sonata No. 32 in C minor, Op. 111
	Chopin:	Preludes, Op. 28

4-Dec-62	Schubert:	Sonata in A major, D. 959
	Beethoven:	Sonata No. 14 in C-sharp minor, Op. 27, No. 2, "Moonlight"
	Beethoven:	Bagatelles, Op. 119
	Schubert:	Wanderer Fantasy, D. 760

11-Dec-63	Schumann:	Etudes Symphoniques, Op. 13
	Beethoven:	Sonata No. 26 in E-flat major, Op. 81a, "Les Adieux"
	Beethoven:	Sonata No. 24 in F-sharp major, Op. 78
	Brahms:	Handel Variations, Op. 24

8-Dec-64	Schumann:	Sonata No. 3 in F minor, Op. 14
	Beethoven:	Sonata No. 28 in A major, Op. 101

	Mendelssohn:	Variations sérieuses, Op. 54
	Brahms:	Klavierstücke, Op. 119
	Chopin:	Barcarolle, Op. 60
	Chopin:	Bolero, Op. 19
7-Dec-65	Bach:	Fugue in A minor, BWV 904
	Haydn:	Sonata in D, Hob. XVI: 19
	Beethoven:	Sonata No. 32 in C minor, Op. 111
	Busoni:	Toccata (1921)
	Busoni:	Berceuse (1909)
	Schumann:	Carnaval, Op. 9
7-Dec-66	Schubert:	Sonata in A major, D. 664
	Schubert:	Impromptus, Op. 142, D. 935
	Beethoven:	Sonata No. 29 in B-flat major, Op. 106, "Hammerklavier"
5-Dec-67	Beethoven:	Sonata No. 1 in F minor, Op. 2, No. 1
	Beethoven:	Sonata No. 26 in E-flat major, Op. 81a, "Les Adieux"
	Beethoven:	Diabelli Variations, Op. 120
2-Feb-69	Beethoven:	Sonata No. 24 in F-sharp major, Op. 78
	Schubert:	Sonata in C minor, D. 958
	Chopin:	Preludes, Op. 28
8-Oct-70	Beethoven:	Sonata No. 1 in F minor, Op. 2, No. 1
	Beethoven:	Sonata No. 6 in F major , Op. 10, No. 2
	Beethoven:	Sonata No. 8 in C minor, Op. 13, "Pathétique"
	Beethoven:	Sonata No. 21 in C major, Op. 53, "Waldstein"
16-Oct-70	Beethoven:	Fantasia in G minor/B-flat major, Op. 77
	Beethoven:	Sonata No. 24 in F-sharp major, Op. 78
	Beethoven:	Sonata No. 28 in A major, Op. 101
	Beethoven:	Sonata No. 23 in F minor, Op. 57, "Appassionata"
9-Dec-70	Beethoven:	Sonata No. 13 in E-flat major, Op. 27, No. 1
	Beethoven:	Sonata No. 16 in G major, Op. 31, No. 1
	Beethoven:	Sonata No. 12 in A-flat major, Op. 26
	Beethoven:	Sonata No. 31 in A-flat major, Op. 110
16-Dec-70	Beethoven:	Sonata No. 11 in B-flat major, Op. 22
	Beethoven:	Sonata No. 14 in C-sharp minor, Op. 27, No. 2, "Moonlight"
	Beethoven:	Sonata No. 29 in B-flat major, Op. 106, "Hammerklavier"
17-Dec-72	Beethoven:	Sonata No. 8 in C minor, Op. 13, "Pathétique"
	Beethoven:	Sonata No. 26 in E-flat major, Op. 81a, "Les Adieux"
	Schubert:	Sonata in B-flat major, D. 960
4-Dec-73	Bach:	Italian Concerto, BWV 971
	Reger:	Bach Variations, Op. 81
	Beethoven:	Sonata No. 6 in F major, Op. 10, No. 2
	Beethoven:	Sonata No. 30 in E major, Op. 109
4-Dec-74	Beethoven:	Sonata No. 1 in F minor, Op. 2, No. 1
	Brahms:	Klavierstücke, Op. 119
	Beethoven:	Diabelli Variations, Op. 120

26-Jan-77	Beethoven:	Sonata No. 1 in F minor, Op. 2, No. 1
	Beethoven:	Sonata No. 23 in F minor, Op. 57, "Appassionata"
	Beethoven:	Sonata No. 29 in B-flat major, Op. 106, "Hammerklavier"
14-Dec-77	Haydn:	Sonata in E-flat major, Hob. XVI: 49
	Mozart:	Rondo in A minor, K. 511
	Beethoven:	Sonata No. 26 in E-flat major, Op. 81a, "Les Adieux"
	Schubert:	Sonata in B-flat major, D. 960
11-Dec-78	Beethoven:	Sonata No. 24 in F-sharp major, Op. 78
	Schubert:	Impromptus, Op. 142, D. 935
	Brahms:	Handel Variations, Op. 24
3-Dec-80	Bach:	Italian Concerto, BWV 971
	Reger:	Bach Variations, Op. 81
	Beethoven:	Sonata No. 21 in C major, Op. 53, "Waldstein"
9-Dec-81	Beethoven:	Sonata No. 8 in C minor, Op. 13, "Pathétique"
	Brahms:	Klavierstücke, Op. 119
	Beethoven:	Sonata No. 30 in E major, Op. 109
	Schubert:	Wanderer Fantasy, D. 760
8-Dec-82	Beethoven:	Sonata No. 30 in E major, Op. 109
	Beethoven:	Sonata No. 31 in A-flat major, Op. 110
	Beethoven:	Sonata No. 32 in C minor, Op. 111
7-Dec-83	Haydn:	Sonata in C major, Hob: XVI: 50
	Beethoven:	Sonata No. 14 in C-sharp minor, Op. 27, No. 2, "Moonlight"
	Schubert:	Moments Musicaux, D. 780
	Beethoven:	Sonata No. 23 in F minor, Op. 57, "Appassionata"
5-Dec-84	Beethoven:	Sonata No. 24 in F-sharp major, Op. 78
	Beethoven:	Sonata No. 26 in E-flat major, Op. 81a, "Les Adieux"
	Beethoven:	Diabelli Variations, Op. 120
29-Jan-86	Mozart:	Fantasy in C minor, K. 475
	Mozart:	Sonata in C minor, K. 457
	Beethoven:	Sonata No. 53 in C major, Op. 53, "Waldstein"
	Schubert:	Sonata in A major, D. 959
8-April-87	Beethoven:	Sonata No. 30 in E major, Op. 109
	Beethoven:	Sonata No. 31 in A-flat major, Op. 110
	Beethoven:	Sonata No. 32 in C minor, Op. 111

The Recorded Legacy of Rudolf Serkin

As was the case for several other musicians of the generation whose musical maturation just preceded the advent and rapid growth of electrical recording technology, Rudolf Serkin harbored negative feelings about recordings throughout his life. It was not simply that he found the process of making recordings arduous; even listening to records, particularly his own, held little appeal for him. His son Peter is unequivocal about this: "My dad hated to record. Absolutely hated it. And he didn't listen to recordings, but because he didn't *like* to listen to records: 'It's always the same, it never improves!'"* In interviews he spoke of "frozen performances" and "snapshots." As Richard Goode has noted in his interview in this volume, Serkin's distaste speaks directly to the way he experienced music. The distinction between the composition and its realization is unique to the Western musical tradition; when Schnabel famously remarked that great music was "better than it can ever be played," he was articulating a kind of musical Platonism that Serkin undoubtedly shared. For Serkin, the activity of playing, of engaging directly with the score as an unending source of musical meaning, was to experience music with the greatest intensity. Listening to others similarly engaged could also involve

---

* Interview, New York, November 18, 2000.

him powerfully, as attested to by his many students and those who sat with him at Marlboro. Mere listening to a recording was, at best, a much paler musical experience.

There was also another factor that played into his attitude toward recordings, one that might be called his ethics of performance. Serkin as a teacher was famously unwilling to play for his students; he wanted them to confront the music directly, unmediated by another performance (particularly a conception as powerful as his own). Similarly, he seems to have regarded recordings as an almost illegitimate means of initially approaching a piece of music; a true musician must first form his own idea of a work before listening to others. Again, Peter Serkin: "My dad would warn me and say, 'Don't listen to recordings and be influenced by the way other people play.'"

Despite his reservations, however, Serkin left an enormous recorded legacy. He clearly was more comfortable with collaborative efforts. With the exception of his 1936 *Appassionata*, all of his European recordings were with Adolf Busch or Busch ensembles. In the United States, too, his concerto and chamber music recordings far outnumbered those of solo works. His core concerto repertoire of Mozart, Beethoven, Schumann, and Brahms received, for the most part, multiple "snapshots." These recordings provide an endlessly fascinating documentation of his musicianship as it evolved during the sixty years of his career.

This survey of Serkin's recorded performances is divided into four sections. Part I lists all of the commercial recordings, both studio and live, that either he or his family authorized for release. Part II contains recordings taken from broadcasts and live performances that were released commercially but never approved. Most of these items, published predominantly in Italy, appeared during the heady introduction of CDs into the market from the mid-1980s through the early 1990s; their performance documentation is occasionally incomplete or inaccurate and many are now out of print.

Several guidelines have been followed in compiling the discographies that make up these first two sections. First, the recorded formats are limited to 78s, LPs, and CDs. Thus, no 45s, reel-to-reel tapes, cassettes, laserdiscs, or videocassettes are listed. I have tried to include all recordings that were available in the United States, either as domestic issues or as imports. In many cases I have listed Japanese LPs and, to a lesser extent, CDs. For a period in the late 1960s and throughout the 1970s, the Japanese were enthusiastically and comprehensively issuing on LP performances of many major musicians of the first half of the century, while the American and European markets were allowing these performances to languish on 78s and long out-of-print LPs. Until the Odyssey Busch-Serkin set was issued in 1977, almost all of their recorded performances together, both European and American, were available only on Japanese records imported in only one or two locations in the United States; so, despite the restricted availability of these records, it is essential that they be included. For 78s I have included matrix numbers and have placed the British issue number first for the recordings made prior to 1940.

Recordings with orchestra and recordings made in London and New York do not have place names listed under the date. With just one exception, studio recordings prior to 1940 were all made in London; the one exception is the Bach G major Violin Sonata with Busch, which was not only Serkin's first released recording but the last authorized recording he ever made in Germany.

Complete recording dates have been given when possible, but in several instances, month and year, or only year, reflects the best information obtainable as of this writing.

Part III of this survey discusses the tapes made at Marlboro and highlights the performances of those works that were otherwise unrepresented in Serkin's recording career. Similarly, Part IV lists tapes of live performances from other sources, most notably those recorded in the Library of Congress between 1937 and 1959. Here again, there are performances of pieces that Serkin played often in concert but never recorded in the studio (or, in several instances, made studio recordings but would not authorize their release).

There are also three appendixes. The first is a compilation of all the performances given by Serkin in the Library of Congress, complete with dates and call numbers. The second lists all of the piano rolls that Serkin made for the Welte company in 1928. Here there are some tantalizing items, foremost of which is a nearly complete *Goldberg Variations*, a work with which Serkin was closely identified early in his career. But unfortunately, piano rolls, even at their best, cannot begin to capture the individual nuances of pianists that are apparent in even the most primitive electrical recordings, and it would be misleading to include them in the main body of recordings. The third appendix lists the studio recordings Serkin made but did not approve for release. The 1989 *Waldstein* and *Appassionata* were his last recording efforts; he was already quite ill, and his family did not deem the results acceptable for issue, especially in light of extant versions of both works showing him at the height of his artistry.

This survey of Serkin's recording career could not have been accomplished without the help of many individuals, and it gives me great pleasure to acknowledge them now. First, I would like to thank Stephen Lehmann and Marion Faber for including me in this project from the outset and for sharing with me over the years the ever more intriguing fruits of their research.

The work of Jacques Delalande, Francis Dresel, Philip Hart, and Tully Potter, all compilers of previous discographies of Busch or Serkin, both published and unpublished, provided a comprehensive foundation on which to build. The following people were extremely generous with their time and efforts in providing information and verifying the myriad details that arise in an endeavor such as this: Bryan Cornell (Library of Congress), Rebecca Koblick (Rogers and Hammerstein Archives of Recorded Sound), Alban Kojima, Donald Manildi (International Piano Archives, University of Maryland), Norman Middleton (Library of Congress), Bernard Meillat, Evelyn Mobray (Telarc), Jean Morrow (New England Conservatory of Music), Paola Saffiotti, Tom Sidebotham, Sara Velez (Rodgers and Hammerstein Archives of Recorded Sound), Richard Wandel (New York Philharmonic Archives), Warren Wernick (Sony), and Seth Winner. I am most grateful to each of them.

Three people above all have been unstinting with their help at crucial junctures. Ray Edwards, whose knowledge not only of music but of the classical recording business is enormous, suggested a context in which to begin and supplied personal contacts that proved to be invaluable. Dick Sloane generously shared with me his extensive files on Serkin's recordings and responded graciously and knowledgeably to what must have seemed at times like an unending stream of phone calls and e-mails. Finally, Kaela Farber, as always, provided every kind of support, tangible and intangible, and turned aspects of this project that might have been most onerous into yet another shared pleasure.

RECORDING NUMBER PREFIXES

Columbia/CBS/Sony		EMI	
LPs	*CDs*	*LPs*	*CDs*
ML, MS	JK	COLC	CDCB
D(#)L, D(#)S	MK	COLH	CDH
D(#)M	MBK	GR (Japan)	CHS
GMB	MPK	HQM	
KL	MYK	SH (World Record Club)	
SL	SK		
M	SMK		
MG	SBK		
MGP	SX(#)K		
MP	SRCR (Japan)		
M(#)X	ooDC (Japan)		
MY			
SOCU (Japan)			
SONC (Japan)			

NOTE: Elec. = EMI Electrola (Germany).
ML and MS, D(#)L and D(#)S are mono and stereo versions issued simultaneously.

THE RECORDED LEGACY OF RUDOLF SERKIN

I. AUTHORIZED RECORDINGS

BACH, JOHANN SEBASTIAN (1685–1750)

Canons (14) on the First Eight Notes of the Aria from the Goldberg Variations, BWV1087

F. Galimir, E. Drucker, U. Kamei,	3-Jul-76	LP: Marlboro Rec Soc MRS 12
G. Fulkerson, I. Cohen, N. Tanaka,	Marlboro	CD: SMK 45892
L. Horner, R. Greutter, violins;		
P. Naegele, S. Ansell, I. Serkin,		
C. Levine, violas; J. Goritzki,		
T. Eddy, P. Rejto, cellos;		
M. Marder, double bass;		
J. Bogorad, flute; R. Vrbsky, oboe;		
M. Rosenberg, English horn;		
A. Heller, C. Millard, bassoons		

Capriccio in B-flat major on the Departure of His Beloved Brother, BWV 992

	5-Apr-57	LP: ML 5236
	Puerto Rico	

Brandenburg Concerto No. 1 in F major, BWV 1046

R. Serkin, continuo; Marlboro Festival	9,11-Jul-64	LP: M2S 731
Orch., Casals		D3S 816
		MP 38755
		CD: MK 38755/6
		SK 42274/5
		SMK 46253

Brandenburg Concerto No. 4 in G major, BWV 1049

R. Serkin, continuo; Marlboro Festival	9,11-Jul-64	LP: M2S 731
Orch., Casals		D3S 816
		MP 38756
		CD: MK 38755/6
		SK 42274/5
		SMK 46254

Brandenburg Concerto No. 5 in D major, BWV 1050

M. Moyse, A. Busch,		
Busch Chamber Players	9,11-Oct-35	MX: CAX 7616/18, CAX 7622/4
		78: Col. (G.Br.) LX 444/6
		Col. 68442/4D (M 250)
		LP: COLC 14
		GR 2089
		GR 2251
		Seraphim IC 6043
		Seraphim 60357
		Pathe 2C 151-43068 M
		CD: CHS 7 64047 2

BACH (cont.)

Brandenburg Concerto No. 5 in D major, BWV 1050 (continued)

O. Gulbransen, A. Schneider, Marlboro Festival Orch., Casals	9,11-Jul-64	LP:	M2S 731
			D3S 816
			MP 38756
		CD:	MK 38755/6
			SK 42274/5
			SMK 46254

Chromatic Fantasy and Fugue in D minor, BWV 903

Jun-50	LP:	ML 4350
Prades		MP 39761

Concerto in F major in the Italian Style, BWV 971

Jun-50	LP:	ML 4350
Prades		MP 39761

Concerto for Three Pianos No. 1 in D minor, BWV 1063

M. Horszowski, R. Laredo, Marlboro Festival Orch., Schneider	7-Jul-64	LP:	ML 6247, MS 6847
			MP 39761

Concerto for Three Pianos No. 2 in C major, BWV 1064

M. Horszowski, P. Serkin, Marlboro Festival Orch., Schneider	13-Jul-64	LP:	ML 6247, MS 6847
			MP 39761

French Suite No. 5 in G major, BWV 816

14-Apr-50	CD:	*Rudolf Serkin, A Life*
Library of		Stephen Lehmann and
Congress		Marion Faber
		Oxford University Press,
		2003
		Accompanying CD

Goldberg Variations, BWV 988 (aria only)

3-Jul-76	LP:	Marlboro Rec Soc MRS 12
Marlboro	CD:	SMK 45892

Sonata for Violin and Piano No. 3 in E major, BWV 1016 (mvts 2, 4 only)

A. Busch	18-Nov-33	78:	Announced as M 235 but never released; matrices destroyed. Test pressings for 2nd & 4th movements found in 1996 by Tully Potter in Busch's personal collection.
		CD:	Appian APR 5543
A. Busch	27-Apr-43 Library of Congress		
		LP:	Odyssey Y3 34639
		CD:	Music & Arts CD 877

Sonata for Violin and Piano No. 4 in C minor, BWV 1017 (Siciliano only)

A. Busch	18-Nov-33	MX: HMV 2B-5449 transferred
		to Col. CAX 7671
		78: Col. (G.Br.) LX 438
		LP: GR 2247
		CD: Appian APR 5543
		CDH 7 63494 2

Sonata for Violin and Piano in G major, BWV 1021 (arr. F. Blume & A. Busch)

A. Busch	24-Oct-29	MX: CNR 808/9
	Berlin	78: HMV DB 1434
	[first recording]	LP: GR 2247
		Perennial 2006
		Rococo 2023
		CD: Appian APR 5543
		CDCB 54374
		Pearl GEMM 9942
		Symposium SYMCD 1109

Toccata in E minor, BWV 914

| | 1-May-42 | MX: XCO 32773/4 |
| | | 78: Col. 71594D |

BARTÓK, BÉLA (1881–1945)

Concerto for Piano and Orchestra No. 1

| Columbia Symphony Orch., Szell | 20,21-Apr-62 | LP: ML 5805, MS 6405 |
| | | CD: MPK 46446 |

BEETHOVEN, LUDWIG VAN (1770–1827)

Bagatelles, Op. 119

	16, 18-Feb-66	LP: ML 6238, MS 6838
		MP 38893
		CD: MPK 44837

Concerto for Piano and Orchestra No. 1 in C major, Op. 15

Philadelphia Orch., Ormandy	14-Feb-54	LP: ML 4914
Philadelphia Orch., Ormandy	14-Jan-65	LP: ML 6238, MS 6838,
		D4L 340, D4S 740
		MY 37807
		CD: MK 42259
		MYK 37807
Boston Symphony Orch., Ozawa	5-Oct-83	LP: Telarc DG 10061-5
		Telarc DG 10062
		CD: Telarc CD 80061-5
		Telarc CD 80062

BEETHOVEN (cont.)

Concerto for Piano and Orchestra No. 2 in B-flat major, Op. 19

Philadelphia Orch., Ormandy	14-Feb-54, 24-Apr-55	LP:	ML 5037
Philadelphia Orch., Ormandy	13-Jan-65	LP:	ML 6239, MS 6839
			D4L 340, D4S 740
Boston Symphony Orch., Ozawa	3-Jul-84	LP:	Telarc DG 10061-5
			Telarc DG 10062
		CD:	Telarc CD 80061-5
			Telarc CD 80064

Concerto for Piano and Orchestra No. 3 in C minor, Op. 37

Philadelphia Orch., Ormandy	22-Mar-53	LP:	ML 4738
New York Philharmonic, Bernstein	20-Jan-64	LP:	ML 6016, MS 6616
			D4L 340, D4S 740
			MY 38526
		CD:	MK 42259
			MYK 38526
			SMK 47520
			SMK 63080
Boston Symphony Orch., Ozawa	2,4-Oct-82	LP:	Telarc DG 10061-5
			Telarc DG 10063
		CD:	Telarc CD 80061-5
			Telarc CD 80063

Concerto for Piano and Orchestra No. 4 in G major, Op. 58

NBC Symphony Orch., Toscanini	26-Nov-44	LP:	RCA Victor LM-2797
			RCA AT 106
			RCA AT 1106
		CD:	RCA Gold Seal 60268-2
Philadelphia Orch., Ormandy	11-Mar-55	LP:	ML 5037
Philadelphia Orch., Ormandy	28-Jan-62	LP:	ML 6145, MS 6745
			D4L 340, D4S 740
		CD:	MK 42260
Marlboro Festival Orch., Schneider	7-Jul-74	CD:	SM2K 89200
Boston Symphony Orch., Ozawa	6-Oct-81	LP:	Telarc DG 10061-5
			Telarc DG 10064
		CD:	Telarc CD 80061-5
			Telarc CD 80064

Concerto for Piano and Orch. No. 5 in E-flat major, Op. 73, "Emperor"

New York Philharmonic, Walter	22-Dec-41	MX:	XCO 32041/50
		78:	Col. 11718/22D (M 500)
		LP:	ML 4004
			Odyssey Y 34607
		CD:	SMK 64489
			SX9K 66249
			Biddulph LHW 026
			Dante LYS 308/9
			Enterprise ENT PD 4163
			Hist. Performers HPS 15

Philadelphia Orch., Ormandy	19-Nov-50	MX:	XCO 43741/50
		78:	MM 989
		LP:	ML 4373
		CD:	SM3K 47269
New York Philharmonic, Bernstein	1-May-62	LP:	ML 5766, MS 6366
			D4L 340, D4S 740
			M2X 788
			M4X821
			MG 788
			M 31807
			MY 37223
		CD:	MK42260
			MYK 37223
			SMK 47520
			SMK 63080
			SMK 63076 (2nd mvt. only)
Boston Symphony Orch., Ozawa	24,26-Jan-81	LP:	Telarc DG 10061-5
			Telarc DG 10065
		CD:	Telarc CD 80061-5
			Telarc CD 80065

Concerto for Violin, Cello, and Piano in C major, Op. 56

J. Laredo, L. Parnas, Marlboro Festival Orch., Schneider	23-May-62	LP:	ML 5964, MS 6564
			MP 38895
		CD:	MPK 44842

Fantasia for Piano, Chorus, and Orch. in C minor, Op. 80

Westminster Choir, New York Philharmonic, Bernstein	1-May-62	LP:	ML 6016, MS 6616
			D4L 340, D4S 740
			M2S 794
			MY 38526
		CD:	MYK 38526
			SM2K 47522
			SB2K 63240
Marlboro Festival Orch. and Chorus, P. Serkin, cond.	9-Aug-81	CD:	SM2K 89200
Tanglewood Chorus, Boston Symphony Orch., Ozawa	2,4-Oct-82	LP:	Telarc DG 10061-5
			Telarc DG 10063
		CD:	Telarc CD 80061-5
			Telarc CD 80063

Fantasia in G minor/B-flat major, Op. 77

	1-Dec-47	MX:	XCO 39493/4
		78:	Col. 72793D (MM 816)
		LP:	ML 4128
	7,14,15-Oct-70	LP:	M 32294
			MP 38895
		CD:	SBK 47666
			SRCR 8590-1

BEETHOVEN (cont.)

Quartet for Piano and Strings in C major, WoO 36

F. Galimir, N. Imai, N. Rosen	11-Jul-70 Marlboro	LP:	Marlboro Rec Soc MRS 6

Quintet for Piano and Winds in E-flat major, Op. 16

J. De Lancie, A. Gigliotti, S. Schoenbach, M. Jones	23-Sep-53	LP:	ML 4834
R. Vrbsky, R. Stoltzman, A. Heller, R. Routch	14,18-Aug-74 Marlboro	LP: CD:	M 33527 SMK 47296

Sonata for Piano No. 1 in F minor, Op. 2, No. 1

	7-Oct-70	CD: SM3K 64490

Sonata for Piano No. 6 in F major, Op. 10, No. 2

	7-Oct-70	CD: SM3K 64490

Sonata for Piano No. 8 in C minor, Op. 13, "Pathétique"

	5-Jun-45	MX: XCO 34898/903
		78: Col. 71850/2D (M 648)
		LP: ML 4003
		ML 5164
	8, 15-Dec-62	LP: ML 5881, MS 6481
		M2X 788
		M4X 821
		MG 788
		M 31811
		MY 37219
		MG 31270 (1st mvt only)
		CD: MYK 37219
		SBK 47666
		SBK 64093 (2nd mvt. only)

Sonata for Piano No. 11 in B-flat major, Op. 22

	14,15-Dec-70,	LP: M 32294
	18-May-73	CD: SRCR 8590-1

Sonata for Piano No. 12 in A-flat major, Op. 26, "Funeral March"

	8-Dec-70	CD: SM3K 64490

Sonata for Piano No. 13 in E-flat major, Op. 27, No. 1

	7-Dec-80	CD: SM3K 64490

Sonata for Piano No. 14 in C-sharp minor, Op. 27, No. 2, "Moonlight"

	3-Sept-41,	MX: XCO 31341/4
	30-Apr-42	78: Col. 71470/1D (M 237)
		LP: ML 4003

28,30-May-51	LP:	ML 4432
Brattleboro, VT		ML 5164
14-Dec-62	LP:	ML 5881, MS 6481
		M2X 788
		M4X 821
		MG 788
		MGP 13
		M 31811
		MY 37219
		MS 7406 (1st mvt. only)
	CD:	MYK 37219
		SMK 60993 (1st mvt. only)

Sonata for Piano No. 16 in G major, Op. 31, No. 1

8-Dec-70	CD:	SM3K 64490

Sonata for Piano No. 21 in C major, Op. 53, "Waldstein"

8-10-Sept-52	LP:	ML 4620
24-26-Oct-75	CD:	SM3K 64490
Guilford, VT		

Sonata for Piano No. 23 in F minor, Op. 57, "Appassionata"

3-Nov-36	MX:	2EA 4440/45
[first solo	78:	HMV C2879/81
recording]		Victor 15536/8 (M 583)
	CD:	CDCB 54374
		Philips 456 964
		The Piano Library PL 189
24,29-Jul-47	MX:	XCO 39024/9
	78:	Col. 72356/8D (MM 711)
	LP:	ML 2002
		ML 5164
8,14,15-Dec-62	LP:	ML 5881, MS 6481
		M4X 821
		M2X 788
		MG 788
		M 31811
		MY 37219
	CD:	MYK 37219

Sonata for Piano No. 24 in F-sharp major, Op. 78

1-Dec-47	MX:	XCO 39495/7
	78:	Col. 72786/7D (M 816)
	LP:	ML 4128
28-Apr-73	LP:	M 32294
18-Jun-73		MP 38895
	CD:	SRCR 8590-1

BEETHOVEN (cont.)

Sonata for Piano No. 26 in E-flat major, Op. 81a, "Les Adieux"

1-May-51,	LP:	ML 4432
29-May-51		
Brattleboro, VT		
14,15-Dec-77	LP:	M2 34596
		MY 37807
	CD:	MYK 37807
		SRCR 8585-6

Sonata for Piano No. 28 in A major, Op. 101

7,14,15-Oct-70	LP:	M 31239
	CD:	SRCR 8590-1

Sonata for Piano No. 29 in B-flat major, Op. 106, "Hammerklavier"

8,9,10-Dec-69,	LP:	M 30081
14,15-Dec-70		MP 38893
	CD:	MPK 44838
		SBK 47666
		SRCR 8590-1

Sonata for Piano No. 30 in E major, Op. 109

22-Jul-52	LP:	ML 4620
8-Jun-76	CD:	SM3K 64490
30-Oct-87	CD:	DG 427 498-2
Vienna		

Sonata for Piano No. 31 in A-flat major, Op. 110

28-Aug-60	CD:	SM3K 64490
Marlboro		
12-Jan-71	LP:	M 31239
	CD:	MPK 44838
		SRCR 8590-1
30-Oct-87	CD:	DG 427 498-2
Vienna		

Sonata for Piano No. 32 in C minor, Op. 111

15,16-Mar-67	CD:	SM3K 64490
30-Oct-87	CD:	DG 427 498-2
Vienna		

Sonata for Violin and Piano No. 1 in D major, Op. 12, No. 1
A. Busch

Oct-51	LP:	Odyssey Y3 34639
Brattleboro, VT		SOCU 19

Sonata for Violin and Piano No. 3 in E-flat major, Op. 12, No. 3
A. Busch

5-May-31	MX:	2B 824/7
	78:	HMV DB 1519/20
		Victor 7560/1

		LP:	GR 2210
			GR 2245
			HQM 1219
		CD:	Appian APR 5541
			CDCB 54374
			Naxos 8. 110954
			CHS 5 65308 2
			Pearl GEM 0019
			Pearl GEMM 9942
			The Piano Library PL 189

Sonata for Violin and Piano No. 5 in F major, Op. 24, "Spring"

A. Busch	17-May-33	MX:	2B 6702/7
		78:	HMV DB 1970/72
			Victor 8351/3 (M 228)
		LP:	Elec. 1C 181-01 823M
			GR 2244
			Rococo 2079
		CD:	Appian APR 5541
			CDH 7 63494 2
			Naxos 8. 110954
			Pearl GEM 0019
			Enterprise ENT QT 99310
			Magic Talent 48022

Sonata for Violin and Piano No. 7 in C minor, Op. 30, No. 2

A. Busch	23-Sept-32,	MX:	2B 3888/93
	16-May-33	78:	HMV DB 1973/5
			Victor 8821/3 (M 283)
		LP:	GR 2244
		CD:	Appian APR 5541
			CDH 7 63494 2
			Magic Talent 48022

Sonata for Violin and Piano No. 8 in G major, Op. 30, No. 3

A. Busch	27-Apr-43	LP:	Odyssey Y3 34639
	Library of	CD:	Music & Arts CD 877
	Congress		

Sonata for Violin and Piano No. 9 in A major, Op. 47, "Kreutzer"

A. Busch	12-Dec-41	MX:	XCO 31974/81
		78:	Col. 71344/7D (M 496)
		LP:	ML 4007
			Odyssey Y3 34639
			SOCU 19
			SONC 15118
			Rococo 2079
		CD:	Biddulph LHW 026
			Naxos 8. 110954
			Pearl GEM 0019

BEETHOVEN (cont.)

Sonata for Violin and Piano No. 10 in G major, Op. 96

| A. Busch | 13-Oct-51 | LP: | SOCU 19 |
| | Brattleboro, VT | | |

Sonata for Cello and Piano No. 1 in F major, Op. 5, No. 1

P. Casals	17-May-53	LP:	ML 4876
	Prades		SL 201
			Odyssey 32 36 0016
			M3P 39659
		CD:	MPK 46725
			SM2K 58985

Sonata for Cello and Piano No. 2 in G minor, Op. 5, No. 2

P. Casals	31-Jul-51	LP:	ML 4572
	Perpignan		SL 169
			SL 170
			ML 4877
			SL 201
			Odyssey 32 36 0016
		CD:	MPK 46725
			SM2K 58985

Sonata for Cello and Piano No. 3 in A major, Op. 69

P. Casals	18-May-53	LP:	ML 4878
	Prades		SL 201
			Odyssey 32 36 0016
			M3P 39659
		CD:	MPK 45682
			SM2K 58985

Sonata for Cello and Piano No. 4 in C major, Op. 102, No. 1

P. Casals	19,20-May-53	LP:	ML 4878
	Prades		SL 201
			Odyssey 32 36 0016
			M3P 39659
		CD:	MPK 45682
			SM2K 58985

Sonata for Cello and Piano No. 5 in D major, Op. 102, No. 2

P. Casals	19,20-May-53	LP:	ML 4876
	Prades		SL 201
			Odyssey 32 36 0016
			M3P 39659
		CD:	MPK 45682
			SM2K 58985

Trio for Clarinet, Cello, and Piano in B-flat major, Op. 11

| R. Stoltzman, A. Meunier | 21-Jul-74 | LP: | Marlboro Rec Soc MRS 7 |
| | Marlboro | CD: | SMK 47296 |

Trio for Piano and Strings No. 4 in D major, Op. 70, No. 1, "Ghost"

A. Busch, H. Busch   15-Dec-47   MX: XCO 39656/61
           or 7-Jan-48   78: Col. 72748/50D (MM 804)
                    LP: ML 4128
                        Odyssey 32 16 0361
                        SONC 15118
                        SOCU 15
                    CD: MPK 46447

Variations for Cello and Piano in E-flat major on "Bei Männern," WoO 46

P. Casals   Aug-51   LP: ML 4572
           Perpignan   SL 169
                        SL 170
                        ML 4877
                        SL 201
                        K3L 233
                        Odyssey 32 36 0016
                    CD: SM2K 58985
                        MPK 46724

Variations for Cello and Piano in F major on "Ein Mädchen oder Weibchen," Op. 66

P. Casals   31-Jul-51   LP: ML 4572
           Perpignan   SL 169
                        SL 170
                        ML 4877
                        SL 201
                        Odyssey 32 36 0016
                    CD: SM2K 58985
                        MPK 46724

Variations for Cello and Piano in G major on a Theme from Handel's Judas Maccabaeus, WoO 45

P. Casals   Aug-51   LP: ML 4640
           Perpignan   Odyssey 32 16 0016
                    CD: MPK 46725
                        SMK 58991

Variations in C major on a Waltz by Diabelli, Op. 120

             3-5-Sept-57 LP: ML 5246
             Marlboro   MP 38780
                    CD: MPK 44837

Variations for Violin, Cello, and Piano in C major, Op. 121a, "Ich bin der Schneider Kakadu"

Y. Horigome, P. Wiley   23-Jul-83   LP: Marlboro Rec Soc MRS 14
           Marlboro   CD: SMK 47296

Variations on an Original Theme for Violin, Cello, and Piano in E-flat major, Op. 44

H. Suzuki, R. Leonard   10-Aug-68 LP: Marlboro Rec Soc MRS 4
           Marlboro

BRAHMS, JOHANNES (1833–1897)

Concerto for Piano and Orch. No. 1 in D minor, Op. 15

Pittsburgh Symphony Orch., Reiner	2-Feb-46	MX:	XCO 35764/75
		78:	Col. 12444/9D (M 652)
		LP:	ML 4100
		CD:	Dante LYS 127
			The Piano Library PL 237
Cleveland Orch., Szell	30-Nov-52	LP:	ML 4829
Philadelphia Orch., Ormandy	10-Dec-61	LP:	ML 5704, MS 6304
			D3L 341, D3S 741
		CD:	MK 42261
			MBK 46272
Cleveland Orch., Szell	19,20-Apr-68	LP:	MS 7143
			MG 31421
			MY 37803
		CD:	MYK 37803
			SBK 48166
			SB3K 52516

Concerto for Piano and Orch. No. 2 in B-flat major, Op. 83

Philadelphia Orch., Ormandy	15-Mar-45	MX:	XCO 34450/61
		78:	Col. 12187/9 D (M 584)
		LP:	ML 4014
Philadelphia Orch., Ormandy	11-Mar-56	LP:	ML 5117
		CD:	SM3K 47269
Philadelphia Orch., Ormandy	4-Apr-60	LP:	ML 5491, MS 6156
			D3L 341, D3S 741
		CD:	MBK 46273
Cleveland Orch., Szell	21,22-Jan-66	LP:	ML 6237, MS 6967
			MG 31421
			M 31849
		CD:	MK 42262
			MYK 37258
			SBK 53262

Klavierstücke, Op. 119

	25,26-May-79	LP:	M 35177
	Guilford, VT		MP 39549 (No. 4 only)
		CD:	MK 42262
			J4K 65819 (No. 1 only)
			SMK 60993 (No. 1 only)

Liebeslieder Waltzes, Op. 52

L. Fleisher, B. Valente,	19,22-Aug-60	LP:	ML 5636, MS 6236
M. Kleinman, W. Conner,	Marlboro	CD:	SBK 48176
M. Singher			

Quartet for Piano and Strings No. 1 in G minor, Op. 25

A. Busch, H. Gottesman, H. Busch	25,26-May-49	MX:	CAX 10520/9
	London	78:	Col. (G.Br.) LX 1217/21

Col. 72998/3002 (M 909)
LP: ML 4296
Elec. C 147-01 555/56 M
GR 2163
GR 2238
Odyssey Y 34638
SH 61
CD: CDH 5 65190 2

Quartet for Piano and Strings No. 2 in A major, Op. 26

A. Busch, K. Doktor, H. Busch   21-Sep-32

MX: 2B 3876/83
78: HMV DB 1849/52
Victor 14344/7 (M 346)
LP: Elec C 147-01 555/56 M
GR 2239
SH 612
CD: Biddulph LAB 027
CDH 7 64702 2

Quintet for Piano and Strings in F minor, Op. 34

Busch Quartet   13-Oct-38
(A. Busch, G. Andreasson,
K. Doktor, H. Busch)

MX: 2EA 6735/44
78: HMV DB 3694/8
Victor 15646/50 (M 607)
LP: GR 2241
Pathe 2C 051-43013
SH 613
Turnabout THS 65061
CD: CDH 7 64702 2
Pearl GEMM 9275

Budapest String Quartet   8,9-Sep-63
(J. Roisman, A. Schneider,
B. Kroyt, M. Schneider)

LP: ML 6031, MS 6631
MP 38769
CD: MPK 45686

Sonata for Violin and Piano No. 1 in G major, Op. 78

A. Busch   4-May-31

MX: 2B 817/22
78: HMV DB 1527/9
Victor 7487/9 (M 121)
LP: GR 2210
GR 2245
HQM 1219
SH 617
CD: Appian APR 5542
CDH 7 64495 2
Enterprise ENT QT 99310
Magic Master MM 37044
Magic Talent 48022
Magic Talent 48026
Pearl GEM 0025
Pearl GEMM 9942

BRAHMS (cont.)

Sonata for Violin and Piano No. 2 in A major, Op. 100

A. Busch 20-Sep-32 MX: 2B 3872/5
78: HMV DB 1805/6
Victor 8359/60
LP: COLH 41
GR 2242
SH 617
CD: Appian APR 5542
CDH 7 64495 2
Enterprise ENT QT 99310
Magic Master MM 37044
Magic Talent 48026
Pearl GEM 0025
Pearl GEMM 9942

Sonata for Cello and Piano No. 1 in E minor, Op. 38

M. Rostropovich Jul-82 LP: DG 2532 073
Washington, CD: DG 410 510-2
D.C. DG 449 611-2

Sonata for Cello and Piano No. 2 in F major, Op. 99

M. Rostropovich Jul-82 LP: DG 2532 073
Washington, CD: DG 410 510-2
D.C. DG 449 611-2

Trio for Horn, Violin, and Piano in E-flat major, Op. 40

A. Busch, A. Brain 13-Nov-33 MX: 2B 6708/15
78: HMV DB 2105/8
Victor 7965/8 (M 199)
LP: COLH 41
GR 2033
GR 2242
Seraphim IC 6044
SH 615
CD: CDH 7 64495 2
Enterprise ENT QT 99302
Iron Needle IN 1342/43
Magic Talent 48021
Pearl GEM 0007
Testament SBT 1001

M. Tree, M. Bloom 22-24-Aug-60 LP: ML 5643, MS 6243
Marlboro MS 7266
CD: SMK 46249

Trio for Piano and Strings No. 2 in C major, Op. 87

A. Busch, H. Busch 10-Oct-51 LP: Odyssey 32 16 0361
Brattleboro, VT SOCU 16
SONC 15108
CD: MPK 46447

Variations and Fugue on a Theme by Handel, Op. 24

| | Jan-79 Guilford, VT | LP: M 35177 |

BUSCH, ADOLF (1891–1952)

Quintet for Piano and Strings, Op. 35

| P. Carmirelli, H. Fajima, A. Pellicia, R. Sylvester | 6-Aug-67 Marlboro | LP: Col. RSM 3 (private pressing) Bruder-Busch-Gesellschaft F60.649 M-A |

Sonata for Violin and Piano No. 2 in A minor, Op. 56

| P. Carmirelli | 7-Aug-66 Marlboro | LP: Marlboro Rec Soc MRS 9 |

CHOPIN, FRÉDÉRIC (1810–1849)

Etudes, Op. 25

| | 5-May-48 Library of Congress | CD: *Rudolf Serkin, A Life* Stephen Lehmann and Marion Faber Oxford University Press, 2003 Accompanying CD |

GEMINIANI, FRANCESCO (1687–1762)

Sonata in C minor, Siciliana (arr. A. Busch)

A. Busch	5-May-31	MX: 2B 829
		78: HMV DB 1524
		LP: GR 2247
		Perennial 2006
		CD: Appian APR 5543
		CDCB 54374

HANDEL, GEORGE FRIDERIC (1685–1759)

Dank Sei Dir, Herr (arr. Ochs)

H. Lashanska, sop.; M. Elman, violin; E. Feuermann, cello	14-Jan-39 [first U.S. recording]	MX: CS 31473
		78: HMV DB 3819
		Victor 15365
		CD: Biddulph LAB 048

HAYDN, FRANZ JOSEF (1732–1809)
Sonata in E-flat major, Hob. XVI: 49

14,15-Dec-77	LP:	M2 34596
	CD:	SRCR 8585-6

Sonata in C major, Hob. XVI: 50

14-Apr, 4-Oct-85	LP:	M 39562
Guilford, VT	CD:	MK 39562

Trio for Flute, Cello, and Piano in G major, Hob. XV: 15

M. Debost, P. Wiley   4-Aug-74   LP: Marlboro Rec Soc MRS 7
                                    Marlboro

MENDELSSOHN, FELIX (1809–1847)
Capriccio brillant for Piano and Orch., Op. 22

Philadelphia Orch., Ormandy   4-Apr-67   LP: MS 7423
                                                           MG 32042
                                                           MP 39544
                                                     CD: MPK 45690
                                                           M2YK 45675
                                                           SBK 48166
                                                           SB3K 52516

Concerto for Piano and Orch. No. 1 in G minor, Op. 25

Philadelphia Orch., Ormandy   19-Dec-57   LP: ML 5456, MS 6128
                                                           D3L 341, D3S 741
                                                           GMB 78
                                                           MS 7185
                                                           M 31837
                                                           MG 32042
                                                           MP 39554
                                                     CD: MPK 45690
                                                           M2YK 45675
                                                           SBK 46542
                                                           SBK 89842

Concerto for Piano and Orch. No. 2 in D minor, Op. 40

Columbia Symphony Orch., Ormandy   8-Oct-59   LP: ML 5456, MS 6128
                                                           GMB 78
                                                           MG 32042
                                                           MP 39554
                                                     CD: MPK 45690
                                                           M2YK 45675
                                                           SBK 46542
                                                           SBK 89842

Fantasies, Op. 16

	10-Dec-46	CD:	*Rudolf Serkin: A Life*
	Library of		Stephen Lehmann and
	Congress		Marion Faber
			Oxford University Press
			2003
			Accompanying CD

Rondo capriccioso, Op. 14

	5-May-48	CD:	*Rudolf Serkin: A Life*
	Library of		Stephen Lehmann and
	Congress		Marion Faber
			Oxford University Press
			2003
			Accompanying CD

Songs without Words, Op. 62, No. 1, "May Breezes"

	1-Dec-47	MX:	XCO 39498
		78:	Col. 72785 (MM 816)
	5-May-48	CD:	*Rudolf Serkin: A Life*
	Library of		Stephen Lehmann and
	Congress		Marion Faber
			Oxford University Press
			2003
			Accompanying CD
	8-Dec-62	LP:	MS 7516
			MP 39549
		CD:	M2YK 45675

Songs without Words, Op. 67, No. 4, "Spinning Song"

	10-Dec-46	CD:	*Rudolf Serkin: A Life*
	Library of		Stephen Lehmann and
	Congress		Marion Faber
	(encore)		Oxford University Press
			2003
			Accompanying CD
	8-Dec-62	LP:	MS 7516
			MP 39549
		CD:	M2YK 45675

MOZART, WOLFGANG AMADEUS (1756–1791)

Concerto for Piano and Orch. No. 8 in C major, K.246

London Symphony Orch., Abbado	16-Mar-82	LP:	DG 410 035-1
		CD:	DG 410 035-2

Concerto for Piano and Orch. No. 9 in E-flat major, K.271

Marlboro Festival Orch., Schneider	29-Aug-56	LP:	ML 5209
	[first recording		Odyssey Y3 34642
	at Marlboro]		
London Symphony Orch., Abbado	4-9-Nov-81	LP:	DG 2532 060
		CD:	DG 415 206-2

MOZART (cont.)

Concerto for Two Pianos and Orch. No. 10 in E-flat major, K.365

P. Serkin, Marlboro Festival Orch., Schneider	3-Oct-62	LP:	ML 6247, MS 6847
			MP 39127
		CD:	SMK 46255
			SM3K 47207
			00DC 997-1000

Concerto for Piano and Orch. No. 11 in F major, K.413

Marlboro Festival Orch., Schneider	28-Aug-57	LP:	ML 5367, MS 6049
			M 31728
		CD:	00DC 997-1000

Concerto for Piano and Orch. No. 12 in A major, K.414

Marlboro Festival Orch., Schneider	30-Aug-56	LP:	ML 5209
Marlboro Festival Orch., Schneider	4-Oct-62	LP:	M 31728
		CD:	SMK 46255
			SM3K 47207
			00DC 997-1000
London Symphony Orch., Abbado	5,6-Nov-81	LP:	DG 2532 053
		CD:	DG 400 068-2
			Philips 456 964

Concerto for Piano and Orch. No. 14 in E-flat major, K.449

Busch Chamber Players	11-Oct-38	MX:	2EA 1190/95
		78:	HMV DB 3960/2
			Vic 15912/4 (M 657)
		LP:	GR 2252
			Turnabout THS 65058
		CD:	CDCB 54374
			Pearl GEMM 9278
			Philips 456 964
Columbia Symphony Orch., Schneider	9-Oct-62	LP:	ML 6244, MS 6844
			MP 38771
		CD:	SM3K 47207
			00DC 997-1000

Concerto for Piano and Orch. No. 15 in B-flat major, K.450

London Symphony Orch., Abbado	5,6-Feb-85	CD:	DG 415 488-2

Concerto for Piano and Orch. No. 16 in D major, K.451

Columbia Symphony Orch., Schneider	10-Nov-55	LP:	ML 5297
Chamber Orch. of Europe, Abbado	Apr,May-88 Vienna	CD:	DG 445 597-2 Philips 456 964

Concerto for Piano and Orch. No. 17 in G major, K.453

Columbia Symphony Orch., Schneider	20,21-Nov-55	LP:	ML 5169
			Odyssey Y3 34642

Columbia Symphony Orch., Schneider   8-Oct-62   LP: ML 6244, MS 6844
                                                       MP 38771
                                                   CD: SM3K 47207
                                                       00DC 997-1000
London Symphony Orch., Abbado   7-9-Nov-81   LP: DG 2532 060
                                                   CD: DG 415 206-2s
                                                       Philips 456 964

Concerto for Piano and Orch. No. 18 in B-flat major, K.456

London Symphony Orch., Abbado   26-Nov-86   CD: DG 423 062-2

Concerto for Piano and Orch. No. 19 in F major, K.459

Columbia Symphony Orch., Szell   28-Apr-61   LP: ML 5934, MS 6534
                                                       MY 37236
                                                   CD: MYK 37236
                                                       SM3K 47207
                                                       00DC 997-1000
London Symphony Orch., Abbado   18-20-Mar-83   LP: DG 410 989-1
                                                   CD: DG 410 989-2
                                                       Philips 456 964

Concerto for Piano and Orch. No. 20 in D minor, K.466

Philadelphia Orch., Ormandy   11-Feb-51   LP: ML 4424
Marlboro Festival Orch., Schneider   27-Aug-57   LP: ML 5367, MS 6049
                                                       MP 39127
Columbia Symphony Orch., Szell   26,27-Apr-61   LP: ML 5934, MS 6534
                                                       MY 37236
                                                   CD: MBK 42533
                                                       SM3K 47207
                                                       MYK 37236
                                                       00DC 997-1000
                                                       MDK 45743 (2nd mvt. only)
London Symphony Orch., Abbado   4-6-Nov-81   LP: DG 2532 053
                                                   CD: DG 400 068-2
                                                       DG 431 278-2
                                                       DG 445 597-2

Concerto for Piano and Orch. No. 21 in C major, K.467

Columbia Symphony Orch., Schneider   8-Nov-55,   LP: ML 5013
                                     19-Dec-55   Odyssey Y3 34642
                                                   CD: SM3K 47269
                                                       J4K 65819 (3rd mvt. only)
London Symphony Orch., Abbado   22-24-Oct-82   LP: DG 2532 095
                                    (cadenzas by   CD: DG 410 068-2
                                     Serkin)   DG 445 516-2
                                                       DG 431 278-2
                                                       DG 427 812-2
                                                       DG 439 150-2 (2nd mvt. only)
                                                       DG 439 514 (2nd mvt. only)
                                                       DG 459 903 (2nd mvt. only)

MOZART (cont.)

Concerto for Piano and Orch. No. 22 in E-flat major, K.482

Perpignan Festival Orch., Casals	26-Jul-51 Perpignan (cadenzas by Serkin)	LP:	ML 4569 SL 168 SL 170 M 32772/3 M5X 32768
		CD:	SMK 66570 SMK 66568
London Symphony Orch., Abbado	6,8-Oct-84 (new cadenzas by Serkin)	CD:	DG 415 488-2 DG 429 978-2

Concerto for Piano and Orch. No. 23 in A major, K.488

Columbia Symphony Orch., Schneider	9-Nov-55	LP:	ML 5297 Odyssey Y3 34642
London Symphony Orch., Abbado	22-24-Oct-84	LP:	DG 2532 095
		CD:	DG 410 068-2 DG 431 279-2 DG 445 771 (2nd mvt. only)

Concerto for Piano and Orch. No. 24 in C minor, K.491

London Symphony Orch., Abbado	27,28-Oct-85 (cadenzas by Serkin)	CD:	DG 423 062-2 DG 431 279-2

Concerto for Piano and Orch. No. 25 in C major, K.503

Cleveland Orch., Szell	15, 16-Apr-53, 20, 21-Nov-55	LP:	ML 5169 Odyssey Y3 34642
		CD:	SM3K 47269
London Symphony Orch., Abbado	16,18-Mar-83	LP:	DG 410 989-1
		CD:	DG 410 989-2 DG 429 978-2

Concerto for Piano and Orch. No. 27 in B-flat major, K.595

Columbia Symphony Orch., Schneider	11-Nov-55	LP:	ML 5013 Odyssey Y3 34642
Philadelphia Orch., Ormandy	28-Jan-62	LP:	ML 6239, MS 6839 MG 31267
		CD:	MBK 42533 SM3K 47207 00DC 997-1000
London Symphony Orch., Abbado	19,20-Mar-82 21-Mar-83	LP:	DG 410 035-1
		CD:	DG 410 035-2 DG 445 516-2 DG 427 812-2

Quintet for Piano and Winds in E-flat major, K.452

J. De Lancie, A. Gigliotti, S. Schoenbach, M. Jones	22-Sep-53	LP:	ML 4834

Rondo in a, K.511

	14,15-Dec-77	LP:	M2 34596
			MP 39549
		CD:	SM3K 47207
			SRCR 8585-6

Rondo for Piano and Orch. in D major, K.382

Columbia Symphony Orch., Schneider   14-Nov-55   CD: SM3K 47207

Sonata for Violin, Cello, and Piano in A major, K.12

P. Carmirelli, D. Cole   23-Jul-67   LP: Marlboro Rec Soc MRS 1
Marlboro

Sonata for Violin, Cello, and Piano in F major, K.13

P. Carmirelli, D. Cole   23-Jul-67   LP: Marlboro Rec Soc MRS 1
Marlboro

Sonata for Violin and Piano in F major, K.377

A. Busch	9-Oct-37	MX:	2EA 5484/7
		78:	HMV DB 3373/4
			Victor 15175/6
		LP:	GR 2247
		CD:	Appian APR 5543
			CDCB 57374

Trio for Piano and Strings in B-flat major, K.502

J. Laredo, M. Foley	11,12-Jul-68	LP:	MS 7447
	Marlboro		D3M 33001
		CD:	SMK 46255

PROKOFIEV, SERGE (1891–1953)

Concerto for Piano and Orch. No. 4, Op. 53

| Philadelphia Orch., Ormandy | 30-Mar-58 | LP: | ML 5805, MS 6405 |
| | | CD: | MPK 46452 |

REGER, MAX (1873–1916)

Concerto for Piano and Orch. in F minor, Op. 114

| Philadelphia Orch, Ormandy | 30-Mar-59 | LP: | ML 5635, MS 6235 |
| | | CD: | MPK 46452 |

Sonata for Violin and Piano in F-sharp minor, Op. 84, Allegretto only

A. Busch	7-May-31	MX:	2B 843
		78:	HMV DB 1523
			Victor 7562 (M 132)
		LP:	GR 2246
			Perennial 2006
		CD:	Appian APR 5542
			Biddulph LAB 165
			CDCB 54374

REGER (cont.)

Sonata for Violin and Piano in C minor, Op. 139

| P. Carmirelli | 12-Aug-72 Marlboro | LP: M 32221 |

Sonata for Clarinet and Piano in B-flat major, Op. 107

| D. Singer | 10-Jul-77 Marlboro | LP: Marlboro Rec Soc MRS 12 |

Variations and Fugue on a Theme by J. S. Bach, Op. 81

| | 19,20-Jun-84 Troy, NY | LP: M 39562 CD: MK 39562 |

SCHUBERT, FRANZ (1797–1828)

Auf dem Strom, D.943

| B. Valente, sop.; M. Bloom, horn | 16,17,22-Aug-60 Marlboro | LP: ML 5643, MS 6243 CD: MPK 45559 SMK 60032 SBK 48176 |

Fantasia for Violin and Piano in C major, D.934

A. Busch	6-May-31	MX: 2B 834/8
		78: HMV DB 1521/3
		Victor 7562/4 (M 132)
		LP: Elec. 1C 137 53032/6M
		GR 2246
		Pathé 2C 051-03309
		Perennial 2006
		SH 53
		CD: Appian APR 5543
		CDH 7 61014 2
		Pearl GEMM 9141

Der Hirt auf dem Felsen, D.965

B. Valente, sop.; H. Wright, clarinet	16,17,22-Aug-60 Marlboro	LP: ML 5636, MS 6236 CD: SMK 45901 MPK 45559 SBK 48176
B. Valente, sop.; H. Wright, clarinet	16,17,22-Aug-60 Marlboro [alternate take]	CD: Boston BR 1024CD
B. Valente, sop.; H. Wright, clarinet	20-Jul-69 Marlboro	CD: Bridge 9108 A/B

Impromptus, Op. 142, D.935

| | Jan-79 Guilford, VT | LP: M 35178 MP 34549 (No. 2 only) MP 38766 CD: MPK 44847 SM2K 60033 |

Introduction and Variations for Flute and Piano, D.802, "Trock'ne Blumen"

P. Robison	3-Aug-68 Marlboro	LP:	Marlboro Rec Soc MRS 3

Litanei, D.343 (arr. Pasternack)

H. Lashanska, sop.;	14-Jan-39	MX:	CS 31474
M. Elman, violin;	[first U.S.	78:	HMV DB 3819
E. Feuermann, cello	recording]		Victor 15365
		CD:	Biddulph LAB 048

Moments Musicaux, D.780

	8-Dec-52	LP:	ML 5153
			MS 7526 (No. 3 only)
			MP 34549

Quintet for Piano, Violin, Viola, Cello, and Double Bass in A major, D.667, "Trout"

J. Laredo, P. Naegele, L. Parnas,	15-Aug-67	LP:	ML 6467, MS 7067
J. Levine	Marlboro		MY 37234
			MGP 32
			D3M 33001
		CD:	SMK 46252
			MYK 37234

Sonata for Piano in C major, D.840, "Unfinished"

	22,24-Mar-55	LP:	ML 5153

Sonata for Piano in A major, D.959

	16,18-Feb-66	LP:	ML 6249, MS 6849
			MP 39055
		CD:	MPK 45559
			SM2K 60033

Sonata for Piano in B-flat major, D.960

	24,25-Sept-75 Guilford, VT	LP:	M 33932
			MP 39756
		CD:	SM2K 60033
	14,15-Dec-77	LP:	M2 34596
		CD:	SRCR 8585-6

Trio for Piano and Strings No. 2 in E-flat major, D.929

A. Busch, H. Busch	23-Oct-35	MX:	2EA 2466/75
		78:	HMV DB 2676/80
			Victor 14464/8 (M 374)
		LP:	COLH 43
			Elec. E 80792
			Elec.1C 137 503032/6M
			GR 2243
			Pathé 2C 051-03309
			SH 533
			Turnabout THS 65064
		CD:	CDH 7 61014 2
			Pearl GEMM 9141

SCHUBERT (cont.)

Trio for Piano and Strings No. 2 in E-flat major, D.929 (continued)

A. Busch, H. Busch	11-Oct-51	LP:	ML 4654
			Odyssey Y 34635
		CD:	SMK 48088

SCHUMANN, ROBERT (1810–1856)

Concerto for Piano and Orch. in A minor, Op. 54

Philadelphia Orch., Ormandy	21-Jan-46	MX:	XCO 35661/8
		78:	Col. 12776/9D (M 734)
		LP:	ML 4041
Philadelphia Orch., Ormandy	11-Mar-56,	LP:	ML 5168
	19-Dec-56	CD:	SM3K 47269
Philadelphia Orch., Ormandy	17-Mar-64	LP:	ML 6088, MS 6688
			D3L 341, D3S 741
			MS 7185
			M 31837
			MG 32042
			MY 37256
		CD:	MYK 37256
			SBK 46543
			SMK 60324

Introduction and Allegro Appassionato, Op. 92

Philadelphia Orch., Ormandy	17-Mar-64	LP:	ML 6088, MS 6688
		CD:	MBK 46273
			SBK 46543
			SB3K 52516
			SMK 60324

Introduction and Allegro, Op. 134

Cleveland Orch., Szell	12,14-Mar-59	CD:	Cleveland Orchestra
			TC093-75-5
Philadelphia Orch., Ormandy	10-Apr-68	LP:	MS 7423
			MG 32042
		CD:	SBK 48166
			SMK 60324

Quintet for Piano and Strings in E-flat, Op.44

Busch Quartet	22-May-42	MX:	XCO 32861/8
(A. Busch, G. Andreasson,		78:	Col. 71442/5D (M 533)
K. Doktor, H. Busch)		LP:	ML 2081
			Smithsonian R 032
			SONC 15108
			SOCU 16
		CD:	Biddulph LAB 103
			Pearl GEMM 9275

Budapest String Quartet (J. Roisman, A. Schneider, B. Kroyt, M. Schneider)	10,11-Sept-63	LP: CD:	ML 6194, MS 6794 M2L 334, M2S 734 MS 7266 MY 37256 MPK 45885 MYK 37256

Sonata for Violin and Piano No. 1 in A minor, Op. 105

A. Busch	9-Oct-37	MX: 78: LP: CD:	2EA 5480/3 HMV DB 3371/2 Victor 15393/4 (M 551) GR 2246 Rococo 2023 Appian APR 5542 Biddulph LAB 165 CDCB 54374 Pearl GEM 0025 The Piano Library PL 189
A. Busch	10-Dec-46 Library of Congress	LP: CD:	Odyssey Y3 34639 Music & Arts CD 877

Sonata for Violin and Piano No. 2 in D minor, Op. 121

A. Busch	27-Apr-43 Library of Congress	LP: CD:	Odyssey Y3 34639 Music & Arts CD 877

STRAUSS, RICHARD (1864–1949)

Burleske for Piano and Orch. in D minor, Op. 11

Philadelphia Orch., Ormandy	11-Mar-55	LP: CD:	ML 5168 SM3K 47269
Philadelphia Orch., Ormandy	3-Feb-66	LP: CD:	MS 7423 MK 42261 SBK 53262

VIVALDI, ANTONIO (1678–1741)

Sonata for Violin and Piano No. 2 in A major, Op. 2 (arr. A. Busch)

A. Busch	5-May-31	MX: 78: LP: CD:	2B 828 HMV DB 1524 GR 2247 Perennial 2006 Rococo 2023 CDCB 54374 Appian APR 5543

II. UNAUTHORIZED RECORDINGS

BACH, JOHANN SEBASTIAN

Capriccio in B-flat major on the Departure of His Beloved Brother, BWV 992

| | 22-May-57 | CD: | Aura 124-2 |
| | Lugano | | Ermitage ERM 110 |

BARTÓK, BÉLA

Concerto for Piano and Orch. No. 1

| New York Philharmonic, Reiner | 19-Mar-60 | CD: | AS 526 |
| | | | Arlecchino ARL-198 |

BEETHOVEN, LUDWIG VAN

Concerto for Piano and Orch. No. 1 in C major, Op. 15

New York Philharmonic, Cantelli	29-Mar-53	CD:	AS 623
			Melodram MEL 18.010
RAI Napoli, Caracciolo	3-Jun-58	LP:	Fonit-Cetra LAR 4
			Mov. Musica 04.001
		CD:	Europa Musica 051.040
Bavarian Radio Orch., Kubelik	3,4-Nov-77	CD:	AS NAS 2603
	Munich		Artists Live FED 067

Concerto for Piano and Orch. No. 2 in B-flat major, Op. 19

RAI Roma, Scaglia	7-Jun-58	LP:	Fonit-Cetra LAR 4
			Mov. Musica 04.001
		CD:	Fonit-Cetra CDE 1001
			Fonit-Cetra CDAR 2036
			Europa Musica 051.040
Bavarian Radio Orch., Kubelik	3,4-Nov-77		AS NAS 2603
	Munich		Artists Live FED 067

Concerto for Piano and Orch. No. 3 in C minor, Op. 37

RAI Napoli, Caracciolo	3-Jun-58	LP:	Fonit-Cetra LAR 4
			Mov. Musica 04.001
		CD:	Europa Musica 051.040

Concerto for Piano and Orch. No. 4 in G major, Op. 58

Danish Radio Orch., F. Busch	23-Nov-33	LP:	Danacord DACO 134-138
	Copenhagen		(1st mvt. only)
			RR 487
			(1st mvt. only)
		CD:	Danacord DACO CD 303
			(1st mvt. only)
New York Philharmonic, Toscanini	23-Feb-36	LP:	A. Toscanini Soc. ATS 1052
	[U.S. broadcast	CD:	The Radio Years RY 53
	debut]		
RAI Roma, Scaglia	7-Jun-58	LP:	Fonit-Cetra LAR 4
			Mov. Musica 04.001
		CD:	Europa Musica 051.040

Concerto for Piano and Orch. No. 5 in E-flat major, Op. 73, "Emperor"

New York Philharmonic, Cantelli	29-Mar-53	CD:	AS 114
			Melodram MEL 18.010
			Legend 142
RAI Napoli, Caracciolo	3-Jun-58	LP:	Fonit-Cetra LAR 4
			Mov. Musica 04.001
		CD:	Fonit-Cetra CDE 1001
			Fonit-Cetra CDAR 2036
			Europa Musica 051.040

Sonata for Piano No. 6 in F major, Op. 10, No. 2

9-Jun-72	CD:	Arkadia CDGI 912.1
London		

Sonata for Piano No. 8 in C minor, Op. 13, "Pathétique"

23-Feb-56	LP:	Mov. Musica 01.038
9-Jun-72	CD:	Arkadia CDGI 912.1
London		

Sonata for Piano No. 12 in A-flat major, Op. 26

16-Jun-71	CD:	Arkadia CDGI 911.1
London		

Sonata for Piano No. 13 in E-flat major, Op. 27, No. 1

16-Jun-71	CD:	Arkadia CDGI 911.1
London		

Sonata for Piano No. 16 in G major, Op. 31, No. 1

26-Oct-61	LP:	Mov. Musica 01.038
14-Jun-71	CD:	Arkadia CDGI 912.1
London		

Sonata for Piano No. 21 in C major, Op. 53, "Waldstein"

16-Jun-71	CD:	Arkadia CDGI 911.1
London		

Sonata for Piano No. 23 in F minor, Op. 57, "Appassionata"

22-May-57	CD:	Aura 124-2
Lugano		Ermitage ERM 110
14-Jun-71	CD:	Arkadia CDGI 912.1
London		

Sonata for Piano No. 26 in E-flat major, Op. 81a, "Les Adieux"

9-Jun-72	CD:	Arkadia CDGI 911.1
London		

Trio for Piano and Strings No. 4 in D major, Op. 70, No. 1, "Ghost"

S. Goldberg, P. Casals	18-Jun-54	CD:	Music & Arts CD 688-4
	Prades		

BEETHOVEN (cont.)

Trio for Piano and Strings No. 5 in E-flat major, Op. 70, No. 2

S. Goldberg, P. Casals	18-Jun-54	LP: RR 547
	Prades	CD: AS 351
		Music & Arts CD 688-4
		Notes PGP 11007

Variations for Violin, Cello, and Piano in C major, Op. 121a, "Ich bin der Schneider Kakadu"

S. Goldberg, P. Casals	18-Jun-54	LP: RR 547
	Prades	CD: AS 351
		Music & Arts CD 688-4
		Notes PGP 11007

BRAHMS, JOHANNES

Quartet for Piano and Strings No. 1 in G minor, Op. 25

| A. Busch, H. Gottesman, H. Busch | 6-Nov-49 | LP: RR 534 |
| | Strasbourg | |

Sonata for Violin and Piano No. 3 in D minor, Op. 108

A. Busch	9-Mar-39	CD: Music & Arts 877
	Library of Congress	
A. Busch	28-Aug-49	LP: RR 485
	Edinburgh	CD: Music & Arts 877

Variations and Fugue on a Theme by Handel, Op. 24

| | 22-May-57 | CD: Aura 124-2 |
| | Lugano | Ermitage ERM 110 |

BUSCH, ADOLF

Sonata for Violin and Piano No. 2 in A minor, Op. 56

| A. Busch | 10-Dec-46 | CD: Music & Arts 877 |
| | Library of Congress | |

CHOPIN, FRÉDÉRIC

Etudes Op. 25, Nos. 1, 10

| | 23-Nov-33 | LP: Danacord DACO 134-138 |
| | Copenhagen | CD: Danacord DACO CD 303 |

MENDELSSOHN, FELIX

Rondo capriccioso, Op. 14

| | 22-May-57 | CD: Aura 124-2 |
| | Lugano | Ermitage ERM 110 |

MOZART, WOLFGANG AMADEUS

Concerto for Piano and Orch. No. 16 in D major, K.451

New York Philharmonic, Mitropoulos	23-Oct-55	LP:	Mov. Musica 01.007
		CD:	Arkadia CDMP 408.1
			AS 511
			HUNT CDL SMH 34008
			LGD 151
			Notes PGP 11014

Concerto for Piano and Orch. No. 20 in D minor, K.466

New York Philharmonic, Cantelli	27-Mar-53	CD:	AS 623

Concerto for Piano and Orch. No. 23 in A major, K.488

Orch."Alessandro Scarlatti" de Naples, F. Caracciolo	14-May-57	LP:	Fonit-Cetra (non-commercial limited edition issue)

Concerto for Piano and Orch. No. 25 in C major, K.503

New York Philharmonic, Mitropoulos	23-Oct-55	LP:	Mov. Musica 01.007
		CD:	Arkadia CDMP 408.1
			AS 511
			HUNT CDL SMH 34008
			LGD 151
			Notes PGP 11014

Concerto for Piano and Orch. No. 27 in B-flat major, K.595

New York Philharmonic, Toscanini	23-Feb-36 [U.S. broadcast debut]	LP: CD:	A. Toscanini Soc. ATS 1011 Radio Years RY53

Sonata for Piano No. 9 in D major, K.311

	23-Apr-56 Milan	CD:	Arkadia CDMP 408.1 Hunt CDLSMH 34008

Sonata for Violin and Piano in E-flat major, K.380

A. Busch	19-Jan-42 Library of Congress	CD:	Music & Arts CD 877

Sonata for Violin and Piano in E-flat major, K.481

A. Busch	7-Nov-44 Library of Congress	CD:	Music & Arts CD 877

Trio for Piano and Strings in G major, K.564

A. Busch, H. Busch	9-Jan-44	CD:	Arbiter 112

SCHUBERT, FRANZ

Impromptus, Op. 142, D.935

	22-May-57 Lugano	CD: Aura 124-2 (No. 4 only) Ermitage ERM 110 (No. 4 only)
	13-May-68 London	CD: Arkadia CDGE 913.1

Rondo brillant for Violin and Piano in B minor, D.895

A. Busch	26-Apr-43 Library of Congress	CD: Music & Arts CD 877

Sonata for Piano in B-flat major, D.960

	14-Jun-71 London	CD: Arkadia CDGE 913.1

SCHUMANN, ROBERT

Concerto for Piano and Orch. in A minor, Op. 54

Munich Philharmonic Orch., Rieger	28-Oct-76	CD: Melodram GM40054

Trio for Piano and Strings No. 3 in G minor, Op. 110

Végh, Casals	11-July-56 Prades	LP: RR 498 CD: AS 350 Music and Arts CD 688-4 Stradivarius STR 10019

STRAUSS, RICHARD

Burleske for Piano and Orch. in D minor, Op. 11

New York Philharmonic, Mitropoulos	9-Feb-58	CD: Dante LYS 300 Hunt CD 581

III. MARLBORO TAPES

Serkin's first recordings from Marlboro were two Mozart concertos with Alexander Schneider and the Festival Orchestra, issued in 1956 for the Mozart Bicentennial. In 1960, Columbia's Music from Marlboro series began in earnest with two releases of chamber music by Schubert and Brahms. Regular in-house taping of Marlboro performances was initiated in 1964; after 1967 all performances were recorded. This enormous and treasurable archive of tapes is now held at the Library of Congress.

Over a period of thirty-nine years at Marlboro, Serkin participated in 234 performances in which he played 279 works; over 150 of these date from 1964 and after and, with only a few early exceptions, they are preserved on tape. Although the repertoire at Marlboro was always highly varied, the preponderance of Serkin's post-1964 performances concentrated on four composers: Haydn, Mozart, Beethoven, and Brahms. Bach was limited to the Fifth *Brandenburg*, the Three-Piano Concertos, the Fourteen "Goldberg Ground" Canons (a Marlboro "exclusive"), and two Trio Sonatas, Schubert to *Auf dem Strom, Der Hirt auf dem Felsen*, and the *Trout* Quintet, and versions of all of these (except the Trio Sonatas) were issued commercially. There was one performance each of Schumann *Märchenerzählungen* (Wright, Rhodes; August 2, 1964) and Mendelssohn Quartet in B minor, Op. 3 (Carmirelli, Graham, Leonard; August 1, 1971). The Smetana Sonata in E minor for two pianos, eight hands, another Marlboro "specialty," was taped three times (August 3, 1973; August 9, 1978; July 29, 1984), the Dvořák Piano Quintet in A major, Op. 81, twice (July 22, 1973; August 12, 1977), and the Dvořák Piano Quartet in D major, Op. 23, also twice (August 9, 1969; August 5, 1977). Reger, Busoni, Busch, and Casals are the remaining composers represented during this period.

Of the four composers whose works constituted the bulk of Serkin's performances, Haydn is surely the most neglected in his commercial recordings. Surprisingly, the work he performed most frequently at Marlboro (discounting, of course, the thirty-two performances of the Beethoven Choral Fantasy) was the Haydn Trio in G, Hob. XV:15 for flute, viola, and piano, which he played nine times. The eleven taped Haydn Piano Trio performances are as follows:

Hob. XV:		
	9 in A major	(Chase, Stocker; July 21, 1982)
	12 in E minor	(Tetzlaff, Linfield; July 23, 1988)
	13 in C minor	(Yajima, Wiley; July 30, 1971)
	14 in A-flat major	(Schneider, Parnas; July 8, 1966)
	20 in B-flat major	(Cirillo, Rosen; July 12, 1969)
	22 in E-flat major	(Klausner, Foley; July 16, 1967)
	23 in D minor	(Kato, Sant'Ambrogio; July 20, 1983)
	25 in G major	(Shacht, Bahng; August 3, 1983)
	26 in F-sharp minor	(Phillips, Meell; August 5, 1984)
	30 in E-flat major	(Frank, Vogler; July 29, 1989)
	31 in E-flat minor	(Tsumura, Sylvester; July 9, 1969)
		(Horigome, Spits; August 7, 1982)
		(Frank, Vogler; July 29, 1989)

Serkin also accompanied Benita Valente in selections from the Canzonettas (July 1, 1966).

Although throughout his career Mozart, Beethoven, and Brahms constituted the heart of Serkin's recorded output, there are works by each that are represented only in the Marlboro tapes, as can be seen below. Of particular significance are the Mozart and Brahms piano four-hand works he played with Horszowski annually between 1971 and 1974, the Mozart trios and G minor Piano Quartet, the second and third Beethoven trios, and his only performance of the Brahms C minor Piano Quartet, Op. 60.

Mozart:

Fugue in C minor for two pianos, K.426 (Goode; July 23, 1967)
Quartet for piano and strings in G minor, K.478 (Beths, Appel, Palm; July 26, 1970)
(Urushihara, Rodrigues, Rivinius; July 22, 1989)
Sonata in B-flat major for piano, four hands, K.358 (Horszowski; July 8, 1972)
Sonata in D major for piano, four hands, K.381 (Horszowski; July 10, 1971; July 24, 1976)
Sonata in C major for piano, four hands, K.521 (Horszowski; July 7, 1973)
Sonata in D major for two pianos, K.448 (Perahia; July 7, 1977)
Trio in E-flat major, K.498 (Webster, Rhodes; July 3, 1968)
(Cohen, Vernon; August 4, 1972)
(Newbold, Appel; July 20, 1977)
Trio in G major, K.496 (Swenson, Wiley; August 21, 1980)
(Bell, Schween; July 19, 1986)
Trio in E major, K.542 (Peinemann, Perényi; August 16, 1970)
Trio in C major, K.548 (Phillips, Grossman; August 8, 1974)

Beethoven:

Sonata for Horn and Piano in F major, Op. 17 (Bloom; August 12, 1966)
Marches for Piano, four hands, Op. 45, Nos. 1–3 (1-Bogle, 2-Barrett, 3-Ortiz; August 2, 1970)
Trio in G major, Op. 1, no. 2 (Carmirelli, Leonard; August 22, 1970)
(Beunion, Carr; August 14, 1982)
Trio in C minor, Op. 1, no. 3 (Luca, Foley; August 11, 1967)
(Mullova, Meell; August 10, 1985)

Brahms:

Neue Liebeslieder Walzer, Op. 65 (Batlle, w. Valente, Kopleff, Burgess, Workman; July 27, 1975)
Quartet for Piano and Strings, no. 3 in C minor, Op. 60 (Smukler, Clarke, J. Serkin; August 12, 1978)
Two Songs for Alto, Viola and Piano, Op. 91 (Ciesinski, Kashkashian; August 9, 1975)
Variations on a Theme by Schumann, Op. 23 (Horszowski; July 6, 1974)

Finally, there are major works by Busoni and Adolf Busch.

Busoni:

Sonata for Violin and Piano in E minor, Op. 36a (Carmirelli; August 10, 1974)

Busch:

Prelude and Passacaglia in D minor, Op. 4 (Carmirelli, I. Serkin, violins; August 7, 1968)

Quintet for Piano and Strings, Op. 35 (Carmirelli, Copes, I. Serkin, Leonard;

August 11, 1972)

(Carmirelli, I. Serkin, Appel, Goritzki;

August 6, 1976)

Theme and Variations, piano four hands, Op. 63 (P. Serkin; August 8, 1980)

The tapes from the Marlboro archives are available for listening at the Motion Picture, Broadcasting and Recorded Sound Department at the Library of Congress.

IV. LIVE PERFORMANCE TAPES

The first and largest cache of live Serkin recordings resides, once again, in the Library of Congress. From 1937 to 1950 he played in the Coolidge Auditorium almost annually, usually with Adolf Busch. All of these performances were recorded; most have been preserved on tape. Four were approved for release in the Busch-Serkin Odyssey set in 1977, and five more were issued on CD in the Music and Arts homage to the duo. As can be seen from the complete listing in Appendix A, however, there are many works for which these tapes remain the only source. The two solo recitals are particularly valuable; Serkin played the twelve Chopin Etudes, Op. 25 throughout his career, but this is the only extant recording of the complete set. The same holds true for the Haydn E-flat major Sonata, the Bach Fifth *French* Suite, and the Schumann *Symphonic Etudes*.*

After a hiatus of five years, Serkin resumed playing at the Library, this time with the Budapest Quartet. The five programs they played together between 1955 and 1959 included two performances of Busch's Piano Quintet, Op. 35, and the only recorded instances of this great ensemble playing the Mozart G minor Piano Quartet, K.478 and the Dvořák Piano Quintet in A major, Op. 81.

Another repository of Busch-Serkin recordings is in the Charles E. Rhodes Collection at the New England Conservatory of Music. These were amateur recordings of live performances in New York, and although the acetates are of questionable quality, the following two performances are major additions to the Serkin recorded canon:

Beethoven: Trio in B-flat major, Op. 97 (A. Busch, H. Busch; March 5, 1944)
Dvořák: Trio in F minor, Op. 65 (movements 1–3 only); (A. Busch,
               H. Busch; December 15, 1946)

Rudolf and Peter Serkin gave a recital of Schubert four-hand piano music at the Toscanini house in Riverdale on May 24, 1964. This event was preserved on tape and is

---

* The Chopin Etudes and the Bach French Suite are being released for the first time on the CD accompanying this volume.

available for listening purposes only as part of the Toscanini Legacy in the Rodgers and Hammerstein Archives of Recorded Sound at the New York Public Library for the Performing Arts (tape LT-10-8665):

Schubert:	March militaire No. 2 in G major, D. 733
	Grande marche No. 2 in G minor, D.819
	Variations on an Original Theme in A-flat major, D.813
	Marche caractéristique No. 1 in C major, D.968B (formerly D.886)

Finally, as is inevitably the case for a great artist who concertized frequently, there exist many unauthorized private tapes of Serkin live performances. Many of these "underground" tapes have circulated for years among his admirers. Particularly because the recorded legacy from his vast solo repertoire was relatively meager, these tapes, despite their occasionally poor sound quality and lack of editing, offer a valuable supplement to the appreciation of his artistry. The following otherwise unrecorded works exist on tapes from concerts:

Bach:	Fugue in A minor, BWV 904
Busoni:	Berceuse (Elegy no. 7, 1909)
	Toccata (1921)
Chopin:	Barcarolle in F-sharp major, Op. 60
	Bolero in C major, Op. 19
	Preludes, Op. 28
Haydn:	Sonata in D major, Hob. XVI:19
Mendelssohn:	Prelude and Fugue in E minor, Op. 35, no. 1
	Variations sérieuses, Op. 54
Mozart:	Fantasia and Fugue in C major, K.394
	Fantasia in C minor, K.475
	Sonata in C minor, K.457
	Sonata in A major, K.331
Schubert:	Fantasy in C major, "Wanderer," D. 760
	Sonata in A major, D.664
	Sonata in C minor, D.958
Schumann:	"Abegg" Variations, Op. 1
	Carnaval, Op. 9
	Symphonic Etudes, Op. 13
	Sonata No. 3 in F minor, Op. 14

APPENDIX 1: SERKIN AT THE LIBRARY OF CONGRESS

Date	Program	L.C. Catalogue Number
14-Dec-37	Beethoven: Sonata for Violin and Piano No. 1 in D major, Op. 12, No. 1 Beethoven: Sonata for Violin and Piano No. 3 in E-flat major, Op. 12, No. 3 Beethoven: Sonata for Violin and Piano No. 10 in G major, Op. 96 with A. Busch, violin	LWO 4366, 1B1
15-Dec-37	Beethoven: Sonata for Violin and Piano No. 5 in F major, Op. 24 Beethoven: Sonata for Violin and Piano No. 4 in A minor, Op. 23 Beethoven: Sonata for Violin and Piano No. 6 in A major, Op. 30, No. 1 Beethoven: Sonata for Violin and Piano No. 8 in G, Op. 30, No. 3 with A. Busch, violin	LWO 4366, 1B2
2-Mar-39	Bach: Sonata for Violin and Harpsichord No. 5 in F minor, BWV 1018 Brahms: Sonata for Violin and Piano No. 1 in G major, Op. 78 Schubert: Fantasia for Violin and Piano in C major, D.934 with A. Busch, violin	LWO 5103, 2A2 (Bach only?)
6-Mar-39	Beethoven: Sonata for Violin and Piano No. 7 in C minor, Op. 30, No. 2 Brahms: Sonata for Violin and Piano No. 2 in A, Op. 100 Schubert: Rondo brillant for Violin and Piano in B minor, D.895 with A. Busch, violin	LWO 5103 2B1 (Brahms only?)
9-Mar-39	Beethoven: Sonata for Violin and Piano No. 9 in A major, Op. 47 Brahms: Sonata for Violin and Piano No. 3 in D minor, Op. 108* Mozart: Sonata for Violin and Piano in D major, K. 306 with A. Busch, violin	LWO 5103, 2B2 (Brahms only?)
19,20-Jan-42	Mozart: Sonata for Violin and Piano in E-flat major, K.380* Schubert: Fantasia for Violin and Piano in C major, D.934 with A. Busch, violin Brahms: Variations and Fugue on a Theme by Handel, Op. 24	LWO 5099, 3B2-4B1 (19th) LWO 5099, 3A1-3B (20th)
27-Apr-43	Bach: Sonata for Violin and Harpsichord No. 3 in E major, BWV 1016* Beethoven: Sonata for Violin and Piano No. 8 in G major, Op. 30, No. 3* Schubert: Rondo brillant for Violin and Piano in B minor, D.895* Schumann: Sonata for Violin and Piano No. 2 in D minor, Op. 121* with A. Busch, violin	LWO 5101, 7B2-8B

Date	Program	L.C. Catalogue Number
7-Oct-44	Beethoven: Sonata for Violin and Piano No. 9 in A major, Op. 47 Mozart: Sonata for Violin and Piano in E-flat major, K.481* Brahms: Sonata for Violin and Piano No. 1 in G major, Op. 78 with A. Busch, violin	LWO 5173, 1B2-2A
14-Dec-45	Brahms: Sonata for Violin and Piano No. 1 in G major, Op. 78 Brahms: Sonata for Violin and Piano No. 2 in A major, Op. 100 Brahms: Sonata for Violin and Piano No. 3 in D minor, Op. 108 with A. Busch, violin	LWO 5181, 5B2-6A
10-Dec-46	Busch: Sonata for Violin and Piano in A minor, Op. 56* Schubert: Fantasia for Violin and Piano in C major, D.934 Schumann: Sonata for Violin and Piano No. 1 in A minor, Op. 105* with A. Busch, violin Mendelssohn: Three Fantasies, Op. 16*	LWO 5232, 6B2 ?, 8A2 ?
8-Mar-47	Brahms: Quintet for Piano and Strings in F minor, Op. 34 with Busch Quartet	LWO 5232, A-B1
16-Jan-48	Beethoven: Sonata for Violin and Piano No. 8 in G major, Op. 30, No. 3 Schubert: Rondo brillant for Violin and Piano in B minor, D.895 with A. Busch, violin Brahms: Variations and Fugue on a Theme by Handel, Op. 24	LWO 5257 8B
5-May-48	Mozart: Fantasy in D minor, K.397 Beethoven: Sonata No. 23 in F minor, Op. 57, "Appassionata" Mendelssohn: Songs without Words, Op. 62. No. 1,* Op. 67, No. 4 Mendelssohn: Rondo capriccioso, Op. 14* Chopin: Etudes, Op. 25*	LWO 5282 1B2
18-Nov-48	Brahms: Quartet for Piano and Strings No. 1 in G minor, Op. 25 Schumann: Quintet for Piano and Strings in E-flat major, Op. 44 with Busch Quartet Beethoven: Sonata No. 30 in E major, Op. 109	LWO 5282 8B
14-Apr-50	Haydn: Sonata in E-flat major, Hob. XVI: 52 Bach: French Suite No. 5 in G major, BWV 816* Beethoven: Sonata No. 21 in C major, Op. 53, "Waldstein" Schumann: Symphonic Etudes, Op. 13	RWD 9624, B2-9625
2-Nov-50	Beethoven: Sonata for Violin and Piano No. 10 in G, Op. 96 Brahms: Sonata for Violin and Piano No. 3 in D minor, Op. 108 Mozart: Sonata for Violin and Piano in G, K.379 with A. Busch, violin	LWO 5284, 25B
3-Nov-50	Schubert: Sonatina for Violin and Piano No. 3 in A minor, D.385	See 2-Nov-50
21-Apr-55	Schumann: Quintet for Piano and Strings in E-flat major, Op. 44 Busch: Quintet for Piano and Strings, Op. 35 Brahms: Quintet for Piano and Strings in F minor, Op. 34 with Budapest Quartet	LWO 2370

Date	Program	L.C. Catalogue Number
6-Apr-56	Schumann: Quintet for Piano and Strings in E-flat major, Op. 44 Mozart: Quartet for Piano and Strings in G minor, K. 478 Dvořák: Quintet for Piano and Strings in A major, Op. 81 with Budapest Quartet	LWO 2386
4,5-Apr-57	Brahms: Quartet for Piano and Strings No. 2 in A major, Op. 26 Brahms: Quintet for Piano and Strings in F minor, Op. 34 with Budapest Quartet	LWO 2479
7-Oct-57	Brahms: Quintet for Piano and Strings in F minor, Op. 34 with Budapest Quartet	LWO 2607
16,17-Apr-59	Busch: Quintet for Piano and Strings, Op. 35 Brahms: Trio for Horn, Violin, and Piano in E-flat major, Op. 40 Schubert: Quintet for Piano, Violin, Viola, Cello, and Bass in A major, D.667, "Trout" with Budapest Quartet, M. Jones, horn, J. Levine, bass	LWO 2826

*See Authorized and Unauthorized Recordings

APPENDIX 2: WELTE-MIGNON PIANO ROLLS

4182	Schubert:	Sonata in C minor, D.958, first and second movements
4183	Schubert:	Sonata in C minor, D.958, third and fourth movements
4184	Bach:	Goldberg Variations, BWV 988, Part 1
4185	Bach:	Goldberg Variations, BWV 988, Part 2
4186	Bach:	Goldberg Variations, BWV 988, Part 3
4187	Beethoven:	Sonata in F major, Op. 10, no. 2
4188	Chopin:	Etude in C-sharp minor, Op. 10, no. 4
		Etude in F minor, Op. 25, no. 2
		Etude in A minor, Op. 25, no. 11
4189	Chopin:	Etude in G-flat major, Op. 25, no. 9

NOTES:
In the Goldberg Variations, Variations 6–8 seem not to have been recorded.
Rolls 4182-86 and 4188 have been issued on CD: Archiphon ARC-105.

APPENDIX 3: UNRELEASED RECORDINGS

Columbia/CBS/Sony

Mozart:	Fantasy in C minor, K.475	September 2, 1941
Schumann:	Theme and Variations on "Abegg", Op. 1	September 3, 1941
Schubert:	Fantasy in C major, D. 760, "Wanderer"	December 2, 1947
Schubert:	Moment Musical No. 3 in F minor, D.780	December 2, 1947
Brahms:	Variations on a Theme by Schumann, Op. 9	December 12, 1951
Weber:	Invitation to the Dance, Op. 65	December 12, 1951
Schubert:	Sonata in A major, D.664 (two versions)	March 15, 16; November 18, 19, 1967
Beethoven:	Variations on a Theme by Diabelli, Op. 120	November 18, 19, 1967
Mozart:	Concerto no. 23 in A major, K.488 Philadelphia Orch., Ormandy	May 10, 1968
Chopin:	Preludes, Op. 28	June 7, 8, 1976

Deutsche Grammophon

Beethoven:	Sonata no. 21 in C major, Op. 53, "Waldstein"	March 14, 15, 1986
	Sonata no. 23 in F minor, Op. 57, "Appassionata"	May 30, 31; June 1, 1989

NOTES

ABOUT THE NOTES

Unless otherwise noted, all citations to unpublished sources are to materials housed in the Rudolf Serkin Papers, Rare Book & Manuscript Library, University of Pennsylvania.

We have endeavored to provide as much relevant information in the citations as we could obtain. Where the information had to be inferred, it is given in brackets. Often, however, it has not been possible to date letters or to identify the sources of newspaper clippings with accuracy. We have not provided notes when it has been necessary to protect the privacy of the source and when there is no additional information to give in a reference beyond what is already in the text itself.

Translations (unless otherwise noted) are by the authors.

INTRODUCTION

1. RS to Buffalo Philharmonic Orchestra, March 26, 1942.

2. RS to John McCullough, March 18, 1986.

3. RS to Jürgen Kesting, April 13, 1983.

4. Myriam Anissimov, "Rudolf Serkin: 'Tout le monde a le trac,'" *Le Monde de la Musique*, no. 55 (April 1983): 57.

5. Ibid., 60.

6. Ibid., 61.

CHAPTER 1

1. B. O. Unbegaun, *Russian Surnames* (Oxford: Clarendon Press, 1972), 343.

2. RS to Irving Syrkin, December 20, 1943.

3. Amalie Buchthal, "Rudi und Adolf Busch," 4. Unless otherwise noted, all Buchthal citations are taken from sketches she wrote about her brother and the history of her family that were generously provided by her daughter, Anna Buchthal, and translated by the authors.

4. Wilhelm Serkin to Amalie Buchthal, December 4, 1964.

5. Amalie Buchthal, "Mein Vater," 3.

6. Marthl Serkin (Schmälzle) to Reinhold Schmälzle, 1928.

7. Mordko Serkin to RS, February 6, 1922.

8. Elizabeth Wiskemann, *Czechs and Germans: A Study of the Struggle in the Historic Provinces of Bohemia and Moravia*, 2d ed. (London: Macmillan, 1967), 102.

9. Armin Wilkowitsch, "Geschichte der Juden in Eger," in *Die Juden und Judengemeinden Böhmens in Vergangenheit und Gegenwart* (Brünn-Prag: Jüdischer Buch-und Kunstverlag, 1934), 1: 121–129; Hillel J. Kieval, "Jews, Czechs and Germans in Bohemia before 1914," in *Austrians and Jews in the Twentieth Century*, ed. Robert S. Wistrich (New York: St. Martin's, 1992), 19–37; Rudolf M. Wlaschek, *Juden in Böhmen*, 2. Aufl. (München: Oldenbourg, 1997); Jitka Chmelikova, *Osudy chebsych Zidu* (Cheb: Chebské Muzeum, 2000).

10. "Cheb," in *Encyclopaedia Judaica* (Jerusalem: Keter, 1971), 5: 368.

11. Wiskemann, *Czechs*, 103.

12. Interview with Amalie Buchthal, London, November 2, 1994.

13. Wiskemann, *Czechs*, 59.

14. Christoph Stölzl, *Kafkas böses Böhmen:*

Zur Sozialgeschichte eines Prager Juden (München: Edition Text + Kritik, 1975), 74.

15. Armin Wilkowitsch to Auguste Serkin, February 23, 1927.

16. Bea Bearth to Irene Serkin, May 9, 1991.

17. Amalie Buchthal, "Mein Vater," 5.

18. Wilhelm Serkin to Amalie Buchthal, June 20, 1973.

19. Undated letter, Serkin Papers.

20. "Rudolf Serkin, Master Musician: Rudolf Serkin in Conversation with Isaac Stern." Produced by WETA, Washington D.C. and first broadcast on March 28, 1978. Cited henceforth as Stern interview.

21. Amram Scheinfeld Collection, Music Division, Library of Congress.

22. Amalie Buchthal, "Wie Rudis musikalisches Talent entdeckt wurde," 1.

23. Anissimov, "Rudolf Serkin," 57; Lotte (Serkin) Fischer to RS, March 20, 1978.

24. Dean Elder, "Serkin, As Interviewed by Dean Elder," *Clavier* (November 1970): 9.

25. "An Interview with Charles Rosen," *Piano Quarterly* (winter 1990−91): 22.

26. From an uncited transcription compiled by Karin Michaelis in Serkin Papers, February 1, 1938. Cited henceforth as Michaelis transcription.

27. January 22, 1912.

28. Armin Wilkowitsch, "Ein Egerer Künstler von Weltruf," *Egerer Zeitung* (1926).

29. Stern interview. Also RS to Karl Schumann, January 12, 1978.

30. Carl Flesch, *The Memoirs of Carl Flesch*, trans. Hans Keller (New York: Macmillan, 1958), 181.

31. Walter Niemann, *Meister des Klaviers: Die Pianisten der Gegenwart und der letzten Vergangenheit* (Berlin: Schuster & Loeffler, 1921), 183−184.

32. Stern interview.

33. Alexander Moszkowski, *Die Jüdische Kiste* (Berlin: Verlag der Lustigen Blätter, 1911), 33.

34. Noted by the critic Julius Korngold, copy in Serkin Papers.

35. *Musikalischer Kurier*, April 22, 1921, 91.

36. Amalie Buchthal, "Wie Rudis," 2.

37. Stern interview.

38. Ibid.

39. Jérôme Spycket, *Clara Haskil* (Lausanne: Payot, 1975), 24.

40. RS to Fred Kountz, May 10, 1976.

41. RS to Amalie Buchthal [early 1980s].

42. Irene Serkin, Personal communication to the authors, August 22, 1994.

43. Ibid.,

44. Amalie Buchthal, "Wie Rudis," 2.

45. Amalie Buchthal, "Wie Rudis," 3.

46. Amalie Buchthal, "Mein Vater," 4.

47. Stern interview.

48. Amalie Buchthal, "Mein Vater," 5.

49. Amalie Buchthal, "Wie Rudis," 3.

50. RS to Johanna [no surname given], October 29, 1920.

51. Marthl Serkin (Schmälze) to Reinhold Schmälzle, May 1928.

52. Amalie Buchthal, "Mein Vater," 6.

53. Alice Herdan-Zuckmayer, *Genies sind im Lehrplan nicht vorgesehen* (Frankfurt: S. Fischer, 1979), 26.

54. Elisabeth Serkin, Interview with the authors, June 15, 1994, Doylestown, Pennsylvania.

55. Karin Michaelis, *Little Troll* (New York: Creative Age Press, 1946), 202.

56. Marion K. Sanders, *Dorothy Thompson: A Legend in Her Time* (Boston: Houghton Mifflin, 1973), 240.

57. Robert Streibel, *Eugenie Schwarzwald und ihr Kreis* (Wien: Picus Verlag, 1996) is probably the most informative of the Schwarzwald histories. The most vivid of firsthand accounts of the Schwarzwalds in English is by Peter Drucker in his autobiography *Adventures of a Bystander* (New Brunswick, NJ: Transaction Publishers, 1994), "Hemme and Genia," 24−61.

58. Robert Musil, *Tagebücher* (Reinbek: Rowohlt, 1976), 631.

59. Elias Canetti, *The Play of the Eyes* (New York: Farrar, Straus and Giroux, 1986), 187−188.

60. Herdan-Zuckmayer, *Genies*, 69.

61. Eugenie Schwarzwald to RS, October 27, 1937.

62. Herdan-Zuckmayer, *Genies*, 81.

63. Joan Allen Smith, *Schoenberg and His Circle: A Viennese Portrait* (New York: Schirmer Books, 1986), 160, 165.

64. Amalie Buchthal, "Genia Schwarzwald," 2.

65. Herdan-Zuckmayer, *Genies*, 206−207.

66. Marianne Hotham to RS, October 23, 1977.

67. Karl Popper to Irene Serkin, May 31, 1991.

68. Oskar Kokoschka, *My Life* (New York: Macmillan, 1974), 68–69.

69. *Adolf Loos zum 60. Geburtstag am 10. Dezember 1930* (Wien: Lanyi, 1930), 60–61.

70. Paul Stefan, *Frau Doktor: Ein Bildnis aus dem unbekannten Wien* (München: Drei Masken Verlag, 1922), 13.

71. Ibid., 26–27.

72. Amalie Buchthal, "Mein Vater," 4.

73. Anissimov, "Rudolf Serkin," 57.

74. Michaelis transcription.

75. Ernst Krenek, *Im Atem der Zeit: Erinnerungen an die Moderne* (Hamburg: Hoffmann und Campe, 1998), 206.

76. From an undated draft of a speech.

77. Joseph Marx to Lotte (Serkin) Fischer, September 29, 1959.

78. Jeffrey Kallberg, Personal communication with the authors.

79. Amalie Buchthal, "Mein Vater," 6.

80. Stern interview.

81. Otto Friedrich, *Before the Deluge* (New York: Harper & Row, 1972), 171.

82. Helen Beck to RS, May 31, 1989; Hansi Ungar to RS, January 23, 1976.

83. Stern interview.

84. Charles Rosen, *Arnold Schoenberg* (Princeton, NJ: Princeton University Press, 1981), 9.

85. Allan Janik and Stephen Toulmin, *Wittgenstein's Vienna* (Chicago: Ivan Dee, 1996), 262.

86. Hubert Saal, Interview transcript, 15, Serkin Papers.

87. Stefan, *Frau Doktor*, 32.

88. From an undated draft of a speech.

89. Saal interview, 19.

90. Rosen, *Arnold Schoenberg*, 22, 15.

91. This is vigorously disputed by Richard Taruskin, *New York Times*, June 6, 1999, Arts Section, 25–26.

92. Rosen, *Arnold Schoenberg*, 8.

93. Krenek, *Im Atem*, 373.

94. Eberhard Freitag, *Arnold Schönberg: Mit Selbstzeugnissen und Bilddokumenten* (Reinbek bei Hamburg: Rowohlt Taschenbuch Verlag, 1973), 50.

95. Smith, *Schoenberg*, 169.

96. Friedrich, *Before the Deluge*, 180.

97. Egon Wellesz, *Leben und Werk* (Wien: Zsolnay, 1981), 50.

98. Judith Meibach, "The Society for Musical Private Performances: Antecedents and Foundation," *Journal of the Arnold Schoenberg Institute* 8, no. 2 (November 1984): 165.

99. Willi Reich, *Arnold Schönberg: Oder der konservative Revolutionär* (Wien: Verlag Fritz Molden, 1968), 160.

100. Wellesz, *Leben*, 40.

101. Willi Reich, *Schoenberg: A Critical Biography*, trans. Leo Black (New York: Praeger, 1971), 160.

102. Rosen, *Arnold Schoenberg*, 65. See also Frederick Dorian and Judith Meibach, "Reger's Historic Stature" (notes to Rudolf Serkin's "Reger" CD, CBS MK 39562, 1986).

103. Stern interview.

104. Ibid.

105. Saal interview, 21.

106. Anton Webern to Alban Berg, March 8, 1920. Copy in Serkin Papers.

107. Anton Webern, *Briefe an Heinrich Jalowetz* (Mainz: Schott, 1999).

108. H. H. Stuckenschmidt, *Schönberg: Leben, Umwelt, Werk* (Zürich: Atlantis, 1974), 246.

109. Karl Popper to Irene Serkin, May 31, 1991.

110. Friedrich, *Before the Deluge*, 180.

111. Irving Kolodin, "The Complete Musician," *Horizon* (September 1961): 84.

112. RS to Amalie Serkin (Buchthal), February 3, 1920.

113. Nuria Nono-Schoenberg, ed., *Arnold Schönberg 1874–1951: Lebensgeschichte in Begegnungen* (Klagenfurt: Ritter Klagenfurt, 1992), 175.

114. Arthur Schnitzler, *Tagebuch, 1920–1922* (Wien: Verlag der Österreichischen Akademie der Wissenschaften, 1993), 12, 23.

115. Christopher Serkin, Phone interview with the authors, August 8, 2001.

116. Peter Serkin, Interview with the authors, New York, November 18, 2000 and June 10, 2001.

117. Niemann, *Meister des Klaviers*, 63.

118. Friedrich, *Before the Deluge*, 171.

119. "Rudolf Serkin: Long Biography," 2–3 in Serkin Papers. Also Robert Jacobson, *Reverberations* (London: Vision Press, 1976), 200.

120. Otto Grüters, *Adolf Buschs Lebenslauf*. Numbering close to seven hundred pages, the manuscript is housed in the Reger-Institut's Brüder-Busch-Archiv in Karlsruhe-Durlach. As

the pages are unnumbered, citations are keyed to the dates of the entries.

121. Grüters, *Adolf Buschs Lebenslauf*, 157.

CHAPTER 2

1. Barbara Kempner, Interview with the authors, New York, September 17, 1994.

2. Ludwig Schiedermair, *Musikalische Begegnungen* (Köln: Staufen-Verlag, 1948), 122.

3. Thomas Mann, *Tagebücher, 1933–1934* (Frankfurt: S. Fischer, 1977), 209.

4. Artur Schnabel, *My Life and Music* (London: Longmans, 1961), 58.

5. Amalie Buchthal, "Rudi und Adolf Busch," 2.

6. Yehudi Menuhin, *Unfinished Journey* (New York: Knopf, 1997), 101–102.

7. Julius Bab and Willy Handl, *Wien und Berlin* (Berlin: Deutsche Buch-Gemeinschaft, 1926), 282.

8. Schnabel, *My Life*, 47.

9. Cesar Saerchinger, *Artur Schnabel: A Biography* (New York: Dodd, Mead, 1957), 132.

10. Friedrich Blume, ed., *Die Musik in der Geschichte und Gegenwart* (Kassel: Bärenreiter, 1949–51), 1: 1727.

11. *Hesses Musikerkalender*, 1923.

12. *Musikalisches Kourier*, April 22, 1921, 94.

13. *Allgemeine Musikzeitung*, 1921, 48.

14. Elder, "Serkin, As Interviewed by Dean Elder," 14.

15. *Der Tagespiegel* (Berlin), March 28, 1973.

16. Interview with Oliver Daniels, December 18, 1984, Stokowski Collection, Rare Book & Manuscript Library, University of Pennsylvania.

17. Amalie Buchthal, "Rudi und Busoni," 1–2.

18. Michaelis's transcription.

19. Robert Jacobson, interview, *Lincoln Center Spotlight* (January 1973): 18. Also Kolodin, "The Complete Musician," 84–85.

20. Reviewed in the *Berliner Tageblatt*, September 20, 1922, 2.

21. *Basler Nationalzeitung*, January 29, 1922.

22. *Basler Nationalzeitung*, December 17, 1923.

23. *Münchener Post*, March 24, 1922.

24. *Musikblätter des Anbruch*, May–June 1925, 332.

25. Schnabel, *My Life*, 207.

26. *New York Times*, April 13, 1978.

27. Seymour Lipkin, Interview with the authors, New York, December 14, 1996.

28. Isaiah Berlin, "The 'Naïveté' of Verdi," in *Against the Current* (New York: Viking, 1980), 288–289.

29. Fritz Busch, *Pages from a Musician's Life* (Westport, Conn: Greenwood Press, 1971), 86.

30. Walter Frisch, *The Early Works of Arnold Schoenberg, 1893–1908* (Berkeley: University of California Press, 1993), 14–19, 211–216.

31. Ibid., 214.

32. Adolf Busch, "The Art of Ensemble Playing," *Etude Music Magazine* (August 1938): 499–500.

33. Henry-Louis de la Grange, *Gustav Mahler* (Oxford: Oxford University Press, 1999), 3: 362.

34. *Berliner Tageblatt*, February 21, 1924, 2.

35. Elder, "Serkin, As Interviewed by Dean Elder," 15.

36. *Die Zeit*, March 25, 1983.

37. Grüters, *Adolf Buschs Lebenslauf*, April 8, 1927.

38. Dominik Sackmann, ed., *Adolf Busch: Werkverzeichnis/Liste des Oeuvres* (Zürich: Schweizerisches Musik-Archiv/Archives Musicales Suisses, 1994), 22.

39. Peter Serkin interview.

40. Bärbel Herbig and Doris Schröder, *Die Darmstädter Mathildenhöhe: Architektur im Aufbruch zur Moderne* (Darmstadt: Magistrat der Stadt Darmstadt, Denkmalschutz—Kulturamt, 1998).

41. Grüters, *Adolf Busch Lebenslauf*, February/March 1923.

42. Remy Louis, "Adieu au poète," *Diapason* (July–August 1991): 38.

43. Grüters, *Adolf Busch Lebenslauf*, May 1925.

44. Ibid., January 1924.

45. Amalie Buchthal, "Darmstadt und die neue Geige," 1.

46. Grüters, *Adolf Busch Lebenslauf*, February 1926.

47. *Basel: Geschichte einer städtischen Gesellschaft* (Basel: Christoph-Merian-Verlag, 2000), 410.

48. Yehudi Menuhin, Interview with the authors, London, March 27, 1995.

49. Lionel Gossman in Nicolas Bouvier, *Geneva, Zurich, Basel: History, Culture, and National Identity* (Princeton, NJ: Princeton University Press, 1994), 66.

50. Krenek, *Im Atem*, 413.

51. Eugenie Schwarzwald to RS, May 22, 1928.

52. RS to Rolf A. Merton, December 27, 1977.

53. Charles Berigan, "An Overwhelming Love for Music," notes to *Rudolf Serkin: Great Pianists of the Twentieth Century* (Philips CD 456 964, 1999), 10.

54. Grüters, *Adolf Buschs Lebenslauf*, March 25, 1937. Also Glenn Plaskin, *Horowitz: A Biography of Vladimir Horowitz* (New York: Quill, 1983), 101, 187−188.

55. Robert Jacobson, "Rudolf Serkin," in *Reverberations* (London: Vision Press, 1976), 203.

56. Grüters, *Adolf Busch Lebenslauf*, September 18, 1930.

57. Ibid., 1931.

58. Donald Rosenberg, *The Cleveland Orchestra Story* (Cleveland: Gray & Co., 2000), 240.

59. Jacobson, "Rudolf Serkin," 203.

60. Richard Taruskin, *Text & Act: Essays on Music and Performance* (New York: Oxford University Press, 1995), 223−224.

61. Theodor W. Adorno, "On the Fetish-Character in Music and the Regression of Listening," in *The Essential Frankfurt School Reader* (New York: Continuum, 1992), 284.

62. Jacobson, "Rudolf Serkin," 203.

63. Richard Goode, Interview with the authors, New York, October 7, 2000.

64. Karl Marilaun, 1925, quoted in Michaelis's transcription.

65. *Allgemeine Musikzeitung*, nos. 26−27 (July 5, 1929): 9.

66. *Münchener Post*, April 12, 1924.

67. *Münchener Post*, November 24, 1924.

68. *Berliner Tageblatt*, November 21, 1932.

69. Eugen Schmitz, *Dresdner Nachrichten*, January 4, 1927.

70. *Süddeutsche Zeitung*, January 25, 1928; *Stuttgarter Neues Tageblatt*, January 27 (?), 1928; Basel, December 13 (?), 1928.

71. Bern newspaper [no citation], October 25, 1939.

72. "Klavierabend Serkin," December 6, 1932.

73. Felix Galimir, Interview with the authors, New York, January 4, 1996.

74. *New York Times*, January 21, 1992.

75. Martin Ebel, "Musikalisches Zeitfenster," *Frankfurter Allgemeine Zeitung*, April 10, 1999, "Bilder und Zeiten," 4.

76. Hans Oesch, "Fragen zu Welte-Mignon an Herrn Rudolf Serkin," November 26, 1979.

77. Peter Serkin interview.

78. Pekka Gronow and Ilpo Saunio, *An International History of the Recording Industry* (London: Cassell, 1998), 39.

79. *Basel: Geschichte einer städtischen Gesellschaft*, 412.

80. A. H. Pellegrini, "Erinnerungen an Adolf Busch," *Basler Nachrichten*, October 12, 1952.

81. Mann, *Tagebücher, 1933−1934*, 404.

82. Pellegrini, *Erinnerungen*.

83. Cited in Lukrezia Seiler, "Riehen war ihm sehr lieb," z'Rieche: *Ein heimatliches Jahrbuch* (1991): 55.

84. Hans Ehringer, "Adolf Busch und Basel," 77−78 in *Basler Jahrbuch* 1955 (Basel: Verlag von Helbing & Lichtenhahn, 1954).

85. Sigfried Schibli, ed., *Musikstadt Basel* (Basel: Buchverlag der Basler Zeitung, 1999), especially Schibli's "Exiljahre in Basel: Der Musikerkreis um Adolf Busch," 154−167.

86. *Deutsches Volksblatt*, Stuttgart, February 19 [?], 1933; *Württembergische Zeitung*, February 19 [?], 1933; *Süddeutsche Zeitung*, Stuttgart, February 19, 1933.

87. *Süddeutsche Zeitung*, March 25 [?], 1933.

88. Friedrich, *Before the Deluge*, 384−385.

89. Grüters, *Adolf Busch Lebenslauf*.

90. *Die Musik* 25, no. 8 (May 1933): 626.

91. Irene Busch Serkin, comp., *Adolf Busch: Letters, Pictures, Memories* (Walpole, N.H.: Arts & Letters Press, 1991), 2:. 284.

92. Amalie Buchthal, "Über Adolf Busch," 3.

93. Grüters, *Adolf Buschs Lebenslauf*, April 4, 1933.

94. *Das "Reichs-Brahmsfest" 1933 in Hamburg: Rekonstruktion und Dokumentation* (Hamburg: von Bockel Verlag, 1997), 24.

95. Gabriele Johanna Eder, *Wiener Musikfeste zwischen 1918 und 1938: Ein Beitrag zur Vergangenheitsbewältigung* (Wien: Geyer Edition, 1991), 324−338.

96. Clipping from an unidentified newspaper, [April 21, 1933], Brüder-Busch Archiv.

97. Friedrich, *Before the Deluge*, 385.

98. May 5, 1934.

99. *Das musikalische Juden-ABC* (München: Hans Brückner Verlag, 1935), 90, 210.

100. RS to Fritz Busch, [Basel, 1933], Brüder-Busch Archiv.

101. RS to Reinhold Schmälzle, undated letter [June 1936]

102. Grüters, *Adolf Buschs Lebenslauf*, September 1934.

103. Dagny Björnson Gulbransson, *Das Olaf Gulbransson Buch* (München: Langen Müller, 1997), 253–256. The letter is dated November 8, 1934.

104. Grüters, *Adolf Buschs Lebenslauf*, May 27, 1933.

105. Frieda Busch to Elizabeth Sprague Coolidge, December 4, 1941, Elizabeth Sprague Coolidge Foundation Collection, Music Division, Library of Congress.

106. Alfred Einstein, *Alfred Einstein on Music: Selected Music Criticism* (New York: Greenwood, 1991), 203.

107. Martin Elste, *Meilensteine der Bach Interpretation, 1750–2000: Eine Werkgeschichte im Wandel* (Stuttgart: Metzler, 2000), 123, 125.

108. Jürg Erni, *Paul Sacher: Musiker und Mäzen* (Basel: Schwabe, 1999), 33.

109. Hans Deichmann, *Objects* (New York: Marsilio Publishers, 1997), 57.

110. RS to Otto Grüters, [1935]. Brüder-Busch Archiv.

111. Hermann Reuter to RS, November 24, 1946.

112. I. B. Serkin, *Adolf Busch: Letters, Pictures, Memories*, 2: 326.

113. Henriette Speiser, Interview with the authors, Basel, April 22, 1997.

CHAPTER 3

1. Joseph Mussulman, *Dear People . . . Robert Shaw: A Biography* (Bloomington: Indiana University Press, 1979), 52.

2. RS to Herbert A. Strauss, November 26, 1977.

3. Herbert F. Peyser, "A New Pianist: Berlin Events," *New York Times*, February 15, 1931, sect. 8, 9.

4. *Musical Courier*, May 6, 1933, 5.

5. Saerchinger, *Artur Schnabel*, 55.

6. de la Grange, *Gustav Mahler*, 3: 787.

7. RS to Irene Serkin, May (?) 1954.

8. RS to Irene Serkin, [February 1936].

9. RS to Irene Serkin, [February 1936].

10. Saerchinger, *Artur Schnabel*, 267.

11. Kolodin, "The Complete Musician," 84.

12. Alexander Schneider, *Sasha: A Musician's Life* (N.p: n.p., 1988), 85.

13. RS to Irene Serkin, February 19, 1936.

14. Robert Silverman, "Serkin: An Interview—Part One," *Piano Quarterly*, 26, no. 100 (winter 1977–78): 4.

15. *New York Times*, February 21, 1936, 20.

16. *Musical Courier*, February 29, 1936, 16.

17. Serkin Papers.

18. Paul Schiff to RS, March 9, 1936.

19. Sol Hurok to RS, August 7, 1936.

20. I. B. Serkin, *Adolf Busch: Letters, Pictures, Memories*, 2: 365.

21. *New York Times*, November 16. 1940.

22. *Times* (London), January 2, 1938.

23. *New York Sun*, December 17 (?), 1937.

24. *New York Sun*, February 3, 1938.

25. Samuel Lipmann, *The House of Music: Art in an Era of Institutions* (Boston: David R. Godine, 1984), 114.

26. Saerchinger, *Artur Schnabel*, 239.

27. RS to Irene Serkin, Los Angeles [1945 or 1946].

28. Paul Schiff to RS, March 9, 1936.

29. Irene Serkin to RS [February or early March 1938?].

30. RS to Irene Serkin, undated letter.

31. Hubert Saal interview, 9.

32. Barbara B. Heyman, *Samuel Barber: The Composer and His Music* (New York: Oxford University Press, 1992), 34.

33. Mann, *Tagebücher, 1940–1943*, 109.

34. *New York Post*, February 7, 1976, 13.

35. *New York Times*, October 5, 1940, 15.

36. Rosalie Leventritt to RS, October 6, 1940.

37. Irving Kolodin, *New York Sun*, January 23, 1946.

38. Harold Taubman, *New York Times*, March 5, 1947.

39. I. B. Serkin, *Adolf Busch: Letters, Pictures, Memories*, 2: 416. The sentence about Serkin is missing from the published English translation.

40. Mischa Schneider to RS, March 19, 1944.

41. I. B. Serkin, *Adolf Busch: Lectures, Pictures, Memories*, 2: 437–438.

42. RS to Benedict Vischer, undated letter [1939?].

43. Undated draft.

44. Ira Hirschmann, *Obligato* (New York: Fromm International Publishing, 1994), 35.

45. Frieda Busch to Elizabeth Sprague Coolidge, December 11, 1940, Elizabeth Sprague Coolidge Foundation Collection, Music Division, Library of Congress.

46. Elizabeth Bishop, *One Art: Letters* (New York: Farrar, Straus and Giroux, 1994), 197.

47. Olga Janowitz to RS, March 8, 1941.

48. Adolf Pines to RS, June 30, 1941.

49. RS to Anka Landau, undated letter [July 1938], Anka Bernstein Landau Collection, Juilliard School Archives.

50. RS to Mr. Rothschild, October 20, 1942.

51. Richard Sterba to RS, February 7, 1953.

52. Erich Kahler to RS, October 21, 1945.

53. Erika and Klaus Mann, *Escape to Life* (Boston: Houghton Mifflin, 1939), 259–260.

54. RS to Marthl Schmälzle, [1945].

55. I. B. Serkin, *Adolf Busch: Letters, Pictures, Memories*, 2: 516.

56. "Rudolf Serkin Talking with Elizabeth Harkins," October 6, 1980, 9. Oral History, American Music Archive, Yale University. Cited henceforth as Steinway Project Interview.

57. RS to Frances Dakyns, [1946?].

58. June 8, 1950.

59. John Serkin, communication with the authors, January 6, 2002.

60. *Harvester World*, 42, no. 3 (March 1951): 20.

61. *De Rotterdammer*, February 1, 1965.

62. Irene Serkin to Eugene Ormandy, August 22, 1964, Eugene Ormandy Papers, Rare Book & Manuscript Library, University of Pennsylvania.

63. RS to Ariel Rubstein, undated.

64. RS to Irene, [1958].

65. RS to Irene Serkin, November 21, 1960.

66. Draft in Serkin Papers.

67. RS to Otto Grüters, June 27, 1952.

68. Elisabeth Serkin, Interview with the authors, Doylestown, PA, June 15, 1994.

69. Ursula Serkin, Interview with the authors, New York, January 12, 1997.

70. Marguerite Serkin, Interview with the authors, Guilford, VT, October 26, 1996.

71. Elisabeth Serkin interview.

72. *New York Times*, January 29, 1967, sect. 2, pp. 13, 27.

73. Peter Serkin interview.

74. Deborah Trustman, "Peter Serkin: Playing in a New Key," *New York Times Magazine*, January 13, 1980.

75. David Dubal, *Remembering Horowitz* (New York: Schirmer Books, 1993), 165.

76. RS to Frances Dakyns, [1946?].

77. Frieda Busch to Ira Hirschmann, June 21, 1945.

78. November 29, 1945.

79. RS to Irene Serkin, October 15, 1947.

80. *Tagesanzeiger*, October 18, 1947.

81. RS to Irene Serkin, [1947].

82. RS to Irene Serkin, October 27, 1947.

83. RS to Irene Serkin, [1947].

84. RS to Irene Serkin, October 1947.

85. RS to Irene Serkin, October 11, 1947 [postmark].

86. RS to Irene Serkin, [October 4, 1948].

87. Elisabeth Serkin interview.

88. Marguerite Serkin interview.

89. Robert Baldock, *Pablo Casals* (Boston: Northeastern University Press, 1992), 194.

90. Schneider, *Sasha*, 122; H. L. Kirk, *Pablo Casals* (New York: Holt, Rinehart and Winston, 1974), 450.

91. Kolodin, "The Complete Musician," 82–87.

92. Bice Horszowski Costa, ed., *Miecio: Ricordi di Mieczyslaw Horszowski* (Genova: Erga, 2000), 347.

93. Bernard Meillat, "Serkin Off the Record," *Diapason* (July–August 1991): 41. Also correspondence with the authors, October 15, 2001.

94. RS to Irene Serkin, [June 9, 1950].

95. Ibid.

96. RS to Hermann Hesse, December 1952, Hermann Hesse Collection, Deutsches Literatur Archiv, Marbach.

97. Alexander Schneider to RS, March 7, 1952.

98. RS to Irene Serkin, [October 1952].

99. Uri (Erich) Toeplitz to Irene Serkin, June 29, 1991.

100. Amalie Buchthal (from Lene Mezger), "Treffen Rudi, Jakob."

101. I. B. Serkin, *Adolf Busch*, 2: 519.

102. Schnabel, *My Life*, 204.

103. Schneider, *Sasha*, 96.

104. Albrecht Goes, Interview with the authors, Stuttgart, October 14, 1995.

105. *Rheinische Post*, June 3, 1957.

106. RS to Irene Serkin, undated letter.

107. Freya von Moltke to RS, November 21, 1974.

108. Undated draft.

109. January 18, 1939, Elizabeth Sprague Coolidge Foundation Collection, Music Division, Library of Congress.

110. August 30, 1940, Elizabeth Sprague

Coolidge Foundation Collection, Music Division, Library of Congress.

111. Amalie Buchthal, "Winnie Leventritt," 3.

112. Saerchinger, *Artur Schnabel*, 197.

113. RS to Marthl Schmälze, undated letter.

114. Israel Strauss to RS, March 26, 1954; Israel Strauss to Irene Serkin, May 3, 1954.

115. Mary Lynn Fixler, Interview with the authors, New York, March 23, 2001.

116. Harvey Sachs, *Arthur Rubinstein: A Life* (London: Weidenfeld & Nicolson, 1996), 215, 337; Joseph Horowitz, *Conversations with Arrau* (New York: Knopf, 1982), 187.

117. Marjorie Hassen, *Harry Zelser Concerts: A Study of Musical Taste in Chicago, 1937–1977* (A.M. thesis, University of Chicago, 1981), 191, 209.

118. RS to Fred Kountz, May 31, 1961.

119. March 20, 1957.

120. Franz Mohr, *Große Maestros, hinter der Bühne erlebt* (Basel: Brunnen, 1996), 74.

121. Joseph Horowitz, *The Ivory Trade: Music and the Business of Music at the Van Cliburn International Piano Competition* (New York: Summit Books, 1990), 72.

122. Seymour Lipkin, Interview with the authors, New York, December 14, 1996.

123. Horowitz, *The Ivory Trade*, 75.

124. Ned Rorem, *The Nantucket Diary of Ned Rorem, 1973–1985* (San Francisco: North Point Press, 1987), 34.

125. Horowitz, *The Ivory Trade*, 76.

CHAPTER 4

1. Hugo Buchthal, Interview with the authors, London, November 2, 1994.

2. Paul Schiff to RS, April 23, 1937.

3. RS to Irene Serkin, March 16, 1962.

4. Eugene Ormandy to RS, January 16, 1941.

5. *Washington Post*, May 9, 1991, C5.

6. Franco Buitoni to Irene Serkin, May 19, 1991.

7. Schnabel, *My Life*, 116.

8. Aaron Richmond to RS, March 12, 1941.

9. Arthur Judson to RS, December 11, 1942.

10. Script dated November 11, 1941.

11. Quoted in a letter from Elaine Wilson to RS, Columbia Concerts, October 10, 1942.

12. Aaron Richmond to RS, June 1, 1948.

13. RS to Arthur Judson, October 19, 1942.

14. *New York Times*, January 29, 1975, 38.

15. Arthur Judson to RS, October 26, 1942.

16. Gary Graffman, *I Really Should Be Practicing* (Garden City, NY: Doubleday, 1981), 118.

17. May 15, 1937 contract, and an addendum to the 1938 contract (February 1, 1938).

18. "An Interview with Charles Rosen," *Piano Quarterly*, 39, no. 152 (winter 1990–91): 24.

19. RS to Irene Serkin, November 11, 1960.

20. Irene Serkin to Ruth Seufert, January 1953.

21. Arnold Steinhardt, *Indivisible by Four* (New York: Farrar, Straus, and Giroux, 1998), 255.

22. Alan Rich, "The Serkins," *Bravo* 7, no. 4 (December 26, 1967): 18.

23. RS to Mr. Lipshutz, January 16, 1944.

24. Gordon Claycombe to RS, January 31, 1944.

25. Ursula Serkin interview.

26. RS to Cynthia Raim, January 13, 1979.

27. Christopher Serkin interview.

28. Stephanie Brown, Interview with the authors, New York, January 13, 2001.

29. Bill Wareing to RS, December 21, 1986.

30. RS to Max Gähwyler, [October 1940?]

31. RS to J. M. Williams (RCA), August 3, 1940.

32. Goddard Lieberson to RS, August 9, 1945, Yale Music Library.

33. RS to Goddard Lieberson, August 13, 1949, Yale Music Library.

34. Frank Salomon to Robert Aerenson, November 10, 1966.

35. Ronald Gelatt, *The Fabulous Phonograph, 1877–1977* (New York: Macmillan, 1977), 281.

36. Robert Silverman, "Serkin: An Interview—Part One," *Piano Quarterly* 26, no. 100 (winter 1977–78): 3.

37. Judith Sherman, Phone interview with the authors, April 16, 2001.

38. Steinway Project Interview.

39. Pianofabrik A. Schmidt-Flohr to RS, October 22, 1936, and Serkin's undated reply (draft).

40. William R. Steinway to RS, July 20, 1934.

41. Steinway Project Interview, 2.

42. Ibid., 5.

43. Charles Osborne, "Rudolf Serkin: Musician," *London Magazine*, July 1966, 101.

44. Steinway Project Interview, 3.

45. Alexander Greiner to RS, November 19, 1952.

46. Alexander Greiner to RS, July 28, 1948.

47. Diana Burgwyn, *Marlboro Music: A Fifty Year Portrait* (Marlboro, VT: Marlboro Music School and Festival, 2001), 13.

48. Peter Serkin interviews.

49. Claudette Sorel, "Piano Studies with Serkin and Stokowski," *Clavier* (March 1994): 20.

50. John Serkin, communication to the authors, October 2, 2001. Of related interest is a very informative video of John Serkin's: *The Anatomy of the Piano: How Your Piano Works* (West Brattleboro: JMC Productions, 1991).

51. January 1966.

52. Elder, "Serkin, As Interviewed by Dean Elder," 39.

53. RS to Irene Serkin, [1960s].

54. RS to Irene Serkin, February 1946.

55. RS to Irene Serkin, [late 1940s].

56. *New York Times*, January 27, 1977, 31.

57. Elder, "Serkin, As Interviewed by Dean Elder," 39.

58. Plaskin, *Horowitz*, 400.

59. "An Interview with Charles Rosen," 24.

60. *New York Times*, December 10, 1958, 52.

61. Bernard Meillat, "Serkin Off the Record," *Diapason* (July–August 1991): 41.

62. Peter Serkin, Interview, June 10, 2001.

63. Erik Entwistle's analysis of the sonata, "Form & Fantasy in Martinů's Piano Sonata" (in press) includes a history of Serkin's role in its genesis.

64. William Judd to Frank Salomon, June 9, 1965

65. Kolodin, "The Complete Musician," 83.

66. RS to Eugene Ormandy, June 1967, Eugene Ormandy Papers, Rare Book & Manuscript Library, University of Pennsylvania.

67. *The Gramophone* (May 1969): 1548.

68. RS to Mischa Schneider, May 7, 1976.

69. Peter Serkin interview.

70. Ibid.; also Meillat, "Serkin Off the Record," 41.

71. Costa, *Miecio: Ricordi di Mieczyslaw Horszowski*, 452.

72. Mstislav Rostropovich, Interview with the authors, Philadelphia, March 27, 1995.

73. Peter Serkin interview.

74. RS to Irene Serkin, October 28, 1942 and November 18, 1942.

75. Eugene Ormandy to RS, June 15, 1942.

76. RS to Eugene Ormandy, June 22, 1942.

77. Eugene Ormandy to RS, September 4, 1942.

78. RS to Eugene Ormandy, undated letter, Eugene Ormandy Papers, Rare Book & Manuscript Library, University of Pennsylvania.

79. Claude Frank, "Rudolf Serkin: Servant of Music," *Keynote*, March 1983, 15.

80. Ruth O'Neill to RS, March 22, 1946.

81. RS to Dirk Nabering, March 27, 1979.

82. RS to Georges Payot, Konzertgesellschaft Zürich, July 19, 1978.

83. RS to Emmie Tillett, August 18, 1977.

84. RS to Hanno Rinke, May 9, 1989.

85. RS to Paola Saffioti, February 24, 1989.

86. RS to Hanno Rinke, April 12, 1989.

87. RS to Novello & Co., London, July 28, 1940.

88. David Diamond to RS, [1951]; Jenö Takács to RS, January 2, 1954.

89. Taruskin, *Text & Act*, 283.

90. Saal interview, 18.

91. Paul Badura-Skoda, "Fehlende Takte und korrumpierte Stellen in klassischen Meisterwerken," *Neue Zeitschrift für Musik* 119, no. 11 (November 1958): 635.

92. Wolfgang Amadeus Mozart, *Neue Ausgabe sämtlicher Werke* (Kassel: Bärenreiter, 1960), Serie 5, Werkgruppe 14, Bd. 8, pp. xxiv–xxv; Badura-Skoda, "Fehlende Takte und korrumpierte Stellen in klassischen Meisterwerken," 635–642. Serkin's inclusion of the missing bars occasioned strong disapproval in a review in *The Gramophone* (July 1959), 69, with a rejoinder in Serkin's defense by Alfred Brendel (October 1959), 215.

93. RS to Elfrieda F. Hiebert, August 31, 1979.

94. Elfrieda Hiebert, "Beethoven's *Pathétique* Sonata, Op. 13: Should the Grave Be Repeated?" *Piano Quarterly*, 34 (1986): 33–37.

95. Charles Rosen, *The Frontiers of Meaning* (New York: Hill and Wang, 1994), 30n.

96. Seymour Lipkin to RS, October 10, 1990.

97. RS to Elfrieda F. Hiebert, August 31, 1979.

98. Elder, "Serkin, As Interviewed by Dean Elder," 13.

99. Silverman, "Serkin," 3.

100. RS to Günter Henle, May 12, 1952.

101. Günter Henle, *Three Spheres: A Life in Politics, Business and Music* (Chicago: Regnery Co., 1971), 223–268.

102. RS to Günter Henle, August, 29, 1969.

103. Silverman, "Serkin," 3.

104. Jacobson, *Reverberations*, 204.

105. RS to Irene Serkin, 1957.

106. RS to Irene Serkin, [early 1950s, San Francisco].

107. Stern interview.

108. RS to Irene Serkin, undated letter.

109. RS to Irene Serkin, undated card, [1954].

110. RS to Irene Serkin, undated letter, [1953].

111. RS to Irene Serkin, [early 1950s].

112. Quoted in Plaskin, *Horowitz*, 325.

113. Quoted by Meillat, "Serkin Off the Record," 41.

114. E-mail communication to the authors from Shoji Sato, April 4, 2001.

115. Monica Steegmann and Eva Rieger, eds., *Frauen mit Flügel: Lebensberichte berühmter Pianistinnen von Clara Schumann bis Clara Haskil* (Frankfurt am Main: Insel, 1996), 255.

116. "Rudolf Serkin on Dimitri Mitropoulos: Phone conversation with Oliver Daniel, Brattleboro, Vermont, December 18, 1984," 10, Leopold Stokowski Collection, Rare Book & Manuscript Library, University of Pennsylvania.

117. Leopold Stokowski to RS, December 24, 1959.

118. Schneider, *Sasha: A Musician's Life*, 85.

119. George Szell to RS, January 3, 1954.

120. Personal communication to the authors, August 6, 2000.

121. *New York Times*, January 27, 1977, 31.

122. Peter Serkin interview.

123. Michael Steinberg, *Boston Globe*, December 17, 1973.

124. Peter Serkin interview.

125. *New Orleans States-Item*, December 15, 1967.

126. Lawrence Gilman, *New York Herald Tribune*, February 21, 1936.

127. Olin Downes, *New York Times*, January 12, 1937.

128. *Current Biography* 51, no. 6 (June 1990): 47.

129. *New York Herald Tribune*, November 16, 1940.

130. Edward Said, "Uncertainties of Style," *The Nation*, March 9, 1992.

131. Elisabeth Serkin interview.

132. Burge, *Remembering Horowitz*, 165.

133. Osborne, "Rudolf Serkin," 99.

134. *New York Times*, April 28, 1962, 15.

135. Peter Serkin interview.

136. *Die Zeit*, March 25, 1983.

137. Elder, "Serkin, As Interviewed by Dean Elder," 14.

138. Joachim Kaiser, *Great Pianists of Our Time* (London: George Allen & Unwin, 1971), 104; *Große Pianisten in unserer Zeit* (München: Rütten & Loening, 1965), 116.

139. Harris Goldsmith, "Serkin's Beethoven: Once with Toscanini, Today with Ormandy," *High Fidelity* (October 1965): 80–81.

140. Harris Goldsmith, "A Performance to Treasure: Serkin and Beethoven's *Hammerklavier*," *High Fidelity* (December 1971): 86.

141. *Stuttgarter Zeitung*, November 2, 1961.

142. Richard Sennett, "Pianists in Their Time: A Memoir," in *The Lives of the Piano*, edited by James R. Gaines (New York: Harper & Row, 1981), 205.

143. *Berner Tagblatt*, October 24, 1938, 3.

144. Oscar Levant, *Memoirs of an Amnesiac* (Hollywood: S. French, 1989), 220.

145. *New York Review of Books*, August 9, 2001, 37.

146. Edward Said, "Musical Retrospection," *The Nation*, October 26, 1992.

CHAPTER 5

1. Plaskin, *Horowitz*, 295.

2. Joseph Horowitz, *New York Times*, May 28, 2000.

3. Amalie Buchthal interview.

4. Herdan-Zuckmayer, *Genies*, 209.

5. Menuhin interview.

6. RS to Grace Johnston, April 15, 1935.

7. I. B. Serkin, *Adolf Busch: Letters, Pictures, Memories*, 2: 332.

8. Anton Kuerti, Interview with the authors, Philadelphia, November 24, 1997.

9. The Curtis Institute of Music, *Overtones*, 11, no. 1, Fiftieth Anniversary Issue (October 1, 1974): unpaginated.

10. Diana Burgwyn, *Seventy-Five Years of The Curtis Institute of Music: A Narrative Portrait* (Philadelphia: Curtis Institute, 1999), 11.

11. Carl Flesch, *The Memoirs of Carl Flesch*,

trans. by Hans Keller (New York: Macmillan, 1958), 350.

12. Burgwyn, *Seventy-Five Years*, 23.

13. Curtis Institute, *Overtones*.

14. Philip Hart, *Fritz Reiner* (Evanston, IL.: Northwestern University Press, 1994), 49.

15. Orlando Cole, on a panel celebrating the Curtis's 70th anniversary, Philadelphia, April 17, 1995.

16. Orlando Cole, Interview with the authors, Philadelphia, November 3, 1995.

17. Elza Ann Viles, *Mary Louis Curtis Bok Zimbalist: Founder of the Curtis Institute of Music and Patron of American Arts* (Ph.D. thesis, Bryn Mawr, 1983), 38.

18. Boris Goldovsky, *My Road to Opera: The Recollections of Boris Goldovsky* (Boston: Houghton Mifflin, 1979), 136.

19. RS to Anka Bernstein Landau, [1938], Anka Bernstein Landau Collection, Juilliard School Archives.

20. Reginald Gerig, *Famous Pianists & Their Technique* (Washington, DC: R. B. Luce, 1974), 410. See also Olga Samaroff Stokowski, *An American Musician's Story* (New York: Norton, 1939), 170–210.

21. Irene Serkin to Mary Bok, March, 1939.

22. "Denial by Curtis School: Institute of Music Not to Close, Says Josef Hofmann," *New York Times*, January 12, 1933, p. 20.

23. RS to Mary Bok, undated.

24. Mary Bok to RS, May 8, 1942.

25. Ned Rorem, *Knowing When to Stop* (New York: Simon & Schuster, 1994), 169.

26. Joseph Rezits, *Beloved Tyranna: The Legend and Legacy of Isabelle Vengerova* (Bloomington, IN: David Daniel Music, 1995), i.

27. Gary Graffman, Interview with the authors, Philadelphia, January 24, 2001.

28. Peter Orth, Interview with the authors, Pulheim-Geyen, Germany, November 2, 2000.

29. Rorem, *Knowing*, 169.

30. Kuerti interview.

31. Graffman, *I Really Should Be Practicing*, 64.

32. Graffman interview.

33. Rorem, *Knowing*, 200.

34. Jane Hill to Rudolf and Irene Serkin, April 4, 1942; September 3, 1944; May 27, 1946.

35. Costa, *Miecio: Ricordi di Mieczyslaw Horszowski*, 437.

36. Rezits, *Beloved Tyranna*, 112.

37. May 31, 1961.

38. Humphrey Burton, *Leonard Bernstein* (New York: Doubleday, 1994), 64–65.

39. Lee Luvisi, Written communication to the authors, November 10, 1996.

40. Peter Serkin interview.

41. Rorem, *Knowing*, 168.

42. Claudette Sorel, "Piano Studies with Serkin and Stokowski," *Clavier* (March 1994): 20.

43. RS to Natalie Synhaivsky, February 25, 1976.

44. *Great Pianists Speak with Adele Marcus* (Neptune, NJ: Paganiniana Publications, 1979), 62.

45. Stephen West, ed., "Strength of Fingers, Strength of Thought: A Conference with Rudolf Serkin," *The Etude: Music Magazine* (March 1941): 155.

46. Kuerti interview.

47. Elder, "Serkin, As Interviewed by Dean Elder," 12.

48. Ibid., 10–11.

49. Ruth Laredo, Interview with the authors, New York, January 12, 1997.

50. Felix Witzinger, Interview with the authors, Basel, April 22, 1997.

51. RS to Fern Kletter, April 6, 1977.

52. March 7, 1961.

53. West, "Strength of Fingers," 155.

54. Ibid., 196.

55. Luis Batlle, Interview with the authors, Marlboro, VT, August 23, 1994.

56. Linda J. Noyle, ed., *Pianists on Playing: Interviews with Twelve Concert Pianists* (Metuchen, NJ: Scarecrow, 1987), 30.

57. Claude Frank, Interview with the authors, November 10, 1996.

58. November 16, 1934.

59. September 3, 1935.

60. October 10, 1941.

61. June 2, 1944.

62. Byron Hardin, Letter to the authors, January 5, 1997.

63. Cynthia Raim, Interview with the authors, Philadelphia, March 5, 1997.

64. Cecile Licad, Interview with the authors, New York, January 13, 2001.

65. Jeffrey Wagner, "Artists in Their Own Ways: Arthur Loesser and Rudolf Serkin," *Clavier* (November 1987): 13.

66. Mickey Thomas Terry, "An Interview with George Walker," *Musical Quarterly* 84, no. 3 (fall 2000): 375–376.

67. Wagner, "Artists," 13.

68. The history and culture of the Leventritt Competition is well described in a number of sources, e.g., Helen Epstein, *Music Talks: Conversations with Musicians* (New York: Penguin, 1987); Helen Drees Ruttencutter, *Pianist's Progress* (New York: Crowell, 1979); and Joseph Horowitz, *The Ivory Trade* (New York: Summit Books, 1990).

69. Sol Schoenbach, Interview with the authors, Haverford, PA, November 5, 1996.

70. Daniel Webster, *Philadelphia Inquirer*, December 22, 1968.

71. RS to Abe Fortas.

72. Cole interview.

73. *New York Times*, January 17, 1968.

74. Martin Mayer, *New York Times*, December 7, 1969.

75. Daniel Webster, *Philadelphia Inquirer*, December 22, 1968.

76. Martin Mayer, *New York Times*, December 7, 1969.

77. Burgwyn, *Seventy-Five Years*, 60.

78. Martin Mayer, *New York Times*, December 7, 1969.

79. Graffman interview.

80. Burgwyn, *Seventy-Five Years*, 27.

81. Daniel Webster, *Philadelphia Inquirer*, February 23, 1974.

82. James Felton, *The Evening Bulletin*, Philadelphia, November 20, 1972.

83. Samuel Singer, *Philadelphia Inquirer*, April 10, 1974.

84. Steinway Project Interview, 14.

85. Daniel Webster, *Philadelphia Inquirer*, December 22, 1968.

86. Daniel Webster, "Serkin at Top Speed," *Philadelphia Inquirer*, February 23, 1975.

87. Arianna Stassinopoulos, *Maria Callas: The Woman behind the Legend* (New York: Simon and Schuster, 1981), 311.

88. Peter Schoenbach, Interview with the authors, Haverford, PA, September 10, 1995.

89. Sol Schoenbach interview.

90. Burgwyn, *Seventy-Five Years*, 80.

91. Sol Schoenbach interview.

92. RS to M. Todd Cooke, December 20, 1974.

93. James Felton, *Sunday Bulletin*, January 16, 1977.

94. Ibid.

95. RS to Hsueh-Yung Shen on April 28, 1976.

96. RS to Jonathan Sternberg, April 21, 1977.

97. Ivan Galamian to RS, May 26, 1976.

98. Mieczyslaw Horszowski to RS, May 22, 1975.

99. RS to A. Margaret (Stormy) Bok, October 11, 1982.

100. Stephanie Brown, Interview with the authors, New York, January 13, 2001.

101. [1979].

102. Robert Silverman, "Serkin: An Interview—Part One," *Piano Quarterly* (winter 1977–1978): 4.

103. Peter Orth interview.

CHAPTER 6

1. Sol Schoenbach interview.

2. Irene Serkin, "Then and Now," Memo to Marlboro Trustees, 1998.

3. Rosalie Leventritt to RS, August 1947.

4. Irene Serkin to Agnes Meyer, [summer 1952].

5. RS to Walter Strauss, April 21, 1976.

6. RS to Tilden Wells, March 21, 1961.

7. Schnabel, *My Life and Music,* 209.

8. J. M. Snyder, ed., *Espressivo: Music and Life at Marlboro* (Marlboro, VT: Marlboro Music School and Festival, 1994), ix.

9. David Riesman, Graduation Address, Marlboro College, June 5, 1954, 6.

10. Frieder Reininghaus, "Serkin-Kempff-Arrau," *Kultur-Chronik* [Bonn] (May 1991): 38.

11. Donal Henahan, *New York Times*, July 8, 1975.

12. Dorothy Canfield Fisher, "On Marlboro," 1956, Serkin Papers.

13. RS to Walter Hendl, April 18, 1961.

14. RS to Anthony Checchia, June 3, 1980.

15. RS to E. S. Coolidge, April 11, 1951.

16. Rosalie Leventritt to RS, November 7, 1951.

17. Agnes E. Meyer to RS, April 14, 1951.

18. Burgwyn, *Marlboro: A Fifty-Year Portrait*, 11.

19. *Time*, July 18, 1960, 47.

20. RS to Irene Serkin, [1958].

21. Harvey Olnick, telephone interview with the authors, March 29, 2001.

22. Howard Taubman "Vermont Interlude," *New York Times*, September 2, 1956.

23. RS to Frank Salomon, January 14, 1980.

24. RS to Frank Salomon, January 7, 1976.

25. Felix Wolfes to RS, duplicate of letter to Martial Singher, October 23, 1955.

26. John Browning to RS, July 23, 1960.

27. Helen Epstein, *Music Talks: Conversations with Musicians* (New York: McGraw-Hill, 1987), 100.

28. Felix Galimir, interview with the authors, New York, January 4, 1996; Philadelphia, January 29, 1996.

29. Roger Sessions to Paul Fromm, August 24, 1959.

30. Galimir interview.

31. Peter Heyworth, "Worth Crossing the Atlantic For," *New York Times*, August 31, 1969.

32. Bernard Levin, *The Listener*, July 30, 1981, 69.

33. Milan Turkovic, "Kammermusik-Festival in Marlboro (USA)" *Das Orchester* [Mainz] (November 1969): 487.

34. Samuel Barber to RS, September 12, 1963.

35. Michael Steinberg, *Boston Globe*, February 6, 1967.

36. Burgwyn, *Marlboro*, 13.

37. Cited in Snyder, *Espressivo*, 65.

38. Steinhardt, *Indivisible by Four*, 71.

39. Joseph Horowitz, *Understanding Toscanini* (New York: Knopf, 1987), 394.

40. For an especially fine analysis of Marlboro's importance as an "alternative" ideal in the 1960s, see Sennett, "Pianists in Their Time," 187–208.

41. Donal Henahan, *New York Times*, July 8, 1975.

42. *New York Times*, August 19, 1962.

43. Anthony Checchia, interview with the authors, Philadelphia, November 19, 1996.

44. Sviatoslav Richter to RS, March 3, 1962.

45. Harvey Olnick to RS, June 15, 1956.

46. Robert Baldock, *Pablo Casals* (Boston: Northeastern University Press, 1993), 247.

47. Plaskin, *Horowitz*, 399.

48. *New York Times*, August 16, 1962.

49. Agnes Meyer to RS on June 12, 1959.

50. RS to Agnes Meyer, 1959.

51. RS to Agnes Meyer, 1960.

52. Pablo Casals, as told to Albert E. Kahn, *Joys and Sorrows* (New York: Simon & Schuster, 1970), 281.

53. David Blum, *Quintet: Five Journeys toward Musical Fulfillment* (Ithaca, NY: Cornell University Press, 1998), 18.

54. Steinhardt, *Indivisible*, 140.

55. Evelyne Crochet, letter to the authors, April 3, 1997.

56. Ann McCutchan, *Marcel Moyse: Voice of the Flute* (Portland, OR: Amadeus Press, 1994), 186.

57. Marcel Moyse to Anthony Checchia, April 11, 1966.

58. McCutchan, *Marcel Moyse*, 208.

59. RS, July 15, 1977.

60. *New York Times*, July 8, 1962.

61. Sol Schoenbach interview.

62. Snyder, *Espressivo*, 105.

63. Blum, *Quintet*, 127.

64. Snyder, *Espressivo*, 84.

65. Harold Schonberg, *New York Times*, July 5, 1965.

66. *Boston Globe*, November 5, 1965.

67. Madeline Foley to RS, November 13, 1965.

68. Raymond Ericson, *New York Times*, November 6, 1977.

69. RS to Frank Salomon, November 19, 1977.

70. RS to Frank Salomon, January 14, 1980.

71. Quoted in Allan Kozinn, "The Miracle of Marlboro: Rudolf Serkin's Musical Mecca," *Ovation* (June 1981).

72. András Schiff, letter to the authors, September 7, 2001.

73. RS to Checchia, April 1, 1977.

74. Richard Goode, interview with the authors, New York, October 7, 2000.

75. Galimir interview.

76. Urs Frauchiger, *Der eigene Ton: Gespräche über die Kunst des Geigenspielens* (Zurich: Ammann Verlag, 2000), 184–185.

77. Checchia interview.

78. Frank Salomon, letter to the authors, August 13, 2001.

79. Checchia interview.

80. RS to Sonya Brandt, October 13, 1978.

81. Hubert Saal, *Newsweek*, July 21, 1975, 69.

82. Luis Batlle, interview with the authors, Guilford, VT, May 23, 1998.

83. Kuerti interview.

84. Epstein, *Music Talks*, 103.

85. *New York Times*, September 25, 1991.

EPILOGUE

1. *Michigan State News*, April 5, 1974.

2. Alexander Schneider to RS, December 21, 1985.

3. Mary Lynn Fixler, interview with the authors, New York, March 23, 2001.

4. RS to Walther Bohnke, March 8, 1989.

5. John Serkin, phone communication with the authors, September 26, 2001.

6. Peter Serkin interview.

7. Batlle interview.

8. Peter Serkin interview.

9. Max Rudolf to Irene Serkin, May 10, 1991.

Includes books (and sections of books) and journal articles, but not reviews or newspaper articles.

Anissimov, Myriam. "Rudolf Serkin: 'Tout le monde a le trac.'" *Le Monde de la Musique*, no. 55 (April 1983): 57–61.

Banowetz, Joseph. "Arrau, Horowitz, Serkin: A Walk among Giants." *Piano Quarterly* (fall 1979): 23–30.

Blyth, Alan. "Rudolf Serkin Talks to Alan Blyth." *Gramophone* (May 1969): 1548.

Brusilow, Anshel. "Anshel Brusilow Remembers Arrau and Serkin." *Piano Quarterly* (fall 1979): 31–32.

Burgwyn, Diana. *Marlboro Music: A Fifty Year Portrait.* Marlboro, VT: Marlboro Music School and Festival, 2001.

Busch, Adolf. "The Art of Ensemble Playing." *Etude Music Magazine* (August 1938): 499–500.

Chasins, Abram. "Rudolf Serkin." In *Speaking of Pianists.* 2d ed. New York: Knopf, 1961, 130–135.

Daniel, Oliver. "Rudolf Serkin on Dimitri Mitropoulos: Phone Conversation with Oliver Daniel." Unpublished interview, transcript. Leopold Stokowski Collection, Rare Book & Manuscript Library, University of Pennsylvania.

Deichmann, Hans. "Four Plates in Pieces." In *Objects: A Chronicle of Subversion in Nazi German and Fascist Italy.* New York: Marsilio Publishers, 1997, 55–58.

Dubal, David. "Rudolf Serkin." In *The Art of the Piano.* 2d ed. San Diego: Harcourt Brace, 1995, 238–240.

Elder, Dean. "Serkin, As Interviewed by Dean Elder." *Clavier: A Magazine for Pianists and Organists* (November 1970): 9–15, 37–39. Reprinted in *Pianists at Play: Interviews, Master Lessons, and Technical Regimes* (London: Kahn & Averill, 1986), 55–63 and again, in slightly abridged form, in *Clavier* (July–August 1991): 10–19, 46.

Frank, Claude. "Rudolf Serkin: Servant of Music." *Keynote* (March 1983): 13–16.

Friedrich, Otto. *Before the Deluge: A Portrait of Berlin in the 1920s.* New York: Harper & Row, 1972.

Gillespie, John, and Anna Gillespie. "Rudolf Serkin." In *Notable Twentieth Century Pianists: A Bio-Critical Sourcebook.* Westport, CT: Greenwood, 1995, 2: 811–822.

Graffman, Gary. "Rudolf Serkin." *Proceedings of the American Philosophical Society* (March 1993): 169–171.

Horowitz, Joseph, "Elitists Bite the Dust." In *The Ivory Trade: Music and the Business of Music at the Van Cliburn International Piano Competition.* New York: Summit Books, 1990, 70–77.

Jacobson, Robert. "Rudolf Serkin." In *Reverberations: Interviews with the World's Leading Musicians.* London: Vision Press, 1976, 197–206. (Originally published in a slightly different form in *Lincoln Center for the Performing Arts* [January 1973]: 10, 16–19.)

Jochum, Veronica. "Rudolf Serkin." *Piano Quarterly* (summer 1991): 30.

Kaiser, Joachim. *Great Pianists of Our Time.* Translated from the German by David Wooldridge and George Unwin. London: George Allen & Unwin, 1971, 103–106.

Kolodin, Irving. "The Complete Musician." *Horizon* (September 1961): 82–87.

Kuerti, Anton, as told to Jeffrey Wagner. "Master Portraits: Artists in Their Own Ways—Arthur Loesser and Rudolf Serkin." *Clavier* (November 1987): 10–13.

Mann, Erika, and Klaus Mann. "A Musical Evening." In *Escape to Life.* Boston: Houghton Mifflin, 1939, 258–264.

Marlboro Music: Collected Concert Programs. 3 vols. Marlboro, VT: Marlboro Music School and Festival, 2000.

Meillat, Bernard. "Serkin Off the Record." *Diapason* (July–August 1991): 41.

Mohr, Franz, with Beat Rink. "Rudolf Serkin." In *Große Maestros, hinter der Bühne erlebt.* Basel: Brunnen-Verlag, 1996, 73–99.

O'Harra, Richard. "Serkin: Some Thoughts about Music." *Musical Courier* (May 1960): 10–11.

Osborne, Charles, "Rudolf Serkin: Musician." *London Magazine* (July 1966): 98–102.

Rattalino, Piero. *Da Clementi a Pollini: Duecento anni con i grandi pianisti.* Milan: Ricordi, 1983, 213–219.

Reed, Peter Hugh. "Two Master Musicians: An Exclusive Interview with Adolf Busch and Rudolf Serkin." *The Music Lover* (February 1938): 366–369.

Roddy, Joseph. "Rudolf Serkin: Seraphic and Serious." *High Fidelity Magazine* (July 1961): 24–28, 82.

Saal, Hubert. Unpublished interview with Rudolf Serkin. Transcript in Rudolf Serkin Papers, Rare Book & Manuscript Library, University of Pennsylvania.

Schibli, Sigfried. "Der Pianist Rudolf Serkin und seine Riehener Jahre." In *z'Rieche: Heimatliches Jahrbuch,* 1991, 57–63.

Sennett, Richard. "Pianists in Their Time: A Memoir." In *The Lives of the Piano.* New York: Harper Colophon, 1983, 187–208.

Serkin, Irene Busch, compiler. *Adolf Busch: Letters, Pictures, Memories.* 2 vols. Translated by Russell Stockman. Walpole, NH: Arts & Letters Press, 1991. (German original: *Adolf Busch: Briefe, Bilder, Erinnerungen.* 1 vol. Walpole, NH: Arts & Letters Press, 1991.)

"Serkin, Rudolf." In *Current Biography Yearbook.* New York: H. W. Wilson, 1990, 43–47. (The original article on Serkin in *Current Biography* appeared in the 1940 volume, 725–726.)

Silverman, Robert. "Serkin: An Interview—Part One." *Piano Quarterly* (winter 1977–78): 3–6.

Snyder, J. M., editor. *Espressivo: Music and Life at Marlboro.* Marlboro, VT: Marlboro Music School and Festival, 1994.

Sorel, Claudette. "Piano Studies with Serkin and Stokowski." *Clavier* (March 1994): 19–22.

Steiner, Diana. "Rudolf Serkin, String Player Extraordinaire." *California Music Teacher* (September–October 1983): 10.

Steinway Project Interview. "Rudolf Serkin Talking with Elizabeth Harkins." Brattleboro, VT, October 6, 1980. Unpublished transcript. Oral History, American Music Archive, Vivian Perlis, Yale University.

Svoboda, Wilhelm. "Rudolf Serkin: Eine biographische Skizze." In *Zwischen Aufklärung & Kulturindustrie: Festschrift für Georg Knepler . . . ,* III. Musik/Gesellschaft. Hamburg: von Bockel Verlag, 1993, 191–197.

Tubeuf, André. "Serkin l'Initiateur." *Diapason* (July–August 1991): 40.

West, Stephen. "Strength of Fingers, Strength of Thought: A Conference with Rudolf Serkin." *Etude* (March 1941): 155, 196.

Wolff, Konrad. "Klavierpädagogik in Amerika unter dem Einfluß der Hitler-Emigration." In *Musiktradition im Exil: Zurück aus dem Vergessen.* Köln: Bund-Verlag, 1993, 96–105.

INDEX

Page numbers in italic indicate illustrations.

INDEX

INDEX

INDEX